ALLTHEBEST
recipes

ALLTHEBEST
recipes

300 delicious and extraordinary recipes
Jane Rodmell

Robert
ROSE

For complete cataloguing information, see page 448.

Disclaimer

The recipes in this book have been carefully tested by our kitchen and our
tasters. To the best of our knowledge, they are safe and nutritious for ordinary
use and users. For those people with food or other allergies, or who have
special food requirements or health issues, please read the suggested contents
of each recipe carefully and determine whether or not they may create a
problem for you. All recipes are used at the risk of the consumer.

We cannot be responsible for any hazards, loss or damage that may occur as
a result of any recipe use.

For those with special needs, allergies, requirements or health problems, in
the event of any doubt, please contact your medical adviser prior to the use of
any recipe.

Editor: Carol Sherman
Recipe Editor: Jennifer MacKenzie
Contributor: David Cobb
Copy Editor: Karen Campbell-Sheviak
Design and Production: Kevin Cockburn/PageWave Graphics Inc.
Illustrations: Kveta/Three in a Box
Photography: Colin Erricson
Food Styling: Kate Bush and Kathryn Robertson
Prop Styling: Charlene Erricson

Cover image: Chicken, Shrimp and Mussel Paella (see recipe, page 238)

We acknowledge the financial support of the Government of Canada through
the Book Publishing Industry Development Program (BPIDP) for our
publishing activities.

Published by Robert Rose Inc.
120 Eglinton Avenue East, Suite 800, Toronto, Ontario, Canada M4P 1E2
Tel: (416) 322-6552 Fax: (416) 322-6936

Printed and bound in Canada

1 2 3 4 5 6 7 8 9 CPL 17 16 15 14 13 12 11 10 09

Contents

Acknowledgments

I would need to compile another book to adequately express my gratitude to my family and the many friends, colleagues and customers who have provided me, and All The Best, with much- appreciated support over the past twenty-five years. Without the vision of Michael de Pencier and Ken Burgess we would not have opened the doors of our small bake shop. The comradeship and shared hard work with my partners Jane Lash and Lynda van Velzen and great bakers like Susannah Fleming and David Moore made the early years exciting and a lot of fun. Wise counsel from long-time friends including Don Emerson, Karl Jaffray, Michael Rea, Carole-Ann Hayes, David Lewis, Wendy Cook and Gay Gooderham kept us from going too far astray. Some valued old friends are sorely missed- Philip Greey, Judy Burgess, Mary Ann Brinkman, Elizabeth Hendrie and Allyson Davies.

In the making of this cookbook I gratefully acknowledge the good humor, co-operation and diligent work of many talented cooks, bakers and support staff at All The Best kitchens, including Executive Chef Olivia Bolano; bakers extraordinaire Mario Totaro, Gennelle Bachand and Barry Spackman; chefs Nicole Rumball and Sarah Martins; and catering pros Bob Lamont and Linda Knox. Special thanks to Chef Sarah Visheau and skilled baker, Jill Snider for their invaluable contribution through the many months of tasting and testing recipes, and to Chef Chris Klugman for friendship and inspiration.

We thank our eminent publisher, Bob Dees, for having faith in our endeavors and for being a frequent appreciator of our food. We hope that his early Saturday morning visits will long continue even when the need for subtle, yet diligent, encouragement in the matter of deadlines is no longer needed. Everyone in the Robert Rose team is a star in my book! Editor Carol Sherman made the part of pulling this collection of recipes together a pleasant challenge rather than a stressful exercise. It was a great pleasure for me to work again with longtime friends David Cobb, a writer of much elegant prose, and Kate Bush, inspired food stylist and companion on many culinary adventures. Many thanks also to photographer Colin Erricson, food stylist Kathryn Robertson, illustrator Kveta, designer Kevin Cockburn of PageWave Graphics, and the eagle eyes of Jennifer MacKenzie for recipe editing and testing and Karen Campbell-Sheviak for copy editing.

My heartfelt appreciation is also due to Sue Bowman, who tirelessly guides All The Best everyday, and to Christina Jackson and our whole retail team, whose support is critical in serving our customers with "the best."

Introduction

In 1984 we opened the doors of All The Best, a small bakeshop in a century-old building in midtown Toronto. Our goal was to create delicious products, handmade in small batches from the finest ingredients, and to seek out for our customers all manner of unique and wonderful food products made by other producers who share our passion for quality and natural good taste. We were perhaps a bit ahead of the curve! At that time in our city the bread on supermarket shelves was mainly the squishy, white-sliced variety and we would drive for miles in search of a real kalamata olive! Happily for us, our customers enjoyed the food experiences we offered. The small shop grew, All The Best Catering was born, and our talented chefs, bakers and retail staff continue the same pursuit of excellence and passion for good food today.

For this collection of recipes to celebrate our 25th anniversary we sifted through the boxes of well-worn, handwritten recipe cards from early years and pored over the thousands of recipes in our current database. It quickly became apparent that we should really embark on a dozen cookbooks! The selection process was daunting. However the decision was made: we would include recipes for dishes that our customers have chosen as their favorites over time.

You will find in these pages recipes for simple food to serve the family on a weekday and others to enjoy on special occasions. Many of the early recipes are for familiar, comfortable foods that our customers return for day after day mainly from American and French cooking traditions — creamy *Macaroni and Cheese*, home-style *Chicken Pot Pie*, *Big-Batch Bran Muffins*, *Raisin Pecan Butter Tarts* — and classics like *Coq au Vin*, *Roast Beef with Roasted Garlic Pan Gravy and Yorkshire Pudding* and *Apple Cinnamon Crumble Pie*. The collection expands to include current popular dishes from other cuisines such as spicy *Thai Green Curry Chicken*, South American-inspired grilled meats such as *Marinated Flank Steak with Chimichurri Sauce, Mushroom Risotto* including local wild mushrooms, nutritious salads such as *Soba Noodle Salad with Edamame* and *Five-Grain Pomegranate Salad*, and sweet treats such as *Fresh Ginger Cake* made special with grated fresh ginger or decadent, delicious *Tiramisù*. We encourage you to start off with the best ingredients of the season, develop techniques to bring out the best flavors and maybe add a touch of something special as a tasty surprise.

From our experience a well-informed food shopper is well on the way to becoming a great cook. Throughout the book you will find a collection of short food essays on popular ingredients that we hope you will find entertaining and informative. They were written by David Cobb, a highly esteemed writer, longtime friend and colleague. (We worked together for 18 years or so on "Epicure," a monthly food column in our local successful city magazine *Toronto Life*.) You will also find dozens of tips and hints on ingredients and cooking techniques gathered from experiences working in our professional kitchen.

Whether you are a once-in-a-while baker or a dedicated gourmet cook we hope that you will find this collection of All The Best recipes provides you with inspiration and success in the kitchen and many happy occasions around the dining table. We look forward to sharing exciting food experiences over the next 25 years and wish you all the best!

— *Jane Rodmell, Toronto, 2009*

All About these Recipes

We hope that the following notes will help you have great success in making delicious food from this collection of recipes. There are also food essays on specific foods from Apples to Vinegar throughout this cookbook (see Food Essays, page 440, for a complete list).

About Ingredients

Butter and Oils
Butter
We cook with unsalted butter. Use soft butter for ease of beating into sugar when making cake batters. Chilled butter is best for cutting into flour in making pastry and streusel. Butter has a low smoking point in relation to other fats and burns quickly. Use medium heat or use a mix of butter and oil when sautéing. (See also Butter, page 370.)

Olive Oil
We seek out good-quality extra virgin olive oil with light to medium fruity flavor for use in cooking. We treasure the single-estate premium extra virgin oils and use for seasoning on special occasions. (See also Olive Oil, page 76.)

Vegetable Oil
Our most frequently used vegetable oils are sunflower and canola. Sesame and nut oils are used for essential flavoring.

Dairy Products
Milk, Cream and Yogurt
Dairy products are labeled in different ways in different regions, so it is wise to understand the relationship between the local name and the percentage of fat in the product. We generally use homogenized milk and yogurt of about 3 percent fat. For enrichment of soups and sauces use cream according to your taste. Whipping, or heavy, cream is the most luxurious at 35 percent fat. Coffee, or table, cream has 18 percent fat and half-and-half cream has 10 to 12 percent fat. You need 35 percent cream for whipping.

Parmesan Cheese
When Parmesan is called for our first choice would always be for the real thing, Parmigiano-Reggiano, but we frequently use good-quality Grana Padano in cooking. Freshly grated cheese provides the best flavor.

Eggs
These recipes were tested using large eggs, free-range and hormone-free. Eggs at room temperature will provide more volume in batters when beaten than eggs straight from the refrigerator. Store eggs in original carton in the coldest part of refrigerator. Leftover eggs can be stored in a covered container in the refrigerator for up to 2 days. Egg yolks alone should be covered with cold water to prevent a skin from forming. They may be frozen for up to 4 months. Don't forget to label the container with the date and number of eggs. If freezing whole eggs, blend yolks and whites. Egg whites can be frozen in ice cube trays and then transferred into freezer bags. Thaw in the refrigerator for 12 to 24 hours and use as fresh. (See also Eggs, page 365.)

Flour
Unless otherwise listed we use all-purpose, unbleached white, whole wheat or pastry flour made from Canadian wheat.

Fruits and Vegetables

We recommend that you wash all produce thoroughly. Drain and dry as appropriate. Before cooking trim away inedible stalks, cores, pits, seeds and imperfections. Remove peel as required by the recipe or according to taste. Peel an old carrot but a fresh young carrot only needs a good scrub! Always dry salad greens thoroughly.

Citrus Juices and Zest

The juices of freshly squeezed lemons, limes, oranges and grapefruit are used in these recipes. Bottled or frozen juices do not provide the same taste. When peeling or cutting the fruit into segments, we work over a bowl so we can collect the juices to use in the dish.

Peppers

For bell peppers, remove stem, core and seeds before chopping. For hot chile peppers, remove stems: discard core and seeds also if you wish, either for appearance or to cut back on the heat a little. (See also Sweet and Hot Peppers, page 208.)

Anchovies and Capers

We use anchovies in many dishes as a subtle flavor enhancer (not to actually taste anything fishy), just as cooks used salted fish in Roman times. Seek out imported anchovies from Italy or Spain packed in salt in jars in the refrigerator display case at the market. You will find the flavor superior to canned anchovies. Always rinse off excess salt in cold water for both anchovies and capers before using and pat dry in paper towels. Store in the refrigerator.

Nuts

We use many varieties of nuts in our bakery and each variety adds distinct flavor to baked cookies, cakes, loaves, breads and desserts. Almonds, walnuts, pecans, hazelnuts, macadamia nuts and pine nuts are staples. Always make sure that the nuts you purchase are fresh. They tend to go rancid quickly, especially in warm cupboards. For short storage time toast nuts and store in a covered container in the refrigerator; for longer periods, store in the freezer and toast just before using.

Salt

Sea salt is our preferred salt, especially in cold dishes and coarse kosher salt is frequently used in cooking. We usually do not specify actual amounts of salt and pepper unless it is critical to the dish, as in brining for example. The desired amount of salt varies with the taste of the individual. If you are a salt lover your taste buds will desire more salt than may be tolerated by someone else. It's better to be conservative. Always taste a dish during cooking and before serving. (See also Salt, page 36.)

About Measuring

In our commercial kitchen, the chefs and bakers most frequently use kitchen scales. Weighing ingredients results in increased accuracy and consistency. For these recipes we used the familiar set of dry measuring cups, ranging from $1/4$ cup (50 mL) to 1 cup (250 mL), for measuring ingredients such as flour and sugar. The measurement comes to the top of the cup so that you can sweep off excess with the back of a knife. In the set of measuring spoons, ranging from $1/8$ tsp (0.5 mL) to 1 tbsp (15 mL), the measurement is also level with the top of the spoon. Liquids are measured in 1-cup (250 mL), 2-cup (500 mL) or 4-cup (1 L) measuring cups with handle and pouring spout. Bring the

measuring cup to eye level for accuracy. With practice you will soon begin to eye-ball quantities (e.g. 1 medium carrot, about 7 inches/17.5 cm) long is about 1 cup/250 mL chopped).
Precision in measurement is always necessary in baking.

Produce is assumed to be of medium-size unless otherwise specified. When the exact quantity is not critical we give a number (e.g. 1 stalk celery). When we need to be more precise we give a volume (e.g. ½ cup/ 125 mL chopped onion).

1 clove garlic is one medium clove, about 1 tsp (5 mL) finely chopped (e.g. not a giant clove nor a tiny one from the center of the bulb).

About Equipment

The equipment we used to make all the recipes in this cookbook is basic and familiar to most household kitchens.

The old standbys **food mill** and **blender** do a great job of puréeing soups, the **immersion blender** is useful for puréeing small quantities directly in the pot and the **food processor** takes all the work out of blending ingredients to make a dip, chopping nuts, cutting fat into flour etc.

We love using our **heavy-duty stand mixer** with its multiple whisks, paddles and dough hook for making cookies, cakes and breads, but we are equally at home doing these tasks with a **large bowl**, a **whisk** and a **wooden spoon**.

A heavy ceramic **mortar and pestle** is used for grinding spices or making a paste of garlic and gingerroot. For larger amounts of whole spices to be made into spice blends we have a **small electric grinder** dedicated to the purpose.

Every chef will agree that the most important equipment in the kitchen is a set of high quality sharp **knives**: a chef's knife with 9-inch (23 cm) blade for most chopping tasks, a knife with 6-inch (15 cm) blade for smaller jobs, a paring knife, a small knife with serrated blade, good for slicing tomatoes and cucumbers, and a large knife with serrated blade for breads. Keep knives sharp and safe. Most accidents in the kitchen are caused by using a dull knife and carelessness in handling knives. If a chef walks through our kitchen with a knife, the point is carefully pointing towards the floor and he calls out "KNIFE" to alert his fellow workers.

Don't underestimate the importance of a couple of good **cutting boards**: either plastic or wood is fine, but make sure that they are large enough so that you have room to work comfortably.

An old **box grater** still does the job of grating nutmeg on one fine grating side, lemon zest on another and grating carrots or shredding cheese on the sides with larger shredding teeth. However, handy **Microplane graters** are less hard on the knuckles and a **zester** makes fancy longer shreds of zest for garnish.

Other equipment I would not want to be without: an **instant-read thermometer** that measures the inside temperature of meats and poultry quickly and accurately, **spring-hinged tongs** (short handled ones for working in the kitchen and longer ones for turning foods on the grill), **wooden spoons** of various sizes (one with a flat bottom for scraping the sides of a saucepan), flexible heatproof **spatulas** for folding batters and scraping bowls, an **offset spatula** for icing cakes…and a **salad spinner**. Crisp dry greens are essential to every good salad.

Basic Pots and Pans

Most of the recipes in this cookbook can be made with the following basic pots and pans:

Most frequently we use a **large ovenproof skillet with lid**, about 12 inches (30 cm), and a **heavy-duty Dutch oven** with lid (about 6 quart/6 L) in which to sear foods and then simmer on the stove top or transfer to the oven for gentle braising. **Saucepans** are in constant use (small, about 1 quart/ 1 L, medium, about 2 quart/2 L and large about 3 quart /3 L), a **large pot** 6 to 8 quart (6 to 8 L) for stocks and soups, and a good-quality **roasting pan**, preferably without nonstick coating, in which to roast meats and poultry and deglaze cooking juices on the stovetop.

If baking is your passion, this familiar equipment is often in use: 10- by 15-inch (25 by 37.5 cm) **rimmed baking sheets**, 9-inch (23 cm) **pie plate**, 6-inch (15 cm) **springform pan**, 9- by 5-inch (2 L) **loaf pan**, 13- by 9-inch (3 L) **baking pan**, 8-inch (20 cm) **round cake pan**, **wire cooling racks** and **parchment paper**, and, of course, a **rolling pin**. Short ones are useless! Invest in a solid wooden rolling pin, about 15 inches (37.5 cm) long with smooth rolling action, usually a steel shaft through the center with roller bearings at the handles.

Food Mill or Mouli

One of the most treasured pieces of equipment in my kitchen is a battered, old French "mouli," purchased in my student days in England at a favorite haunt in London, The Elizabeth David Kitchen Shop. In our commercial kitchen today we use an enormous food mill to purée bushels of tomatoes and apples for sauce, mountains of mashed potatoes and loads of legumes and vegetables for soups. It's an agreeably ergonomic and simple tool. It comes with different plates that allow you to purée food to varying degrees of smoothness with a few turns of the handle. The plates also keep back unwanted peel and seeds at the same time. For some tasks a food processor or blender is just too vigorous — starchy vegetables such as potatoes turn gummy in a flash and, unless you work carefully using short bursts of power, your bean soup becomes a smooth purée instead of the pleasantly textured creation you may prefer.

Techniques

Preparing Herbs, Spices and Other Flavorings

What is a Chiffonade of Basil?

Sometimes recipes call for a "chiffonade" of fresh herbs or leafy vegetables, such as basil or baby spinach. This French term refers to a different cut, a fine sliver, instead of a chop. These fine herb strands make an attractive garnish for soups, savory crostini and many main dishes.

1. Stack 2 to 3 washed and trimmed basil leaves on top of each other.
2. Roll them up together lengthwise.
3. Cut across the rolled herb leaves in slices about ⅛-inch (3 mm) wide.

Cutting into Julienne

This is a technique where strips of vegetables are cut finely, about the size and length of a matchstick, and are frequently added to soups and salads as part of a garnish. There are many gadgets to help with the task. Seek out a German-made julienne cutter made by Börner. It rests securely on top of a bowl and is easier to use than the traditional mandolin. Or use your chef's knife.

1. With a sharp chef's knife, cut a thin strip along the length of a vegetable so that it sits flat on the cutting board. Cut the vegetable crosswise into 2-inch

(5 cm) lengths, then lengthwise into thin vertical slices.

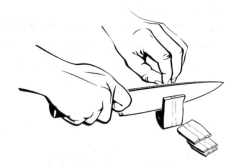

2. Stack the slices and cut lengthwise to make thin strips. For very fine strips, cut continuously keeping the tip of the knife resting on the board. Keep your fingers tucked back away from the blade!

To Dice or Chop? — A Thorny Question!

Dicing is for occasions when the precise shape and small size of the pieces (⅛- to ¼-inch/3 mm to 0.5 cm cubes) is desired for appearance and for even cooking. Chopping is less exact, sometimes defined further as "finely chopped" or "roughly chopped." The shape is less critical, but the pieces should still be of even size so that they cook in the same time period. In long cooking stews and braises, finely chopped vegetables will soften to the point at which they melt into the sauce. Roughly chopped indicates larger pieces that will retain a distinct shape. Different vegetables that are to be cooked together may be chopped or cut into cubes of a specific size so that they cook within the same time period, yet retain their chunky shape.

1. Stack vegetable slices as for julienne and cut into thin strips.
2. Take a bundle of julienned vegetables and cut crosswise to make small dice, $\frac{1}{8}$ to $\frac{1}{4}$ inch (3 mm to 0.5 cm) or medium dice, $\frac{1}{4}$ to $\frac{3}{8}$ (0.5 to 0.75 cm).

Slicing an Onion

1. With a sharp chef's knife, cut peeled onion in half from the stem to the root.
2. Place onion cut side down on a cutting board. Trim off the root end. Make parallel cuts from stem to root about $\frac{1}{8}$ to $\frac{1}{4}$ inch (3 mm to 0.5 cm) apart.

Chopping an Onion

1. With a sharp chef's knife, cut peeled onion in half from the stem to the root.
2. Place onion cut side down on a cutting board. Keep a firm hold of the onion and make parallel horizontal cuts almost to the root but not through it about $\frac{1}{8}$ to $\frac{1}{4}$ inch (3 mm to 0.5 cm) apart.

3. Make parallel cuts from the stem almost to the root end.

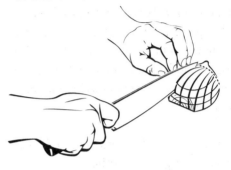

4. Cut across the onion to form small dice.

Chopping Fresh Herbs

1. Strip the leaves of herbs from the stalks and make a pile on the cutting board.
2. Holding the tip of a sharp chef's knife with one hand on the board, chop the herbs into fine or coarse pieces with a continuous up-and-down cutting motion, moving the knife back and forth across the pile of herbs.

Using a Mortar and Pestle

Grinding whole spices by hand with mortar and pestle is a traditional and very satisfying technique. It is also an efficient method of blending ingredients, such as chopped herbs, fresh garlic, coarse salt, nuts, ginger or grated cheese, into wonderful flavorful pastes, dressings and sauces.

1. Place chopped herbs, garlic or other dry ingredients in the mortar. Pound with the pestle until thoroughly combined into a purée or paste.

2. Gradually add oil or other liquid and mix to form a smooth sauce.

Peeling and Chopping Garlic

1. Place the garlic clove on a cutting board. Place the flat side of a chef's knife on top and bang it with your fist.

2. Remove and discard the skin and finely chop the garlic.
3. Use the flat of the knife at the very tip to mash the garlic into a fine paste, if required.

Preparing Fresh Gingerroot

Fresh gingerroot is very fibrous. In some preparations, especially in baking and confectionary, when you are seeking maximum ginger flavor without the fibers grate ginger using a fine grater or rasp.

1. Gingerroot when young and fresh has a fine skin that you can scrape away with the edge of a teaspoon, otherwise peel away brown outer skin with a paring knife.

2. Cut gingerroot into slices and press down on slices with the flat side of a chef's knife to break up the fibers. Chop finely.

Preparing Lemongrass

1. Trim and discard outside dry or damaged leaves from the stalk of lemongrass. Cut off the tough piece at the bottom of the stem.

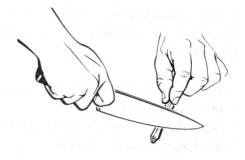

2. Soften the stem of lemongrass with the blunt edge of a chef's knife. Chop the softened stalk into fine pieces. Save the top of the stalk and use to flavor stocks and soups.

Preparing Fresh Chiles

Handle fresh chiles carefully; a hint of the fiery juices can burn if in contact with eyes or lips. Wear protective gloves if your hands are sensitive.

1. Rinse chiles, cut off stem and halve lengthwise.
2. Scrape out seeds and cut away the fleshy ribs on the inside. Chop finely as required.

Seeding a Pomegranate

Extracting the sweet-tart seeds from a pomegranate is a challenge. Release the seeds from between the tough membranes without cutting into them. Rub the seeds in a strainer placed over a bowl when you want to release the juice.

1. Cut around the blossom end with the tip of a sharp knife and discard.
2. Score the tough outer skin into quarters.
3. Working over a bowl, break the pomegranate open into sections with

your fingers and peel back the skin. Release the seeds from between the tough white membranes.

Using a Whole Vanilla Bean

A whole vanilla bean provides pure sweet vanilla flavor. Infuse the bean in a hot liquid, for example in sugar syrup for poaching fruit, or in milk or cream for making custard. The whole bean may be used many times: just rinse and dry it after use. Tuck it into a jar of granulated sugar, and you always have vanilla sugar on hand to flavor desserts.

1. Infuse the whole vanilla bean in a hot liquid. It will soften.
2. For stronger vanilla flavor, cut along the length of the bean and scrape out the seeds. Add seeds to the liquid and let them stand for 10 minutes; then strain. Or crush the seeds and add to the liquid if you wish to add the slight crunch of intense vanilla to your dish.

Working with Poultry, Meat and Seafood

Cutting up Poultry

Learn how to cut up poultry into serving pieces yourself and you'll have neatly trimmed pieces, interesting variety and save money, too.

1. Pull one leg away from the body and cut through the skin between the body and both sides of the thigh. Press down on the leg until the ball at the top of the thigh pops out of the socket. Cut between the ball and socket and release the leg. Repeat with the other leg. Divide the leg at the joint to provide two pieces — thigh and drumstick, if you wish.

2. Press one wing against the body of the bird and locate the joint at the top. Make a cut between the ball and socket at the shoulder, then press down and slice through the skin to release the wing. Repeat with the other wing. Cut off pinions at the ends, if you wish.

3. Put a knife blade through the cavity, or use poultry shears, to cut the rib bones and backbone from the breast on each side. Save for the stockpot. Slit along the breastbone to loosen the meat and cut the breast in half.

4. To cut a larger bird into eight portions, leave the wing attached and divide each breast in half, cutting through the breast and rib bones on the diagonal and leaving some breast meat attached to the top of each wing.

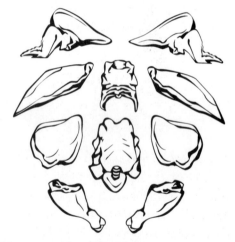

A Note on the Wishbone

The wishbone is the small bone at the front of the breastbone in poultry. The top is joined by cartilage to the breastbone and the ends attach it to the collarbones on either side. If you cut this out with the tip of a knife before, or after, cooking, it is easier to cut neat even slices from the breast. (You also get to make a wish, if you end up with the top piece, after pulling apart the wishbone with a friend.)

Trussing a Chicken or Turkey

1. Fold the flap of skin at the neck under the bird and secure with a small skewer poked through the skin on each side of the backbone. Tuck the wing tips underneath.
2. Center the middle of a length of kitchen string between the legs; bring each end up and over the ends of the legs. Cross the string, pull the legs together and tie.

3. If you want to make a more compact package, pull each end of string back around the thighs and wings and tie at the neck. Cut away string and discard after cooked turkey has rested and before carving.

To Butterfly or Spatchcock a Game Hen or Chicken

1. Place game hen on a cutting board breast-side up; make sure that there is nothing in the cavity. With a sharp chef's knife cut flap of skin hanging off the top of the breasts and cut away wishbone.
2. Push the knife into the bird through the cavity and cut down on one side of the backbone right through the skin, or use poultry shears. Pull the bird open and cut on the other side of the backbone to detach it completely from the body. Discard the backbone, or save it for stock.

3. Spread the bird out on the cutting board with the breast side facing up. With the heel of your hand press down on the breast to flatten.

Carving a Capon or Turkey

After a resting period on a carving board or large platter, remove any trussing strings from the bird and provide yourself with a very sharp long knife with a pointed tip, a sturdy two-pronged fork and a warm serving platter.

1. Steady the bird with a fork and cut through the skin between the thigh and the breast. Bend the thigh outwards and slice down at the joint to release the leg.

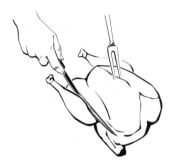

2. Make a horizontal cut straight to the bone across the corner of the breast above the wing.

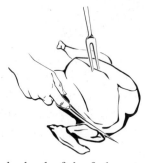

3. Hold the back of the fork against the breast on the side you are about to carve. Make long slices, slightly on the diagonal

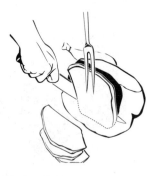

across the length of the breast. (This is easier if you have removed the wishbone, see page 16.)

4. Move the wing to locate the joint, cut through and remove. A small portion of breast meat will be attached. You might leave the wing attached until later, since it helps to steady the bird while you carve the other side

5. Cut through the leg at the joint between the thigh and the drumstick. Slice the dark meat on the thigh portion parallel to the bone into pieces. Slice the meat on each side of the drumstick in the same way, or leave it whole.

6. Arrange all the slices on the warm serving platter.

Making a Neat Package of a Boned Roast

1. Cut off about 5 feet (1.5 m) butcher's string from the roll. Tie one loop around one end of the meat and make a knot.

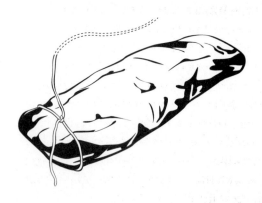

2. Hold the length of string in your right hand (if you're right-handed), 6 to 8 inches (15 to 20 cm) to the right of the meat. With your other hand make a loop with the string that stretches between the meat and your right hand.

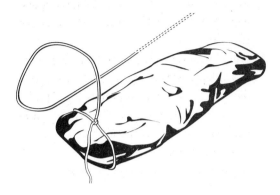

3. Put this loop around the meat about $\frac{1}{2}$ to 1 inch (1 to 2.5 cm) from the first loop. Tighten the loop by gently pulling the string to the right. Repeat until the entire roast is neatly tied with loops of string. Make a knot with the last loop and cut off extra string.

Frenching a Lamb or Pork Rib

On a restaurant plate, your lamb loin rib chops arrive with meat moist and pink and rib bones nicely browned, clean and glistening. To prepare the racks ready for roasting takes a bit of work. The technique used to trim the fat and silver skin from around and in between the bones is called "frenching." Your friendly butcher will help you with this, or arm yourself with a small sharp knife and give it a try.

1. Score across the length of each rack about 2 inches (5 cm) down from the tip of the bones on both sides.

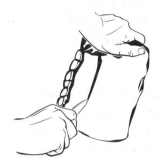

2. Make 2 cuts down to the score line between each rib bone, keeping close to the bones. Remove the fat and sinew between the bones.

3. Place your sharp blade across the score line on the top of each bone and scrape up the bone, carefully pulling away the tough sinewy covering. Repeat on the underside.

Very conscientious chefs will clean the bones thoroughly with an abrasive pad or scrape them with a taut length of string! However you can wrap the bones with foil to prevent any remaining bits of sinew from burning during the roasting or grilling period.

Cutting up a Live Lobster

1. Protecting your hand with a cloth, hold the lobster firmly over the back, insert the point of a chef's knife in the cross mark at the head and press swiftly down. (The lobster is instantly dispatched.)

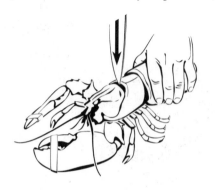

2. Still protecting your hand with a cloth, hold the lobster firmly by the head, slice down through the middle to the tail. Remove and discard the spongy head sac and the line of intestine, scrape out the tomalley (the soft greenish liver) and the coral (present in female lobsters) — it will be blackish when uncooked and turns pink when cooked. The tomalley and the

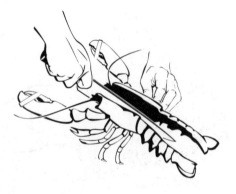

coral can be reserved for use in soups and sauces. Crack the claws. Save any accumulated juices and add to a sauce.

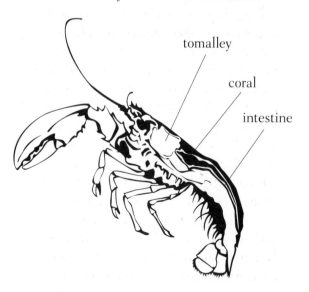

tomalley

coral

intestine

Cutting up a Cooked Lobster

1. Hold lobster firmly at the head, twist and pull away the tail section. With strong kitchen shears, cut along the underside of the tail on both sides, pull back the shell to release the meat in one piece.

2. Cut off and crack claws. Use the body shell and legs for seasoning shellfish stews and sauces.

Perfecting Pastry

Rolling Pastry

Rolling out pastry can be intimidating if it's something you don't do very often. Here are a few tips from our pastry chef: If refrigerated, let pastry stand for 10 to 15 minutes at room temperature to warm up a bit. Cold pastry is hard to handle. Lightly dust clean, uncluttered work surface with flour. Dust a little flour on the surface of the pastry and on the rolling pin. Working from the center of the disk, roll out pastry in each direction until about $\frac{1}{2}$ inch (1 cm) thick. Slide a metal spatula under the pastry to loosen it from the work surface. If it seems to be sticking, sprinkle a little flour underneath. Continue to roll from the center until about $\frac{1}{8}$ inch (3 mm) thick.

Assembling a Two-Crust Pie

1. Prepare 2 disks of pastry. Roll out one pastry circle about $\frac{1}{8}$ inch (3 mm) thick and cut a circle about 1 inch (2.5 cm) larger than the top of the pie plate.
2. Loosen pastry from work surface with a metal spatula. Fold the pastry circle in half and lift it onto the center of the pie plate. Gently unfold the circle and ease the pastry to fit the bottom of the pie plate.

3. Fill pastry shell with cool filling. Using a pastry brush lightly brush the edges of the pastry shell with egg wash.

4. Roll out another pastry circle about $\frac{1}{8}$ inch (3 mm) thick and cut a circle about 1 inch (2.5 cm) larger than the top of the pie plate. Loosen pastry from work surface with a metal spatula. Fold pastry circle in half and lift it onto the center of the pie plate over the filling. Gently unfold the circle over the filling and press the edges of the pastry together.

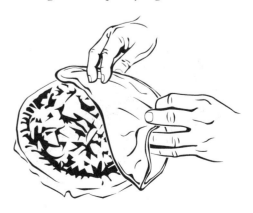

5. Trim excess pastry and crimp around the edge. To crimp, place your thumb and middle finger on the pastry edge about 1 inch (2.5 cm) apart and pull back on the pastry in between with your index finger, either pull straight back or with a slight twist. Turn the pie plate in a clockwise direction and repeat all around the edge. Or you can simply seal the edge with the tines of a fork or make a scallop pattern with a knife. Make small slits in top to allow steam to escape.

pan. Unfold the pastry circle and gently smooth the pastry to line the bottom of the pan and up the sides, allowing the pastry to hang over the edge of the pan by an inch (2.5 cm) or so. Press the pastry against the sides so it is smooth and there are no folds. (If you leave folds in the pastry it will cause problems when you unmold your cooked pie.) Arrange filling in the pastry case.

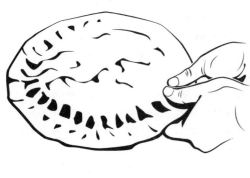

Lining a Springform Pan

1. Grease the inside of the springform pan. Cut a circle of parchment to line the bottom and a strip of parchment to line the sides. Take two-thirds of the pastry and roll into a large circle, about 12 inches (30 cm) in diameter. Roll out the remaining pastry to make a circle about 7 inches (18 cm) in diameter.
2. Fold the large pastry circle in quarters. Place the point of the folded circle in the middle of the bottom of the springform

3. Beat the remaining egg to make an egg wash. Brush the edges of the pastry in the pan with egg wash. Lay the smaller pastry circle on top. Trim away excess pastry. Lift up the edges and crimp to form a decorative stand-up edge and brush top of pie with egg wash. Make small slits in pastry top to allow steam to escape.

Lining a Tart Pan

We recommend using a tart pan with a removable base for preparing special occasion tarts and flans. It is easy to unmold the tart for serving and makes an elegant presentation.

4. Roll the pin over the top of the pan to release excess dough. With your thumb and index finger gently press the pastry up around the edge and smooth the rim. Do not let excess pastry overhang the edge of the pan. Prick the bottom of the pastry shell to prevent it from bubbling during baking. Chill until firm, at least 15 minutes.

1. Lightly grease the pan. On a lightly floured surface, roll pastry about $\frac{1}{8}$ inch (3 mm) thick into a circle about 2 inches (5 cm) larger than the pan.
2. Roll the pastry around the rolling pin and lift it over the pan. Unroll gently.

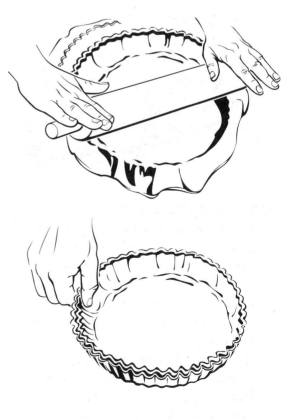

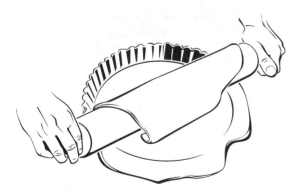

3. Lift the edges of the pastry and use your fingers to smooth the dough over the bottom, around the inside edge and up the sides of the pan.

Forming a Samosa

It takes practice to create a perfect samosa! Seal the edges of the pastry cone securely so that the stuffing stays inside and the samosa remains intact during deep-frying (see recipe, page 347).

1. On a lightly floured surface, roll samosa dough ⅛ inch (3 mm) thick. Stamp out circles about 6 inches (15 cm) in diameter. Cut each circle of dough in half. Dip your finger in water and moisten half of the straight edge of a semicircle of dough.

3. Fill the cone with 1 tbsp (15 mL) stuffing. Moisten the inside edges of the opening and pinch closed to make a secure seam. Place samosa, seam side down, on a baking tray in a cool spot while you complete assembling the rest. Deep-fry as described on page 346.

2. Pick up the dough and bring the half with the dry edge over the half with the moistened edge overlapping by about ¼ inch (0.5 cm) to form a cone. Pinch to seal the seam.

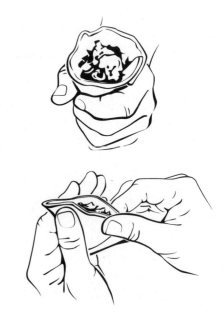

Soups

Carrot Ginger Soup

This friendly soup is a year-round winner — tasty and comforting whatever the weather. A dash of fresh lime juice squeezed into the soup at the table adds a burst of tingling flavor.

Tips

Letting the soup cool for 1 to 2 minutes before puréeing prevents you from being burned with hot splatters.

Puréeing soup in a blender will produce the smoothest results. Stray bits of vegetables usually get left behind when using the food processor or hand-held immersion blender.

Adding a small quantity of rice to some vegetable soups when the basic mix does not include other starchy vegetables, such as potato or sweet potato, will act as a thickener.

● Blender or food processor

2 tsp	vegetable oil	10 mL
1 tsp	butter	5 mL
1	onion, chopped	1
1	clove garlic, chopped	1
2 tbsp	chopped gingerroot	25 mL
2 tbsp	basmati rice	25 mL
1 lb	carrots, chopped (5 to 6 medium)	500 g
1 tsp	ground cumin	5 mL
½ tsp	cayenne pepper	2 mL
	Kosher or sea salt	
6 cups	Vegetable Stock (page 56) or ready-to-use broth	1.5 L
1 tbsp	chopped cilantro	15 mL
6 tbsp	yogurt, optional	90 mL
1	lime, sliced into wedges, optional	1

1. In a large pot, heat oil and butter over medium heat. Add onion and sauté until softened but not browned, 4 to 5 minutes. Add garlic, ginger and rice and toss for 1 minute. Add carrots.

2. Sprinkle cumin, cayenne and ½ tsp (2 mL) salt over vegetables and stir to coat with the spicy, seasoned cooking juices. Stir in vegetable stock and bring to a boil. Reduce heat to low and simmer until carrots are tender, 30 to 40 minutes.

3. Remove from heat and let soup cool for a few minutes (see Tips, left). In a blender, purée soup in batches. Return to pot, reheat over medium heat until steaming. Taste and adjust seasoning. Serve in warm bowls and garnish with a sprinkling of fresh cilantro. Top with a spoonful of yogurt and serve slices of lime on the side, if you like.

Fresh Herbs

The magic ingredient in the kitchen

In our commercial kitchen one whole shelf in the produce walk-in refrigerator is set aside for the chef's selection of fresh, aromatic herbs supplied regularly by local farmers. Herbs contain essential oils and aromatic compounds that heighten the flavor of food and lend distinction to a dish. Some of our favorites are:

- Flat-leaf or Italian parsley is used in quantity every day in stocks, soups, stews, sauces, salads and pestos. This variety has four times the essential oil of curly parsley and is a great flavor enhancer.
- Fresh thyme, oregano, rosemary, tarragon, sage and bay leaf are always on hand and used extensively in cool weather dishes. Basil is a favorite salad herb, particularly to use alongside the season's fresh ripe tomatoes, together with dill, chives and chervil.
- Cilantro, lemongrass and mint are added to the mix when Asian, North African or Mexican dishes are included on the weekly menu.
- Bouquet garni (aka herb bouquet): This bundle of herbs is tied with kitchen string and dropped into a pot of simmering broth or stew to add flavor. The classic mix includes sprigs of fresh thyme, parsley and a bay leaf. Sometimes other aromatics are included, such as a piece of leek green, a celery stalk or a strip of orange zest.

  If spices are added, such as whole peppercorns, cloves, allspice berries, juniper berries or fennel seeds, they should be enclosed in a small cheesecloth bag. Cut a triple layer of cheesecloth, about a 6-inch (15 cm) square, add the spices and tie in a bundle with a length of string.

  Remove and discard the herb bundle at the end of the cooking time. Squeeze the flavorful juices from the bag into the cooking pot before discarding.

  Prepackaged bouquet garni are available that include a mix of dried herbs. Occasionally the mix is labeled Herbes de Provence and may include thyme, savory, fennel, sage, rosemary and bay leaves.

Cream of Mushroom Soup

SERVES 6 TO 8

A richly flavored, elegant soup to serve as a first course at lunch or dinner. Make your selection of mushrooms at the market, depending on what varieties look fresh and good. White button, cremini, shiitake and oyster mushrooms are widely available. Include wild mushrooms in season or dried porcini mushrooms to intensify the flavor.

Tip

To clean mushrooms: Brush off any dirt or rinse mushroom briefly. Although the mushroom won't absorb water as commonly thought, rinsing can discolor them.

● **Blender or food processor**

1½ lbs	assorted mushrooms	750 g
3 tbsp	butter	45 mL
1	leek, white and tender green parts only, thinly sliced	1
¼ cup	coarsely chopped shallots	50 mL
2	cloves garlic, coarsely chopped	2
1½ tbsp	chopped thyme	22 mL
	Salt and freshly ground black pepper	
2 tbsp	sherry or brandy	25 mL
3 tbsp	sherry vinegar	45 mL
1	small potato, peeled and thinly sliced	1
7 cups	Vegetable Stock (page 56) or ready-to-use broth	1.75 L
½ cup	half-and-half (10%) cream	125 mL
2 tsp	chopped tarragon	10 mL
	Mushroom Asparagus Garnish, optional (page 29)	

1. Clean and thinly slice mushrooms. Set aside.
2. In a large pot, melt butter over medium heat. Add leek and cook, stirring, for 5 minutes. Add shallots and garlic and sauté for 5 minutes. Add mushrooms, thyme, salt and pepper and sauté until mushrooms are softened, 6 to 7 minutes. Add sherry and sherry vinegar. Increase heat to medium-high and cook until liquid is reduced to a syrupy glaze, about 5 minutes.
3. Add potato and vegetable stock. Bring to a boil. Reduce heat and simmer until potato is tender, about 15 minutes.
4. Remove from heat. Stir in cream and let cool for a few minutes. In a blender, purée soup, in batches, until smooth, but still retaining some texture. Return to pot and reheat over medium-low until steaming. Taste and adjust seasoning. Serve in warm bowls and sprinkle with tarragon or Mushroom Asparagus Garnish, if using.

Mushroom Asparagus Garnish

Makes enough for 6 to 8 servings

4 oz	assorted wild or exotic mushrooms, trimmed	125 g
6	spears asparagus, halved lengthwise	6
2 tsp	vegetable oil	10 mL
1 tsp	butter	5 mL
2 tsp	minced garlic	10 mL
	Salt and freshly ground black pepper	
2 tsp	finely chopped tarragon	10 mL

1. Clean and thinly slice mushrooms. Slice asparagus into pieces on the bias, $1^{1}/_{2}$ inches (4 cm) thick.
2. In a skillet, heat oil and butter over medium-high heat. Add mushrooms, asparagus and garlic and sauté for 1 to 2 minutes. Toss with salt and pepper to taste. Set aside.
3. Use sautéed mushrooms and asparagus to garnish individual soup bowls and sprinkle with tarragon.

Butternut Squash and Apple Soup

This soup is delicious when served as a smooth creamy purée. Press puréed soup through a sieve for extra smoothness. For a pleasing contrast in textures top each serving with crunchy herb croutons or accompany with a crisp herb crostini topped with grated Gruyère and broiled briefly until cheese melts.

- **Preheat oven to 400°F (200°C)**
- **Blender or food processor**
- **Roasting pan**

1	butternut squash, peeled and chopped, about 4 cups (1 L)	1
1 tbsp	olive oil	15 mL
	Kosher or sea salt	
2 tbsp	butter	25 mL
2	leeks, white and tender green parts only, chopped	2
1	clove garlic, chopped	1
1	large potato, peeled and chopped	1
1	large apple, peeled and chopped	1
1 tsp	chopped thyme or ½ tsp (2 mL) dried thyme	5 mL
½ tsp	chopped rosemary or ¼ tsp (1 mL) dried rosemary	2 mL
5 cups	Vegetable Stock (page 56) or ready-to-use broth or water	1.25 L
	Freshly ground black pepper	
¼ cup	whipping (35%) cream, optional	50 mL
1 tbsp	chopped flat-leaf parsley	15 mL
	Croutons (page 31)	

1. In a large bowl, toss butternut squash with olive oil and ½ tsp (2 mL) salt. Spread in a single layer in a roasting pan. Roast in preheated oven for 10 minutes. Shake the pan to turn the squash pieces over and continue roasting until edges of vegetables are nicely caramelized, about 10 minutes more. Remove from oven and set aside.

2. In a large pot, melt butter over medium heat. Add leeks and garlic and sauté until soft. Add roasted squash, potato, apple, thyme and rosemary. Stir in stock and bring to a boil. Reduce heat and simmer until vegetables are tender, 20 to 25 minutes.

3. Remove from heat and let cool for a few minutes. In a blender, purée soup, in batches, until smooth. Return to pot and reheat over medium heat until steaming. Taste and adjust seasoning. Stir in cream, if using. Serve in warm bowls and garnish with parsley and/or top with crispy croutons.

Crispy Croutons

Homemade croutons are so much better than any store-bought version and justify the extra effort involved. They're a handy item to have around to add to soups and salads or to crunch up and use as a casserole topping.

Cut homemade-style bread, white or whole wheat, into cubes to make about 6 cups (1.5 L). Place in a large bowl. Add salt, freshly ground black pepper, herbs and seasoning of your choice to taste. Add a minced garlic clove, a dash of hot sauce and/or 2 tbsp (25 mL) grated Parmesan cheese, if you like. Toss seasoned bread cubes with 3 tbsp (45 mL) olive oil or a mixture of oil and melted butter. Spread in a single layer on baking sheets and bake in preheated 375°F (190°C) oven, shaking the pans a few times to ensure croutons brown evenly, until bread cubes are crisp and golden, 10 to 15 minutes. Let cool and store in a covered container for up to 2 days.

Makes 6 cups (1.5 L).

Dried Herbs 101

Dried herbs have a more concentrated flavor than fresh herbs. To replace 1 tbsp (15 mL) fresh herbs it is recommended to use $\frac{1}{2}$ to $1\frac{1}{2}$ tsp (2 to 7 mL) of dried. The amount is determined by the intensity of the flavor of the herb and how finely it is crumbled or ground. Strongly flavored herbs such as rosemary, sage and tarragon are best used with discretion.

Since the aromatic compounds in herbs tend to be more soluble in fat than in water, the flavor is enhanced if you toss herbs with other ingredients in a little oil or fat at the beginning of the cooking process before adding liquids.

To release the aromatic components of dried herb leaves, bruise them gently with your fingers before adding to a dish. Measure the amount of herbs to be included in a dish into the palm of your hand, bruise them gently and add them to the pot. If you shake herbs from the jar directly into the pot, heat and moisture can get into the jar and ruin the remaining herbs.

Tomato Basil Soup

Without a doubt this is the most popular soup in our repertoire. But, be warned, the essential good flavor rests completely on the quality of the ingredients — fresh, field-ripened tomatoes in season or premium canned plum tomatoes and fresh basil is the only way to go!

Variations

Sunshine Tomato Basil Soup:
Wonderful heirloom tomatoes in glorious colors are showing up at roadside markets. Surprise your guests and make your Tomato Basil Soup with ripe sunny yellow tomatoes instead.

This soup is also refreshing and delicious served chilled on a hot day.

● **Blender or food processor**

1 tbsp	olive oil	15 mL
2 tsp	butter	10 mL
1	onion, chopped	1
2	cloves garlic, chopped	2
3 lbs	Roma (plum) tomatoes, peeled, seeded and chopped (about 6 cups/1.5 L), or 2 cans (each 28 oz/796 mL) plum tomatoes with juice	1.5 kg
	Kosher or sea salt	
Pinch	granulated sugar, optional	Pinch
2 tbsp	basil chiffonade (approx.) (page 12)	25 mL
6 tbsp	Crème Fraîche (page 33), optional	90 mL

1. In a large pot, heat olive oil and butter over medium heat. Add onion and sauté until softened but not browned, 4 to 5 minutes. Add garlic and sauté for 1 minute. Stir in tomatoes and $\frac{1}{2}$ tsp (2 mL) salt. Bring to a simmer. Reduce heat to low and simmer for about 20 minutes.

2. Remove from heat and let cool for a few minutes. In a blender, purée soup, in batches, until smooth. Return to pot and reheat over medium heat until steaming. Taste and adjust seasoning, adding a little sugar, if needed. Stir in basil. Serve in warm bowls and garnish with a spoonful of crème fraîche and a little additional slivered basil, if you like.

Crème Fraîche

A spoonful of this thick, slightly tangy cream makes an enriching addition to a sauce or soup as well as a delicious topping to a fruit tart. Unlike yogurt and sour cream, it has the advantage of withstanding heat without separating when added to soups and sauces.

In a small saucepan, combine 1 cup (250 mL) whipping (35%) cream with $\frac{1}{3}$ cup (75 mL) buttermilk and 1 tbsp (15 mL) lemon juice. Stir over low heat until cream is lukewarm (e.g. body temperature when tested on the inside of your wrist). Pour into a bowl and set aside, partially covered, at room temperature, for 12 to 24 hours, until cream thickens and develops a slightly tart flavor. Use immediately or cover and refrigerate for up to 2 weeks.

Makes $1\frac{1}{3}$ cups (325 mL).

Easy Crème Fraîche

Combine equal parts of whipping (35%) cream and sour cream. Set aside, partially covered, at room temperature, for 12 to 24 hours, until cream thickens and develops a slightly tart flavor. Use immediately or cover and refrigerate for up to 2 weeks. The quality of taste depends on whether you can find good 35% cream and sour cream that has not been ultra-pasteurized and stabilized.

Gazpacho

The flavors of summer in a bowl! This classic Spanish soup is perfect for a summer lunch or supper or to tote along on a picnic. When local plum tomatoes are at their peak we include them instead of using canned tomatoes, and sometimes we grill the peppers, onions and tomatoes to add a pleasing smoky flavor to the soup.

Tip

If gazpacho is too thick, add ice water or chilled vegetable stock. On a hot summer's day, add an ice cube per serving to keep the soup chilled.

Variation

Grilled Gazpacho: Before chopping, toss peppers, onion and fresh tomatoes with a spoonful of olive oil and grill over a moderate fire until nicely charred. Follow Gazpacho recipe Steps 1 through 3.

Food processor or blender

1 tsp	finely chopped garlic	5 mL
½ tsp	kosher or sea salt	2 mL
¼ cup	fresh white bread crumbs	50 mL
1 tbsp	extra virgin olive oil	15 mL
1	English cucumber, peeled, seeded and roughly chopped	1
½	green bell pepper, roughly chopped	½
½	red bell pepper, roughly chopped	½
½	red onion, roughly chopped	½
2 tbsp	chopped seeded jalapeño pepper	25 mL
1	can (28 oz/796 mL) plum tomatoes, drained and chopped, juice reserved, or 2 cups (500 mL) chopped seeded ripe Roma (plum) tomatoes	1
2 tbsp	red wine vinegar	25 mL
Dash	hot pepper sauce, optional	Dash
4 tbsp	sour cream, optional	60 mL
1	green onion, finely chopped, optional	1

1. In a large bowl, crush garlic and salt together. Stir in bread crumbs and oil.

2. In food processor, pulse cucumber, green and red peppers, red onion, jalapeño and tomatoes, in batches, until finely chopped. Add to bread crumb mixture. Stir in vinegar and enough of the reserved tomato juice to reach desired consistency. Add hot pepper sauce, if using. Taste and adjust seasoning. Let chill in a covered container in the refrigerator.

3. Serve chilled with a garnish of sour cream and chopped green onions, if desired.

Roasted Red Pepper Soup

A soup to celebrate the pure, sweet flavor of roasted peppers. Adjust the richness of the purée by using light cream, instead of table cream or omit cream altogether. Enjoy the soup chilled on a summer's day.

Tip

Roasted Peppers: Toss peppers in 1 tbsp (15 mL) oil and place on a barbecue grill over high heat or under the broiler. Roast, turning occasionally, until skins are evenly charred, 15 to 20 minutes. Transfer peppers to a bowl and cover. Let steam for 10 minutes. Remove and discard charred skins and seeds. Complete this task over a bowl to catch the good pepper juices. Roughly chop peppers.

Blender or food processor

2 tbsp	olive oil	25 mL
1	onion, chopped	1
2	cloves garlic, chopped	2
4	large red bell peppers, roasted, juices reserved (see Tip, left)	4
	Salt and freshly ground black pepper	
5 cups	Vegetable Stock (page 56) or ready-to-use broth	1.25 L
½ cup	table (18%) cream	125 mL
1½ tsp	balsamic vinegar	7 mL
1 tbsp	chopped basil	15 mL
	Basil chiffonade	

1. In a large pot, heat oil over medium heat. Add onion and sauté until softened but not browned, 4 to 5 minutes. Add garlic and sauté for 1 minute. Stir in peppers, pepper juices, ½ tsp (2 mL) salt and a few grinds of pepper. Stir in stock. Bring to a simmer. Reduce heat to low and cook gently for 20 minutes.

2. Remove from heat and let cool for a few minutes. In a blender, purée soup, in batches, until smooth. Return to saucepan and stir in cream. Reheat over medium heat until steaming. Taste and adjust seasoning. Add lively flavor with a splash of balsamic vinegar and stir in chopped basil. Serve in warm bowls and garnish with basil chiffonade.

> ### Grilling Bell Peppers
> Here is a quick and easy way to remove the core and seeds from bell peppers while ensuring the pepper slices lie flat on the barbecue grill for quick, even charring. Slice each pepper from top to bottom on all sides around the core. (You will have 4 or 5 large flat slices of pepper, and the core with seeds attached can be discarded.) Lightly oil pepper slices and place on a barbecue over high heat or under broiler. Grill, turning occasionally, until skin is evenly charred, about 10 minutes. Transfer to a bowl and cover. Let steam for 10 minutes. Remove and discard charred skin; remember to save the good pepper juices. (See also Roasted Peppers, left.)

Salt

What happened to salt? One of the foundations of civilization, it has been preserving food, the organic deep-freeze of the ages, since the Chinese used it for pickling in 2700 BC, and 1,000 years after that the Egyptians used it to help preserve their mummies. No wonder it was valued, or that Jesus used it in a metaphor that lasts to this day, telling his disciples in the Sermon on the Mount: "Ye are the salt of the earth." And Jewish folklore held that salt delivered wisdom and good health, both.

And now? Salt as we generally know it (sodium chloride, or NaCl), has become one of the great kitchen Satans. Food commentators and wellness people (the growth industry of our time) are forever warning that too much salt leads to asthma, heartburn, osteoporosis, stomach cancer, high blood pressure — all leading to death, and the common cold.

Surely matters saline cannot have come to such a terminal pass. They have not. Used as it is meant to be used, salt is a preservative, a taste enhancer, and, though you wouldn't know it from its critics, a necessity for health and a staff of life. Simple, inexpensive iodized table salt (a mere five percent of North American salt production, by the way) may not be on the true foodie's must-have condiment list today, but new specialized versions have sprung up to take its place.

In the Kitchen

Sea salt, generically named and coarsely ground (some finely ground varieties are available), gathered from almost any country with a coast, is the most widely available, with many aromatic variants, but there are others gaining ground every year. Types include **Maldon salt**, a chefs' favorite from an estuary in Essex, England, prized for salads and light dishes; **Celtic Gray salt**, robustly flavored, fine for meats; **Fleur de sel**, from France's Guérande Peninsula (or **flor do sal**, from Portugal's Algarve), harvested in seawater ponds from the first formation of surface salt, sweetly and delicately flavored, called the queen of salts, composed of small, flaky crystals; and **Halen Môn**, sea salt filtered over Welsh mussel beds in Anglesey, stiff with magnesium and calcium. **Hawaiian red sea salt** gets its color from the clay of the salt ponds where it's harvested, earthy, lots of minerals, good with fish.

Himalayan pink salt, subject to some wild hyping on the 'Net ("essential for regulation of your blood pressure"), and said to come from 250-million-year-old salt stocks located so high in Nepal (and so far from the increasingly contaminated sea) that they're free of all the toxins we're warned so much about down here below.

Kosher salt is a coarse-grained refined rock salt that does not contain iodine, giving it a fresher, cleaner taste than regular table salt. Its name came from kosher butchering — the large absorbent crystals remain on the surface of meat, drawing out the blood, a component of koshering.

These "new" specialty salts, coarse or fine, have two things in common. They tend to come in small amounts at large prices, and they work their alchemic best as finishing salts. That is, their subtle flavors and their prices would be wasted if you cook with them. But judiciously added at the end of your labors, they will give dividends in taste back to the dish, just as they did thousands of years ago when salt was truly prized.

Sweet Potato Soup

The common orange-fleshed sweet potato is a favorite in our winter kitchen, adding a sweet, squash-like flavor to soups, stews and vegetable purées. This is a "feel good" soup made lively with the addition of fresh dill.

Blender or food processor

1 tbsp	vegetable oil	15 mL
1	onion, chopped	1
1	leek, white and tender green parts only, chopped	1
2	cloves garlic, chopped	2
2	sweet potatoes, peeled and roughly chopped (about 3 cups/750 mL)	2
1	large carrot, roughly chopped	1
¼ cup	dry white wine	50 mL
	Kosher or sea salt	
5 cups	Vegetable Stock (page 56) or ready-to-use broth	1.25 L
½ cup	whipping (35%) cream	125 mL
2 tbsp	chopped dill, divided	25 mL
1 tbsp	chopped flat-leaf parsley	15 mL
	Freshly ground black pepper	

1. In a large pot, heat oil over medium heat. Add onion and leek and sauté until softened but not browned, 4 to 5 minutes. Add garlic, sweet potatoes, carrot, wine and a pinch of salt and sauté for 3 minutes. Stir in stock and bring to a boil. Reduce heat and simmer, covered, until sweet potatoes are tender, 20 to 25 minutes.

2. Remove from heat and let cool for a few minutes. Using a blender, purée soup, in batches, until smooth. Return to saucepan. Stir in cream, 1 tbsp (15 mL) of the dill and parsley. Reheat over medium heat until steaming. Season with pepper to taste. Serve in warm bowls and garnish with remaining dill.

Corn Chowder with Double-Smoked Bacon

SERVES 6 TO 8

There's something irresistible about the combination of sweet corn and smoky bacon. A hearty meal-in-a-bowl for lunch or supper on a crisp late summer's day. Chunks of grilled sourdough bread complete the meal.

● **Food processor or blender**

2 oz	double-smoked bacon, cut into pieces	60 g
1	onion, chopped	1
1	potato, diced	1
1	clove garlic, chopped	1
1 tbsp	chopped thyme or 1 tsp (5 mL) dried thyme	15 mL
¼ tsp	hot pepper flakes	1 mL
2	ripe Roma (plum) tomatoes, seeded and chopped	2
1	small zucchini, chopped	1
3 cups	corn kernels, frozen or fresh	750 mL
4 cups	Vegetable Stock (page 56) or ready-to-use broth	1 L
1 cup	whole (3.25%) milk	250 mL
¼ cup	finely chopped red bell pepper	50 mL
	Salt and freshly ground black pepper	

1. In a large pot over medium heat, cook bacon until brown and crisp. Remove with a slotted spoon and set aside. Drain on paper towels.

2. Toss onion in rendered bacon fat and sauté until soft, 5 to 6 minutes. Add potato, garlic, thyme and hot pepper flakes and sauté for 2 minutes.

3. Add tomatoes, zucchini, corn and stock. Bring to a boil. Reduce heat and simmer until vegetables are tender, about 20 minutes.

4. Remove from heat and let cool for a few minutes. In a food processor, purée half the soup in batches. Return the puréed soup to the vegetables in the pot. Stir in milk and bell pepper. Reheat over medium heat until steaming. Season with salt and pepper to taste. Serve in warm bowls and garnish with crisp smoked bacon bits.

Cream of Roasted Fennel Soup

Fennel imparts a sweet licorice-like flavor to a soothing soup.

Tips

Trim the fennel bulb and remove tough outer layers; discard fibrous stalks and dill-like fronds, which will not contribute to the dish.

Add the finishing touch to a serving of Cream of Roasted Fennel Soup with an attractive garnish that complements the soup's flavor and texture. Something crispy would be delicious, such as small (1/2 inch/1 cm) toasted croutons (page 31), seasoned with a hint of fennel, cumin and thyme.

- Preheat oven to 400°F (200°C)
- Roasting pan
- Spice mill or mortar and pestle
- Food processor or blender

1	bulb fennel, trimmed and chopped (see Tips, left)	1
1	onion, chopped	1
2 tbsp	olive oil, divided	25 mL
	Kosher or sea salt	
1/2 tsp	fennel seeds	2 mL
1/2 tsp	cumin seeds	2 mL
1	large potato, peeled and cubed	1
3 cups	Vegetable Stock (page 56) or ready-to-use broth	750 mL
1/2 cup	whipping (35%) cream	125 mL
1 to 2 tbsp	freshly squeezed grapefruit or lemon juice	15 to 25 mL
	Freshly ground black pepper	

1. In a large bowl, toss fennel and onion with 1 tbsp (15 mL) of the oil and 1/2 tsp (2 mL) salt. Spread vegetables in a roasting pan and roast in preheated oven until vegetables are just beginning to color, 10 to 15 minutes. Set aside.

2. In a small dry skillet, toast fennel and cumin seeds over medium heat, swirling pan, until the aromas are released, 2 to 3 minutes. Remove from heat. Grind toasted seeds in a spice mill or with a mortar and pestle until fine. Set aside.

3. In a large pot, heat remaining oil over medium heat. Add roasted vegetables, potato and toasted seeds and sauté for 2 minutes. Stir in stock and bring to a simmer. Reduce heat to low and simmer until vegetables are tender, about 20 minutes.

4. Remove from heat and let cool for a few minutes. In a food processor, purée soup, in batches, until smooth. Force through a sieve for a super smooth texture. Return to saucepan and stir in cream. Add grapefruit juice to bring out the flavors. Reheat over medium heat until steaming. Season with salt and pepper to taste. Serve in warm bowls.

Borscht

There are probably as many recipes for borscht as there are European grandmothers. This version, with lots of chunky vegetables and the enrichment of a smoky pork hock, is our favorite. For a vegetarian version, omit the pork hock and replace chicken stock with vegetable stock.

6 cups	Chicken Stock (page 54) or ready-to-use broth	1.5 L
½	smoked pork hock	½
1	beet, roughly chopped	1
1	onion, quartered	1
2	beets, grated or finely chopped	2
1	carrot, grated or finely chopped	1
1	potato, grated or finely chopped	1
3 tbsp	red wine vinegar	45 mL
	Kosher or sea salt	
1 cup	finely chopped Savoy cabbage	250 mL
2 tbsp	chopped dill, divided	25 mL
	Freshly ground black pepper	
6 tbsp	sour cream, optional	90 mL

1. In a large pot over medium-high heat, combine stock, pork hock, roughly chopped beet and onion. Bring to a boil. Reduce heat to low and simmer, covered, for 1½ hours. Strain the broth and set aside. Pull meat from pork hock and set aside. Discard vegetables.

2. Return stock and pork to the pot over medium heat. Add grated beets, carrot and potato and season with vinegar and 1 tsp (5 mL) salt. Bring to a boil. Reduce heat to low, cover and cook for about 30 minutes.

3. Add cabbage and 1 tbsp (15 mL) of the dill and cook, covered, until vegetables are tender, about 10 minutes.

4. Season with pepper to taste. Serve in warm bowls, topped with a spoonful of sour cream, if using, and a sprinkling of dill.

When to salt?

When you watch our chefs at work in the kitchen they add a pinch of salt now and again at various times throughout the cooking process in order to build and bring out flavors as they go. With a final taste and seasoning at the end and at time of service. You can always add later, but add too much, too soon and the dish is ruined.

Inside Scoop on Sandwiches

Sandwiches are a great way to feed a group of two or 20. Make a large pot of soup and set out a selection of sandwich fixings on the table. Let each person create his or her own masterpiece, plain or grilled. If you have an electric sandwich grill or electric skillet, plug it in close by and if you are outside, light up the barbecue and have an iron skillet or griddle handy.

Basic sandwich ingredients would include your favorites from each of the following sections:

1. Great bread: a whole wheat bread (but not so grainy that it will overwhelm the filling) and a crusty white country bread, baguette, Focaccia (page 385), calabrese rolls, pitas or plain wheat tortillas.
2. A selection of thinly sliced cold meats such as country ham, Genoa salami, spicy soprosetta, prosciutto, or cold sliced beef, chicken, pork, lamb or sausage.
3. One or two cheeses that slice and melt well, such as Havarti, Monterey Jack, Cheddar, Provolone, Emmental, Gruyère, Fontina or smoked Gouda.
4. Sliced vegetables for garnish, such as firm ripe tomatoes, avocado, red onion, cucumber, grilled eggplant or zucchini, roasted bell peppers and grilled or marinated artichoke hearts.
5. Condiments and spreads, either homemade or store-bought, such as Mayonnaise (page 96), aïoli, mustard, sliced dill pickles, Pesto (page 320), Tapenade (page 324), garlic or herb butter.
6. Crunchy greens such as lettuce, arugula, watercress or leaf spinach…and don't forget sea salt and the pepper mill.

Sandwich Serving Suggestions

Pair one of our soups with a sandwich to make a perfect lunch or casual supper. Here are some suggestions:

- Serve Carrot Ginger Soup (page 26) with sliced Grilled Boned Leg of Lamb (Variation, page 196) tucked in a grilled pita bread with Tabbouleh, Tzatziki and a drizzle of Hummus (pages 84, 172 and 313). *Other option:* Tomato Basil Soup (page 32).
- Serve Butternut Squash and Apple Soup (page 30) with a hearty sandwich of Barbecued Pulled Pork (page 180), Monterey Jack Cheese and Chipotle Mayonnaise (page 96) on a toasted ciabatta. *Other option:* Carrot Ginger Soup (page 26).
- Serve Sweet Potato Soup (page 37) with slices of rare grilled steak, Fontina cheese and Chimichurri Sauce (page 145) on a crusty ciabatta.
  Other option: Gazpacho (page 34).
- Serve Tomato Basil Soup (page 32) with grilled portobello mushrooms, slivers of Parmigiano-Reggiano and Sun-Dried Tomato Pesto (page 321) on a crusty panini.
  Other option: Roasted Red Pepper Soup (page 35).
- Serve Cream of Roasted Fennel Soup (page 39) with a delicious sandwich of Herbed-Roasted Salmon (page 219) mixed with a little mayonnaise and watercress on a whole wheat or country white bread. *Other options:* Spring Green Soup (page 48) or Tomato Basil Soup (page 32).
- Serve Spring Green Soup (page 48) with a hearty sandwich of hot Chicken Piccata (page 108) with roasted peppers and a spoonful of tomato sauce on a crusty warm kaiser roll.
- Enjoy Chilled Zucchini Basil Soup (page 51) with a whole wheat tortilla spread with Basil Pesto (page 320) and creamy goat's cheese and wrapped around roasted yellow and red bell peppers.
- A perfect match! French Canadian Split Pea Soup with Dill (page 43) accompanied by a classic grilled sandwich of country ham and Gruyère cheese on whole wheat or country white bread.
- Serve Vichyssoise (page 50) with a grilled chicken club sandwich of sliced Italian Grilled Chicken (page 104), crispy bacon slices, sliced tomato and leaf lettuce on a baguette or ciabatta.
- Serve Asparagus Soup (page 53) with a Crab Cake (page 340), capers, red onion and a little mayonnaise on challah.

Manhattan Clam Chowder

A meal-in-a-bowl that is satisfying and delicious. It's a useful soup to have in your repertoire since the essential ingredients are staples that you can keep on hand in the kitchen cupboard.

Tip

A jar or two of bottled clam juice is an acceptable substitute for fish stock in fish soups and stews. Be sure to test the saltiness before adding more seasoning.

Variation

Manhattan Clam Chowder with Fresh Clams: Replace canned clams with steamed fresh clams. Combine ½ cup (125 mL) each water and dry white wine in a large shallow pot. Add a handful of aromatics including roughly chopped onion, celery and leek, sprigs of parsley and thyme, a bay leaf and a few black peppercorns. Simmer all together for about 10 minutes. Add 3 lbs (1.5 kg) washed and scrubbed clams. Discard any clams that are not tightly closed. Cover pot and steam clams until shells open, 6 to 10 minutes. Discard any clams that do not open. Remove clams from the shells. Discard shells and strain the cooking broth. Follow recipe, right, adding clams and cooking liquid to chowder in place of canned clams.

3	slices bacon or salt pork, about 2 oz (60 g), diced	3
½	onion, diced	½
1	stalk celery, diced	1
1	carrot, diced	1
½	green bell pepper, diced	½
1	clove garlic, finely chopped	1
1	bay leaf	1
1 tsp	dried oregano	5 mL
1 tsp	dried thyme	5 mL
½ tsp	hot pepper flakes, or to taste	2 mL
1	potato, peeled and diced	1
1	can (28 oz/796 mL) plum tomatoes, chopped, juice reserved	1
1	can (5 oz/142 g) clams, drained, juice reserved	1
1 cup	Vegetable or Chicken Stock (pages 56 and 54), fish stock or ready-to-use broth	250 mL
	Kosher or sea salt	
2 tbsp	chopped flat-leaf parsley	25 mL
	Freshly ground black pepper	

1. In a large pot over medium heat, sauté bacon until brown and crisp. Remove with a slotted spoon. Drain on paper towels and set aside. Reserve fat in pot.

2. Add onion, celery, carrot and bell pepper to pot with reserved bacon fat and sauté until soft, 5 to 7 minutes. Add garlic, bay leaf, oregano, thyme and hot pepper flakes and sauté for 1 minute.

3. Stir in potato, tomatoes, reserved clam juice, stock and 1 tsp (5 mL) salt. Bring to a boil. Reduce heat, cover and simmer until vegetables are tender, 20 to 25 minutes.

4. Stir in clams, reserved bacon and parsley and cook over low heat to blend all the flavors together, 5 to 10 minutes. If more liquid is required, use reserved tomato juice. Season with pepper to taste. Serve in warm bowls.

French Canadian Split Pea Soup with Dill

Tip

Unlike dried beans and chickpeas, split peas and lentils do not need to be soaked. Salt may be added at the beginning of cooking.

Variation

Split Pea and Ham Soup: In a large pot, combine 1 small smoked pork hock with 6 cups (1.5 L) water. Add a bouquet garni including a couple of sprigs each of parsley and thyme, a piece of celery stalk, a bay leaf and 6 to 8 black peppercorns. Bring to a boil. Reduce heat and simmer for 45 minutes. Remove pork hock and, when it is cool enough to handle, trim away skin and remove tender meat from the bone. Chop roughly and reserve. Strain broth and set aside. Replace vegetable stock with pork hock cooking liquid. Stir in pork hock meat with dill at the final cooking stage.

Food Processor or blender

1 tbsp	butter	15 mL
1	onion, finely chopped	1
1	carrot, finely chopped	1
1	parsnip, finely chopped	1
1	clove garlic, finely chopped	1
1	potato, peeled and diced	1
½ cup	yellow split peas (see Tip, left)	125 mL
	Kosher or sea salt	
4 cups	Vegetable Stock (page 56) or ready-to-use broth or water	1 L
¼ cup	chopped dill	50 mL
	Freshly ground black pepper	

1. In a large pot, melt butter over medium heat. Add onion, carrot and parsnip and sauté until onion is soft, 5 to 7 minutes.

2. Add garlic, potato, split peas and a pinch of salt and toss together for 2 minutes. Stir in stock and bring to a boil. Reduce heat and simmer, partially covered, until peas are tender, about 45 minutes.

3. Remove from heat and let cool for a few minutes. In a food processor, purée about two thirds of the soup. Return puréed soup to pot and combine with chunky vegetables. Stir in dill. Reheat over medium heat until steaming. Season with pepper to taste. Serve in warm bowls.

Miso Soup with Mushrooms and Lotus Root

A light, nourishing soup. We recommend that you make your own dashi (see below) because the instant variety is sadly lacking!

Tip

Avoid gritty leeks! Leeks notoriously hide quantities of sandy soil between their leaves. Careful washing is mandatory. Cut off and discard root end, keeping white bulb and about 2 inches (5 cm) of tender green leaves. Make a deep slit down the length of the leek almost to the root end, force the sections of leaves apart and run under cold water, green end down, to wash away the grit. Shake and squeeze off excess water. Or slice leeks and set in a large bowl of cold water. Swish them around to release any grit and scoop out of the bowl into a colander to drain.

4 cups	dashi	1 L
1	carrot, julienned	1
1/2	leek, white and tender green parts only, julienned (see Tip, left)	1/2
1/4 cup	yellow miso	50 mL
1 cup	diced firm tofu	250 mL
2	shiitake mushrooms, stems removed, slivered	2
1	lotus root, very thinly sliced	1
1	green onion, sliced thinly on the diagonal	1

1. In a large pot over medium heat, bring dashi to a boil. Add carrot and leek. Reduce heat to medium and simmer for 5 minutes.

2. In a small bowl, combine miso with 1 cup (250 mL) hot dashi. Stir until smooth. Stir dissolved miso into soup with tofu, mushrooms and lotus root. Simmer very gently (do not allow to boil) until flavors are combined and mushrooms are tender, 3 to 4 minutes. Serve in warm bowls and garnish with green onion.

Homemade Dashi

Dashi is a basic stock, fundamental to Japanese cuisine that imparts a distinctive flavor to many dishes. The ingredients are kelp (a kind of seaweed, also called kombu) and dried bonito flakes (a type of shredded tuna). Both kombu and bonito flakes are available at Asian markets.

In a saucepan over medium heat, combine a piece of dried kelp, about 6 inches (15 cm) long, and 8 cups (2 L) water. Heat slowly. Just as water is about to come to a boil, remove pan from heat and remove kelp. Immediately stir in 1/2 to 1 cup (125 to 250 mL) bonito flakes. (The higher amount of bonito flakes added and the longer the bonito sits in the liquid, the stronger flavored the stock becomes.) Let stand for 1 to 2 minutes. Strain. Use dashi immediately or let cool, cover and refrigerate and use within 2 days.

Lemongrass Chicken Soup

Not quite the chicken soup your grandmother likely made yet equally tasty and good. Prepare all the ingredients and have them ready at the stove; this soup is ready in a few minutes. Accompanied by a bowl of rice noodles or jasmine rice, the soup makes a delicious light meal.

Tips

Cut top part of lemongrass stalk in half and toss into the pot to intensify the citrus flavor, if you like. Discard before serving.

Wild lime leaf (aka makrut) is an intensely fragrant citrus leaf used extensively in Thai cuisine. It is sometimes referred to as "kaffir" lime but because that term is derogatory in the native language "wild" lime is a more appropriate name.

1 tbsp	vegetable oil	15 mL
1 tbsp	finely chopped lemongrass (see Tips, left and page 14)	15 mL
1 tsp	finely chopped gingerroot	5 mL
1 tsp	finely chopped garlic	5 mL
1 to 2 tsp	Thai green curry paste	5 to 10 mL
8 oz	skinless boneless chicken breast, thinly sliced	250 g
1	wild lime leaf (see Tips, left)	1
4 cups	Chicken Stock (page 54) or ready-to-use broth	1 L
1	can (14 oz/400 mL) coconut milk	1
4	shiitake mushrooms, stems removed, thinly sliced	4
1 tbsp	freshly squeezed lime juice	15 mL
2 tsp	fish sauce	10 mL
	Kosher or sea salt	
¼ cup	thinly sliced green onion	50 mL
¼ cup	coarsely chopped cilantro	50 mL

1. In a large pot, heat oil over medium heat. Add lemongrass, ginger and garlic and sauté for 1 to 2 minutes. Add curry paste, chicken and lime leaf and sauté for 2 minutes.

2. Stir in stock, coconut milk and mushrooms. Reduce heat to low and simmer until chicken is no longer pink inside and mushrooms are tender, 5 to 6 minutes.

3. Add lime juice and fish sauce. Season with salt to taste. Serve in warm bowls and garnish with green onion and cilantro.

Tomatoes

There are something north of 10,000 varieties of tomato in existence, from the smallest (about $\frac{1}{2}$ inch/1 cm in diameter) to the largest single specimen (the 7 lb 12 oz/3.5 kg spawn of the Delicious cultivar, grown in Edmond, Oklahoma in 1986 and recognized by Guinness). All of them probably descended from green plants in the Andean highlands of Peru, and by 500 BC cultivated as far north as Mexico. Then came Spanish colonization, and the tomato spread through the Caribbean to Asia. It took its time reaching Europe (the earliest tomato recipes were published in Naples in 1692), and even longer arriving in the U.S. and Canada, where it was introduced via European immigrants and not, strangely, via Mexicans, who had been eating them for two millennia. Hardly a beeline.

Early in our own colonizing history, people were leery about the tomato. Beautiful, yes, and fine as ornaments, but the plant looked depressingly like deadly nightshade (or belladonna), 10 of whose berries can kill. Indeed, apart from the fruit itself, the stems and leaves of the tomato plant, though hardly lethal, are poisonous, which did nothing for its early P.R.

Still, nothing tasting so good could be kept down forever, and among its first popularizers was Thomas Jefferson, who grew them at his Monticello farm and whose daughters promoted their use in cooking. And so to today, when North Americans consume some 25 lbs (11 kg) of tomatoes per head per year, much of them in ketchup, and when the U.S. exports about $275 million worth of tomatoes annually — mostly to Canada and (a nice irony) Mexico.

Of the 10,000 varieties, among the most common ones marketed today are the **beefsteak** and the **big boy**, which are large, red and delicious raw and cooked; similarly the **globe**, medium-size; the **plum** (aka **Roma**), smaller, egg-shaped, excellent for canning; the **cherry**, red or gold, about 1 inch (2.5 cm) in diameter, prized both for taste (eaten whole it explodes in the mouth) and as a garnish; the **green**, firm and medium-size, with a sharper flavor than the reds (and yellows), making it a cooks' choice for broiling, frying, and adding to sauces and chutneys.

The most flavorful are the **heirloom** cultivars — open-pollinated, non-hybrid tomatoes, developed as far as possibly distant from the hybrid varieties of the commercial seed trade. Best of all heirlooms might come from seeds handed down, family to family, from just after Columbus. Since these are rare, the ones to look out for, with farmers to trust, would include: Aunt Ruby's German Green, Andrew Rahart Jumbo Red, Box Car Willie, Brandywine, Cherokee Purple, Great Divide, Marianna's Peace, Mortgage Lifter and Rose (all beefsteak variants).

Tomatoes are good for us no matter what or whence the brand. All are rich in vitamins A and C, potassium and iron. Best of all are the red varieties, and the redder the better; this comes from the red pigment called lycopene, a powerful cancer-fighting antioxidant (particularly strong in fighting cancers of the colon, stomach, lung and prostate). Raw is fine, but cooked is finer still, since the cooking releases more of the lycopene.

Best of all is homegrown, naturally; second best, "vine-ripened." Store (if necessary) out of direct sunlight. Never refrigerate: the cold kills the flavor and makes them mushy. To force ripen, put them in a paper bag with an apple. Leave at room temperature for a few days. Time will tell.

In the Kitchen

Canned tomatoes: It would be hard to function in a northern kitchen without canned tomatoes! They are a pantry essential and used extensively in many of our most popular soups, sauces, curries, salsas and stews. The many brands on the market vary hugely in quality and flavor: some are pale and tasteless and have a hard core that has to be removed. It's best to sample a few and find a favorite. The varieties picked when ripe and touched by the Mediterranean sun (e.g. Italian San Marzano) seem to be the sweetest.

Fresh tomatoes: When in season we use fresh tomatoes, both field and plum varieties, in our kitchen in all kinds of cooked preparations from a hearty bolognese sauce to a delicate fresh tomato coulis — including sauces, soups, braises and curries. In season we relish the flavor of fresh, field-ripened tomatoes in salads and sandwiches.

There are a welcome assortment of small tomato varieties (e.g. **Sweet Grape**, **Sweet Cocktail**, **Sweet Berry**, **Grape Roma** and multicolor **Sweet Rainbow**) now being grown hydroponically and in hot houses all year long. They all look very appealing but sometimes their flavor is disappointing, probably as a result of differences in cultivation and distance traveled. Experiment to find your favorites. Sweet cherry tomatoes are more than a garnish. They make a delicious side dish, tossed over medium heat in a little extra virgin olive oil with minced shallots and a pinch of salt. They are perfect to thread on a skewer to cook over the coals and a sweet, juicy bite to include with an antipasto selection.

Many recipes call for tomatoes to be peeled and seeded. This is for reasons of appearance and taste. Tomato flesh softens during cooking and blends into a dish. Pieces of skin detract from the appearance and make for an unpleasant mouthful. The seeds add bitterness and also contain a lot of moisture that may be undesirable.

To peel tomatoes: Cut a cross in the skin at the bottom of the tomato (the side opposite the stem). Drop into a pan of boiling water and leave for 30 seconds. Remove with tongs. When cool enough to handle peel away skins.

To seed tomatoes: Cut tomato in half crosswise. Release and discard seeds. Your fingers are the best tools for the job. If you want to retain more tomato juice, you can toss the seeds in a sieve over a bowl.

To remove seeds from canned tomatoes, force them through a fine sieve or "mouli."

Slow-Roasted Tomatoes

Slow-roasted cherry or Campari tomatoes acquire a sweet, intense flavor that is delicious as a garnish for salads or pizza.

Cut tomatoes in half. Release and discard seeds. Toss tomatoes with a little extra virgin olive oil, dried oregano or basil and a pinch of coarse kosher or sea salt and freshly ground black pepper. Spread, cut side up, in a single layer on a baking sheet. Place in a preheated 200°F (100°C) oven and slow-roast until the flesh is tender and deep red and has shrunken slightly, about 3 to 4 hours, depending on the size of the tomatoes.

Slow-Roasted Tomato Coulis: Press slow-roasted tomatoes through a fine sieve. Add extra virgin olive oil, fresh chopped herbs (e.g. basil, oregano, chervil, chives), salt and pepper to taste.

Spring Green Soup

Spring in a bowl! Light in flavor with a vibrant green color.

● **Blender or food processor**

1 tbsp	butter	15 mL
2	shallots, chopped	2
¼ cup	basmati rice	50 mL
5 cups	Vegetable Stock (page 56) or ready-to-use broth	1.25 L
	Kosher or sea salt	
2 cups	baby spinach	500 mL
1 cup	green peas, frozen	250 mL
1	head Boston lettuce, chopped	1
1	green onion, chopped	1
2 tbsp	chopped mint, divided	25 mL
4 tbsp	Crème Fraîche (page 33) or store-bought	60 mL

1. In a large pot, melt butter over medium heat. Add shallots, reduce heat and cook gently, stirring, until softened but not browned, 4 to 5 minutes.

2. Add rice and stir for 1 minute. Add stock and ½ tsp (2 mL) salt and bring to a boil. Reduce heat and simmer, partially covered, until rice is tender, 10 to 12 minutes.

3. Stir in spinach, peas, lettuce and green onion and simmer until vegetables are wilted and soft, 2 to 3 minutes.

4. Remove from heat and let cool for a few minutes. In a blender, purée soup, in batches, until smooth. Return to saucepan and stir in 1 tbsp (15 mL) of the mint. Reheat over medium-low heat until steaming. Taste and adjust seasoning. Serve in warm bowls and garnish with crème fraîche and remaining mint.

Classic Minestrone Soup

SERVES 6 TO 8

Don't think of minestrone soup only as a winter warmer. It makes an amazing lunch with grilled garlic bread on the deck in sunshine. The flavors are pure Mediterranean, and you can change the greens with the seasons, including spinach in spring and savoy cabbage or kale in fall. It's essential to have a bowl of freshly grated Parmigiano-Reggiano on the side.

Tip

Save the rinds of Parmigiano-Reggiano cheese and add to the pot when making robust vegetable soups like this one. The cheese enriches the flavor and texture of the broth.

Variation

For convenience we include canned beans in this minestrone soup. If time allows we recommend that you use dried beans cooked from scratch. The texture and taste will be superior. Soak beans in water to cover by 2 inches (5 cm) in refrigerator for 8 hours or overnight. Drain. Place beans in a large pot and add fresh cold water to cover by 2 inches (5 cm). Bring to a boil over high heat. Reduce heat and simmer, uncovered, until beans are tender, 45 to 50 minutes. Remove from heat. Add ½ tsp (2 mL) salt and let stand for 5 minutes. Drain and set aside.

1 tbsp	olive oil	15 mL
2 oz	pancetta or lean bacon, chopped	60 g
1	onion, finely chopped	1
1	stalk celery, finely chopped	1
1	leek, white and tender green parts only, chopped (see Tip, page 44)	1
½	green bell pepper, finely chopped	½
2 to 3	cloves garlic, finely chopped	2 to 3
1 tsp	chopped thyme	5 mL
1 tsp	chopped oregano	5 mL
6 cups	Vegetable or Chicken Stock (pages 56 and 54) or ready-to-use broth	1.5 L
1	can (28 oz/796 mL) plum tomatoes with juice	1
1	zucchini, chopped	1
2 cups	shredded Savoy cabbage	500 mL
1	can (14 to 19 oz/398 to 540 mL) white beans, drained and rinsed	1
1 tsp	basil chiffonade	5 mL
	Freshly grated Parmigiano-Reggiano cheese	
	Salt and freshly ground black pepper	

1. In a large pot, heat oil over medium heat. Add pancetta and cook, stirring, until crisp and brown. Remove with a slotted spoon and drain on paper towels. Set aside.

2. Add onion, celery, leek, bell pepper, garlic to taste, thyme and oregano to the rendered fat and sauté until soft and lightly browned, 5 to 7 minutes.

3. Add stock and tomatoes with juice and bring to a boil. Reduce heat and simmer until vegetables are tender, about 20 minutes. Add zucchini, cabbage, beans and reserved pancetta and simmer until cabbage is tender, about 20 minutes.

4. Stir in basil. Taste and adjust seasoning. Serve in warm bowls and garnish with Parmesan and a sprinkling of freshly ground black pepper.

Vichyssoise

Simple ingredients combine to make a sublime chilled creamy soup.

Variations

Country-Style Leek and Potato Soup: Proceed as in Vichyssoise, right. Omit cream enrichment and do not strain to a smooth cream. Return puréed soup to saucepan. Reheat over medium-low heat until steaming. Taste and adjust seasoning. To garnish, reserve the tender greens of one of the leeks and cut into thin lengthwise slivers. Add slivered leek to the puréed soup before reheating. Serve in warm bowls and garnish with Crème Fraîche (page 33).

Cream of Watercress Soup: Replace one of the leeks with 4 cups (1 L) watercress, trimmed of thick stalks. Blanch an extra handful of watercress leaves for garnish.

Cream of Sorrel Soup: Replace one of the leeks with 8 cups (2 L) chopped sorrel leaves.

Blender or food processor

2 tbsp	butter	25 mL
4	leeks, white and tender green parts only, chopped (see Tip, page 44)	4
1	onion, chopped	1
1 lb	potatoes, Russets or Yukon Gold, peeled and chopped	500 g
4 cups	water or Vegetable Stock (page 56) or ready-to-use broth	1 L
1 tsp	kosher or sea salt	5 mL
1½ cups	half-and-half (10%) cream	375 mL
½ cup	whipping (35%) cream, optional	125 mL
	Freshly ground black pepper	
1 tbsp	chopped chives	15 mL

1. In a large pot, melt butter over low heat. Add leeks and onion and cook gently, covered, until soft, 7 to 10 minutes.

2. Add potatoes, water and salt. Increase heat and bring to a boil. Reduce heat to low and simmer, covered, until potatoes are tender, 20 to 30 minutes. Stir in half-and-half cream and bring just to the boil.

3. Remove from heat and let cool for a few minutes. In a blender, purée soup, in batches, until smooth. Force through a fine sieve for super smooth texture. Let cool and refrigerate until needed. Enrich with whipping cream, if you like. Season with pepper to taste. Serve chilled and garnish with chives.

Chilled Zucchini Basil Soup

In many dishes the flavor of mild summer squash gets lost. In this light, chilly soup you can actually taste the zucchini. Enjoy it with clear conscience because it is virtually fat free.

- **Blender or food processor**
- **Steamer**

1½ lbs	zucchini	750 g
2	shallots, quartered	2
2	small cloves garlic, smashed	2
	Kosher or sea salt	
1 cup	Vegetable Stock (page 56) or ready-to-use broth	250 mL
1½ cups	plain yogurt	375 mL
1 tbsp	basil chiffonade, divided	15 mL
	Freshly ground black pepper	
	Freshly grated Parmigiano-Reggiano cheese, optional	
	Parmesan Crostini (page 320), optional	

1. Cut zucchini into quarters lengthwise and cut away seedy core.

2. In a steamer basket set in a pot over simmering water, cook zucchini, shallots and garlic until soft, 7 to 8 minutes. Remove from heat. Sprinkle with a little salt and set aside to cool.

3. In a blender, purée vegetables with vegetable stock until smooth. Add yogurt and process briefly to combine. Pour into a bowl and stir in 2 tsp (10 mL) of the basil.

4. Chill soup, covered, in the refrigerator, 1 to 2 hours. Taste and adjust seasoning before serving. Serve in chilled bowls with a garnish of remaining slivered basil. Sprinkle black pepper and a little Parmesan cheese on top or serve a Parmesan crostini on the side.

Chilled Watermelon Soup

SERVES 6 TO 8

When the temperatures soar, this delightful soup cools and refreshes. Perfect for a summer wedding or bridal shower, or to serve in small "shooter" glasses at a summer cocktail party.

Blender

¼	seedless watermelon, about 3 lbs (1.5 kg) (rind removed)	¼
2 tsp	finely grated gingerroot	10 mL
1 tbsp	grated lime zest	15 mL
¼ cup	freshly squeezed lime juice	50 mL
3 tbsp	Triple Sec or other orange-flavored liquor	45 mL
1 tbsp	cassis	15 mL
½ tsp	ground cardamom	2 mL
1 tbsp	brown sugar	15 mL
¼ tsp	hot pepper sauce	1 mL
¼ tsp	kosher or sea salt	1 mL
1 tbsp	chopped fresh mint	15 mL
3 to 4	whole mint leaves, chiffonade	3 to 4

1. Reserve one slice of watermelon for garnish and cut the rest into 1-inch (2.5 cm) cubes. You should have about 6 cups (1.5 L).

2. In a large bowl, combine watermelon, ginger, lime zest and juice, Triple Sec, cassis, cardamom, brown sugar, hot pepper sauce and salt. Cover and marinate at room temperature, stirring occasionally, for 1 hour.

3. Add chopped mint. In a blender, purée watermelon mixture in batches. Strain through a sieve to remove pulp. Taste and adjust balance of sweet, spicy and tart flavors with a pinch of sugar or salt or a dash of hot pepper sauce or lime juice.

4. Place soup and serving bowls in the freezer for 30 minutes before serving to ensure that soup is well chilled.

5. Cut reserved watermelon into ¼-inch (0.5 cm) cubes and toss with whole mint. Serve soup in chilled bowls and garnish with watermelon and mint.

Asparagus Soup

SERVES 6

Asparagus season is eagerly awaited and all too short: by mid-June in our part of the world commercial crops are finished. For that reason in a few short months we feast on asparagus steamed, roasted, stir-fried or grilled: served hot in soups, side dishes, quiches, and tarts or chilled in a variety of salads.

Variations

To enhance the color of the soup to a bright, rich green, stir in about 1 cup (250 mL) puréed spinach. In boiling lightly salted water, blanch 4 oz (125 g) spinach for 30 seconds. Strain spinach and plunge into ice water to stop cooking. Strain and squeeze out all moisture. Blend to a bright green purée with ¼ to ½ cup (50 to 125 mL) vegetable stock.

Garnish asparagus soup with fresh crabmeat. In a small nonstick skillet, heat cooked crabmeat over medium heat until hot, 1 to 2 minutes. Ladle soup into warm serving bowls and garnish each serving with asparagus spears and crabmeat.

● **Blender**

3 lbs	asparagus (see Tips, page 276)	1.5 kg
2 tbsp	butter	25 mL
1 tbsp	olive oil	15 mL
1 cup	sliced leeks, white and tender green parts only (see Tip, page 44)	250 mL
¼ cup	roughly chopped shallots	50 mL
¼ cup	white wine vinegar	50 mL
½ cup	dry white wine	125 mL
	Salt and freshly ground black pepper	
6 cups	Vegetable Stock (page 56) or ready-to-use broth	1.5 L
2	potatoes, peeled and sliced	2

1. Break off tough ends of asparagus and discard (see Tips, page 276). Cut off tips, about 1 inch (2.5 cm) from top; set aside. Chop asparagus stems into 2-inch (5 cm) pieces. Set aside separately.

2. In a large pot, heat butter and oil over medium heat. Add leeks and shallots and sauté until soft, 4 to 5 minutes. Add vinegar and wine and a pinch of salt and pepper. Simmer until liquid is reduced to a syrupy glaze, about 5 minutes.

3. Add vegetable stock, potatoes and asparagus pieces (keep the tips for Step 5). Bring to a boil. Reduce heat and simmer until asparagus is tender, 15 to 20 minutes.

4. Remove from heat and let cool for a few minutes. In blender, purée soup, in batches, until smooth. Strain through a sieve and press on vegetables with the back of a spoon to extract all the flavor. Set aside. Discard pulp in strainer.

5. Bring a small pot of lightly salted water to a boil. Place a few ice cubes in a bowl of water. Blanch asparagus tips in boiling water for 1 minute. Remove with a slotted spoon and immediately plunge in ice water to stop cooking and retain bright color. Remove tips from ice water after a few minutes, pat dry, slice in half lengthwise and set aside.

6. Return soup to a clean pot. Add blanched asparagus and reheat over medium heat until steaming. Taste and adjust seasoning.

Chicken Stock

A batch of stock simmering away in the large tilt kettle is a common sight in our commercial kitchen. Homemade stock adds extra goodness to soups, stews and sauces without excess salt or chemical flavor enhancers and preservatives often found in store-bought options.

Tip

Add a small amount of salt to help bring out flavors of other ingredients during cooking, but do not add more salt to finished stock since it will be used in many applications and seasoned again later. Here is the opportunity to make a salt-free stock if health concerns dictate.

Variation

Turkey Stock: Replace chicken pieces with turkey and include any giblets (neck, heart, gizzard) that you have saved in the freezer. The liver makes stock bitter. Discard it or save separately for later use.

- 8-quart (8 L) stockpot
- Fine sieve, lined with cheesecloth

2 lbs	whole chicken or chicken pieces	1 kg
2	onions, quartered	2
1	carrot, quartered	1
1	stalk celery, quartered	1
1	leek, halved (see Tip, page 44)	1
1	tomato, quartered	1
4 quarts	cold water	4 L
1	bay leaf	1
2	sprigs thyme	2
2	sprigs parsley	2
1	sprig rosemary	1
1 tsp	whole black peppercorns	5 mL
1 tsp	kosher salt	5 mL

1. Rinse chicken in cold water. Place in stockpot. Add onions, carrot, celery, leek, tomato and water. Tie bay leaf, thyme, parsley and rosemary in a bundle with kitchen string and add to the pot with peppercorns and salt.

2. Bring to a boil over medium heat. Reduce heat to low and simmer until liquid is flavorful, 3 to 4 hours. Regularly skim off and discard foam and impurities that come to the surface.

3. Remove pot from heat and lift out chicken and vegetables with a slotted spoon. Pour stock into a large bowl through prepared sieve. Discard solids. Let cool.

4. Refrigerate, covered, until cold. Remove fat that congeals on top. Simmer stock to reduce and intensify flavor, if needed. Keep in refrigerator in a covered container for up to 4 days or freeze for up to 3 months.

Beef or Veal Stock

*The secret to a fine beef
stock is in the roasting
of the bones, careful
skimming during the
simmering stage and
diligent removal of fat in
final stage.*

Tips

There's no need to peel the
onions when making brown
stock: the skins add color
and flavor. It is important,
however, to wash them, as
with all produce.

Freeze reduced stock in ice
cube trays and, when frozen,
turn out into sealed freezer
bags and store in the freezer.
Reduced stock is an instant
enrichment for sauces.

- Preheat oven to 450°F (230°C)
- Roasting pan, preferably one safe for stovetop use
- 8-quart (8 L) stockpot
- Fine sieve, lined with cheesecloth

4 lbs	beef and or veal bones	2 kg
2	onions, unpeeled, quartered	2
2	carrots, roughly chopped	2
2	stalks celery, roughly chopped	2
1 tbsp	tomato paste	15 mL
4 quarts	cold water, divided	4 L
1	bay leaf	1
4	sprigs thyme	4
4	sprigs parsley	4
1 tsp	whole black peppercorns	5 mL
1 tsp	kosher or sea salt	5 mL

1. In a large roasting pan, arrange bones in a single layer
and roast in preheated oven, turning bones every
15 minutes, for 45 minutes. Add onions, carrots, celery
and tomato paste and stir to coat bones and vegetables
in the tomato paste and roasting juices. Roast until
bones and vegetables are nicely browned, 30 minutes.

2. Transfer bones and vegetables to stockpot. Pour off fat
from roasting pan. Add 2 cups (500 mL) of the cold
water to the pan and set over high heat and deglaze pan,
scraping up browned bits on the bottom. Pour into the
stockpot and add remaining 3.5 quarts (3.5 L) water.

3. Tie bay leaf, thyme and parsley in a bundle with kitchen
string and add to the pot with peppercorns and salt.
Bring to a boil over medium-high heat. Reduce heat and
simmer until liquid is flavorful, 3 to 5 hours. Regularly
skim off and discard foam and impurities that come to
the surface.

4. Remove pot from heat and lift out bones and vegetables
with a slotted spoon. Pour stock into a large bowl
through prepared sieve. Discard solids. Let cool.
Refrigerate, covered, until cold. Remove fat that
congeals on top. Simmer stock to reduce and intensify
flavor, if desired. Keep in refrigerator in a covered
container for up to 4 days or freeze for up to 3 months.

Vegetable Stock

A kitchen staple. Save trimmings from vegetables in a freezer bag and make up a batch of vegetable stock when you have enough.

- **8-quart (8 L) stockpot**
- **Fine sieve, lined with cheesecloth**

2	carrots, roughly chopped	2
2	stalks celery, roughly chopped	2
1	onion, roughly chopped	1
1	leek, top green leaves only, roughly chopped (see Tip, page 44)	1
1 cup	mushroom stems	250 mL
2	cloves garlic, smashed	2
6 cups	cold water	1.5 L
1	bay leaf	1
4	sprigs thyme	4
4	sprigs parsley	4
1 tsp	whole black peppercorns	5 mL
½ tsp	kosher or sea salt	2 mL

1. In a stockpot, place carrots, celery, onion, leek, mushrooms, garlic and water. Tie bay leaf, thyme and parsley in a bundle with kitchen string and add to pot with peppercorns and salt.

2. Bring to a boil over medium heat. Reduce heat to low and simmer until liquid is flavorful, about 30 minutes.

3. Remove pot from heat. Pour stock into a large bowl through prepared sieve. Discard solids. Simmer stock to reduce and intensify flavor, if needed. Let cool. Keep in refrigerator in a covered container for up to 4 days or freeze for up to 3 months.

Salads and Dressings

Three-Pea and Mint Salad

SERVES 6

Here's a vibrant salad to welcome spring. Combine peas with dressing shortly before serving, since the bright color fades within a few hours.

Tip

To string edible-pod peas: With a sharp paring knife, cut across the stem end of the peas towards the inside edge and pull away the thin cellulose string that holds the two sides of the pod together.

3 cups	peas, fresh or frozen	750 mL
2 cups	snow peas (see Tip, left)	500 mL
1 cup	sugar snap peas	250 mL
1 tbsp	finely chopped shallot	15 mL
1 tbsp	mint chiffonade	15 mL
½ cup	White Wine Vinaigrette, omitting garlic (see Variation, page 93)	125 mL
	Kosher or sea salt	

1. Bring a large pot of lightly salted water to a boil. Add peas and cook until tender, 5 to 15 minutes. (Timing will vary depending on whether you are using fresh or frozen peas.) String snow peas and snap peas and blanch briefly, for 30 seconds. Drain and rinse under cold water to stop the cooking. Set aside.
2. In a large bowl, combine peas, shallot and mint. Toss with vinaigrette. Season with salt to taste.

Southwest Slaw

Northern winters are long and chilly, and the variety of available fresh vegetables shrinks dramatically. That's when we have to get creative with cabbage and carrots and such. This tasty creamy slaw is popular all year long.

Food processor with slicing blade or mandolin, optional

¼	head red cabbage	¼
¼	head green cabbage	¼
1	carrot	1
1	red bell pepper	1
1	jalapeño pepper, seeded	1
¾ cup	Mayonnaise (page 96) or store-bought	175 mL
1 tbsp	Dijon mustard	15 mL
1 tbsp	natural rice vinegar	15 mL
2 tsp	freshly squeezed lime juice	10 mL
2 tsp	brown sugar	10 mL
1 tsp	minced garlic	5 mL
1 tsp	toasted cumin seeds	5 mL
	Kosher or sea salt	
2 tbsp	chopped cilantro	25 mL

1. Cut out and discard hard core of red and green cabbages. Cut cabbages into fine slivers or shred in a food processor with a slicing blade or using a mandolin. Transfer to a large bowl and set aside.
2. Slice carrot and bell and jalapeño peppers into juliennes. Add to cabbage.
3. In a small bowl, combine mayonnaise, mustard, vinegar, lime juice, brown sugar, garlic and cumin. Add dressing to vegetables and mix thoroughly. Season with salt to taste. Garnish with cilantro.

Asian Slaw

A crisp, refreshing salad to enjoy all year long, especially with Asian-inspired food from the grill.

Tip

For preparing slaws all you really need is a chef's knife with a sturdy sharp blade about 9 inches (23 cm) long with the part nearest the handle (the tang), about 2 inches (5 cm) wide. (This prevents your knuckles from banging on the cutting surface as you chop.) If you are preparing large amounts of shredded green or red cabbage a food processor with slicing blade does the job quickly. However the shape and texture of napa cabbage makes it easy to shred with a knife.

Dressing Tips

Bird's eye chiles are tiny, thin-skinned red Thai chiles that pack quite a heat (40,000 to 60,000 SU on the unit scale devised by pharmacologist Wilbur Scoville that measures hotness of a spice). Add amounts that suit your taste.

Sesame oil, used in dishes from East Asia, is made from toasted sesame seeds. It has a rich, very nutty flavor and is most commonly used sparingly at the end of the cooking process as a flavoring.

4 cups	thinly sliced napa cabbage (see Tip, left)	1 L
¼	green bell pepper, julienned	¼
¼	red bell pepper, julienned	¼
1	small carrot, shredded	1
1	stalk celery, thinly sliced on the diagonal	1
½ cup	bean sprouts	125 mL
¼ cup	sliced drained water chestnuts	50 mL
1	green onion, thinly sliced on the diagonal	1
	Asian Dressing and Dip (see below)	
	Kosher or sea salt	

1. In a large bowl, combine cabbage, green and red bell peppers, carrot, celery, bean sprouts, water chestnuts and green onion.
2. Add dressing to vegetables and mix thoroughly. Season with salt to taste.

Asian Dressing and Dip

Makes about ½ cup (125 mL)

3 tbsp	natural rice vinegar	45 mL
2 tbsp	freshly squeezed lime juice	25 mL
2 tbsp	granulated sugar	25 mL
1 tbsp	finely chopped gingerroot	15 mL
1 tbsp	finely chopped lemongrass	15 mL
2 tsp	fish sauce	10 mL
½ to 1	bird's eye (Thai) chile, seeded and finely chopped (see Dressing Tips, left)	½ to 1
¼ cup	vegetable oil	50 mL
1 tbsp	sesame oil (see Dressing Tips, left)	15 mL
	Kosher or sea salt	

1. In a small bowl, combine vinegar, lime juice, sugar, ginger, lemongrass, fish sauce and chile. Whisk in vegetable and sesame oils. Season with salt to taste.

Tuscan Pepper and Tomato Salad

Enjoy summer in every bite of this vibrant salad. Adjust the spiciness of the mixture with your choice of peppers.

1	red bell pepper	1
1	yellow bell pepper	1
½	green bell pepper	½
1	banana pepper	1
1	jalapeño pepper, seeded, optional	1
1 cup	halved cherry tomatoes	250 mL
¼ cup	finely sliced red onion	50 mL
¼ cup	halved pitted kalamata olives	50 mL
3 tbsp	olive oil	45 mL
2 tbsp	red wine vinegar	25 mL
1	clove garlic, minced	1
½ tsp	kosher or sea salt	2 mL
Pinch	hot pepper flakes, optional	Pinch
1 tbsp	basil chiffonade	15 mL

1. Cut red, yellow, green and banana peppers and jalapeño, if using, into very fine slivers (see Techniques, page 12). Transfer to a large bowl. Add tomatoes, red onion and olives.

2. In a small bowl, combine oil, vinegar, garlic, salt and hot pepper flakes, if using. Taste and adjust seasoning. Add dressing to vegetables and mix thoroughly. Garnish with basil.

Greek Salad

SERVES 6

This simple classic summer salad celebrates vegetables at their peak of flavor. Seek out dried oregano leaves imported from Greece to provide distinctive aroma and flavor. Fine imported Greek extra virgin olive oil and feta will add authenticity to all your Greek-inspired dishes.

½	English cucumber	½
1	green bell pepper, cut into chunky bite-size pieces	1
2	ripe tomatoes, seeded and cut into chunky bite-size pieces	2
1	small red onion, thinly sliced and separated into rings	1
½ cup	kalamata olives, pitted	125 mL
3 tbsp	extra virgin olive oil	45 mL
2 tsp	dried oregano leaves, crumbled	10 mL
	Salt and freshly ground black pepper	
1 tbsp	red wine vinegar, optional	15 mL
4 oz	feta cheese, broken into chunks	125 g

1. Slice cucumber lengthwise and scoop out seeds. Cut into bite-size pieces.
2. In a large bowl, combine cucumber, bell pepper, tomatoes, red onion and olives. Sprinkle with olive oil, oregano and salt and pepper to taste. Toss to combine and taste. Add a splash of vinegar if salad needs a touch of acidity; it all depends on the flavor of the tomatoes. Fold in chunks of feta.

Japanese Cucumber Salad

This sweetly spiced cucumber salad is a light crispy accompaniment to Asian-inspired foods from the grill. The garnish of toasted nori and black sesame seeds may be omitted, but it accentuates the Japanese flavors.

Tips

Seaweed has been consumed around the world for centuries. It's natural, nutritious and a flavor enhancer. Nori is most familiar as a toasted sheet used as a wrap (as for sushi), or as a condiment or garnish. Use also to add nutty, salty flavor to soup, rice or a stir-fry. Toast nori sheets in a hot pan, or hold with tongs and pass briefly and carefully over an open flame.

Sesame seeds come in colors of black, brown or beige. They all have sweet nutty flavor and pleasing crunch. Don't keep sesame seeds around for long since they turn rancid. Buy in small quantities and keep in closed containers in refrigerator or freezer. Toast sesame seeds before using. Place in a small heavy skillet over medium heat. Swirl the pan until aromas are released and seeds begin to color, about 2 minutes.

1	English cucumber	1
1 tsp	kosher or sea salt	5 mL
1½ tbsp	natural rice vinegar	22 mL
1 tsp	soy sauce	5 mL
1 tsp	mirin	5 mL
1 tsp	granulated sugar	5 mL
1	sheet nori, toasted (see Tips, left)	1
1 tsp	black sesame seeds (see Tips, left)	5 mL

1. Cut cucumber in half lengthwise and scoop out seeds. Slice thinly. Sprinkle cucumber slices with salt and set aside in a sieve to drain off excess moisture, about 30 minutes. Rinse cucumbers and pat dry.

2. In a bowl, combine vinegar, soy sauce, mirin and sugar. Add cucumber slices and toss to combine.

3. Using kitchen scissors, cut sheet of nori lengthwise into thirds and then into fine strips. Garnish cucumber salad with nori strips and sesame seeds.

Green Beans and Roasted Red Onion Salad

Yellow and green beans are one of our most prolific local summer crops, and we include them in a host of summer dishes. This is a tasty, colorful salad with the added pleasing crunch of toasted pine nuts. In our experience, green beans are popular with everyone, including the kids. Just don't overcook them!

Preheat oven to 450°F (230°C) or grill to medium-high

½	red onion, cut into wedges	½
1 tbsp	olive oil	15 mL
	Salt and freshly ground black pepper	
8 oz	green beans, trimmed	250 g
½	radicchio, torn	½
	Balsamic Vinaigrette (page 92)	
2 tbsp	pine nuts, toasted	25 mL

1. Toss red onion with oil and spread in a single layer on a baking sheet. Season with salt and pepper to taste. Place in preheated oven and roast until tender and just beginning to caramelize, 10 to 15 minutes. If using the grill, toss onion wedges with oil and seasoning and thread onto presoaked bamboo skewers. Grill, turning occasionally, until tender and nicely charred, 10 to 12 minutes. Let cool.

2. In a large saucepan of boiling lightly salted water, blanch green beans until bright green and just resistant to the bite, 2 to 3 minutes. Drain and rinse under cold water to stop cooking and retain bright green color.

3. In a large bowl, combine green beans, red onion and radicchio. Add vinaigrette and toss well to combine. Taste and adjust seasoning. Garnish with toasted pine nuts just before serving.

Grilled Onions

Unless you are equipped with a fancy vegetable grilling basket, cooking sliced onions on a barbecue grill is a challenge. They persistently fall through the grill. The following method works well. Peel onions and slice into wedges or into rings ½ inch (1 cm) thick. Pierce through the onion ring horizontally with two presoaked bamboo skewers, spaced about 1 inch (2.5 cm) apart. Brush lightly with olive oil and place on an oiled grill over medium-high heat, turning occasionally, until onions are tender and nicely charred, 10 to 12 minutes. Season with salt and pepper to taste and a splash of balsamic vinegar. Delicious!

Caesar Salad

Legend has it that this salad was created in the early 1900s by Caesar Cardini, a Tijuana restaurateur. The powerful creamy garlic dressing has become a classic and makes the salad a favorite to serve with Italian-inspired meals and also as a popular dip for crudités.

1	romaine lettuce, torn into bite-size pieces (about 6 cups/1.5 L)	1
1 cup	croutons (page 31) or store-bought	250 mL
¾ cup	Caesar Salad Dressing (see below)	175 mL
6	pieces bacon, cooked until crisp, optional	6
⅓ cup	shaved Parmigiano-Reggiano cheese	75 mL
	Freshly ground black pepper	
1	lemon, cut into wedges	1

1. In a large bowl, toss romaine and croutons with dressing until all leaves are well coated. Crumble bacon over top, if using. Garnish with shaved Parmesan and a few grinds of fresh pepper. Serve lemon wedges on the side.

Caesar Salad Dressing

Makes 1 cup (250 mL)

1	clove garlic, minced	1
1 to 2	anchovy fillets, rinsed, dried and minced (see Dressing Tips, left)	1 to 2
½ tsp	Dijon mustard	2 mL
½ tsp	Worcestershire Sauce	2 mL
2	egg yolks (see Tips, page 96)	2
1 tbsp	freshly squeezed lemon juice	15 mL
1 tbsp	white wine vinegar	15 mL
¼ tsp	hot pepper sauce, optional	1 mL
½ cup	olive oil	125 mL
	Freshly ground black pepper	
2 tbsp	freshly grated Parmigiano-Reggiano, optional	25 mL

1. In a large bowl, crush together garlic, anchovy, mustard and Worcestershire sauce to make a fine paste. Stir in egg yolks. Add lemon juice, vinegar and hot pepper sauce, if using. Slowly whisk in oil. Season with pepper to taste. Stir in Parmesan cheese, if making a vegetable dip. Because of the egg yolks, this dressing does not store well. Make it fresh and use it right away.

Tip

Parmigiano-Reggiano is the real Parmesan imported from Italy, made for more than 800 years in the areas of Parma, Reggio Emilia, Modena, Mantova and Bologna according to strictly guarded traditions. It has a slightly grainy consistency and a salty, nutty flavor unlike any others. Serve it freshly grated over soups or pasta, slivered in a salad or antipasto platter or just nibble as a special snack with olives, prosciutto and a glass of wine, of course.

Dressing Tips

The distinctive saltiness of anchovies has flavor-enhancing properties but it is not to everybody's taste. Add 1 or 2 fillets according to your preference.

Using a blender or hand-held immersion blender, combine ingredients as directed in recipe and slowly blend in oil. Whisk in 1 to 2 tbsp (15 to 25 mL) water if dressing is too thick.

Broccoli Primavera

We like to offer our customers lots of variety and we have tried to take this salad off the menu now and again over the past 25 years, but our customers just won't let us! Lots of crunchy, colorful vegetables, including super-good-for-you broccoli, and our popular Mustard Vinaigrette — that must be the secret. This rich creamy dressing is particularly delicious with blanched asparagus, a variety of other vegetables and seafood salads.

Variation

To make a milder, less assertive vinaigrette substitute natural rice vinegar for part, or all, of the white wine vinegar and use vegetable oil in place of olive oil.

1	head broccoli, florets only	1
2	carrots	2
½ cup	peas, fresh or frozen	125 mL
1	zucchini	1
½	each red and yellow bell peppers, diced	½
2 tbsp	coarsely chopped flat-leaf parsley	25 mL
1 tbsp	grated lemon zest	15 mL
	Mustard Vinaigrette (see below)	
	Salt and freshly ground black pepper	

1. In a saucepan of boiling lightly salted water, blanch broccoli until bright green and tender, 2 to 3 minutes. Drain and rinse under cold water. Drain and set aside.
2. Cut carrots in half lengthwise and slice thinly on the diagonal. Blanch carrots and peas as above. Set aside.
3. Slice zucchini in half lengthwise and slice thinly on the diagonal.
4. In a large bowl, combine blanched broccoli, carrots and peas, zucchini, red and yellow peppers, parsley and lemon zest. Add vinaigrette and toss well to combine. Season with salt and pepper to taste.

Mustard Vinaigrette

Makes 1 cup (250 mL)

1	clove garlic	1
1 tsp	kosher or sea salt	5 mL
2	hard-boiled egg yolks (see page 68)	2
3 tbsp	white wine vinegar	45 mL
1 tsp	Dijon mustard	5 mL
½ tsp	dry mustard	2 mL
⅔ cup	olive oil	150 mL
1 tsp	Worcestershire sauce	5 mL
¼ tsp	freshly ground black pepper	1 mL
1 tsp	honey or granulated sugar, optional	5 mL

1. In a small bowl, grind garlic and salt to a paste. Mix in egg yolks, vinegar and Dijon and dry mustards. Slowly whisk in oil. Add Worcestershire and pepper. Add honey to taste, if desired.

Vinegar

Vinegar, from the French *vin aigre* (sour wine), owes its mouth-shivering taste to acetic acid, itself the child of bacteria interacting with the alcohol in fermented cider, beer or wine. With its many-thousand-year history, not all of it pleasant, it has endured, as tough a survivor as an olive tree. It has long been recognized as multipurpose: offered to Christ on the cross as a quenching painkiller, it was also one of the four favorite food seasonings of the Prophet Mohammed, who called it "blessed." To today, when it is still used, generically, as much outside the kitchen (hair rinsing, toilet cleaning, fighting fleas and bedbugs) as it is inside.

We have taken our time but we have come to realize the wondrous and transformative effect good vinegar can have on our food. The result of this culinary light bulb snapping on in our brains is the great variety of vinegars now available in grocery stores throughout North America.

In the Kitchen

Balsamic vinegar is the most expensive because it is aged the longest. Top of the list (though Spanish sherry vinegars are also highly prized and similarly aged) is *Aceto Balsamico Tradizionale* that comes from Modena, Italy (home, too, to the Ferrari and Luciano Pavarotti); cooked from the must of Trebbiano white grapes until it is dark, rich, thick, aromatic and sweetly pungent, it is aged in barrels like fine wine, often for decades, and is often drunk neat, in small treasured amounts, at Italian family gatherings. Less expensive *Balsamico Condimento*, a blend of grape must and aged red wine vinegar, still offers a unique depth of flavor, and makes wonderful mixes for marinades and salad dressings. A few drops go a long way.

Red and white wine vinegars are the chef's Chevrolets. Well-aged wine vinegars such as Bunyuls from the foothills of the Pyrenees are made from fine regional wines and aged in oak barrels to develop smooth spicy flavor. Taste vinegars to identify the bouquet and choose for flavor rather than simply for a splash of acidity. Either red or white wine vinegar is fine for salad dressings and marinades. The red is better used with hearty flavors, and meats like pork and beef. The white works well with fish, chicken, and the lighter vegetables.

Apple cider vinegar also makes for light dressings. A small amount with water and ice is a great summer drink. Inexpensive and mild.

Malt vinegar, a full-bodied mix from malted barley, is popular in the U.K., particularly at fish and chips stands.

Rice vinegar, having little acidity, is the mildest of vinegars. Much used in Asian cooking and in light-flavored dressings.

Coconut vinegar is a sharper, more acidic vinegar, popular in India and in the Philippines, where it is made. Similarly **cane vinegar**, also produced in France and the U.S.; despite its name and being made from the juice of sugar canes, is not noticeably sweet.

Plain distilled vinegar is made from grain alcohol, and is best used for cleaning. It's acrid and unpleasant, but can be used in small amounts, added to milk, to make a substitute for buttermilk.

Storage

All vinegars should be firmly closed and stored somewhere dark and cool. They should be used within a year after opening. Left longer, the flavors will decline — a particular waste with expensive varieties, which should be bought in small amounts and savored.

Super Creamy Potato Salad

Every recipe collection has to include a creamy potato salad. It's a must to have in the repertoire for summer parties to serve with cold roast beef or glazed ham. The trickiest part of making a good potato salad is to find tasty mini potatoes (freshly harvested is best) and to cook them just right. Potatoes continue to cook and soften during cooling time. Remove them from the heat when they are still a bit resistant when tested. We keep a bamboo skewer at the stove for testing.

1½ lbs	mini white-skinned potatoes	750 g
2 tbsp	natural rice vinegar	25 mL
2 tbsp	olive oil	25 mL
	Salt and freshly ground black pepper	
1	stalk celery, thinly sliced on the diagonal	1
¼	red onion, thinly sliced	¼
¼ cup	Mayonnaise (page 96) or store-bought	50 mL
1 tbsp	Dijon mustard	15 mL
3	hard-cooked eggs, peeled and sliced	3
2 tbsp	chopped flat-leaf parsley	25 mL

1. In a large saucepan, cover potatoes with cold water, salt lightly and bring to a gentle boil. Cook until just tender, 10 to 15 minutes. Test frequently after 10 minutes. Potatoes should be just resistant to the test. Drain and let cool slightly.

2. When potatoes are cool enough to handle, cut each into quarters or halves, depending on size. Place in a large bowl and sprinkle warm potatoes with vinegar, oil and salt and pepper to taste.

3. Add celery, red onion, mayonnaise and mustard and mix together well. Taste and adjust seasoning. Gently fold in eggs and parsley.

How to Hard Boil an Egg
In a small saucepan, cover egg with cold water by ½ inch (1 cm) and place over medium heat. As soon as water is simmering remove pan from heat. Cover and set aside for 7 minutes. Immediately plunge egg in cold water and cool. Crack the shell all over (gently tap on the counter a few times) and remove the shell under cold running water. To prevent black rings from forming around the yolk, let eggs cool as quickly as possible. Fresh eggs are difficult to peel; they should be at least 2 to 3 days old.

French Potato Salad

This salad is as colorful as an Impressionist painting! Make it when vegetables are at their peak of color and flavor.

Variation

Salade Niçoise: Prepare potatoes and green beans as in Steps 1 to 3. Toss potatoes with onions, celery and green onions with enough White Wine Vinaigrette to flavor and coat the vegetables (about 1/4 cup/50 mL), and arrange in the center of a large platter. Edge the platter with Boston lettuce leaves. Toss beans and tomatoes separately with a scant 1/4 cup (50 mL) of vinaigrette and arrange in clusters around the edge of the platter. Garnish platter with hard-cooked eggs, cut in half, a handful of pitted dry-cured Nyons olives, 5 or 6 anchovy fillets and a scattering of fresh basil. To complete the dish, add chunks of drained canned tuna packed in oil or grilled fresh tuna.

1½ lbs	mini red-skinned potatoes	750 g
1 tbsp	white wine vinegar	15 mL
	Salt and freshly ground black pepper	
8 oz	green beans, trimmed	250 g
¼	red onion, thinly sliced	¼
1	stalk celery, thinly sliced	1
1 cup	halved cherry tomatoes	250 mL
1	green onion, thinly sliced on the diagonal	1
	White Wine Vinaigrette (see Variation, page 93)	
2 tbsp	capers, drained	25 mL
1 tbsp	basil chiffonade	15 mL

1. In a large saucepan, cover potatoes with cold water, salt lightly and bring to a gentle boil. Cook until just tender, 10 to 15 minutes. Test frequently after 10 minutes. Potatoes should be just resistant to the test. Drain and let cool slightly.

2. When potatoes are cool enough to handle, cut each into quarters or halves, depending on size. Place in a large bowl and sprinkle warm potatoes with vinegar and salt and pepper to taste. Set aside.

3. In a saucepan of boiling lightly salted water, blanch green beans until just tender, 2 to 3 minutes. Drain and rinse under cold water to stop cooking and retain bright color. Cut beans in half, or quarters, if long.

4. Add beans, red onion, celery, tomatoes, green onion and vinaigrette to potatoes. Toss gently to combine. Taste and adjust seasoning. Garnish with capers and basil.

Spanish Grilled Potato Salad

A rustic salad with rich, smoky Mediterranean flavors. Serve with a salad of radicchio and frisée and warm crusty bread on the side and you have the makings of a spectacular lunch. The spicy roasted potatoes are delicious to serve as a side dish with grilled pork or fish.

Tip

Paprika is not just the obligatory sprinkle on a piece of fish! The Extremadura and Murcia regions of Spain produce a wonderful range of paprika made from sweet, bittersweet and hot peppers. They all impart unique flavor to stews, sauces, rubs, pickles and especially sausages. Smoked bittersweet paprika is produced from peppers smoked over smoldering oak fires following traditional methods. The peppers are ground into a smooth powder that has an unmistakable rich, smoky aroma and taste.

- **Preheat oven to 400°F (200°C)**
- **Roasting pan**

2 lbs	mini red-skinned potatoes	1 kg
¼ cup	olive oil, divided	50 mL
1 tbsp	smoked paprika (see Tip, left)	15 mL
2 tsp	cayenne pepper	10 mL
2 tsp	kosher or sea salt	10 mL
1 tsp	ground cumin	5 mL
½ tsp	freshly ground black pepper	2 mL
1	onion, cut into ½-inch (1 cm) pieces	1
2	cloves garlic, thinly sliced lengthwise	2
1	red bell pepper, thinly sliced	1
8 oz	dry-cured chorizo sausage, thinly sliced, optional	250 g
2 tbsp	balsamic vinegar (approx.)	25 mL
2 tbsp	extra virgin olive oil	25 mL
½ cup	coarsely chopped cilantro	125 mL

1. Cut potatoes into halves or quarters, depending on size. In a large bowl, toss potatoes with 2 tbsp (25 mL) of the olive oil, paprika, cayenne, salt, cumin and pepper.

2. Spread potatoes in a single layer in a roasting pan and roast in preheated oven, stirring occasionally, until tender and nicely browned, 20 to 25 minutes. Set aside.

3. In a skillet, heat remaining olive oil over medium heat. Add onion, garlic and bell pepper. Season lightly with salt and pepper and sauté until onions are tender and lightly browned, 5 to 7 minutes. Stir in chorizo, if using, and sauté until lightly browned. Add vinegar and deglaze pan, scraping up browned bits on the bottom. Transfer vegetables and sausage to a large bowl and add roasted potatoes. Let cool completely.

4. Add extra virgin olive oil and cilantro. Taste and adjust seasoning, adding a splash more balsamic vinegar, if needed. Serve at room temperature.

Sesame Noodle Salad

This is a great salad to serve a crowd, especially with food from the grill marinated in Asian flavors.

Dressing Tips

For times when processors and blenders are not around, a mortar and pestle does a great job. Grind the chopped and dry ingredients (garlic, gingerroot, sugar etc.) together first. Stir in liquid flavoring ingredients and lastly whisk in the oil until sauce is smooth and of the desired consistency.

Tahini is a creamy paste made from ground sesame seeds and is available in jars in most markets. It is used in many Middle Eastern sauces and dressings to drizzle over legumes, vegetables and salads and in popular dips such as Hummus (with chickpeas) (page 313) and Baba Ghanoush (with eggplant) (page 312).

Variation

Peanut Sauce: Replace tahini with natural unsweetened peanut butter to make an irresistible sauce to accompany salad rolls, or indeed anything that needs a peanut dip. Kids have been known to eat this with a spoon!

7 oz	rice vermicelli noodles	200 g
1/2	each red and green bell peppers	1/2
2 oz	snow peas, trimmed (see Tip, page 58)	60 g
1	stalk celery	1
2	green onions	2
1 cup	bean sprouts	250 mL
1 to 1 1/4 cups	Sesame Ginger Dressing and Dip (see below)	250 to 300 mL

1. Blanch rice vermicelli in a large pot of boiling water for 1 minute, or prepare noodles according to package instructions. Drain and rinse under cold water. Set aside.
2. Cut bell peppers into julienne. Cut snow peas, celery and green onions into fine slivers on the diagonal.
3. In a large bowl, combine noodles, bell peppers, snow peas, celery, green onions and beans sprouts and toss with dressing.

Sesame Ginger Dressing and Dip

Makes 1 3/4 cups (425 mL)

● **Food processor or blender**

1/3 cup	tahini (see Dressing Tips, left)	75 mL
1/4 cup	soy sauce	50 mL
3 tbsp	sweet chili sauce	45 mL
3 tbsp	mirin	45 mL
2 tbsp	brown sugar or palm sugar	25 mL
1 tbsp	chopped gingerroot	15 mL
2 tsp	chopped garlic	10 mL
1/2 tsp	sambal oelek	2 mL
1/3 cup	vegetable oil	75 mL

1. In a food processor, combine tahini, soy sauce, chili sauce, mirin, brown sugar, ginger, garlic and sambal oelek. With motor running, slowly drizzle in oil through the feed tube. Add about 1/4 cup (50 mL) water. Add more water, 1 tbsp (15 mL) at a time, to make sauce a thick, creamy consistency.

Soba Noodle Salad with Edamame

A great salad is all about creating a pleasing combination of taste, texture and color. We feast with our eyes! Here we combine soba noodles with crisp vegetables for a nourishing salad tossed with an Asian-inspired Miso Dressing.

Tips

You will find that salads that include noodles absorb a lot of dressing as they stand. Taste and add more dressing before serving, if needed.

Soba noodles are a staple in Japanese cuisine and enjoyed often as a simple light meal. The flavorful brown noodles are made from wheat and buckwheat. Cook noodles in a pot of boiling lightly salted water until tender but not too soft, 6 to 8 minutes. Drain and, if serving cold, rinse quickly under cold running water and drain again. Somen are thin brown wheat noodles that are also served hot and cold. Prepare the same way, but cook for a shorter time.

Edamame are young tender soybeans available shelled and frozen in the pod. Cook before eating, following package instructions. Do not overcook. They have a pleasing crunch and are good for you, too!

8 oz	soba noodles (see Tips, left)	250 g
	Kosher or sea salt	
8 oz	edamame in the pod, frozen (see Tips, left)	250 g
4 oz	snow peas, trimmed (see Tip, page 58)	125 g
2	radishes, julienned	2
2	green onions, thinly sliced on the diagonal	2
Pinch	hot pepper flakes	Pinch
½ to ⅔ cup	Miso Dressing (page 73) (see Tip, page 230)	125 to 150 mL
1	sheet toasted nori, optional (see Tips, page 63)	1
1 tbsp	toasted white sesame seeds, optional (see Tips, page 63)	15 mL
1 tbsp	toasted black sesame seeds, optional	15 mL

1. In a large saucepan of boiling salted water, cook noodles until tender, 6 to 8 minutes, or prepare noodles according to package instructions. Drain and rinse under cold water. (You should have 4 cups/1 L cooked soba noodles.) Set aside.

2. Cook edamame in ½ cup (125 mL) lightly salted water, covered, according to package instructions, about 4 minutes. Gently squeeze beans from pod. (You should have about ¾ cup/175 mL.)

3. Blanch snow peas for 30 seconds. Drain and rinse under cold water. Cut into fine slivers.

4. In a large bowl, combine noodles, edamame, snow peas, radishes, green onions and hot pepper flakes. Toss with dressing.

5. Using kitchen scissors, cut sheet of nori lengthwise into thirds and then into fine strips. Sprinkle on top of salad and garnish with white and black sesame seeds, if using.

Miso Dressing

Makes 1¾ cups (425 mL)

● **Food processor or blender**

⅔ cup	natural rice vinegar	150 mL
¼ cup	yellow or white miso	50 mL
2 tbsp	chopped gingerroot	25 mL
2 tbsp	granulated sugar	25 mL
1 tbsp	chopped garlic	15 mL
	Salt and freshly ground black pepper	
1 cup	vegetable oil	250 mL
1 tbsp	sesame oil, optional	15 mL

1. In a food processor, combine vinegar, miso, ginger, sugar, garlic and salt and pepper to taste. Slowly drizzle in vegetable oil and sesame oil, if using, through the feed tube. Add water, 1 tbsp (15 mL) at a time, to make sauce a light, creamy consistency. Taste and adjust seasoning.

Dressing Tip

In our kitchen, the chefs make frequent use of a giant immersion blender (about 3 feet/1 m high) for some puréeing tasks. In the home kitchen, a hand-held immersion blender does a great job of blending small quantities of dressings, sauces and even soups. It's also a handy piece of equipment for quickly puréeing a small amount of food for babies and young tots.

Fusilli, Feta and Arugula Salad

A favorite pasta salad, fortunately prepared all year long using baby arugula from local greenhouses in winter months.

Tip

Salads made with pasta, grains and legumes absorb dressing over time and tend to dry out and lose flavor. Citrus flavors, in particular, fade rapidly. Toss ingredients with dressing and let stand for an hour or so for flavors to blend, and always taste and adjust seasoning and amount of dressing again before serving. Add a splash of vinegar, lemon juice or oil as needed.

2 cups	fusilli	500 mL
1 tbsp	olive oil	15 mL
1	red bell pepper, julienne	1
½	red onion, thinly sliced	½
¼ cup	oil-packed sun-dried tomatoes, drained and chopped	50 mL
½ cup	Red Wine Vinaigrette (page 93)	125 mL
1 cup	baby arugula	250 mL
½ cup	crumbled feta cheese	125 mL
	Salt and freshly ground black pepper	

1. In a large pot of boiling lightly salted water, cook pasta until tender, 8 to 10 minutes, or according to package directions. Drain, rinse under cold water and drain well. Transfer to a large bowl and toss with olive oil.

2. Add bell pepper, red onion and sun-dried tomatoes.

3. Add dressing and mix thoroughly to combine. Gently fold in arugula and feta. Season with salt and pepper to taste.

Herbed Penne Salad

For visual appeal and variety we use dried pasta of many different shapes in our pasta salads. The shape of the pasta, whether it's a butterfly (farfalle), a spiral (rotini or fusilli) or a long tube (penne) determines how the vegetables are chopped, diced or slivered. The creamy dill dressing is delicious with cucumbers, on pasta and a pleasing condiment to serve with cold salmon or trout. Try it as a dip for Crab Cakes (page 340).

2 cups	penne	500 mL
1 tbsp	olive oil	15 mL
1	carrot	1
½	red bell pepper	½
½	English cucumber	½
½ cup	Fresh Herb Dressing and Dip (see below)	125 mL
	Kosher or sea salt	

1. In a large pot of boiling lightly salted water, cook pasta until tender, 8 to 10 minutes, or according to package directions. Drain, rinse under cold water and drain well. Transfer to a large bowl and toss with olive oil. (You should have 3½ cups/875 mL cooked pasta.)
2. Cut carrot and red pepper into fine slivers. Cut cucumber in half lengthwise and slice thinly. Add vegetables to pasta.
3. Add dressing and mix thoroughly to combine. Season with salt to taste.

Fresh Herb Dressing and Dip

Makes 1 cup (250 mL)

½ cup	Mayonnaise (page 96) or store-bought	125 mL
½ cup	sour cream	125 mL
2	green onions, finely chopped	2
2 tbsp	chopped dill	25 mL
1 tbsp	chopped mint	15 mL
1 tbsp	chopped flat-leaf parsley	15 mL
	Salt and freshly ground black pepper	

1. In a small bowl, combine mayonnaise, sour cream, green onions, dill, mint and parsley. Season with salt and pepper to taste.

Olive Oil

Born wild in the Mediterranean basin some 8,000 years BC, and domesticated there about 2,000 years later, the olive tree may be the basin's greatest boon to mankind. We know its oil best — Homer called it "liquid gold," Greek athletes rubbed it over their bodies because it highlighted the beauty of the male body, lamps were lit with it and Roman charioteers used it to grease their axles.

In our time we recognize it as the prime oil deliverer of monounsaturated fat, hailed for both its taste and its health benefits, and the prime component of the Mediterranean diet. Also known as the French Paradox, this holds that though people in Mediterranean countries, home to 95 percent of the world's olive trees, consume great amounts of fat, they are generally not obese, and have much lower rates of cardiovascular disease than do North Americans (who gobble up similar amounts of fat and have an obesity prevalence of 60 percent).

It is not the only heart-healthy part of the diet, of course — red wine, plenty of fresh fruit and vegetables play their part — but studies have shown that olive oil has powerful antioxidant properties, regulates cholesterol (and helps lower rates of bad LDL), and can improve general heart health.

One study in particular, approved by the U.S. Food and Drug Administration, suggests that people who consume 2 tbsp (25 mL) of olive oil daily will reduce the risk of coronary heart disease, thanks to olive oil's high levels of monounsaturates (73 percent, compared, for instance, with butter's 21 percent and safflower oil's 13 percent).

The oil's health benefits are constant, but its range is not: Olive oil offers a huge range of flavors ranging from robust and spicy to delicate and fruity. The flavor is influenced by the variety of olive, the soil and climate where the olives are grown, the care taken during cultivation of the olive trees, the quality and ripeness of the olives at time of harvest and the methods used in extracting and processing the oil.

The finest olive oils are produced from olives grown on carefully nurtured groves from an accredited region or single estate. They are made from the first cold-pressing of hand-picked olives selected as to degree of ripeness within 24 hours of harvesting. Some are submitted to a gentle filtering that provides a smooth, clear greenish to gold oil, others retain some of the tiny olive particles, which results in an opaque greenish oil with intense fruity flavor. Newly pressed oil, eagerly awaited in our markets in early spring, is intense. The flavor mellows in the bottle over time.

Nationally, Italian extra virgin olive oil from Tuscany is probably the one most recognized for its robust, earthy olive flavor with lingering hint of pepperiness (similar to the oil from Puglia, in southern Italy, and from Andalusia in southern Spain). Extra virgin olive oil from other regions such as Liguria in Italy, Catalonia in Spain and Provence in France has a more delicate, smooth, fruity flavor. Now coming to the marketplace are fine extra virgin olive oils from California, New Zealand, Greece, Portugal and South Africa. Some of these olive estates grow popular Tuscan olive varieties such as Frantoia and Leccino, producing oil with intense, earthy flavor. Each will have the uniqueness of the growing and processing conditions. Find out the story behind the oil and take every opportunity to sample the aroma and taste.

Jeanne Calment, though, was no respecter of brands. The oldest recorded person in history, if we discount

Methuselah, Calment died in 1997 at age 122. She ascribed her longevity — and her relatively youthful looks — to olive oil, any olive oil, which she poured on all her food and rubbed vigorously into her skin. She was also a lover of port wine, and ate 2 lbs (1 kg) of chocolate a week. Without the olive oil, who knows?

In the Kitchen

The finest extra virgin olive oils are used to dress pasta, to drizzle over grilled vegetables or ripe tomatoes and to brush on grilled bread for bruschetta. The mellow oil from Liguria and Provence is fabulous over grilled fish, for special salads or to make an authentic basil pesto. Less expensive extra virgin olive oil is the workhorse of our kitchen, especially for sautéing, roasting and grilling vegetables.

The chef always tastes before making an olive oil purchase. Follow the vintner's methods. Pour a sample of oil into a glass and warm it in the hand. Take a deep sniff to capture the aroma. Sip, taking in air with your sip, and spread the oil around your mouth. Savor sweet fruitiness in the front, any bitterness at the back and wait for spicy pepperiness to come later. It's a rewarding experience and leads to many great culinary adventures.

Estate-bottled extra virgin olive oil from the first cold pressing of hand-picked olives is considered the best. The name of the estate, the varieties of olive used and the careful methods used in production are usually all identified on the olive oil label. Finest and fruitiest, and most expensive. The acidity level must be less than 1 percent. Commercial and house brands of extra virgin olive oil are widely available. They do not have the complexity of flavor but are fine for everyday use and very versatile. You may get lucky with quality of some house brands, so they're worth a try.

Virgin olive oil comes from the first and second pressings and largely from lesser-quality olives. It is less flavorful and has a higher acidity level than extra virgin olive oil.

Pure olive oil, also simply olive oil, is usually a blend of refined, processed and virgin oils. Typically lacks the flavor of the full virgins.

Light and extra-light olive oil (American marketing labels) have been heavily filtered and offer a very mild olive taste. However, they contain the same monounsaturated health benefits as the others — and the same number of calories. Good for baking and high-heat cooking.

Lampante is not suitable for food; used mainly for oil-burning lamps, as the ancients did.

The oils with most intense flavor are made from a blend of red-ripe and green olives picked early in the season. The only difference between green and black olives is that green are unripe and black are ripe. Red-ripe, no longer green, are on their way to blackness.

Storage

The finest extra virgin olive oils are best used within a year of pressing. Find out from your supplier when the pressing took place. Frequently the "best before" date stamped on the bottle refers to the date of bottling, which is misleading. Store in a cool place out of direct sunlight to preserve flavor and prevent oil from going rancid.

Bulgur and Grilled Vegetable Salad

SERVES 6

This summer mainstay salad is a great way to make use of harvest vegetables and any leftover grilled vegetables. The mix can be adjusted to whatever vegetables you have on hand. It's a perfect salad to accompany grilled steak and a delicious main dish for vegetarians in the group with the addition of crumbled feta cheese.

Tip

Bite into a Taggiasche olive and you taste the Mediterranean sun! The typically small olives grow in west Liguria region in Italy. They ripen late in the season, which probably contributes to their smooth, rich flavor. You will find them in specialty food stores, both pitted and with pits, sometimes in bulk packs or in small jars preserved in olive oil. They are our first choice to make a luxurious Tapenade (page 324). If you can't find them, use your favorite ripe olive from the deli counter.

Variation

In Step 1, replace bulgur with couscous for a tasty variation of color, taste and texture.

Preheated barbecue or indoor grill

1 cup	fine bulgur	250 mL
1¼ cups	boiling water	300 mL
1	red bell pepper, halved	1
1	yellow bell pepper, halved	1
1	zucchini, sliced lengthwise	1
1	red onion, sliced	1
2 tbsp	olive oil	25 mL
	Kosher or sea salt	
1	can (14 to 19 oz/398 to 540 mL) chickpeas, rinsed and drained	1
¼ cup	oil-packed sun-dried tomatoes, drained and chopped	50 mL
¼ cup	Taggiasche or kalamata olives, pitted and chopped (see Tip, left)	50 mL
¼ cup	Balsamic Vinaigrette (page 92)	50 mL
	Freshly ground black pepper	
2 tbsp	basil chiffonade	25 mL
1 tbsp	chopped flat-leaf parsley	15 mL

1. Place bulgur in a large bowl and cover with boiling water. Cover bowl tightly with plastic wrap and set aside for 20 minutes. Place bulgur in a sieve to remove any excess water and set aside in a large bowl. (You should have 3 cups/750 mL bulgur after soaking.)

2. In another large bowl, toss red and yellow bell peppers, zucchini and red onion with oil and a pinch of salt. Grill in batches over medium-high heat until tender and lightly browned, 10 to 15 minutes. Let cool and chop coarsely.

3. In a large bowl, combine bulgur, grilled vegetables, chickpeas, sun-dried tomatoes and olives. Add vinaigrette and mix together well. Season with black pepper to taste. Taste and adjust seasoning. Garnish with basil and parsley.

Tuscan White Bean and Tomato Salad

A simple excellent salad that is very quick to prepare when using good quality canned white beans. We like to add variety and texture by making this salad with different varieties of dried beans or fava beans cooked in the kitchen.

Tip

For speed and convenience, replace dried beans with 1 can (14 to 19 oz/398 to 540 mL) white beans, rinsed and drained.

1 cup	dried white navy beans (see Tip, left)	250 mL
	Kosher or sea salt	
¼ cup	olive oil	50 mL
2 tsp	finely chopped garlic	10 mL
	Freshly ground black pepper	
2 cups	diced seeded ripe tomatoes	500 mL
¼	red onion, diced	¼
1 tbsp	coarsely chopped oregano	15 mL
2 tbsp	balsamic vinegar	25 mL

1. Place beans in a bowl and add water to cover. Set aside to soak overnight in the refrigerator. Drain beans.

2. In a saucepan over medium heat, add beans and cover with cold water, about 4 cups (1 L). Bring to a boil and cook until soft, 40 to 45 minutes. Remove from heat. Add a pinch of salt and let stand for 5 minutes. Drain and set aside.

3. In a large skillet, heat oil over medium-low heat. Add garlic and sauté until soft and just beginning to caramelize, 1 to 2 minutes. Add beans and toss to combine with garlic-infused oil. Season lightly with salt and pepper. Let cool.

4. In a large bowl, combine cooled beans, tomatoes, red onion, oregano and vinegar. Toss to combine well. Season with black pepper to taste.

Chickpea and Roasted Pepper Salad

This salad is quick and easy to prepare, tastes good and travels well. It's a perfect stand-by for summer picnics.

Tip

All canned chickpeas and beans are not created equal. In our kitchen we periodically taste-test different brands of canned goods. We advise you to do the same. We are always amazed at the different qualities of taste and texture. Even the same brand will differ from year to year. In this case we find a quality brand of organic legumes is superior. Remember to rinse off the preserving liquid and drain well before using.

1	roasted red bell pepper, diced (page 35)	1
1	carrot, grated	1
2	cans (each 14 to 19 oz/398 to 540 mL) chickpeas, rinsed and drained (see Tip, left)	2
½ cup	Red Wine Vinaigrette (page 93)	125 mL
2 tbsp	chopped flat-leaf parsley	25 mL
2 tsp	chopped oregano	10 mL
	Salt and freshly ground black pepper	

1. In a large bowl, combine roasted pepper, carrot and chickpeas.
2. Add vinaigrette, parsley and oregano and toss to combine. Season with salt and pepper to taste.

Black-Eyed Pea Salad with Tomato and Feta

Tip

For speed and convenience, replace dried beans with 1 can (14 to 19 oz/398 to 540 mL) black-eyed peas, rinsed and drained.

1 cup	dried black-eyed peas (see Tip, left)	250 mL
	Kosher or sea salt	
1	large ripe tomato, seeded and diced	1
1/2	red onion, chopped	1/2
1/4 cup	kalamata olives, pitted and halved	50 mL
1/4 cup	Red Wine Vinaigrette (page 93)	50 mL
2 tbsp	coarsely chopped flat-leaf parsley	25 mL
1 tbsp	finely chopped oregano	15 mL
1/2 cup	crumbled feta cheese	125 mL
	Freshly ground black pepper	

1. Place black-eyed peas in a bowl and add water to cover. Set aside to soak overnight in the refrigerator. Drain peas.

2. In a saucepan over medium heat, add black-eyed peas and cover with cold water, about 4 cups (1 L). Bring to a boil and cook until soft, 35 to 45 minutes. Remove from heat. Add a pinch of salt and let stand for 5 minutes. Drain. Transfer to a large bowl. Let cool.

3. Add tomato, red onion and olives. Add vinaigrette, parsley and oregano and toss to mix well. Season with salt to taste. Garnish with feta and a few grindings of black pepper.

Four Beans with Basil Salad

This is another good robust salad to take on a picnic. The taste improves when the beans have had time to absorb all the flavors. It keeps well in the refrigerator for 2 to 3 days.

Tip

The mix of black and red beans, green mung beans and pale chickpeas in this recipe is an appetizing combination of color, texture, shape and size. When you start from scratch with the dried varieties you gain a distinct taste and texture difference. However, for convenience, substitute 2 cans (14 to 19 oz/398 to 540 mL) of your favorite beans, rinsed and drained.

½ cup	dried black turtle beans	125 mL
½ cup	dried pinto beans	125 mL
	Kosher or sea salt	
½ cup	dried mung beans	125 mL
1	can (14 to 19 oz/398 to 540 mL) chickpeas, drained and rinsed	1
½	red bell pepper, diced	½
½	red onion, diced	½
2	green onions, thinly sliced on the diagonal	2
½ cup	Basil Vinaigrette (page 92)	125 mL
	Freshly ground black pepper	

1. Place black turtle and pinto beans in separate small bowls and add water to cover. Set aside to soak overnight in the refrigerator. Drain beans.

2. In a saucepan, combine turtle beans and pinto beans and cover with cold water, about 4 cups (1 L). Bring to a boil and cook until soft, 40 to 45 minutes. Remove from heat. Add a pinch of salt and let stand for 5 minutes. Drain. Transfer to a large bowl. Let cool.

3. Follow the same cooking method for the mung beans but omit soaking and reduce cooking time to 15 to 20 minutes. Drain and add to turtle and pinto beans.

4. Add chickpeas, bell pepper and red and green onions. Add vinaigrette and toss to combine. Season with black pepper to taste.

Grilled Corn and Lima Bean Salad

Of the hundreds of salads we have created over the years, this has proven to be a runaway bestseller! We thought of keeping the recipe a secret, but it's too good not to share. It's a colorful, refreshing salad and makes a satisfying lunch all by itself.

Tip

Slicing kernels from a cob of corn: Make a slice across the bottom of the corncob so that it stands upright on a large cutting board. Hold the blade of a sharp knife against the cob at the top and slice downwards firmly following the shape of the cob and releasing the kernels as you go.

● **Preheated barbecue or indoor grill**

2	ears corn, husk and silk removed (see Tip, left)	2
3 tbsp	olive oil, divided	45 mL
	Kosher or sea salt	
2 cups	frozen lima beans	500 mL
1 cup	halved cherry tomatoes	250 mL
1	shallot, diced	1
1/4 cup	kalamata olives, pitted and roughly chopped	50 mL
2 tbsp	apple cider vinegar	25 mL
	Freshly ground black pepper	
1 cup	baby arugula	250 mL
1/2 cup	crumbled feta cheese	125 mL

1. Brush corn lightly with 1 tbsp (15 mL) of the oil and sprinkle with salt. Place on a lightly oiled grill over medium-high heat and grill until lightly charred on all sides. Let cool and slice kernels from the cob. Transfer to a large bowl and set aside.

2. In a saucepan of boiling lightly salted water, blanch lima beans until tender, 3 to 5 minutes. Drain and let cool. Add to corn with tomatoes, shallot and olives.

3. In a small bowl, whisk vinegar with remaining oil and season with salt and pepper to taste.

4. Pour dressing over vegetables and mix together well. Taste and adjust seasoning. Gently fold in arugula and feta.

Tabbouleh

Here's a light refreshing salad with origins in Greek cuisine. The secret to a stellar tabbouleh is the freshness of all ingredients, especially in the clean bright taste of a large quantity of fresh parsley.

Tip

Parsley is an herb of astounding value. Lots of health-giving properties and it acts as a taste enhancer, accentuating the flavors of accompanying ingredients. In our kitchen we primarily use Italian flat-leaf parsley (not the curly variety). The flavor is more intense, the leaves are more robust and hold well as a garnish, either coarsely or finely chopped.

1 cup	fine bulgur	250 mL
1¼ cups	boiling vegetable stock or water	300 mL
3 tbsp	freshly squeezed lemon juice	45 mL
3 tbsp	olive oil	45 mL
	Kosher or sea salt	
½	English cucumber, peeled, seeded and diced	½
1	large ripe tomato, seeded and diced	1
2	green onions, thinly sliced	2
1	clove garlic, minced	1
1 cup	finely chopped flat-leaf parsley (see Tip, left)	250 mL
2 tbsp	chopped mint	25 mL
	Freshly ground black pepper	

1. Place bulgur in a large bowl and cover with boiling vegetable stock. Cover bowl tightly with plastic wrap and set aside for 20 minutes. Place bulgur in a sieve to remove any excess liquid and set aside in a large bowl. Sprinkle with lemon juice, oil and a little salt.

2. Add cucumber, tomato, green onions, garlic, parsley and mint and mix together well. Season with black pepper to taste. Add a dash more lemon juice and oil, if needed.

Almond Tabbouleh

1 cup	fine bulgur	250 mL
1¼ cups	boiling vegetable stock or water	300 mL
3 tbsp	freshly squeezed lemon juice	45 mL
3 tbsp	olive oil	45 mL
	Kosher or sea salt	
2	green onions, thinly sliced	2
1 cup	finely chopped flat-leaf parsley	250 mL
⅓ cup	chopped toasted slivered almonds	75 mL
¼ cup	currants	50 mL
1 tbsp	chopped mint	15 mL
	Freshly ground black pepper	

1. Place bulgur in a large bowl and cover with boiling vegetable stock. Cover bowl tightly with plastic wrap and set aside for 20 minutes. Place bulgur in a sieve to remove any excess liquid and set aside in a large bowl. Sprinkle with lemon juice, oil and a little salt.

2. Add green onions, parsley, almonds, currants and mint and mix together well. Season with black pepper to taste. Add a dash more lemon juice and oil, if needed.

Tortellini and Dill Salad

SERVES 4 TO 6

Light in taste yet quite satisfying enough to make a nice summer lunch when served over tossed greens.

12 oz	mini cheese tortellini pasta	375 g
1 tbsp	olive oil	15 mL
1	carrot, julienned	1
½	green bell pepper, julienned	½
2	green onions, thinly sliced on the diagonal	2
2 tbsp	coarsely chopped dill	25 mL
2 tbsp	coarsely chopped flat-leaf parsley	25 mL
	Lemon Vinaigrette (page 90)	
	Salt and freshly ground black pepper	

1. In a large pot, bring 12 cups (3 L) of lightly salted water to a boil. Add tortellini and cook until tender, about 12 minutes, or according to package directions. Drain and rinse in cold water. In a large bowl, toss pasta with oil. Let cool.

2. Add carrot, bell pepper, green onions, dill and parsley to the pasta and toss with vinaigrette. Season with salt and pepper to taste.

Beet Salad with Chèvre and Tarragon

1¼ lbs	beets (about 3 large)	625 g
¼	red onion, thinly sliced	¼
½ cup	White Wine Vinaigrette (see Variation, page 93)	125 mL
1 tbsp	chopped tarragon	15 mL
1 tsp	grated orange zest	5 mL
	Salt and freshly ground black pepper	
4 tbsp	crumbled soft chèvre	60 mL

1. In a large saucepan, cover beets with cold, lightly salted water. Bring to a boil, reduce heat and simmer until beets are tender, 30 minutes depending on size. Adjust timing if your beets are smaller or larger. Drain. Let cool and remove skins.

2. Cut beets in half and slice or coarsely chop. In a large bowl, combine beets, red onion, vinaigrette, tarragon and orange zest. Toss well to blend flavors. Season with salt and black pepper to taste. Sprinkle chèvre on beet salad just before serving.

Moroccan Carrot Salad

SERVES 4 TO 6

A tasty salad to accompany foods from the grill seasoned with North African flavors. The salad keeps and travels well and improves when flavors have had time to mingle.

Spice mill or mortar and pestle

1 tsp	cumin seeds or ½ tsp (2 mL) ground cumin	5 mL
1 tbsp	apple cider vinegar	15 mL
1 tsp	grated orange zest	5 mL
1 tbsp	freshly squeezed orange juice	15 mL
½ tsp	ground cinnamon	2 mL
½ tsp	kosher or sea salt, divided	2 mL
3 tbsp	vegetable oil	45 mL
3 tbsp	olive oil	45 mL
	Freshly ground black pepper	
1 lb	carrots, grated (about 5)	500 g
2	green onions, thinly sliced on the diagonal	2
2 tbsp	currants	25 mL
2 tbsp	toasted pine nuts	25 mL
2 tbsp	chopped mint	25 mL
2 tbsp	chopped cilantro	25 mL

1. In a small skillet over medium heat, toast cumin seeds until aromas are released, 1 to 2 minutes. Grind to a powder in a spice mill or with mortar and pestle.

2. In a bowl, mix together vinegar, orange zest and juice, cumin, cinnamon and ¼ tsp (1 mL) of the salt. Whisk in vegetable and olive oils. Taste and adjust seasoning. Set aside.

3. In a large bowl, combine carrots, green onions, currants, pine nuts, mint and cilantro. Pour dressing over carrot mixture and toss well to combine.

Five-Grain Pomegranate Salad

SERVES 6

This salad contains sweet and fruity pomegranate, a hint of anise from fennel and a crunchy mix of grains. A salad that is so tasty and pretty to look at, you can hardly believe it's good for you, too!

Tips

Grain Mixes: Many delicious high-protein grain and legume mixes are available in health food markets. For convenience sake, they are processed to cook quickly in a large pot of boiling water in 12 to 15 minutes. For this salad, the grain mix contains brown rice, barley, couscous, lentils and quinoa. Sometimes we make our own grain mix and then we cook or prepare each grain separately. A favorite blend is brown rice, mung beans, de Puys lentils, barley and quinoa. (See pages 257 and 271 for cooking instructions.)

The pomegranate has a lot going for it. The crimson fruit with thin deep pink skin is filled with tart, juicy seeds that are used as a dye and also a flavoring in Middle Eastern and West Indian cooking. Recent studies show that pomegranate juice is rich in antioxidants with accompanying health benefits, so the juice is now a popular item at the market. Our chefs in both the sweet and savory kitchens love the pomegranate for singular tart flavor and brilliant color.

1½ cups	Jade Grain Mix (10 oz/300 g) (see Tips, left)	375 mL
¼ cup	red wine vinegar	50 mL
2 tbsp	freshly squeezed lemon juice	25 mL
1 tsp	kosher or sea salt	5 mL
½ tsp	freshly ground black pepper	2 mL
⅓ cup	extra virgin olive oil	75 mL
1¼ cups	pomegranate seeds (about 1 pomegranate) (see Tips, left and Techniques, page 15)	300 mL
½	bulb fennel, quartered and thinly sliced	½
2	green onions, thinly sliced on the diagonal	2
¼ cup	coarsely chopped flat-leaf parsley	50 mL

1. In a large pot, bring 6 quarts (6 L) of lightly salted water to a boil. Add grain mix, return to a boil, reduce heat and simmer until tender, 12 to 15 minutes. Drain. Transfer to a large bowl. Let cool completely.

2. In a small bowl, combine vinegar, lemon juice, salt and pepper. Slowly whisk in olive oil.

3. Add pomegranate seeds, fennel, green onions and parsley to grain mix. Add vinaigrette and mix together well. Taste and adjust seasoning.

Lemon Vinaigrette

This bright and lively vinaigrette is delicious with many vegetables, such as artichokes, asparagus and winter greens, and perfect for seafood and fruity salads. We recommend making the vinaigrette shortly before using to enjoy the fresh citrus flavor at its best.

Tips

In some salads for aesthetic reasons and taste preferences you may not wish to include black pepper. You may choose to add a dash of hot pepper sauce or smoky paprika instead.

The flavor and sweetness of lemons and limes varies greatly throughout the year. Sometimes a pinch of sugar, or a drizzle of honey, is needed.

Variation

Greek Vinaigrette: Proceed as in Lemon Vinaigrette but replace half the lemon juice with white wine vinegar. Add 1 tsp (5 mL) chopped capers, 2 tsp (10 mL) coarsely chopped oregano and freshly ground black pepper to taste.

1	clove garlic, minced	1
1 tsp	Dijon mustard	5 mL
½ tsp	kosher or sea salt	2 mL
¼ cup	freshly squeezed lemon juice	50 mL
⅔ cup	light extra virgin olive oil	150 mL
Pinch	granulated sugar, optional (see Tips, left)	Pinch
	Freshly ground black pepper, optional	

1. In a small bowl, mash together, garlic, mustard and salt. Stir in lemon juice. Slowly whisk in oil. Taste and adjust seasoning. Add a little sugar, if necessary. Add pepper depending on how you plan to use the vinaigrette (see Tips, left).

Niçoise Vinaigrette

This robustly flavored dressing is ideal for Mediterranean-style vegetable salads.

Tip

Anchovies, like liver and cilantro, are not to everyone's taste. We use them in many dishes as a subtle flavor enhancer (not to actually taste anything fishy), just as cooks used salted fish in Roman times. Seek out imported anchovies from Italy or Spain packed in salt in jars in the refrigerator display case at the market. You will find the flavor superior to canned anchovies. Always rinse off excess salt in cold water before using and pat dry in paper towels. Store in the refrigerator.

1 to 2	anchovy fillets, rinsed, dried and chopped, optional (see Tip, left)	1 to 2
2 tsp	Dijon mustard	10 mL
1 tsp	finely chopped garlic	5 mL
¼ tsp	kosher or sea salt	1 mL
1 tbsp	freshly squeezed lemon juice	15 mL
1 tbsp	red wine vinegar	15 mL
⅓ cup	extra virgin olive oil	75 mL
Pinch	freshly ground black pepper	Pinch

1. In a small bowl, mash together anchovy, mustard, garlic and salt. Stir in lemon juice and vinegar. Slowly whisk in oil. Season with black pepper to taste.

Basil Vinaigrette

MAKES ABOUT ½ CUP (125 ML)

A basic vinaigrette with the addition of finely chopped shallots and fresh herbs is one of our favorite, and most frequently used, salad dressings.

1 tsp	finely chopped garlic	5 mL
1 tsp	Dijon mustard	5 mL
¼ tsp	kosher or sea salt	1 mL
1 tbsp	freshly squeezed lemon juice	15 mL
1 tbsp	white wine vinegar	15 mL
1 tsp	finely chopped shallot	5 mL
⅓ cup	extra virgin olive oil	75 mL
	Freshly ground black pepper	
1 tbsp	chopped basil	15 mL

1. In a small bowl, mash together garlic, mustard and salt. Stir in lemon juice, vinegar and shallot. Slowly whisk in oil. Season with black pepper to taste. Add basil.

Balsamic Vinaigrette

MAKES ABOUT ½ CUP (125 ML)

If you are lucky enough to have high quality balsamic vinegar in the cupboard, keep your dressing very simple: equal amounts of balsamic and olive oil and a pinch of salt and pepper, if appropriate to the dish. Sometimes a dash of balsamic vinegar all alone is all you need.

1 tsp	finely chopped garlic, optional	5 mL
1 tsp	Dijon mustard	5 mL
¼ tsp	kosher or sea salt	1 mL
2 tbsp	balsamic vinegar	25 mL
6 tbsp	extra virgin olive oil	90 mL
Pinch	freshly ground black pepper	Pinch
1 tbsp	freshly squeezed lemon juice, optional	15 mL

1. In a small bowl, mash together garlic, if using, mustard and salt. Add vinegar. Slowly whisk in oil. Season with pepper to taste. Add lemon juice for a little extra fruity acidity, if needed.

Red Wine Vinaigrette

We most frequently use the proportion of three parts oil to one part acidic ingredient (vinegar or citrus juice or a combination) in our salad dressings. However, the proportion may be adjusted to taste and will vary according to the individual characteristics of the oil and vinegar being used and the salad ingredients (e.g. bean salads benefit from a splash more acidity).

Tip
Read the ingredient label on most commercial salad dressings and you will see sugar fairly high on the list. Our collective taste buds obviously favor sweetness. If you find your homemade dressing too acidic to your taste, add a pinch of sugar or drizzle of honey.

Variation
White Wine Vinaigrette:
Substitute white wine vinegar for red wine vinegar and proceed as above.

1 tsp	finely chopped garlic, optional	5 mL
1 tsp	Dijon mustard	5 mL
¼ tsp	kosher or sea salt	1 mL
2 tbsp	red wine vinegar	25 mL
6 tbsp	extra virgin olive oil	90 mL
Pinch	freshly ground black pepper	Pinch
1 tbsp	freshly squeezed lemon juice, optional	15 mL

1. In a small bowl, mash together garlic, if using, mustard and salt. Add vinegar. Slowly whisk in oil. Season with pepper to taste. Add lemon juice for a little fruity acidity, if needed.

Grapefruit Poppy Seed Dressing

*This slightly sweet citrus
dressing was developed
to toss with one of our
popular composed
appetizer salads that
includes buttery Boston
lettuce, sliced avocados
and segments of fresh
ruby grapefruit. The
flavor is best when
freshly made.*

Tip

When you cut segments of
grapefruit and orange to serve
as garnish for a salad, collect
the juices in a bowl to include
in the salad dressing.

1 tbsp	freshly squeezed grapefruit juice (see Tip, left)	15 mL
2 tsp	liquid honey	10 mL
1 tsp	freshly squeezed orange juice	5 mL
1 tsp	freshly squeezed lemon juice	5 mL
2 tsp	white wine vinegar	10 mL
	Kosher or sea salt	
¼ cup	vegetable oil	50 mL
Pinch	freshly grated nutmeg	Pinch
½ tsp	poppy seeds	2 mL

1. In a bowl, combine grapefruit juice, honey, orange and
   lemons juices, vinegar and a pinch of salt. Whisk in
   oil. Stir in poppy seeds and nutmeg. Taste and adjust
   seasoning.

> **Mesclun greens**
> This is a popular mix of "wild" salad leaves, which
> originated in Nice. Today packages of cultivated leaves are
> widely available in our produce markets and a wonderful
> selection of field grown greens can be found on farmer's
> stalls at country markets. Be "picky" in your selection
> to make sure they are as fresh as possible and wash
> thoroughly and dry well before serving. The "wild" green
> selection most often includes dandelion, baby arugula,
> oak leaf lettuce, lamb's lettuce and chervil.

Composed Salads

These artful combinations of salad ingredients can be served as a first course to a formal dinner or as a light lunch.

Here are some favorite combinations served at some of our catered dinner parties. Prepare the elements ahead. Just prior to serving, toss greens in a bowl with a little dressing and arrange on individual chilled plates. Arrange the other elements on top and drizzle with a little more dressing. To serve a crowd, arrange elements of a salad on large platters as part of a summer buffet.

1. Watercress, fresh orange segments and crumbled goat's cheese with Basil Vinaigrette (page 92).
2. Boston lettuce tossed in Grapefruit Poppy Seed Dressing (page 94), garnished with sliced avocado and grapefruit segments.
3. Baby arugula, tossed with Lemon Vinaigrette (page 90), garnished with a salad of baby beets and crumbled Gorgonzola.
4. Mesclun greens, grilled pear and crumbled Roquefort with Red Wine Vinaigrette (page 93) sweetened with a drizzle of honey.
5. Baby arugula with Slow-Roasted Tomatoes (page 47) and crumbled chèvre with Balsamic Vinaigrette (page 92).
6. Sauté sliced mushrooms tossed with Balsamic Vinaigrette (page 92) and served over frisée and radicchio garnished with shaved Parmigiano-Reggiano.
7. Salade Niçoise (see Variation, page 69).
8. Baby spinach tossed with Mustard Vinaigrette (page 66), garnished with crispy pieces of bacon, sliced marinated mushrooms and slivered Gruyère or Parmigiano-Reggiano
9. Mesclun greens, tossed in Grapefruit Poppy Seed Dressing (page 94), omitting nutmeg and poppy seeds, but adding 2 tbsp (25 mL) chopped dill, garnished with grapefruit or orange segments and mini bocconcini.

Mayonnaise

The classic creamy dressing has countless uses. The homemade version has character and deep, rich flavor that is quite different from the commercial varieties.

2	egg yolks (see Tips, left)	2
1 tbsp	freshly squeezed lemon juice or white wine vinegar, divided	15 mL
½ tsp	Dijon mustard	2 mL
½ tsp	kosher or sea salt	2 mL
¼ tsp	freshly ground black pepper	1 mL
¾ cup	extra virgin olive oil (or half olive oil, half vegetable oil)	175 mL

1. In a bowl, combine egg yolks, 1 tsp (5 mL) of the lemon juice, mustard, salt and pepper. Whisk until mixture is smooth and lightly thickened.

2. Pour oil into a small measuring cup. Very slowly, a few drops at a time, whisk into egg mixture. Whisk diligently until all oil is added and mixture is thick and smooth. Whisk in the remaining lemon juice. Taste and adjust seasoning. Because of the egg yolks, this dressing does not store well. Make it fresh and use it right away.

Tips

This recipe contains raw egg yolks. If you are concerned about the safety of using raw eggs, use pasteurized eggs in the shell or ¼ cup (50 mL) pasteurized liquid whole eggs.

One tablespoon (15 mL) boiling water whisked into the completed mayonnaise keeps the mixture stable.

If mayonnaise separates during whisking, take a clean bowl and add another egg yolk. Gradually whisk in the separated mayonnaise and beat until smooth.

Variations

Aïoli (Garlic Mayonnaise): Mash 2 to 3 cloves garlic to a fine paste with a little salt and stir into the mayonnaise. Serve with vegetables, as a sandwich spread or soup enrichment.

Chipotle Mayonnaise: Add about 1 tsp (5 mL) minced chipotles in adobo sauce to the mayonnaise. Serve as a dip or sandwich spread.

Lemon Dill Mayonnaise: Add chopped dill, grated lemon zest and freshly squeezed lemon juice to taste. Delicious to serve with asparagus and salmon.

Corn Chowder with Double-Smoked Bacon (page 38)

Spring Green Soup (page 48)

Tuscan Pepper and Tomato Salad (page 61)

Soba Noodle Salad with Edamame (page 72)

Chicken Puttanesca (page 100)

Coq au Vin (page 106)

Smoky Spicy Grilled Cornish Game Hen (page 130)

Grilled Beef Short Ribs Korean-Style (page 148)

Osso Buco with Gremolata (page 162)

Pork Stir-Fry with Spicy Orange Sauce (page 186)

Maple-Brined Pork Chops (page 188)

Herb-Crusted Rack of Lamb (page 216)

Poultry

Roast Chicken with Fresh Herbs and Lemon

There is nothing more delicious than a roast chicken fresh from the oven with glistening golden brown crispy skin and succulent herb-infused flesh. Add a light tangy sauce, maybe some skinny "pommes frites" or Rosemary Roasted Potatoes (page 297) and certainly a cool glass of white Burgundy and that has to be heaven on earth!

- **Preheat oven to 350°F (180°C)**
- **Roasting pan**
- **Instant-read thermometer**

2 to 3 lbs	roasting chicken	1 to 1.5 kg
4	unpeeled garlic cloves	4
1	lemon, quartered lengthwise	1
1	small onion, quartered lengthwise	1
5	sprigs thyme	5
5	sage leaves	5
2	sprigs flat-leaf parsley	2
1	sprig rosemary	1
	Salt and freshly ground black pepper	
2 tbsp	extra virgin olive oil	25 mL
	Stock, wine or water	
	Chicken Pan Gravy (page 99)	

1. Rinse chicken and thoroughly pat dry. Place in roasting pan with wings neatly tucked underneath.
2. Stuff cavity with garlic, lemon, onion, thyme, sage, parsley, rosemary, and a pinch of salt. Rub chicken all over with olive oil. Season lightly with salt and pepper. Tie legs together with butcher's string.
3. Roast chicken in preheated oven, basting occasionally with pan juices, until an instant-read thermometer inserted into the thickest part of the meat registers 165°F (74°C), 1½ to 1¾ hours. Let chicken stand for 10 minutes before carving. Skim fat from pan into a small saucepan and deglaze pan with a little stock, wine or water (see Deglazing the Pan, page 143). Reserve pan juices to make Chicken Pan Gravy.

Chicken Pan Gravy

1 tbsp	fat skimmed from chicken pan juices, or butter	15 mL
2 tbsp	all-purpose flour	25 mL
1½ cups	Chicken Stock (page 54) or ready-to-use broth	375 mL
½ cup	white wine	125 mL
½ cup	deglazed pan juices	125 mL
1 tsp	chopped thyme	5 mL
	Salt and freshly ground black pepper	
¼ cup	whipping (35%) cream, optional	50 mL

1. In a small saucepan, heat fat over medium-low heat. Stir in flour and cook, stirring, 2 to 3 minutes.

2. Add chicken stock, wine and pan juices, whisking vigorously until sauce is smooth. Bring to a boil. Reduce heat and let sauce simmer until desired flavor and consistency is reached, 5 to 10 minutes. Add thyme and salt and pepper to taste. For added richness, stir in cream.

Chicken Puttanesca

This robust saucy chicken dish is named for the zesty "ladies of the night" (puttana is Italian for "whore.") Serve over chunky pasta, such as penne or rotini, with fresh crusty bread and a simple green salad on the side.

Variation

Puttanesca Sauce: Follow recipe but omit the chicken. Enjoy as is with pasta, or serve with spicy sausages, or over firm white fish, such as cod or halibut.

2 tbsp	extra virgin olive oil	25 mL
1	chicken, cut into serving pieces (2 to 2½ lbs/1 to 1.25 kg)	1
	Salt and freshly ground black pepper	
2	onions, halved lengthwise and thinly sliced	2
12	cloves garlic, thinly sliced	12
2	cans (each 28 oz/796 mL) plum tomatoes, juice reserved	2
½ cup	sliced oil-packed sun-dried tomatoes	125 mL
¼ cup	coarsely chopped drained capers	50 mL
2	anchovy fillets, rinsed and chopped (see Tip, page 91)	2
2 tbsp	chopped basil or 2 tsp (10 mL) dried basil	25 mL
2 tbsp	chopped oregano or 2 tsp (10 mL) dried oregano	25 mL
1 tsp	hot pepper flakes	5 mL
½ cup	pitted Niçoise olives	125 mL
¼ cup	chopped flat-leaf parsley	50 mL

1. In a large heavy skillet, heat oil over medium-high heat. Season chicken pieces lightly with salt and pepper. Add to skillet and brown well on all sides, 3 to 4 minutes per side. Remove chicken and set aside.

2. Add onions to the skillet. Reduce heat to medium and sauté until onions are soft and beginning to brown, 5 to 7 minutes. Add garlic and sauté for 1 to 2 minutes.

3. Strain plum tomatoes, reserving the juice, and chop tomatoes roughly. Add tomatoes to the pan with sun-dried tomatoes, capers, anchovies, basil, oregano and hot pepper flakes. Bring sauce to a simmer, stirring occasionally.

4. Return browned chicken to the pan and coat with sauce. Cover pan, reduce heat and simmer until juices run clear when chicken is pierced, 30 to 40 minutes. Add some of the reserved tomato juices if sauce is too thick. Stir in olives and parsley. Taste and adjust seasoning.

Honey Rosemary Chicken

Sweet cherry tomatoes add their own special flavor to this quick and easy dish. Add the smaller quantity of honey to the sauce at first and adjust to your taste. After initial browning we braise the chicken breasts in the oven to provide even, gentle heat. You could also continue the cooking on the stovetop. Just be watchful not to overcook the chicken breasts.

- Preheat oven to 350°F (180°C)
- Large ovenproof skillet with lid

1 tbsp	olive oil	15 mL
6	skinless boneless chicken breasts	6
	Salt and freshly ground black pepper	
2	cloves garlic, sliced	2
¼ tsp	hot pepper flakes	1 mL
1 cup	Chicken Stock (page 54) or ready-to-use broth	250 mL
1 to 2 tbsp	liquid honey	15 to 25 mL
1 pint	cherry tomatoes, halved	500 mL
2 tbsp	chopped rosemary or 2 tsp (10 mL) dried rosemary	25 mL
1 tbsp	red wine vinegar	15 mL
1 tbsp	butter, optional	15 mL

1. In large ovenproof skillet, heat oil over medium-high heat. Season chicken breasts lightly with salt and pepper. Add chicken to skillet and brown on both sides, about 3 minutes per side. You may need to do this in two batches. Do not crowd the pan. Transfer to a platter and set aside.

2. Reduce heat to medium. Add garlic and hot pepper flakes and sauté for 1 to 2 minutes. Add chicken stock and bring to a boil, scraping up browned bits on the bottom of pan.

3. Return chicken to the pan and drizzle with 1 tbsp (15 mL) of the honey. Scatter tomatoes around and sprinkle with rosemary. Cover pan and cook in preheated oven until juices run clear when chicken is pierced, 10 to 12 minutes.

4. Lift chicken and tomatoes from the pan with a slotted spoon and set aside. Place pan on the stovetop over medium heat and bring to a simmer until sauce is slightly reduced, 1 to 2 minutes. Add a splash of vinegar. Taste and add salt, pepper and a drizzle more honey, if needed, and swirl in butter to add sheen and viscosity to the sauce. Return chicken and tomatoes to pan and reheat briefly to allow flavors to meld.

Chicken Supremes Stuffed with Chèvre and Sun-Dried Tomatoes

A chicken supreme is a boned chicken breast that has the small wing bone attached. It covers the desires of the cook to have a lean, tender, easy-to-eat chicken breast with the advantage of flavor from a little dark meat and bone. It also lends itself to being stuffed in many interesting ways.

Tip

Chicken supremes are not a common prepackaged item at the supermarket but you sometimes find them at the butcher's counter. It's worth a visit to your local specialty butcher or a specialty online butcher to find chicken supremes and other less familiar cuts of meat.

- Preheat oven to 350°F (180°C)
- Large ovenproof skillet
- Instant-read thermometer

6 oz	fresh chèvre (goat's cheese)	175 g
¼ cup	finely chopped oil-packed sun-dried tomatoes, patted dry	50 mL
½ cup	chopped basil, divided	125 mL
1 tsp	finely chopped garlic	5 mL
	Salt and freshly ground black pepper	
6	chicken supremes (see Tip, left)	6
2 tbsp	extra virgin olive oil	25 mL

1. In a small bowl, combine goat's cheese, sun-dried tomatoes, ¼ cup (50 mL) of the basil and garlic. Season with salt and pepper to taste. Set aside.

2. Rinse chicken and thoroughly pat dry. Make a small slit in the breast portion of each chicken supreme and, using your fingers or the handle of a wooden spoon, form a small tunnel to hold the goat's cheese stuffing. Lightly pack about 2 tbsp (25 mL) of goat's cheese mixture into each portion.

3. In a large ovenproof skillet, heat oil over medium-high heat. Add stuffed chicken supremes and brown on both sides, about 3 minutes per side. You may need to do this in two batches. Do not crowd the pan.

4. Transfer pan to preheated oven and roast until juices run clear when chicken is pierced, 15 to 20 minutes. Set aside, loosely covered with foil, for 5 minutes. Garnish with remaining basil before serving.

Southern Fried Chicken

We make this light, crispy golden chicken fresh every day. It's a year-round favorite.

● **Deep-fryer or large saucepan with frying basket**

2 cups	buttermilk, divided	500 mL
2	cloves garlic, finely chopped	2
1 tsp	kosher or sea salt	5 mL
½ tsp	freshly ground black pepper	2 mL
¼ tsp	cayenne pepper	1 mL
1¼ lbs	skinless boneless chicken breasts, cut in half lengthwise	625 g
8 to 12 cups	vegetable oil for deep-frying	2 to 3 L
1 cup	all-purpose flour	250 mL

1. In a shallow dish, combine 1 cup (250 mL) of the buttermilk, garlic, ½ tsp (2 mL) of the salt, ¼ tsp (1 mL) of the pepper and cayenne. Add chicken. Cover and refrigerate for several hours or overnight.

2. Preheat oil for deep-frying to about 350°F (180°C).

3. In another shallow dish, mix flour with remaining ½ tsp (2 mL) of salt and ¼ tsp (1 mL) of pepper. Pour remaining buttermilk in another shallow dish.

4. Lift chicken pieces from the marinade, discarding marinade. Dip in seasoned flour to coat on all sides, dip in plain buttermilk and back again in the seasoned flour. Shake off excess flour and set aside on a rack until ready to cook.

5. Preheat oven to 300°F (150°C). Deep-fry chicken pieces in hot oil a few pieces at a time, according to the size of your deep-fryer. Do not crowd the pot. Cook until the chicken is nicely golden and no longer pink inside, 6 to 7 minutes. Lift cooked chicken from the hot oil with a slotted spoon and set aside on a rack set over a tray, lined with paper towel. Keep warm in preheated oven until all chicken is cooked and ready to be enjoyed.

Italian Grilled Chicken

Summery, light and simply delicious served straight from the grill or chilled and served cold with a salad or in a sandwich.

In the marinade, fresh herbs impart the most refreshing flavors, but in a pinch dried herbs can be used.

Ovenproof grill pan, lightly oiled (if using oven)

6	skinless boneless chicken breasts	6
	Fresh Herb Marinade, divided (page 105)	
1 tbsp	olive oil	15 mL
	Salt and freshly ground black pepper	

1. In a large bowl, toss chicken breasts with half of the Fresh Herb Marinade. Set aside, covered, in the refrigerator for 1 hour. Reserve the remaining marinade.
2. Preheat oven to 350°F (180°C) or barbecue to medium.
3. *To use oven and grill pan:* Set grill pan over medium-high heat on stovetop. Wipe chicken dry and brush lightly with oil. Discard excess used marinade. Grill chicken breasts until nicely marked, about 2 minutes per side. Brush chicken with some of the reserved marinade. Set grill pan in preheated oven and bake until juices run clear when chicken is pierced, 10 to 12 minutes. Brush with more marinade partway through cooking period.
4. *To cook on the barbecue:* Lightly brush clean hot cooking grill with a little vegetable oil. Place chicken breasts, skinned side down, over medium indirect heat with thickest side towards the source of heat (coals or lit burner). Close lid and cook for about 5 minutes. Turn chicken breasts over with thinner edge towards the heat and continue to cook with lid down for another 5 minutes. Brush one side of chicken breasts with Fresh Herb Marinade and grill over direct heat, uncovered, 1 to 2 minutes. Baste chicken breasts with mixture again, turn and cook over direct heat until juices run clear, 1 or 2 minutes more.
5. Let stand, loosely covered with foil, for 5 minutes. Season with salt and pepper to taste.

Fresh Herb Marinade

Makes about ½ cup (150 mL)

¼ cup	extra virgin olive oil	50 mL
2 tbsp	dry white wine or freshly squeezed lemon juice	25 mL
2	cloves garlic, finely chopped	2
3 tbsp	chopped basil or 1 tbsp (15 mL) dried basil	45 mL
3 tbsp	chopped oregano or 1 tbsp (15 mL) dried oregano	45 mL
1 tbsp	chopped rosemary or 1 tsp (5 mL) dried rosemary	15 mL

1. In a bowl, combine oil, wine, garlic, basil, oregano and rosemary. Use at once for best fresh flavor.

Italian Grilled Chicken...let me count the ways!

It always astonishes us to learn the many ways this popular grilled chicken is used by our customers. Here are a few suggestions:

- In a quick and easy sandwich: Slice a baguette in half horizontally. Arrange layers of sliced chicken breast, sliced tomato, leaf lettuce and a touch of mayonnaise. Add a slice of grilled bacon to make a Chicken Club.
- Chopped with celery, green onions and a dash of mayonnaise for a quick chicken salad.
- In a quick and easy salad: Sliced and served on top of a Caesar Salad (page 65).
- In a quick and easy main dish: Sliced and heated with Chunky Tomato Sauce (page 133) to serve over pasta.
- Sliced and heated in a creamy Alfredo Sauce (page 263) to serve over fettuccini.
- Sliced and added to Puttanesca Sauce (Variation, page 100) to serve over penne.

Coq au Vin

For a delicious comforting dish in true bistro-style it's hard to beat a chicken stew that includes onions, mushrooms, bacon and generous quantities of rich red wine sauce. As in all good stews, key elements are cooked separately and joined together for the final braise. All the work can be done ahead and the final result is even tastier on the following day. Serve with simple boiled baby potatoes and steamed green beans.

Tip

Cut a sheet of cooking parchment just ½ inch (1 cm) larger than the surface of your pot or casserole. Lay the parchment directly on the surface of the meat and vegetables, with edges turned up around the edge of the pot. Cover the pot. During braising time the parchment sheet catches any evaporated moisture that drips into the casserole from the lid. Carefully lift off parchment and pour away accumulated water. Your sauce will not be diluted.

- **6-quart (6 L) Dutch oven or wide shallow pot with lid**
- **Parchment paper, optional**

2 tbsp	butter	25 mL
3 oz	bacon or lean salt pork, cut into ½-inch (1 cm) strips	90 g
3 lbs	chicken, cut into serving-size pieces	1.5 kg
1	carrot, finely chopped	1
1	onion, finely chopped	1
1	stalk celery, finely chopped	1
2	cloves garlic, finely chopped	2
1 tbsp	tomato paste	15 mL
3 cups	dry red wine	750 mL
	Salt and freshly ground black pepper	
½ to 1 cup	Chicken Stock (page 54) or ready-to-use broth	125 to 250 mL
1 tsp	finely chopped thyme	5 mL
1	bay leaf	1
	Sautéed Mushrooms (page 151)	
	Caramelized Pearl Onions (page 151)	
2 tbsp	finely chopped flat-leaf parsley	25 mL

1. In large Dutch oven, melt butter over medium heat. Add bacon and sauté until lightly browned. Remove with a slotted spoon and set aside to drain on paper towel.
2. Pat chicken dry. Add to pot and brown well on all sides. (You may need to do this in batches. Do not crowd the pan.) Transfer chicken to a platter and set aside.
3. Add carrot, onion, celery and garlic to the pot and sauté for about 5 minutes. Add tomato paste and cook for 2 minutes. Stir in wine and deglaze pan, scraping up browned bits on the bottom. Return chicken and bacon to the pot. Season lightly with salt and pepper.

4. Add stock, as needed, just to cover the chicken, and thyme and bay leaf. Bring to a simmer. Cover, reduce heat to low and simmer the chicken on the stovetop until tender, or braise in preheated 325°F (160°C) oven. (Now is the time when you prepare the Sautéed Mushrooms and Caramelized Pearl Onions.) Test chicken for doneness after 20 minutes since the breast meat will cook more quickly. Remove chicken pieces as they are cooked (when the juices run clear when chicken is pierced) and set them aside. Continue simmering until all chicken is cooked, 5 to 10 minutes more.

5. Bring cooking liquids to a boil and skim off any fat. Taste, adjust seasoning, and continue to boil and reduce until sauce is richly flavored and thickened to your taste, 1 to 2 minutes. If you like lots of sauce and do not want to reduce the amount of liquid too long, prepare a "beurre manié" (page 111).

6. Return chicken and bacon to the casserole and add Sautéed Mushrooms and Caramelized Pearl Onions. Gently stir all together to coat with sauce and heat briefly to blend flavors, about 5 minutes. The dish is now ready to be served. For best flavor, let cool, cover and refrigerate for a day or for up to 3 days. About 1 hour before serving, remove pot from refrigerator, bring to room temperature for about 30 minutes and reheat on stovetop over medium-low heat or in 325°F (160°C) oven. Simmer until all the contents are hot, 20 to 30 minutes. Garnish with parsley.

Tip

If space and time allows we recommend long, slow cooking of stews to take place in a slow oven, around 325°F (160°C), rather than on top of the stove. In the confined space you are able to control a more even low heat and adjust the temperature to keep liquid at a steady gentle simmer.

Chicken Piccata

Chicken Piccata

A light crispy coating keeps the skinless boneless chicken breast moist and flavorful. For extra piquancy you could include 1 tbsp (15 mL) grated Parmesan cheese. Add a topping of Chunky Tomato Sauce (page 133) and pile in a crusty bun for a delicious, if messy, hot sandwich.

Tip

When is chicken cooked? Perfectly cooked chicken is tender and moist and the juices run clear. Recommended internal temperature is 165°F (74°C). Meat continues to cook and the internal temperature rises during the first 5 to 10 minutes when removed from the heat. If cooking a whole chicken, we recommend removing chicken from the heat when the internal temperature registered at the thickest part of the meat (without touching bone) is 160°F (71°C).

Variation

Pork or Veal Cutlets: Use the seasoned bread crumbs to coat thin cutlets of pork or veal. Bake in preheated oven as for Chicken Piccata, or sauté in a skillet over medium heat.

- **Preheat oven to 400°F (200°C)**
- **Baking sheet, lightly oiled**

6	skinless boneless chicken breasts	6
1 tsp	grated lemon zest	5 mL
1½ cups	fresh bread crumbs or Panko (see Tips, page 119)	375 mL
2 tbsp	freshly squeezed lemon juice	25 mL
2 tbsp	finely chopped basil or 2 tsp (10 mL) dried basil	25 mL
2 tbsp	finely chopped flat-leaf parsley	25 mL
2 tsp	finely chopped rosemary or ½ tsp (2 mL) dried rosemary	10 mL
½ tsp	kosher or sea salt	2 mL
½ tsp	freshly ground black pepper	2 mL
Pinch	cayenne pepper	Pinch
¼ cup	butter	50 mL
¼ cup	olive oil	50 mL

1. Pound chicken breasts between sheets of plastic wrap or parchment to an even thickness of about ½ inch (1 cm). Drizzle with lemon juice.

2. In a bowl, combine bread crumbs, lemon zest, basil, parsley, rosemary, salt, pepper and cayenne. Spread seasoned bread crumbs in a shallow dish.

3. In a small saucepan, melt butter and oil over low heat. Pat chicken dry. Dip chicken in melted butter and oil, one piece at a time, then coat in seasoned bread crumbs. Arrange in a single layer on prepared baking sheet. Discard any excess butter and bread crumb mixtures.

4. Bake in preheated oven until crust is crisp and golden and chicken is no longer pink inside, 12 to 15 minutes.

Chicken Dijonnaise

This mustard-flavored creamy sauce is a favorite with our customers. We prepare this dish sometimes with boneless chicken breasts, chicken pieces or with pork tenderloin, adjusting the cooking times as needed. Serve with crispy roasted lemon garlic potatoes or egg noodles, with something green on the side, such as sautéed rapini, green beans or grilled asparagus.

Tip

There are several ways to finish and thicken a sauce. Frequently we use the reduction method: Set the pan over high heat for a few minutes to reduce the amount of liquid and intensify flavor. If you do not want to reduce the volume of sauce, see other methods (Sauce-Thickening Dilemma, page 111).

2 lbs	bone-in chicken thighs	1 kg
	Salt and freshly ground black pepper	
2 tbsp	olive oil	25 mL
1 tbsp	butter	15 mL
¼ cup	finely chopped shallots	50 mL
2 tsp	minced garlic	10 mL
¾ cup	dry white wine	175 mL
1 cup	Chicken Stock (page 54) or ready-to-use broth	250 mL
¼ cup	Dijon mustard	50 mL
1 tbsp	coarsely chopped thyme	15 mL
2 tbsp	half-and-half (10%) cream, optional	25 mL
2 tbsp	coarsely chopped flat-leaf parsley	25 mL
2 tsp	coarsely chopped tarragon	10 mL

1. Pat chicken dry. Lightly season chicken thighs with salt and pepper. In a large skillet, heat oil and butter over medium-high heat. Add chicken thighs, smooth side down. Sear chicken on all sides until nicely browned, 2 to 3 minutes per side. Transfer to a platter and set aside.

2. Reduce heat to medium. Add shallots and garlic and sauté for 30 seconds. Add white wine and deglaze pan, scraping up browned bits on the bottom. Add chicken stock, mustard, thyme and salt and pepper to taste.

3. Return chicken to pan with the juices that have collected on the platter. Reduce heat to medium-low and partially cover. Leave a small space for the steam to escape; this will let the sauce reduce slightly while chicken is cooking. Continue cooking gently until juices run clear when chicken is pierced, about 20 minutes

4. Remove chicken from pan with a slotted spoon and set aside, cover and keep warm while you finish the sauce. The sauce should coat the chicken nicely. If it is too thin, increase heat, skim off fat and boil and reduce for 2 to 3 minutes. Swirl in cream, if using, parsley and tarragon. Taste and adjust seasoning. Return chicken to sauce and reheat over low heat, 1 to 2 minutes.

Chicken with Porcini Ragoût

This is a popular dish to serve a crowd buffet-style. Prepare using boneless chicken breasts and slice into convenient serving pieces before returning to the sauce in Step 5. Porcini mushrooms impart a rich flavor to the ragoût, which is also delicious to serve with pork tenderloin or chops.

Tip

Many recipes for braised chicken are equally delicious using various chicken pieces or a whole cut up chicken. Simply adjust the cooking time: Chicken breasts on the bone take 15 to 18 minutes, legs and thighs, about 5 minutes longer. When we cook a whole cut up chicken we remove the breast pieces when tender and leave the dark meat in the pan 5 to 10 minutes longer. Skinless boneless breasts cook quickly, 5 to 6 minutes, but remember to reduce heat to medium-low after the brief initial browning step or the result is dry and tasteless. Chicken cooked on the bone is moister and more flavorful.

Large ovenproof skillet with lid

1 oz	dried porcini mushrooms	30 g
1 cup	hot water	250 mL
2 tbsp	olive oil	25 mL
1 tbsp	butter	15 mL
2 lbs	bone-in chicken breasts or 3 lbs (1.5 kg) chicken, cut into serving-size pieces	1 kg
	Salt and freshly ground black pepper	
¼ cup	finely chopped shallots	50 mL
2 tsp	minced garlic	10 mL
½ cup	dry white wine	125 mL
1 cup	Chicken Stock (page 54) or ready-to-use broth	250 mL
2 tbsp	Marsala wine	25 mL
1½ tsp	chopped thyme	7 mL
1 tsp	chopped rosemary	5 mL
2 tbsp	coarsely chopped flat-leaf parsley	25 mL
2 tbsp	all-purpose flour, optional	25 mL
1 tbsp	butter, optional	15 mL

1. Soak mushrooms in hot water for 5 minutes. Remove mushrooms and chop roughly. Set aside. Strain the soaking liquid through cheesecloth or a coffee filter to remove any sand and grit and reserve.

2. In a large skillet, heat oil and butter over medium-high heat. Season chicken lightly with salt and pepper. Add chicken and sear on all sides until nicely browned, 2 to 3 minutes per side. Transfer to a platter and set aside.

3. Reduce heat to medium. Add shallots, garlic and mushrooms and sauté for 30 seconds. Add white wine and deglaze pan, scraping up browned bits on the bottom. Stir in mushroom soaking liquid, stock, Marsala, thyme and rosemary and bring to a simmer.

4. Return chicken to the skillet with any collected juices. Reduce heat to medium-low and partially cover. Leave a small space for the steam to escape; this will let the sauce reduce slightly while chicken is cooking. Continue cooking gently until juices run clear when chicken is pierced, about 20 minutes

5. Remove chicken from the skillet with a slotted spoon, cover and keep warm while you finish the sauce. Bring braising liquid to a boil, skimming off any fat. Taste, adjust seasoning, and continue to boil and reduce until sauce is richly flavored and of light sauce consistency, 1 to 2 minutes. If you like lots of sauce and do not want to reduce the amount of liquid too long, prepare a "beurre manié" using the flour and butter (see below). Return chicken to sauce and reheat over low heat, 1 to 2 minutes. Serve garnished with parsley.

Sauce-Thickening Dilemma

Here are some ways to thicken a sauce:

1. *Beurre manié:* This makes enough to thicken about 2 cups (500 mL) sauce. Make a paste of 2 tbsp (25 mL) all-purpose flour and 1 tbsp (15 mL) soft butter. With your fingers, sprinkle small pieces of the butter-flour paste into boiling liquid and whisk vigorously. Boil for a couple of minutes to remove raw flour taste and continue cooking until sauce thickens.

2. *Working with roux in the roasting pan:* When cooking roasts there are lots of flavorful cooking juices left in the pan to work with. Pour away all but 2 to 3 tbsp (25 to 45 mL) fat from roasting pan. Stir in 3 to 4 tbsp (45 to 60 mL) all-purpose flour and cook, stirring, over medium heat until nicely browned. Gradually stir in $1\frac{1}{2}$ to 2 cups (375 to 500 mL) stock and whisk briskly until smooth. Bring to a boil. Reduce heat and simmer, stirring often, until desired flavor and consistency is reached, 5 to 10 minutes. Add any accumulated juices from the meat. Taste and adjust seasoning. Add port or Madeira for flavor and a splash of cream for enrichment, if you like.

3. *Cornstarch as thickener:* Mix 1 tsp (5 mL) cornstarch dissolved in 1 tbsp (15 mL) water to make a slurry or thin paste. Stir slowly into liquid and bring to a boil for 1 minute.

4. *Make a reduction:* Place pan containing the cooking/braising liquid over medium-high heat and cook until volume has decreased by one-third to one-half — the sauce thickens slightly and the flavor intensifies. Remove from heat and swirl in a spoonful of soft butter to enrich and emulsify the sauce.

Chicken

For a bird we take so much for granted and treat, in the main, so poorly, the history of *Gallus gallus* has the kind of dramatic arc that defines Oscar Wilde's remark that nothing succeeds like excess. It just took time. First domesticated and bred for food in what is now Vietnam some 10,000 years ago, it took them 8,000 years to reach Europe, via ancient Rome, where for centuries they were treated as oracles (if they ate hungrily, the omen was good; if not, watch out) as well as delicacies for the well-fed table.

Hard as it is to imagine today, when they outnumber every other bird on earth and humans by at least five to one, they remained delicacies until a nanosecond ago in recorded time. The estimable King Henry IV of France in 1589 made his suffering subjects a promise of a chicken in every pot, every Sunday, but fine pragmatic ruler though he was, he could not make good on it. Nobody could, for about 400 years. Well into the 1950s the storied chicken was storied only on the tables of the well to do, or of the farmers who bred them. Simply put, demand exceeded supply, which made the hen, and its eggs, expensive.

The problem had always been winter. Chickens do not thrive without sunlight. But then came vitamin D, which coped with sun deficiency and made it possible to keep chickens in confinement all year round. Coupled with intensive scientific breeding, this confinement led to battery-raised chickens. Until the early '50s, 1,500 hens would keep a farm family busy; the battery system — half a dozen chickens to a tiny cage, half a dozen weeks of fattening life indoors — enabled a family to farm them by the hundred thousand.

Result: Chicken as we mostly know it today — available to all, tender, bland, with little structural, color or taste difference between breast, wing, thigh or leg. Good enough when it can fill out a sandwich with something else.

In the Kitchen

If we spare a thought for a chicken's existence and seek out those advertised as *free-range*, we will be repaid in taste dividends, even as we pay a bit more. Free-range is not a legally defined term, and sometimes the hens will, in fact, spend little time outside being truly free. Some unscrupulous farmers label their product free-range because their cages are a couple of inches off the floor and there's a window down there at the end.

Best of all choices is *pastured* poultry, which are raised in outdoor rotating pens with year-round access to grass and give full meaning to "free-range." Happier chickens live longer, get to exercise, and produce the tastiest meat of all: the dark is dark, the light light, and both are juicier and much more flavorful than the mass variety.

Chicken Types

Broiler or **fryer:** 2 to 3 lbs (1 to 1.5 kg). All-purpose bird to roast whole or cut into portions for sautéing, braising, grilling and pies.

Boiling fowl (aka **stewing hen** or **baking hen**): 5 to 6 lbs (2.5 to 3 kg). Save this older bird for the stockpot and soup; requires long, slow cooking.

Capon: 6 to 10 lbs (3 to 5 kg). A fattened castrated rooster. An excellent juicy bird to roast for a family feast.

Rock Cornish hen: 1 to 2 lbs (500 g to 1 kg). A small chicken cross between White Plymouth Rock and Cornish breeds. Roast or split and grill.

Thai Green Curry Chicken

This is a light chicken and vegetable curry vibrant with Thai flavors of lemongrass, fresh ginger and chiles. Serve hot with steamed jasmine rice and a fresh garnish of green onion and cilantro.

Tips

Fresh lemongrass is commonly available in city markets nowadays. It lends a subtle, distinctive citrus flavor to sauces, soups, stews and marinade, and is an essential ingredient in Indonesian and Thai cooking. Look for bright green stalks with a moist, flexible root end.

To prepare lemongrass for cooking: Trim off root end and peel away any discolored outer layers from stalk. Smash the root end with the blunt edge of a heavy kitchen knife and slice through the smashed fibers to make a very fine chop (see Techniques, page 14).

2 lbs	skinless boneless chicken breasts and thighs, cut into 1-inch (5 cm) pieces	1 kg
2 tbsp	Thai green curry paste	25 mL
2 tbsp	vegetable oil	25 mL
1 tbsp	finely chopped lemongrass (see Tips, left)	15 mL
1 tsp	grated gingerroot	5 mL
1	clove garlic, finely chopped	1
	Kosher or sea salt	
1	can (14 oz/400 mL) coconut milk	1
1 tbsp	freshly squeezed lime juice	15 mL
1	wild lime leaf	1
1	red bell pepper, diced	1
1	green bell pepper, diced	1
½ tsp	brown sugar, optional	2 mL
1	green onion, thinly sliced on the bias	1
1 tbsp	chopped cilantro	15 mL

1. Coat chicken pieces with green curry paste and set aside.

2. In a large sauté pan, heat oil over medium heat. Add lemongrass, ginger, garlic and a pinch of salt. Stir-fry for 3 to 4 minutes.

3. Add chicken to pan and stir-fry until lightly colored, 4 to 5 minutes. Stir in coconut milk, lime juice and lime leaf. Bring to a simmer. Add red and green bell peppers. Cover and cook until chicken is no longer pink inside for breasts and juices run clear when thighs are pierced, 15 to 18 minutes. Taste and adjust flavors. You may like to add brown sugar, lime juice or salt. Serve hot and garnish with green onion and cilantro.

Chicken Saag

A simple chicken curry cooked in a creamy spinach yogurt sauce. It's very aromatic, but not spicy hot. Serve with bowls of steamed basmati rice.

2 tbsp	butter	25 mL
2 tbsp	vegetable oil	25 mL
1	onion, diced	1
1 tbsp	minced garlic	15 mL
1 tbsp	minced gingerroot	15 mL
2 to 3 tbsp	Curry Masala (page 116)	25 to 45 mL
	Salt and freshly ground black pepper	
2 lbs	skinless boneless chicken thighs, cut into 1-inch (2.5 cm) pieces	1 kg
½ cup	Chicken Stock (page 54) or ready-to-use broth	125 mL
2 cups	cooked spinach, fresh or frozen	500 mL
3 cups	plain yogurt (see page 115)	750 mL
1 tsp	Garam Masala, optional (page 117)	5 mL

1. In a large heavy saucepan, melt butter and oil over medium-low heat. Add onion and cook, stirring often, until softened and deeply browned, 10 to 12 minutes. Do not rush this step as the caramelized onion adds depth to the finished dish. Add garlic and ginger and cook, stirring, 4 to 5 minutes.

2. Stir in Curry Masala, 1 tsp (5 mL) salt and ¼ tsp (1 mL) pepper and cook, stirring, 2 to 3 minutes. Add chicken and toss in the spicy juices. Add chicken stock. Cover and simmer for 15 minutes.

3. Add spinach. Cover and cook over low heat until juices run clear when chicken is pierced, about 10 minutes.

4. Stir in yogurt and heat through gently. Sprinkle with garam masala, if using. Taste and adjust seasoning.

Cooking with Yogurt

Yogurt adds light creaminess to sauces, soups, stews and dressings with a pleasant acidity. In cooking use only natural yogurt, with no stabilizers added. The higher the fat content of the yogurt used the creamier and richer the result. Regular (3.5%) or low-fat (2%) yogurts are fine, but fat-free yogurt provides only acidity, no body to the dish. Luxurious yogurts of 6 to 8% butterfat add delicious richness to a sauce.

Yogurt is stirred in at the end of the cooking period. Do not bring to a boil or the sauce will separate.

Strained Yogurt

Place a small sieve, lined with a coffee filter over a bowl; spoon in yogurt. Place in the refrigerator overnight to drain. The longer the yogurt drains, the thicker it becomes until it reaches thick sour cream consistency. This thick yogurt can be swirled into a sauce, curry or dip. It is also a fabulous substitute for whipped cream in desserts. Sweeten with a little honey or maple syrup and flavor as you wish with vanilla, fresh mint or fruit liqueur.

Curry Masala

**MAKES ABOUT
½ CUP (125 ML)**

*In India "masala" vary
widely from region to
region, and even from
one family to the next,
based upon geography,
heritage and custom.
"Masala" refers to an
intricate blend of spices.
The mixture may be mild
or strong, gently aromatic
or mouth-numbingly fiery.
Each mixture is designed
to create the levels of
flavor suited to a specific
dish. A "wet masala" is
a paste that includes the
aromatic spice blend
with caramelized onions,
garlic, gingerroot and
sometimes ground nuts
or coconut. It is prepared
before any meat, fish
or vegetables are added
and forms the basis of
an authentic curry. If
you like a spicier blend,
increase the number
of chiles.*

- **Preheat oven to 200°F (100°C)**
- **Baking sheet**
- **Spice mill or mortar and pestle**

¼ cup	cumin seeds	50 mL
¼ cup	coriander seeds	50 mL
1 tbsp	fennel seeds	15 mL
2 to 3	small dried hot red chiles	2 to 3
2 tbsp	ground turmeric	25 mL

1. Spread cumin, coriander and fennel seeds and chiles on a baking sheet. Toast in preheated oven until fragrant, about 30 minutes.

2. Using a spice mill, grind toasted spices to a fine powder. You may need to do this in several batches. Sieve, if necessary, to remove any remaining chunky pieces. Combine with turmeric. Store in a covered container in a cool dark cupboard for up to 6 months as aromas fade over time.

Curry Spices

A blend of aromatic spices, that when combined with fresh garlic, ginger and caramelized onions, forms the basis of an authentic curry. The dry spice blend is also used in marinades and spice rubs for fish, poultry and meats. The blend most commonly includes powdered cumin, coriander, chiles, turmeric and salt. Purchase a good brand of prepared curry powder or create your own. Store in a covered container in a cool dark cupboard. Use within 6 months as aromas fade over time.

Garam Masala

An aromatic spice blend most often used as a marinade or a finishing spice toward the end of cooking. The name means "warm mixture" in Hindi. The traditional mix of spices usually includes coriander seeds, cumin seeds, cinnamon, peppercorns, cardamom and cloves. Depending on your dish you may also include fennel seeds, nutmeg, star anise and bay leaf.

- **Preheat oven to 200°F (100°C)**
- **2 baking sheets**
- **Spice mill or mortar and pestle**

30	green cardamom pods	30
2	pieces (3 inches/7.5 cm) cinnamon sticks, crushed	2
1 tbsp	black cumin seeds	15 mL
1 tbsp	whole cloves	15 mL
1 tbsp	black peppercorns	15 mL
1½ tsp	coriander seeds	7 mL

1. Spread cardamom pods on one baking sheet. Spread cinnamon sticks, cumin seeds, cloves, peppercorns and coriander seeds on another baking sheet. Toast in preheated oven until aromas are released, about 30 minutes.

2. Place cardamom pods on a clean tea towel, fold over cloth to enclose the spices and smash the pods with a rolling pin to crush the shells. Pick out the small green seeds and discard the shells.

3. Use a spice mill to grind spices to a fine powder. You may need to do this in several batches. Sieve, if necessary, to remove any remaining chunky pieces. Store in airtight jar in cool cupboard for up to 6 months.

Indonesian Chicken Satays

MAKES 24 SKEWERS

*Enjoy these delicious
satays as a main course
with Sesame Noodle
Salad (page 71) or Asian
Slaw (page 60) or serve as
a party snack.*

*Use the highly aromatic
spice paste with chicken
and pork. Tiny red
bird's-eye chiles (also
known as Thai chiles)
pack quite a heat, so add
according to your taste.*

- **8-inch (20 cm) bamboo skewers, soaked for 30 minutes**
- **Barbecue or indoor grill**

⅓ cup	Indonesian Spice Paste (see below)	75 mL
1 tbsp	palm sugar or brown sugar	15 mL
3	skinless boneless chicken breasts (about 1½ lbs/750 g)	3
	Kosher or sea salt	
1 tbsp	finely chopped cilantro	15 mL
	Sesame Ginger Dressing and Dip (page 71)	

1. Sweeten spice paste with palm or brown sugar. Set aside.
2. Cut each chicken breast lengthwise into 8 strips. Coat with spice paste and marinate overnight in a covered container in the refrigerator.
3. Preheat barbecue or indoor grill to medium heat.
4. Thread a skewer through each chicken strip. Grill skewers until chicken is golden and no longer pink inside, 3 to 4 minutes per side. Sprinkle with salt and garnish with cilantro. Serve dipping sauce on the side.

Indonesian Spice Paste

Makes about ¾ cup (175 mL)

- **Food processor**

2 tbsp	roughly chopped macadamia nuts	25 mL
2 tbsp	finely chopped garlic	25 mL
2 tbsp	finely chopped gingerroot	25 mL
1 tbsp	finely chopped lemongrass	15 mL
3 to 6	bird's-eye (Thai) chiles, finely chopped	3 to 6
1	shallot, finely chopped	1
1 tsp	ground turmeric	5 mL
2 tbsp	vegetable oil	25 mL

1. In a food processor, combine nuts, garlic, ginger, lemongrass, chiles, shallot and turmeric. Pulse ingredients into a rough paste. Drizzle in oil through hole in feed tube and whirl briefly.
2. Store in a covered container in the refrigerator. Use within 2 to 3 days or freeze for longer storage.

Chicken Fingers for Kids

SERVES 3 TO 4

Who would have thought that our customers would want us to make chicken fingers? Believe it or not, we make mountains of them! They're a favorite for kids' parties — with the obligatory plum sauce, of course! At least our version is freshly prepared from good-quality chicken, simple ingredients and no questionable additives.

Tips

Panko is light, flaky Japanese-style bread crumbs available in packages at the market. Made from wheat flour with dextrose, shortening, yeast and salt. They're useful in the kitchen for quick, easy breading of chicken, fish, pork or vegetables.

A note on the kids' favorite plum sauce. Read the label. There often isn't a plum in sight, the main ingredient is pumpkin!

Variation

Instead of deep-frying, place breaded chicken fingers on lightly oiled baking sheets and bake in preheated 350°F (180°C) oven, turning partway, until chicken is no longer pink inside and coating is crisp and lightly browned, 10 to 12 minutes.

- Deep-fryer or large heavy saucepan with frying basket
- Preheat deep-fryer to 325° to 350°F (160° to 180°C)
- Preheat oven to 300°F (150°C)

12 oz	skinless boneless chicken breasts, sliced lengthwise into strips	375 g
	Salt and freshly ground black pepper	
½ cup	all-purpose flour	125 mL
2	eggs, beaten	2
½ cup	Panko bread crumbs (see Tips, left)	125 mL
8 to 12 cups	vegetable oil for deep-frying	2 to 3 L
	Plum Sauce (see Tips, left)	

1. Season chicken lightly with salt and pepper. Place flour in a shallow dish and beaten eggs in another. Add a pinch of salt and pepper to bread crumbs and place in another shallow dish or on a baking sheet.

2. Dip chicken pieces in flour to coat on all sides, then dip in beaten eggs. Let excess egg drip off and coat chicken on all sides with seasoned bread crumbs. Shake off excess crumbs and set aside on a rack until ready to cook. Discard any excess flour, egg and bread crumbs.

3. Deep-fry chicken pieces in hot oil, a few pieces at a time, according to the size of your deep-fryer. Do not crowd the pot. Cook until the chicken is nicely golden and no longer pink inside, 3 to 4 minutes. Lift cooked chicken from hot oil with a slotted spoon and set aside on a rack set over a tray lined with paper towel. Keep warm in preheated oven until all chicken is cooked and ready to be enjoyed. And don't forget the plum sauce.

Chicken Pot Pie

SERVES 6

This home-style chicken pie is one of the most popular items on our weekly menu, particularly in cooler months. A good pie has moist juicy chunks of chicken and tender vegetables that retain their flavor — all combined in a well-seasoned sauce under a crisp, golden crust.

Variations

If you wish to make a pie from previously roasted chicken or turkey, omit Step 1 and proceed through the remaining steps, using about 3 cups (750 mL) cubed chicken or turkey.

To make individual chicken pies: Spoon filling into 5 individual 3-inch (7.5 cm) pie plates and top with circles of pastry, about 4 inches (10 cm) in diameter. Egg wash as indicated in recipe and bake until golden, 15 to 20 minutes.

- **Preheat oven to 350°F (180°C)**
- **9-inch (23 cm) deep-dish glass pie plate or shallow casserole**

1½ lbs	skinless boneless chicken breasts and thighs	750 g
	Salt and freshly ground black pepper	
2	carrots, cut into ½-inch (1 cm) dice	2
1	stalk celery, cut into ½-inch (1 cm) pieces	1
1 cup	green peas, frozen	250 mL
2 cups	Chicken Velouté Sauce (page 121)	500 mL
4 oz	puff pastry	125 g
1	egg, lightly beaten with a splash of water	1

1. Season chicken with salt and pepper and place in a small casserole dish. Bake in preheated oven until breasts are no longer pink inside, 10 to 15 minutes. Continue to bake thighs until juices run clear when pierced, 10 minutes longer. Let cool. Trim and cut chicken into 1-inch (2.5 cm) cubes. Set aside in a large bowl.

2. In a saucepan of boiling lightly salted water, cook carrots and celery until tender, 5 to 10 minutes. Lift out with a slotted spoon and run briefly under cold water to stop the cooking process. Drain and add to chicken in bowl.

3. Increase oven temperature to 400°F (200°C).

4. Combine cooked chicken, carrots, celery, green peas and Chicken Velouté Sauce. Taste and adjust seasoning. The filling may be prepared ahead to this point and refrigerated in a covered container for up to 3 days.

5. Spoon chicken and vegetable filling into the pie plate. Place on a baking sheet.

6. Roll out puff pastry and cut into a circle, ⅛ inch (3 mm) thick and about 10½ inches (26 cm) in diameter. Carefully lift pastry circle and lay on top of the filling, letting the pastry hang over the sides. Brush pastry with egg mixture and grind a little black pepper over top. Bake in preheated oven until the top is golden brown and the pastry is cooked through, about 25 minutes.

Chicken Velouté Sauce

Makes 2 cups (500 mL)

2 cups	Chicken Stock (page 54) or ready-to-use broth	500 mL
¼ cup	butter	50 mL
1	leek, white part only, chopped	1
¼ cup	all-purpose flour	50 mL
1 tbsp	coarsely chopped tarragon	15 mL
1 tbsp	finely sliced chives	15 mL
1 tsp	kosher or sea salt	5 mL
½ tsp	freshly ground black pepper	2 mL

1. In small saucepan, heat chicken stock over medium-low heat until just simmering.

2. In a large saucepan, melt butter over medium heat. Add leek and sauté until soft, 4 to 5 minutes. Add flour and cook, stirring, 1 to 2 minutes. Slowly whisk in warm stock, about ¼ cup (50 mL) at a time, whisking diligently to ensure sauce is smooth. Continue cooking and stirring until sauce reaches consistency to coat the back of the spoon, 5 to 10 minutes.

3. Stir in tarragon and chives and season with salt and pepper.

Roast Turkey with Apple Sage Stuffing and Madeira Gravy

At holiday times our kitchen is filled with wonderful aromas of roasting turkeys, herbed stuffing and simmering gravy. There is a buzz of electricity in the air as all the chefs and bakers work at fever pitch to prepare the festive meal at the appointed time for our customers. At home there is no need for stress: make a list and plan and prepare most of the meal ahead of time so that you can relax and enjoy the festivities. We roast our turkeys with aromatic vegetables and herbs in the central cavity and bake stuffing on the side.

- Large stovetop safe roasting pan
- Preheat oven to 325°F (160°C)
- Instant-read thermometer

1	turkey (16 lbs/8 kg)	1
1	lemon, quartered	1
	Salt and freshly ground black pepper	
1	onion, quartered	1
1	stalk celery with leaves, roughly chopped	1
1	head garlic, loose skins removed and cut in half horizontally	1
3	sprigs thyme	3
3	sprigs flat-leaf parsley	3
2	bay leaves	2
2 tbsp	melted butter or olive oil	25 mL
1 tbsp	dried sage	15 mL
1 tbsp	dried thyme	15 mL

Madeira Gravy

1 cup	Madeira	250 mL
3½ cups	Turkey or Chicken Stock (page 54) or ready-to-use broth (approx.)	875 mL
¼ cup	butter, optional	50 mL
3	shallots, finely chopped	3
6 tbsp	all-purpose flour	90 mL
1 tsp	chopped thyme	5 mL
	Salt and freshly ground black pepper	

1. Remove giblets from turkey cavity; set aside for stock, if desired. Rinse turkey inside and out with cold water and pat dry thoroughly. Squeeze juice of one section of lemon into central cavity and season with salt and pepper. Add remaining lemon quarters, onion, celery, garlic, thyme sprigs, parsley sprigs and bay leaves. Rub skin of bird with butter, dried sage, dried thyme, salt and pepper. To truss your turkey: Tuck the flap of skin at the neck and the wing tips under the bird. Loosely tie the drumsticks together. If you like to truss the bird in a more compact shape see Techniques, page 17.

2. Place turkey in a large roasting pan. Some cooks like to roast the turkey breast-side down for the first hour to keep the breast meat juicy, others prefer to baste with pan juices every 20 minutes or so. Roast turkey, basting occasionally with pan juices, until an instant-read thermometer inserted into the thickest part of the thigh registers 165°F (74°C) and when pierced the juices run clear, $3\frac{1}{2}$ to 4 hours. It is important to turn the pan in the oven several times so that the bird cooks evenly and to cover the breast loosely with foil if it seems to be browning too quickly.

3. Remove pan from oven and let rest for 5 minutes. Lift turkey from pan, transfer to a warm platter and cover loosely with foil for about 30 minutes.

4. *Madeira Gravy:* Pour off fat and juices from roasting pan into a large measuring cup and place in the freezer for 2 to 3 minutes so that fat quickly rises to the surface. Transfer $\frac{1}{4}$ cup (50 mL) fat to a saucepan and skim off and discard the rest. Reserve the juices underneath.

5. Set roasting pan over medium-high heat. Carefully add Madeira and bring to a boil, scraping up browned bits on the bottom. Reduce heat and simmer for 5 minutes. Strain liquid and add to measuring cup. Add enough stock to make 4 cups (1 L).

6. In a saucepan, heat reserved turkey fat or butter over medium heat. Add shallots and sauté until soft and lightly browned, 4 to 5 minutes. Add flour and cook, stirring, until lightly browned, 3 to 4 minutes. Slowly whisk in Madeira mixture until smooth. Reduce heat. Add thyme and let sauce simmer, stirring occasionally, until desired flavor and consistency is reached, 5 to 10 minutes. Season with salt and pepper to taste.

7. Carve turkey and serve with Madeira Gravy and Apple Sage Stuffing (page 124).

Variations

Brined turkey: Prepare brine (page 127). Place turkey in double layer of turkey-size oven bags and place bags in roasting pan. Pour in brine and secure with a twist tie. Place in refrigerator and marinate, turning occasionally, 12 to 18 hours. When its time to start cooking, remove turkey from brine, rinse under cold water and pat dry thoroughly inside and out. Turkey is seasoned from the brine and does not need extra seasoning. Use reduced-sodium broth for the gravy and do not add extra salt before tasting. Brining the turkey is particularly good if you plan to roast the bird over charcoal.

Sage Butter Baste: A thin layer of flavored butter smoothed over the turkey breast under the skin adds moisture and flavor while the bird is cooking. Combine $\frac{1}{3}$ cup (75 mL) soft butter with 2 tbsp (25 mL) chopped sage, 1 tsp (5 mL) grated lemon zest, $\frac{1}{4}$ tsp (1 mL) kosher salt and $\frac{1}{4}$ tsp (1 mL) freshly ground pepper. Use your hands to loosen the skin of the turkey from the breast meat and from the tops of the legs. Spread the herb butter over the meat and pat the skin to distribute the butter in an even layer.

To cook the stuffing in the turkey: Loosely pack the central cavity and under the neck flap using about 8 cups (2 L) stuffing. Increase roasting time to 4 to $4\frac{1}{2}$ hours, ensuring the center of the stuffing reaches 165°F (74°C).

Use a country-style bread with good texture for stuffings — white, whole wheat or a mixture. It should be 1 to 2 days old and cut into ½-inch (1 cm) cubes or roughly torn. One large loaf yields 10 to 12 cups (2.5 to 3 L) bread cubes, to fill a 13- by 9-inch (3 L) shallow baking dish, about 10 servings, or to stuff a 16-lb (8 kg) turkey with extra on the side. Onions, celery and a generous amount of fresh herbs make up the basic flavorings, but other popular additions include apples, mushrooms, fennel, sausage meat and sun-dried tomatoes. Stuffing ingredients should be moist enough to just hold together when mixed. Add a little more moisture (melted butter, stock or eggs) if the stuffing is to be baked in a separate casserole. Prepare stuffing and store separately in refrigerator up to 2 days ahead. If using eggs in your stuffing, add them just before stuffing the bird or baking. Always stuff your turkey just prior to roasting and insert an instant-read thermometer into the center of the stuffing to make sure it is properly cooked to 165°F (74°C): to disregard these precautions may cause illness.

Apple Sage Stuffing

Serves 10 or enough to stuff one 14- to 16-lb (7 to 8 kg) turkey

● **13- by 9-inch (3 L) shallow baking dish, lightly buttered**

½ cup	butter, divided	125 mL
2 cups	chopped onions	500 mL
2 cups	chopped peeled firm tart apples	500 mL
1½ cups	chopped celery	375 mL
½ cup	chopped shallots	125 mL
¾ cup	chopped flat-leaf parsley	175 mL
1 tbsp	chopped sage	15 mL
1 tbsp	chopped thyme	15 mL
1 tsp	grated lemon zest	5 mL
¼ tsp	ground cloves	1 mL
	Salt and freshly ground black pepper	
1	large loaf country-style bread, cut into ½-inch (1 cm) cubes (10 to 12 cups/2.5 to 3 L)	1
½ to 1 cup	Turkey or Chicken Stock (page 54) or ready-to-use broth	125 to 250 mL

1. In a large skillet, melt 2 tbsp (25 mL) of the butter over medium heat. Add onions and sauté until soft and lightly browned, 5 to 7 minutes. Scrape into a large bowl. Return skillet to heat and add remaining butter. Add apples, celery and shallots and sauté until soft, 5 to 7 minutes. Add parsley, sage, thyme, lemon zest, cloves, 1 tsp (5 mL) salt and ¼ tsp (1 mL) pepper and sauté for 1 minute, then add to onions in bowl. Add bread cubes to bowl, moisten with enough stock until stuffing just holds together. Season with salt and pepper to taste.

2. Spread stuffing in prepared dish and cover with foil. About 30 minutes before the turkey is cooked, place casserole in oven and bake for 30 minutes. Remove foil and bake until top is lightly browned, about 15 minutes more.

Turkey Roasting Primer

Since many of us prepare a turkey feast only once, or maybe twice, a year, the following notes may be helpful.

Make-Ahead Tips: Prepare stock ahead and freeze. Prepare the stuffing a day ahead and keep covered in the refrigerator. Remove stuffing from refrigerator about 15 minutes before stuffing the turkey or baking.

You can never have too much turkey gravy! Allow at least $\frac{1}{3}$ cup (75 mL) per person. Make Turkey Stock (see Variation, page 54) including turkey pieces and any giblets (neck, heart, gizzard) that you have saved in the freezer. The liver makes the stock bitter: discard or sauté it in a little butter, chop and add to finished gravy or stuffing, if you like.

    As a rule of thumb: for each cup (250 mL) of gravy, allow 1 tbsp (15 mL) turkey fat, $1\frac{1}{2}$ tsp (7 mL) all-purpose flour and 1 cup (250 mL) pan juices and/or stock.

A large rectangular roasting pan made of heavy gauge aluminum for good heat distribution is indispensable in the kitchen for roasting turkeys and large cuts of meat. Select one that has a sturdy stand up handle at each end: swinging handles that hang down are sometimes difficult to grab in a hot oven. Avoid nonstick coated ones because they often are not safe for use on the stovetop. A large V-shaped roasting rack keeps turkey suspended above the roasting fat and makes basting and handling easier.

When is Turkey Done?

For an unstuffed turkey, allow 15 to 18 minutes per lb (500 g) in a 325°F (160°C) oven. For example, a 14- to 16-lb (7 to 8 kg) turkey takes $3\frac{1}{2}$ to 4 hours to reach an internal temperature of 165°F (74°C) at the thickest part of the thigh. The juices will run clear when the thigh is pierced when it's properly cooked.

For a stuffed turkey, allow 18 to 20 minutes per lb (500 g) in a 325°F (160°C) oven. So a 14- to 16-lb (7 to 8 kg) turkey will take 4 to $4\frac{1}{2}$ hours to reach an internal temperature of 165°F (74°C) at the thickest part of the thigh and in the center of the stuffing. The juices will run clear when the thigh is pierced when it's properly cooked and the skin will be pulled back from the ends of the drumstick.

Lifting a heavy turkey from roasting pan to platter is often a two-man job. Make sure a large warm platter is placed right beside the pan. Let turkey rest in the pan for 5 minutes. Stick the handle of a large wooden spoon into the cavity of the bird between the stuffing (if stuffed) and the breast bone and lift straight up and out of the pan The helper is at hand to steady pan and platter and to guide the bird on both sides with hands protected by paper or tea towels. Cover loosely with foil and let rest while you complete the gravy.

Brined Duck Breast

A period in an aromatic brine adds moisture and flavor to duck and other poultry. Duck breasts cooked in this classic method are juicy and tender.

6	duck breasts	6
	Herbed Brine for Duck or Turkey (page 127), chilled	
2 tbsp	balsamic vinegar	25 mL
1 cup	Chicken Stock (page 54) or ready-to-use broth, preferably reduced-sodium	250 mL
2 tbsp	Port or Madeira	25 mL
	Freshly ground black pepper	
	Kosher or sea salt, optional	

1. Add duck breasts to cold brine, making sure that they are completely submerged; you may need to weight them down. (We insert a plate that fits into the pot weighed down with a plastic container filled with water.) Cover and refrigerate for at least 6 hours or for up to 18 hours.

2. Drain duck and pat dry. Discard brine. Score the fat on the duck breast before cooking. Lay duck breast on a cutting board parallel to your body, take a sharp knife and run it through the fat at a slight angle all the way across the fat to within $1/4$ inch (0.5 cm) of the flesh; do not cut all the way through to the flesh. Turn the duck breast 180 degrees and cut lines perpendicular to the first set of cuts.

3. Heat a large heavy skillet over medium heat. Lay the duck breasts in pan, fat side down. You may have to cook duck in batches. Do not crowd the pan. Let duck breasts cook undisturbed for 5 minutes. Drain off fat regularly. (Keep this fat for other purposes, see pages 128 and 129, but remember that it is seasoned from the brining process.) Continue gentle cooking and rendering off fat until all but a scant $1/4$ inch (0.5 cm) of fat remains on the duck and the skin of the duck has browned to a rich, deep gold, 15 to 20 minutes. If the duck skin is getting too dark before enough fat has melted away, simply reduce the heat.

4. Turn duck breasts over and remove from heat. Let stand, loosely covered with foil, 5 to 6 minutes. The duck will be cooked to a succulent rare to medium-rare.

5. Discard fat from skillet. Add vinegar and deglaze pan over high heat, scraping up browned bits on the bottom. Add stock and continue to cook until liquid is reduced to about ¾ cup (175 mL). Stir in Port and season with pepper to taste. (Use reduced-sodium stock and taste carefully before adding more salt: initial brining adds saltiness.) Spoon jus over duck breasts to serve.

Herbed Brine for Duck or Turkey

8 cups	water	2 L
½ cup	kosher salt	125 mL
¼ cup	packed brown sugar	50 mL
12	sage leaves	12
6	sprigs thyme	6
2	bay leaves	2
2	cloves garlic, coarsely chopped	2
1 tbsp	black peppercorns, crushed	15 mL
2 tsp	coriander seeds	10 mL
1 tsp	juniper berries	5 mL

1. In a stockpot, combine water, salt, brown sugar, sage, thyme, bay leaves, garlic, peppercorns, coriander seeds and juniper berries over medium heat. Bring to a boil, stirring to dissolve salt and sugar. Reduce heat and simmer for 5 minutes. Pour into a large deep bowl and let cool. Refrigerate, covered, until cold.

Duck Confit

Since duck breasts are the preferred part of the bird for delicious entrées, it makes sense to have a brilliant way of dealing with all the legs and the saved duck fat! Confit keeps in the refrigerator up to a month. Use the meat in salads, pastas and soups, with beans, and, of course, a little duck fat adds a whole new dimension to home fries.

Variation

Change the flavor of the confit. Add a strip of orange zest or 6 crushed juniper berries.

• **Deep Dutch oven or stockpot**

6	duck legs	6
6 tbsp	kosher salt	90 mL
6 tbsp	packed brown sugar	90 mL
3	cloves garlic, sliced	3
6	bay leaves	6
2 tbsp	coarsely chopped thyme	25 mL
6	black peppercorns, crushed	6
4	whole cloves, crushed	4
4 cups	rendered duck fat	1 L

1. Rub duck legs all over with salt and brown sugar and place in a nonreactive dish (glass or ceramic). Press garlic, bay leaf, thyme, peppercorns and cloves into surface of each duck leg. Cover with plastic wrap and refrigerate overnight.

2. Preheat oven to 200°F (100°C).

3. Rinse duck legs under cold water to remove all seasonings and dry thoroughly. Set aside.

4. Melt duck fat slowly in Dutch oven over medium-low heat and arrange duck legs in pot so that they are completely covered by melted fat. Place in preheated oven and bake until legs are completely tender and have settled in the bottom of the pot, about 6 hours.

5. Remove from oven and let cool to room temperature. Store in refrigerator, covered in fat, for up to 1 month.

Duck Rillettes

**MAKES 1 CUP
(250 ML)**

*A tasty, decadent spread
for crostini or baguette
slices. Enjoy alone as
a snack with sliced
gherkins or Shallot Port
Marmalade (see below)
or serve beside a salad of
sharp baby greens.*

● **2 small serving ramekins**

8 oz	duck confit (about 2 legs preserved in duck fat)	250 g
6 tbsp	fat from Duck Confit (page 128), or as needed	90 mL
2 tsp	chopped thyme	10 mL
	Salt and freshly ground black pepper	

1. Remove meat from bones, discard skin and chop meat coarsely. Combine with ¼ cup (50 mL) fat, thyme and salt and pepper to taste. Blend thoroughly until fat is evenly distributed and meat is finely shredded and creamy (a standing electric mixer on medium-high speed does the job quickly and easily). The rillettes should be moist and spreadable. Taste and adjust seasoning. Pack into ramekins. Seal with a thin layer of remaining duck fat and refrigerate for 4 hours or overnight.

Shallot Port Marmalade

**MAKES 2 CUPS
(500 ML)**

*You will find many
occasions to use
this savory sweet
condiment — with Duck
Rillettes (see above),
patés and terrines, glazed
ham and to accompany a
cheese board.*

¼ cup	butter	50 mL
2 lbs	shallots, thinly sliced	1 kg
½ cup	Port	125 mL
¼ cup	white wine vinegar	50 mL
¼ cup	liquid honey	50 mL
	Salt and freshly ground black pepper	

1. In a saucepan, melt butter over medium heat. Add shallots. Reduce heat to low and cook, stirring occasionally, until softened and caramelized, 30 to 45 minutes.

2. Add Port and vinegar to pan. Increase heat and deglaze pan, scraping up browned bits on the bottom. Add honey and a pinch of salt and pepper. Continue to cook until almost all the liquid has evaporated. Taste and adjust seasoning. Remove from heat and let cool. Chill before serving. Store marmalade in a covered container in the refrigerator for up to 3 weeks.

Smoky Spicy Grilled Cornish Game Hen

Tips

A cautionary tip: Always separate marinating and basting liquid into two small bowls with a separate clean basting brush in each. Use one for basting on raw meat and during the cooking process and reserve the other for brushing on cooked meat at end of cooking process. It's a safeguard against cross-contamination.

A safe food-handling reminder: Wash all knives, cutting boards, platters (and hands) used for preparing raw meats at once in hot soapy water. Clean knives, cutting boards and platters must be used for the cooked meat.

● **Barbecue or indoor grill**

4	Cornish game hens	4
1 cup	olive oil	250 mL
3 tbsp	smoked paprika	45 mL
2 tbsp	freshly ground black pepper	25 mL
2 tbsp	minced garlic	25 mL
1 tbsp	dry mustard	15 mL
1 tsp	ground ginger	5 mL
	Kosher or sea salt	

1. Butterfly or spatchcock the game hens (see Techniques, page 17). Rinse and pat dry.

2. In a small bowl, combine oil, paprika, pepper, garlic, mustard and ginger. Rub 2 tbsp (25 mL) of the spicy mixture all over each hen. Reserve the rest. Marinate hens, covered, in the refrigerator overnight or for at least 4 hours.

3. Preheat barbecue or indoor grill to medium. Stir remaining marinade and pour half of it into a small bowl. Set aside. Brush hen on both sides with marinade and season with salt. Place on lightly oiled grill, skin-side down, and grill for 10 to 12 minutes. Using two strong spatulas, turn game hen over to grill the other side. Brush the cooked skin side with reserved marinade. Grill until the juices run clear in the leg when pierced, 10 to 12 minutes more.

4. Remove from grill and brush game hens with more reserved marinade. Cover loosely with foil for 5 minutes before serving.

Beef and Veal

Italian Meatballs with Chunky Tomato Sauce

This recipe is easily multiplied and is a favorite dish when families get together. Serve over spaghetti with extra grated Parmesan to sprinkle on top, and a dish of hot pepper flakes on the table for those who like to spice it up a little.

Tip

Multiply this recipe to serve a large party or to make-ahead and store in the freezer. For large quantities, instead of browning in a skillet, arrange the meatballs in single layers on large baking sheets and roast in a preheated 350°F (180°C) oven for about 20 minutes, shaking the pan occasionally so that the meatballs brown evenly on all sides. Heat Chunky Tomato Sauce in a large pot and combine browned meatballs with sauce and continue with Step 3.

1½ lbs	lean ground beef	750 g
8 oz	ground pork	250 g
1	small onion, finely chopped	1
2	cloves garlic, finely chopped	2
¼ cup	fresh bread crumbs	50 mL
¼ cup	chopped flat-leaf parsley	50 mL
2 tbsp	grated Parmesan cheese	25 mL
1 tbsp	chopped basil or 1 tsp (5 mL) dried basil	15 mL
1 tbsp	chopped oregano or 1 tsp (5 mL) dried oregano	15 mL
1½ tsp	kosher or sea salt	7 mL
½ tsp	freshly ground black pepper	2 mL
1	egg, lightly beaten	1
2 tbsp	olive oil	25 mL
	Chunky Tomato Sauce (page 133)	

1. In a large bowl, using a fork, combine beef and pork with onion, garlic, bread crumbs, parsley, Parmesan, basil, oregano, salt, pepper and egg. Scoop ¼ cup (50 mL) of the mixture and shape into a ball. Repeat with remaining mixture.
2. In a large skillet, heat oil over medium-high heat. Add meatballs, in batches, and brown lightly on all sides. Do not crowd the pan. Set aside.
3. In a large pot, heat Chunky Tomato Sauce over medium heat until bubbling. Reduce heat to medium-low and add meatballs to the sauce. Use a wooden spoon to make room in the pot for all the meatballs and to ensure that they are all immersed in the sauce. Partially cover the pot and simmer until meatballs are no longer pink inside, 20 to 30 minutes.

Chunky Tomato Sauce

**MAKES ABOUT
5 CUPS (1.25 L)**

*If you plan to make only
one homemade sauce,
this is the one. It is used
in dozens of ways and
tastes 100 percent better
than any commercial
variety. Seek out good
quality canned plum
tomatoes or, best of all,
use field-ripened fresh
plum tomatoes in season.*

Tip

If using dried herbs, add earlier
in the cooking with the garlic
in Step 1 but not with the
onions and celery.

2 tbsp	extra virgin olive oil	25 mL
2	onions, chopped	2
2	stalks celery, chopped	2
2	cloves garlic, finely chopped	2
¼ cup	tomato paste	50 mL
2	cans (each 28 oz/796 mL) plum tomatoes with juice, chopped	2
1 tbsp	chopped basil, divided, or 1 tsp (5 mL) dried basil (see Tip, left)	15 mL
1 tbsp	chopped oregano, divided, or 1 tsp (5 mL) dried oregano	15 mL
	Salt and freshly ground pepper	
Pinch	granulated sugar, optional	Pinch

1. In a large saucepan, heat oil over medium heat. Add onions and celery and sauté until softened but not browned, 5 to 6 minutes. Add garlic and sauté for 1 to 2 minutes. Add tomato paste and cook, stirring, for 1 minute. Add tomatoes with juice and bring to a simmer.

2. Reduce heat and stir in 1 tsp (5 mL) basil, 1 tsp (5 mL) oregano, ½ tsp (2 mL) salt and ¼ tsp (1 mL) pepper. Simmer, stirring occasionally and breaking up tomatoes with a wooden spoon as they soften, until sauce is smooth and nicely thickened, about 45 minutes. Add remaining basil and oregano and taste and adjust seasoning. Add sugar, if needed.

Classic Roast Beef with Garlic Pan Gravy and Yorkshire Pudding

This premier roast is for special occasions and a fine piece of beef needs no fancy treatment. Beef roasted on the bone is extra juicy and flavorful. We recommend that you do not roast beef for longer than required to reach medium-rare to medium degree of doneness (see Guide for Roasting Beef, page 139).

Tip

Avoid nonstick coated roasting pans because they often are not safe for use on the stovetop.

Variation

For ease of carving, you may prefer to ask your butcher to prepare a boneless roast for you, such as rib-eye or sirloin Follow Step 2 for roasting, allowing 15 to 18 minutes per pound (500 g) for medium-rare.

- **Preheat oven to 325°F (160°C)**
- **Stovetop-safe roasting pan (see Tip, left)**
- **Instant-read thermometer**

6 lbs	beef prime rib roast, bone-in	3 kg
	Salt and freshly ground pepper	
2	cloves garlic, cut in half	2
1 tbsp	extra virgin olive oil	15 mL
5	sprigs thyme	5
3	sprigs rosemary	3

Roasted Garlic Pan Gravy

2 tbsp	all-purpose flour	25 mL
1/2 cup	red wine	125 mL
1 1/2 cups	Beef or Veal Stock (page 55) or ready-to-use broth	375 mL
1	head Roasted Garlic (page 135), or to taste	1
	Salt and freshly ground pepper	
1 tbsp	soft butter, optional	15 mL
	Yorkshire Pudding (page 136)	

1. Season beef well on all sides with salt and pepper and rub with cut sides of garlic cloves. In a large skillet, heat oil over medium-high heat. Place beef, fat side down, in pan and sear until nicely browned. Remove from heat and transfer, fat side up, to roasting pan. Arrange thyme and rosemary sprigs on top of roast.

2. Roast beef in preheated oven until cooked to your taste. For most accurate results test internal temperature with an instant-read thermometer inserted in the thickest part of the meat, not touching a bone. For beef cooked medium-rare the flesh will be slightly resilient to the touch and the juices will run pink, and the internal temperature will be 140° to 145°F (60° to 63°C). This roast will take 1 1/2 to 2 1/4 hours (or 18 to 22 minutes per lb/500 g) to reach medium-rare.

3. Transfer beef to a warm platter and let stand for 10 minutes. Drape foil loosely over the roast for a longer wait. The internal temperature will rise 5° to 10°F (3° to 6°C) while meat rests.

4. *Roasted Garlic Pan Gravy:* Skim away all but 2 tbsp (25 mL) fat from pan. (Save excess for Yorkshire Pudding, see page 136, or discard). Place over medium heat, stir in flour and cook, stirring constantly, until brown, 2 to 3 minutes.

5. Gradually stir in wine and deglaze pan, scraping up browned bits on the bottom. Slowly add stock and whisk vigorously until smooth. Bring to a boil. Reduce heat to low and simmer, stirring often, until desired flavor and consistency, 5 to 10 minutes. Squeeze several cloves of soft roasted garlic into the sauce and stir to combine. Season to taste with salt and pepper. If you like to give the sauce a finishing sheen, stir in butter before serving.

6. Slice the roast across the grain and serve with Roasted Garlic Pan Gravy and Yorkshire Pudding.

> **Roasted Garlic**
> Remove the papery skin from a head of garlic. Slice across the tips of all the cloves about $\frac{1}{2}$ inch (1 cm) down from the top. Place garlic on a square of foil, add a splash of olive oil and a small sprig of rosemary, if you like. Wrap securely. Bake in a preheated 350°F (180°C) oven, or roast on the barbecue grill, until cloves are soft, 45 to 60 minutes. Let cool. Squeeze out the soft caramelized garlic from each clove and use to add sweet garlic flavor to sauces, vegetable purées and mayonnaise.

Yorkshire Pudding

MAKES 12 PUDDINGS

In our catering kitchen we make small Yorkshire Puddings in mini muffin cups for elegant cocktail parties and serve them topped with rich mushroom ragoût: a nod to our current fondness for homey comfort food. Members of the Royal Society of Chemistry have strong feelings about the definitive Yorkshire pudding. They claim that if you don't hail from Yorkshire you're not likely to produce a worthy one since it has to be at least 4 inches (10 cm) high!

Tip

A large 4-cup (1 L) measuring cup is a good container to mix the batter in, making it easier to pour into hot tins.

Variations

For great beefy flavor, replace butter and oil mixture with rendered beef fat from the roast.

Use mini muffin tins to make bite-size Yorkshire puddings for tasty party snacks. Increase the amount of fat to ⅓ cup (75 mL) and divide among 24 mini muffin cups (about ¾ tsp/3 mL in each). Proceed with recipe. Bake in preheated oven until well risen, 8 to 10 minutes. Reduce heat to 350°F (180°C) and continue to bake until golden, 3 to 5 minutes more.

- **Preheat oven to 400°F (200°C)**
- **Muffin pan or 9-inch (2.5 L) square baking pan**

¾ cup + 2 tbsp	all-purpose flour	200 mL
½ tsp	kosher or sea salt	2 mL
2	eggs, beaten	2
½ cup	milk	125 mL
⅓ cup	water (approx.)	75 mL
2 tbsp	melted butter	25 mL
2 tbsp	vegetable oil	25 mL

1. In a large bowl, mix together flour and salt. Make a well in the center. In another bowl, combine eggs and milk and slowly add to flour mixture. Whisk until smooth. Whisk in enough water to make a smooth creamy batter. Set aside, covered in plastic wrap, for 10 minutes.

2. In a small measuring cup, combine butter and oil. Pour 1 tsp (5 mL) fat into each muffin cup or all fat into baking pan. Place in preheated oven until fat is hot, 3 to 4 minutes. Let it smoke, but not burn! Carefully remove pan from oven. Give batter a stir and pour into muffin cups or pan. Bake in preheated oven until well risen, 10 to 15 minutes. Reduce heat to 350°F (180°C) and continue to bake until puddings are puffed and golden, about 5 minutes more. Serve hot.

Sicilian Meat Loaf

Serve this tasty meat loaf with penne and a topping of Chunky Tomato Sauce and grated Parmesan. It freezes and reheats well and makes a mighty fine grilled sandwich with grilled peppers and an extra slice of provolone.

- Preheat oven to 350°F (180°C)
- Parchment paper
- Roasting pan
- Instant-read thermometer

1 lb	medium ground beef	500 g
½	onion, finely chopped	½
2	cloves garlic, finely chopped	2
1 cup	fresh bread crumbs	250 mL
¼ cup	chopped flat-leaf parsley	50 mL
1 tbsp	chopped basil or 1 tsp (5 mL) dried basil	15 mL
1 tbsp	chopped oregano or 1 tsp (5 mL) dried oregano	15 mL
1½ tsp	kosher or sea salt	7 mL
½ tsp	freshly ground black pepper	2 mL
2 tbsp	tomato paste	25 mL
1	egg, lightly beaten	1
3	slices provolone cheese	3
3	slices capicollo or prosciutto	3
	Chunky Tomato Sauce (page 133) or store-bought	
	Grated Parmesan cheese	

1. In a large bowl, combine beef with onion, garlic, bread crumbs, parsley, basil, oregano, salt and pepper. Mix tomato paste with ¼ cup (50 mL) water and add to the meat mixture. Add beaten egg and combine.

2. On a large sheet of parchment paper, spread meat mixture into a rectangle, about 15 by 10 inches (38 by 25 cm), with longer side towards you. Arrange cheese and capicollo slices down the middle.

3. Roll the beef mixture around the filling, forming a neat, tight roll. Bring the parchment up and around the meat roll and twist the ends. Wrap the package securely in foil and place in a roasting pan. Roast in preheated oven until an instant-read thermometer inserted in the center reads 160°F (71°C), for 1 hour. Let stand for 10 minutes before unwrapping and slicing. Serve with a topping of Chunky Tomato Sauce and a sprinkling of Parmesan cheese.

Roast Beef Tenderloin with Madeira Pan Jus

This lean luxury cut of beef is delicious party fare, either served hot or at room temperature. Accompany with a variety of sauces, horseradish and mustards.

Variations

Roast Tenderloin of Bison: Substitute bison tenderloin for the beef tenderloin. Crumble 4 oz (125 g) Stilton cheese over the top of the roasted meat when it is taken from the oven. The cheese enhances the Madeira sauce, adds moisture to the meat and smoothes out gamy flavors.

Bacon-Wrapped Fillets: A whole tenderloin may be sliced into 12 to 15 steaks of equal thickness, 1 to 1½ inches (2.5 to 4 cm). Sauté slices of double-smoked bacon until half-cooked. Remove from pan and set aside. Wrap a slice of bacon around each fillet and secure with toothpicks. In a large ovenproof skillet, sear fillets in reserved bacon fat, in batches as necessary, until nicely browned, 2 to 3 minutes per side. Place in preheated 400°F (200°C) oven to finish cooking, about 5 minutes for medium-rare.

- Preheat oven to 400°F (200°C)
- Butcher's string
- Stovetop-safe roasting pan, optional (see Tips, page 134)
- Instant-read thermometer

1	beef tenderloin, trimmed, 4¾ lbs (2.375 kg)	1
	Kosher or sea salt	
2 tbsp	olive oil	25 mL
¼ cup	Dijon mustard	50 mL
¼ cup	freshly cracked black pepper	50 mL

Madeira Pan Jus

2 tbsp	butter, divided	25 mL
1 tbsp	minced shallots	15 mL
¼ cup	Madeira	50 mL
1 cup	Beef Stock (page 55) or ready-to-use broth	250 mL
1 tbsp	minced tarragon or ½ tsp (2 mL) dried tarragon	15 mL
	Salt and freshly ground pepper	
1 tbsp	balsamic vinegar, optional	15 mL

1. Fold the narrow end of the tenderloin underneath and tie the meat with butcher's string to make a neat package. Season lightly with salt.

2. Preheat indoor grill to high, or set roasting pan over two burners on the stovetop. Rub meat with oil and sear on all sides over high heat. Remove from heat, transfer to roasting pan, if necessary, brush with mustard and sprinkle with an even coating of cracked pepper.

3. Roast in preheated oven until an instant-read thermometer inserted in the thickest part registers 125° to 135°F (52° to 57°C) for rare to medium rare, 30 to 35 minutes. Meat will be slightly resistant to the touch and the juices will run pink. Let stand loosely covered with foil for 10 minutes before carving.

4. Meanwhile, prepare the *Madeira Pan Jus*: Place roasting pan over medium-high heat and add 1 tbsp (15 mL) butter. Add shallots and sauté until soft, 2 to 3 minutes. Deglaze the pan with Madeira, scraping up browned bits on the bottom.

5. Transfer shallots and pan juices to a small saucepan. Add stock, tarragon and a pinch of salt and pepper. Bring to a boil and cook until reduced to about ¾ cup (175 mL). Taste and adjust seasoning. Add a splash of vinegar to sharpen the flavor, if needed, and swirl in the rest of the butter. Slice the tenderloin across the grain and serve with Madeira Pan Jus.

Guide for Roasting Beef

For most accurate results test internal temperature with an instant-read thermometer inserted in the thickest part of the meat, not touching a bone.

- *Rare:* 125°F (52°C)
- *Medium-rare:* 135° (57°C)
- *Medium:* 145°F (63°C)

Remember that the internal temperature of the roast will increase about 5°F (3°C) while it rests after being removed from the oven.

For roasting method when meat is browned initially on top of the stove and then roasted at a consistent lower temperature allow approximately 20 minutes per pound (500 g) for rare beef and 25 minutes per pound (500 g) for medium. A steady moderate roasting temperature keeps meat juicy and results in less shrinkage than when meat is roasted at a high temperature.

Cottage Pie

This homey dish started life as "Shepherd's Pie," traditionally made with leftover roast lamb. Our version, made with moist flavorful beef under a creamy topping of fluffy mashed potatoes, is a favorite family weekday supper.

Tip

Sweet and tangy Worcestershire sauce is a standard on our kitchen shelves and used quite frequently to lift the flavor of a sauce or stew, especially for a dish of British heritage. Lee & Perrin's recipe is a closely guarded secret, but we have word that the ingredients include mature anchovies, tamarind, vinegar, sherry, brandy, soy sauce, pork liver, salt, sugar, cayenne pepper, black pepper, coriander, mace, shallots and caramel. We will not suggest that you make your own! The bottle is fine and will last on your shelf indefinitely, always ready to make that batch of Bloody Marys!

- **Preheat oven to 350°F (180°C)**
- **8- to 10-cup (2 to 2.5 L) glass baking dish, lightly oiled**

1 tbsp	vegetable oil	15 mL
2	onions, chopped	2
2	cloves garlic, chopped	2
2 lbs	medium ground beef	1 kg
	Salt and freshly ground black pepper	
1½ tbsp	all-purpose flour	22 mL
⅓ cup	red wine, optional	75 mL
1 cup	Beef Stock (page 55) or ready-to-use broth	250 mL
2 tbsp	Worcestershire sauce (see Tip, left)	25 mL
2 tsp	chopped thyme or 1 tsp (5 mL) dried thyme	10 mL
1 tsp	chopped rosemary or ½ tsp (2 mL) dried rosemary	5 mL
1 tbsp	coarsely chopped flat-leaf parsley	15 mL
	Mashed Potato Topping (page 141)	

1. In a large skillet, heat oil over medium heat. Add onions and sauté until soft, 4 to 5 minutes. Add garlic and sauté for 1 to 2 minutes.

2. Add beef, season with 1 tsp (5 mL) salt and ¼ tsp (1 mL) pepper and cook, breaking up meat with a wooden spoon, until no longer pink. Sprinkle with flour and cook, stirring, 1 to 2 minutes. Deglaze pan with wine, if using, scraping up browned bits on the bottom. Add stock, Worcestershire sauce, thyme, rosemary, salt and pepper. Partially cover and bring to a simmer. Reduce heat to medium-low and simmer for 5 minutes. Taste and adjust seasoning and stir in parsley.

3. Spoon meat into prepared baking dish. Spread an even layer of Mashed Potato Topping over top. Cover dish with foil. Dish may be prepared ahead to this point and refrigerated, covered, for 24 hours.

4. Bake in preheated oven until heated through, 30 to 40 minutes. (If meat filling has been stored in the refrigerator, increase baking time by 5 to 10 minutes.) Remove foil and continue to bake until pie is hot and top is lightly browned, 10 to 15 minutes more.

Mashed Potato Topping

Makes about 3½ cups (875 mL)

3 to 4	baking potatoes (about 1½ lbs/750 g)	3 to 4
½ to ¾ cup	milk or half-and-half (10%) cream	125 to 175 mL
3 tbsp	butter	45 mL
	Salt and freshly ground pepper	

1. Place potatoes in a large saucepan with lightly salted cold water to cover (or peel and cook potatoes, if preferred, see Tip, page 293). Boil until potatoes are tender when tested, about 30 minutes. Drain potatoes and peel away skin. (Hold them in a dry tea towel and peel away the skin with a paring knife. It will slip off easily). Return peeled potatoes to the pot and keep warm.

2. Add ½ cup (125 mL) of the milk and butter. Mash until smooth, adding more milk as needed to acquire a smooth, light texture. Season with salt and pepper to taste.

Bolognese Sauce

**MAKES 5 CUPS
(1.25 L)**

*There is much
controversy surrounding
this noble Italian pasta
sauce. Should it include
diced prosciutto? Should
cream be added? Perhaps
a touch of nutmeg?
To reach the stature it
deserves the sauce must
be made with care and
begin with a "soffritto" —
gently cooked aromatics
including carrot, onion,
celery and garlic.*

Tip

Make batches of Bolognese
sauce and store in the freezer
ready for a quick pasta supper
when there is no time to cook.

1 lb	medium ground beef	500 g
8 oz	ground veal	250 g
8 oz	ground pork or mild sausage, removed from casing	250 g
	Salt and freshly ground black pepper	
½ cup	red wine	125 mL
1 tbsp	olive oil	15 mL
1 tbsp	butter	15 mL
1 cup	finely chopped onion	250 mL
½ cup	finely chopped celery	125 mL
¼ cup	finely chopped carrot	50 mL
1 tsp	finely minced garlic	5 mL
2 tbsp	tomato paste	25 mL
2 cups	drained and chopped canned plum tomatoes	500 mL
1½ cups	Beef Stock (page 55) or ready-to-use broth	375 mL
1 tbsp	chopped thyme or 1 tsp (5 mL) dried thyme	15 mL
1 tbsp	chopped oregano or 1 tsp (5 mL) dried oregano	15 mL
1 tbsp	chopped flat-leaf parsley	15 mL

1. In a large skillet over medium-high heat, sauté beef, veal and pork, breaking up with a wooden spoon to hasten even cooking and to help moisture evaporate, until lightly browned, 8 to 10 minutes. You may have to do this in batches. Season lightly with salt and pepper. Deglaze pan with wine, scraping up browned bits on the bottom and cook for 1 to 2 minutes. Using a slotted spoon, transfer meat to a bowl and set aside. Reserve 1 tbsp (15 mL) fat in pan and discard the rest.

2. In the same pan, add oil and butter to the fat and heat. Add onion, celery, carrot and garlic and sauté for 1 to 2 minutes. Stir in tomato paste and cook, stirring, for 1 minute. Return meat to pan with any collected juices and stir in tomatoes, stock, thyme, oregano, ½ tsp (2 mL) salt and ¼ tsp (1 mL) pepper.

3. Partially cover and bring to a simmer. Reduce heat to low and simmer, stirring occasionally, until sauce is cooked and richly flavored, about 45 minutes. Stir in parsley. Taste and adjust seasoning.

Deglazing the Pan

To capture the goodness of the flavorful browned bits that stick to the bottom of the pan after browning, sautéing or roasting meats, add liquid, such as wine and/or stock, to the cooking pan. Scrape and stir vigorously while bringing the liquid to a boil. Cook over high heat for a minute or 2 to burn off alcohol, if using, and intensify flavor. Use to make gravy and sauces.

Pour off cooking fat before deglazing if making a simple "jus"; strain if necessary. Add flour and cook for a few minutes in the fat before deglazing when making thickened pan gravy.

When deglazing a pan with brandy, rum or bourbon, warm the liquor in a ladle, ignite with a lighted match and carefully add the flaming liquor to the pan. Gently move the pan over the heat while the flames subside. The flaming burns off alcohol leaving flavor behind.

Marinated Flank Steak with Chimichurri Sauce

Chimichurri is a popular all-purpose sauce originating in Argentina. We use it as a marinade and condiment, particularly with beef cooked on the grill. Don't pass over flank steak, the flat cut taken from the fleshy part of the side of beef between the rib and the hip — it's tender and flavorful and grills to perfection in minutes.

Variations

Grilled Beef Kebabs: Replace flank steak with cubes of boneless beef sirloin, approximately 1½ inches (4 cm). Marinate as directed in Step 2. Dry the meat and thread on bamboo skewers, previously soaked in water for 30 minutes. Grill over a hot fire until done to your liking, 3 to 4 minutes per side.

Grilled Beef Satays: Replace flank steak with strips of boneless beef sirloin, ¼ to ½ inch (0.5 to 1 cm) thick. Marinate as directed in Step 2. Dry the meat and thread on bamboo skewers, previously soaked in water for 30 minutes. Grill over a hot fire until done to your liking, 2 to 3 minutes per side.

Barbecue or indoor grill

1 cup	red wine	250 mL
½ cup	vegetable oil	125 mL
¼ cup	natural rice vinegar	50 mL
¼ cup	soy sauce	50 mL
2 tbsp	brown sugar	25 mL
4	cloves garlic, coarsely chopped	4
2 tbsp	Dijon mustard	25 mL
1 tsp	freshly ground black pepper	5 mL
1½ to 2 lbs	beef flank steak	750 to 1 kg
	Kosher or sea salt	
	Chimichurri Sauce (page 145)	

1. In a small bowl, combine wine, oil, vinegar, soy sauce, brown sugar, garlic, mustard and pepper.

2. In a nonreactive container (a stainless steel or ceramic dish, or a heavy-duty plastic bag), thoroughly coat flank steak with marinade. Cover and refrigerate for at least 4 hours or overnight.

3. Remove steak from refrigerator 30 minutes before grilling. (Meat cooks more evenly when started at room temperature.) Preheat barbecue to high and brush lightly with oil. Lift steak from marinade, discarding marinade, and pat dry with paper towel to remove excess liquid and garlic. Season with salt and pepper.

4. Grill steak until well-marked and browned, 3 to 4 minutes per side for rare or 4 to 5 minutes per side for medium. Let stand, loosely covered in foil, for 5 minutes.

5. Cut flank steak in fine slices across the grain and serve with a generous spoonful of Chimichurri Sauce.

Chimichurri Sauce

The basic ingredients for this sauce are lots of fresh parsley and oregano with onion, garlic, lemon and oil. In Argentina, where it originates, it is used as an all-purpose condiment, particularly tasty with barbecued beef.

1	tomato, seeded and diced	1
½ cup	coarsely chopped flat-leaf parsley	125 mL
2 tbsp	chopped red onion	25 mL
2 tsp	coarsely chopped oregano	10 mL
1 tbsp	minced garlic	15 mL
1 tbsp	sherry vinegar	15 mL
½ tsp	grated lemon zest	2 mL
1 tbsp	freshly squeezed lemon juice	15 mL
1 tsp	kosher or sea salt	5 mL
1 tsp	ground cumin	5 mL
½ tsp	paprika	2 mL
¼ tsp	cayenne pepper	1 mL
¼ tsp	freshly ground black pepper	1 mL
½ cup	olive oil	125 mL

1. In a bowl, combine tomato, parsley, red onion, oregano, garlic, vinegar, lemon zest and juice, salt, cumin, paprika, cayenne and black pepper. Add oil. Let mixture stand for at least 1 hour for the flavors to meld. For freshest flavor enjoy on the same day it is made.

Bourbon-Glazed Braised Beef Short Ribs

This hearty dish is designed to feed sports fans around Super Bowl or World Series time! Ribs are braised with lots of seasonings; this can be done ahead of time. The final flourish is a short period in the oven, or on the grill, slathered with a sweet Bourbon-spiked Sauce. These finger-lickin' ribs are great to serve with baked potatoes, baked beans or corn on the cob.

Tips

Beef short ribs may be available whole or sliced. If you have whole ribs, cut them into 2- or 3-rib portions. If purchasing sliced ribs, get the butcher to slice them into 2-inch (5 cm) thick slices so they hold together when braising and glazing.

To finish ribs on the grill: A half hour before serving, remove ribs from refrigerator and preheat grill to medium-high. Place ribs on lightly oiled grill rack. Turn ribs over after 10 minutes and turn and baste frequently with bourbon sauce until ribs are heated through and nicely glazed, 10 to 15 minutes more. Serve with additional warm bourbon sauce on the side.

- Preheat oven to 350°F (180°C)
- 8-quart (8 L) heavy-bottomed pot
- Baking sheets, lined with parchment paper

1 cup	all-purpose flour	250 mL
	Salt and freshly ground black pepper	
8 lbs	beef short ribs (see Tips, left)	4 kg
1/3 cup	vegetable oil, divided (approx.)	75 mL
1 cup	red wine	250 mL
1/4 cup	tomato paste	50 mL
1	onion, quartered	1
3	stalks celery, quartered	3
2	carrots, quartered	2
24	cloves garlic	24
3 tbsp	black peppercorns	45 mL
10	sprigs flat-leaf parsley	10
6	bay leaves (see Tip, right)	6
6	sprigs thyme	6
10 to 12 cups	Beef or Chicken Stock (pages 55 and 54) or reduced-sodium ready-to-use broth	2.5 to 3 L
2 tbsp	packed brown sugar (approx.)	25 mL
1 1/2 cups	bourbon	375 mL

1. In a large bowl, combine flour, 1 tbsp (15 mL) salt and 1 tsp (5 mL) ground pepper. Coat beef ribs in seasoned flour. Shake ribs in a sieve to remove excess flour; discard excess flour mixture.

2. In a large skillet, heat 2 tbsp (25 mL) of the oil over medium-high heat. Sear beef ribs, in batches, turning often, until deeply golden brown on all sides, 6 to 8 minutes. Do not crowd pan. Add oil as needed. Transfer ribs to a large pot. Deglaze skillet with wine, scraping up browned bits on the bottom. Pour liquid over ribs.

3. Add tomato paste, onion, celery, carrots, garlic, peppercorns, parsley, bay leaves and thyme to pot with ribs. Pour in enough stock to cover ribs. Bring to a boil over medium-high heat. Reduce heat to low. Cover and simmer gently until ribs are very tender and the meat begins to pull back from the ends of the bones, 2 to $2\frac{1}{2}$ hours.

4. Remove ribs from braising liquid and set aside. Ribs may be prepared to this point up to 3 days ahead. Cover and refrigerate until time to glaze in the oven or on the grill (see Tips, left). Strain braising liquid through a sieve into another large pot, pressing down on vegetables to extract good juices. Discard vegetables. Skim off fat from liquid.

5. Place pot over medium-high heat. Add brown sugar and stir to dissolve. Add bourbon. Boil until liquid is reduced to a smooth barbecue sauce consistency, about $1\frac{1}{2}$ hours, stirring often as the sauce gets thick. Taste and adjust seasoning and sweetness.

6. A half hour before serving, remove ribs from refrigerator and preheat oven to 350°F (180°C). Place ribs on prepared baking sheets and brush with bourbon sauce. Bake for 10 to 15 minutes. Remove, turn ribs over and coat again with bourbon sauce. Return to the oven for 10 to 15 minutes more. Serve with additional warm bourbon sauce on the side.

Tip

Whole bay leaves add fragrance to many stocks, soups, stews and braises. They remain intact over long cooking periods. If you like, remove and discard before serving for aesthetic reasons and to prevent family or guests inadvertently putting one in their mouth.

Grilled Beef Short Ribs
Korean-Style

SERVE 4

Ask your butcher to cut a strip of meaty short ribs across the bones into narrow strips. Use the sweet-salty marinade with other beef cuts such as steaks, or kebabs of rib-eye steak or sirloin. It is also excellent on grilled firm fish and seafood such as tuna and scallops.

● **Barbecue or indoor grill**

3 lbs	beef short ribs	1.5 kg
	Korean-Style Marinade and Grill Sauce (see below)	
1 tbsp	vegetable oil	15 mL
1	green onion, thinly sliced on the diagonal	1
2 tbsp	toasted sesame seeds, optional	25 mL

1. In a nonreactive container (a stainless steel or ceramic dish, or a heavy-duty plastic bag), thoroughly coat ribs with marinade. Cover and refrigerate for at least 4 hours or overnight.

2. Preheat barbecue grill to medium-high. Drain ribs and pat dry. Brush ribs lightly with oil and grill (you may have to work in batches) until browned and cooked to medium-rare, 3 to 5 minutes per side. Serve hot and garnish with slivered green onions and sesame seeds, if you like.

Korean-Style Marinade and Grill Sauce

Makes 1 cup (250 mL)

½ cup	soy sauce	125 mL
¼ cup	mirin or sherry	50 mL
¼ cup	packed brown sugar	50 mL
2 tbsp	natural rice vinegar	25 mL
2 tbsp	sesame oil	25 mL
2 tbsp	minced garlic	25 mL
2	green onions, thinly sliced on the diagonal	2
¼ tsp	hot pepper flakes, optional	1 mL

1. In a small bowl, combine soy sauce, mirin, brown sugar, vinegar, oil, garlic, green onions and hot pepper flakes, if using.

Beef

Antonin Carême, the first international celebrity chef and the inventor of haute cuisine, once decreed beef to be "the soul of cooking." In Paris and other smart western capitals where he touted his trade, Carême saw beef as the ultimate good, but in North America — where cattle have been raised for more than 400 years — the soul of cooking for centuries centered more on pork and poultry. In the U.S. beef came into its own at last as a result of the Civil War, when its meat rivals were suddenly in short supply. What pushed America's consumption truly over the top was the explosion of burger chains, starting in the 1960s, along every major and minor travel artery and blood vessel north of the Rio Grande.

But food matters, particularly, tend to be faddish, and since 1970, when U.S. beef consumption hit a peak of an annual 80 pounds per capita, beef has been getting it in the chops (reasons of price, health and ecology: a dread apocalypse troika if ever there was one). And who's been giving it the going over? Chicken again! In 1970 we fed ourselves three times more beef than chicken; today our cow consumption is down 25 percent, that of chicken has more than doubled — and now we eat more chicken than beef.

Still, our love of beef is not about to vanish. The U.S. ranks a steady second in global consumption per person, well behind league-leader Argentina, but comfortably ahead of runners-up Australia, Brazil and Canada. The trick today, for the alert consumer, is to choose the type of beef best suited to individual health and/or pocketbook concerns. And alert doesn't mean going to the supermarket's beef counter and pointing.

In the Kitchen

First, check the source. Find a good butcher and ask where he buys his meat, and (if possible) what the animals feed on, if hormones have been used, how many and what kind they are dealt, how and for how long the meat is aged. Second, choose the right cut for the right dish. No point in shelling out for prime rib and porterhouse if you're just brewing up a meat mess in the slow-cooker while you go out for a round of golf. Thus **rib** and **loin** for roasts and steaks; **chuck**, **brisket** and **shank** for stews and braising.

At the very other end of the scale, there's the increasingly popular, heavily marbled, lusciously tender and full of flavor (also, in some quarters, wretchedly overrated) **Kobe** beef, originating in Japan, where wagyu cattle are fed beer and massaged with sake, and are now also bred (as "Kobe-style," wagyus crossed with Angus) on some ranches in the U.S. and Canada. The cost is so extreme — about $150 per pound — that breeders sell directly to top restaurants.

Somewhere in between there's **organic** and **natural** beef. Their combined share of the market is tiny (natural accounts for barely 1 percent of the beef market, organic for much less) but they are growing like Topsy (natural at a rate of 20 percent a year). The difference is that organic beef, to be so labeled, must pass stringent federal standards for production, husbandry and processing (no antibiotics, no artificial growth boosters). Producers of natural beef, not nearly so strictly defined, may choose not to use antibiotics or growth hormones, but there is no strict overview. The label does mean that it may not contain artificial flavors, colorings or chemical preservatives, and should have been raised on grass. Not the usual production line, so there's soul there.

Boeuf Bourguignon

Beef cooked gently until tender in a richly flavored wine sauce is the most heart-warming food for a cool, dreary day. We take the time to sauté the mushrooms and brown the onions separately in order to preserve their taste and texture. As with all stews, the flavor improves when made ahead, which makes it an excellent dish to serve to large groups of family and friends. Serve with boiled potatoes, tossed with a little butter and chopped parsley, or buttered noodles.

Tip

When buying meat for stews we recommend buying the piece and cutting it up yourself, rather than buying the already cut up and packaged pieces. You can then be sure that all the meat is from the cut you want and you can cut into uniform pieces of the size required by your recipe. Sometimes markets will combine pieces labeled "stewing beef" from different parts of the animal that respond to cooking in different ways. Beef cut from the shoulder with connective tissue and fat becomes tender and remains moist over a long, slow cooking period. Beef cut from the rump, round or sirloin will become dry when cooked for a long time.

2 tbsp	olive oil	25 mL
4 oz	bacon, cut into ½-inch (1 cm) strips	125 g
3 lbs	boneless chunk beef, trimmed and cut into 1½-inch (4 cm) pieces (see Tip, left)	1.5 kg
¼ cup	all-purpose flour	50 mL
	Salt and freshly ground black pepper	
1	onion, chopped	1
1	carrot, chopped	1
3	cloves garlic, finely chopped	3
1 tbsp	tomato paste	15 mL
2 tsp	chopped thyme	10 mL
3 cups	full-bodied red wine	750 mL
1 cup	Beef or Veal Stock (page 55) or ready-to-use broth (approx.)	250 mL
	Sautéed Mushrooms (page 151)	
	Caramelized Pearl Onions (page 151)	
2 tbsp	finely chopped flat-leaf parsley	25 mL

1. In a large heavy pot, heat oil over medium heat. Add bacon pieces and sauté until lightly browned. Remove from heat. With a slotted spoon, transfer bacon to drain on paper towels and set aside.

2. Pat beef dry. Dredge meat pieces with flour; put in a sieve to shake off excess. Discard excess flour. Return pot to medium heat. Add beef pieces and brown well on all sides. You may need to do this in batches, adding more oil if needed. Do not crowd the pan. Season lightly with salt and pepper. Remove and set aside.

3. Add onion and carrot to the pot and sauté until soft, about 5 minutes. Add garlic, tomato paste and thyme and cook, stirring, for 2 minutes. Increase heat to medium-high. Stir in wine and cook, scraping up browned bits on bottom of pot, 3 to 4 minutes.

4. Return beef with any collected juices to the pot with enough stock to cover the meat. Season lightly. Bring to a simmer. Reduce heat to medium-low. Cover and simmer, stirring occasionally, until meat is tender, 1½ to 2 hours. Remove beef from pot with a slotted spoon and set aside while you finish the sauce.

5. Bring sauce to a boil and skim off any fat. Continue to boil and reduce until sauce is richly flavored and of light sauce consistency, 1 to 2 minutes. Taste and adjust seasoning.

6. Return beef and bacon to the pot and add Sautéed Mushrooms and Caramelized Pearl Onions. Gently stir all together to coat with sauce. Let cool. Cover and refrigerate for up to 2 days. About 1 hour before serving, remove pot from refrigerator. Place over medium-low heat or in preheated oven and bring to a simmer. Heat through until meat and vegetables are hot, 30 to 45 minutes. Garnish with parsley.

Sautéed Mushrooms

Serves 6

1 tbsp	olive oil	15 mL
1 lb	cremini mushrooms, whole if small, quartered if large	500 g
	Salt and freshly ground black pepper	

1. In a large skillet, heat oil over medium-high heat. Add mushrooms and sauté until lightly browned, 6 to 8 minutes. Season with salt and pepper to taste. Set aside until needed.

Caramelized Pearl Onions

Serves 6

1 tbsp	olive oil	15 mL
8 oz	pearl onions, peeled	250 g
	Salt and freshly ground black pepper	

1. In a medium saucepan, heat oil over medium-high heat. Add onions and sauté for about 10 minutes, rolling the onions around so that they brown on all sides. Season with salt and pepper. Set aside until needed.

Tex-Mex Chili

We use good quality finely chopped beef instead of ground beef in our basic chili and include a mixture of chiles (jalapeños and chipotles) to boost the flavor. Begin with the smaller amount of heat and adjust to suit your taste. We prefer the texture of dried beans cooked from scratch but canned beans are just fine. Serve with hot Cornbread (page 383) and accompany with your favorite condiments, sour cream and shredded Cheddar cheese. A chili is great party fare, especially for a hoard of ravenous teenagers.

Tip

For convenience, replace cooked beans with 1 can (14 to 19 oz/398 to 540 mL) red kidney or black beans, rinsed and drained.

2 tbsp	vegetable oil	25 mL
2 lbs	boneless chuck beef, finely chopped	1 kg
	Salt and freshly ground black pepper	
2	onions, chopped	2
2	cloves garlic, finely chopped	2
1	jalapeño pepper, seeded and chopped	1
1 to 2 tbsp	chili powder	15 to 25 mL
1 tsp	ground cumin	5 mL
1 tsp	paprika	5 mL
1 tsp	dried oregano	5 mL
1	chipotle pepper in adobo sauce, chopped	1
1 cup	chopped fresh or canned tomatoes	250 mL
1 cup	beer	250 mL
2 cups	Beef Stock (page 55) or ready-to-use broth (approx.)	500 mL
1½ cups	cooked red kidney or black beans (see Tip, left)	375 mL

1. In a large heavy pot, heat oil over medium-high heat. Add beef and brown well on all sides. You may need to do this in batches, adding more oil if needed. Do not crowd pan. Remove from pot. Season lightly with salt and pepper and set aside.

2. Reduce heat to medium. Add onions and sauté until soft and lightly browned, 5 to 6 minutes. Add garlic, jalapeño, chili powder to taste, cumin, paprika and oregano and cook, stirring, 1 to 2 minutes.

3. Return beef to the pot with any collected juices. Stir in chipotle, tomatoes, beer and stock to cover. Bring to a simmer. Reduce heat and simmer, partially covered, stirring occasionally, until beef is tender, 1½ to 2 hours. Add beans and heat through. Taste and adjust seasoning.

Beef Enchiladas

SERVES 4

Tortillas stuffed with grilled beef, chicken or just vegetables are great for a snack or a quick easy supper. They are very forgiving. Use corn or wheat tortillas and include grilled onions, peppers, refried beans and your favorite salsas. Have fiery hot sauce at hand for those who like to spice it up.

- **Preheat oven to 375°F (190°C)**
- **11- by 7-inch (2 L) baking dish**

1	clove garlic, finely chopped	1
1	serrano chile, seeded and finely chopped	1
1 tbsp	freshly squeezed lime juice	15 mL
3 tbsp	vegetable oil, divided	45 mL
1 lb	boneless beef sirloin or skirt steak, 1 inch (2.5 cm) thick	500 g
	Salt and freshly ground black pepper	
2½ cups	Salsa Roja (page 318) or store-bought	625 mL
8	corn tortillas	8
1½ cups	shredded Monterey Jack or mild Cheddar cheese	375 mL
2 tbsp	chopped cilantro	25 mL

1. In a small bowl, combine garlic, chile, lime juice and 1 tbsp (15 mL) of the oil. Pour marinade over steak in a nonreactive container. Cover and refrigerate for at least 1 hour or for up to 8 hours.

2. Remove steak from marinade, discarding marinade. Wipe steak dry, brush lightly with some of the remaining oil and season with salt and pepper. Place a large skillet over medium-high heat, or preheat barbecue grill. Cook steak, turning once, until nicely browned and cooked to your taste, 3 to 4 minutes per side. Set aside. Let rest for 5 minutes. Cut across the grain in thin slices.

3. Spread a thin layer of salsa on the bottom of baking dish. Set aside

4. In a clean skillet, heat 1 tbsp (15 mL) of oil over medium heat. Add tortillas, one at a time, and fry quickly until soft and warm, about 10 seconds per side. Arrange tortillas on your work counter. Spread 2 tbsp (25 mL) of the salsa on each tortilla; top with strips of steak and sprinkle with cheese and cilantro. Roll up and place, seam side down, in the baking dish. Spoon remaining salsa on top and sprinkle with cheese. Bake in preheated oven until heated through and cheese is melted and lightly browned, about 15 minutes.

Beef and Beer Pie

Tip

Do not be deterred from making tasty pies by the (to some ominous) task of making pastry. Flaky Pie Pastry (page 409) can be made ahead and stored in the refrigerator or freezer and many good options for store-bought pastry are available. Flaky pie pastry is available at the market already rolled into pie shells and frozen or in blocks. Thaw the pastry circles and mold or cut them to suit your purpose, if necessary. Frozen puff pastry is available in convenient blocks, with detailed usage instructions on the package. If you are lucky, your local French patisserie may provide you with some all-butter, handmade puff pastry — the taste and texture will be fabulous, so it's worth asking!

● **8- to 10-cup (2 to 2.5 L) baking dish or casserole**

2 oz	double-smoked bacon, cut into ½-inch (1 cm) strips	60 g
¼ cup	all-purpose flour	50 mL
½ tsp	mustard powder	2 mL
2 lbs	boneless chuck beef, cut into 1-inch (2.5 cm) cubes	1 kg
3 tbsp	olive oil, divided	45 mL
	Salt and freshly ground black pepper	
1	onion, chopped	1
2	carrots, chopped into pieces	2
1	leek, white and tender green parts only, sliced (see Tip, page 44)	1
1	clove garlic, chopped	1
1 cup	beer	250 mL
3 to 4 cups	Beef Stock (page 55) or ready-to-use broth	750 mL to 1 L
1 tsp	Worcestershire sauce	5 mL
1 to 2 tsp	brown sugar	5 to 10 mL
2	portobello mushrooms, caps only, chopped into pieces	2
1	potato, peeled and cubed	1
	Puff Pastry or Flaky Pie Pastry (page 409) for single-crust pie	
1	egg, beaten with 1 tsp (5 mL) cold water	1

1. In a large heavy pot, sauté bacon over medium heat until browned, 3 to 4 minutes. Remove from heat. Transfer bacon to drain on paper towels and set aside. Reserve rendered bacon fat in the pot.

2. In a large bowl, combine flour and mustard powder. Toss beef pieces in seasoned flour. Sieve to remove excess flour, discarding excess flour mixture.

3. Add 2 tbsp (25 mL) of the oil to pot with the bacon fat and place over medium-high heat. Add beef, in batches, and brown well on all sides. Do not crowd the pot. Season lightly with salt and pepper. Remove and set aside.

4. Add onion, carrots and leek to the pot and sauté until soft, 5 to 6 minutes. Return beef with any collected juices and bacon to pot. Add garlic and toss for 1 minute. Stir in beer and deglaze pot, scraping up browned bits on the bottom. Add stock to cover and stir in Worcestershire sauce and brown sugar to taste. Bring to a simmer. Reduce heat to low and simmer, partially covered, stirring occasionally, until beef is tender, about $1\frac{1}{2}$ hours.

5. In a skillet, heat 1 tbsp (15 mL) of oil over medium-high heat. Add mushrooms and sauté until nicely browned, 6 to 8 minutes. Add sautéed mushrooms and potato to the stew and simmer for 10 minutes more. Taste and adjust seasoning. Let cool. Refrigerate, covered, if pie is to be assembled later, for up to 3 days.

6. Preheat oven to 350°F (180°C). Transfer beef and vegetables to prepared baking dish. Cover with pastry. Brush surface with egg wash and cut 2 or 3 slits in the top to allow steam to escape. Bake in preheated oven until filling is hot and pastry is golden, 40 to 45 minutes.

Thai Beef Curry

Tip

Red curry paste is a fiery mix of dried red chiles, galangal, lemongrass, garlic and shrimp paste. Seek out a good imported brand widely available in small tins and jars. Add to pork and beef curries for authentic Asian flavor.

2 tbsp	vegetable oil	25 mL
2 lbs	boneless chuck beef, cut into 1-inch (2.5 cm) cubes	1 kg
	Salt and freshly ground black pepper	
2	cloves garlic, finely chopped	2
1 tbsp	grated gingerroot	15 mL
2 tsp	finely chopped lemongrass	10 mL
3 to 4 tbsp	red curry paste (see Tip, left)	45 to 60 mL
2	cans (each 14 oz/400 mL) coconut milk	2
2	wild lime leaves (see Tip, page 45)	2
2 tsp	grated lime zest	10 mL
1 tsp	fish sauce	5 mL
	Beef Stock (page 55) or water, optional	
1	red bell pepper, thinly sliced	1
1 tbsp	chopped Thai basil or cilantro	15 mL

1. In a large heavy pot, heat oil over medium-high heat. Add beef, in batches, and brown well on all sides. Season lightly with salt and pepper. Remove and set aside.
2. Reduce heat to medium. Add garlic, ginger and lemongrass and sauté for 2 to 3 minutes. Stir in curry paste to taste and cook, stirring, 1 to 2 minutes.
3. Return beef to the pot with any collected juices. Add coconut milk, lime leaves, lime zest, fish sauce and stock to cover, if needed. Bring to a boil. Reduce heat and simmer, partially covered, stirring occasionally, until beef is almost tender, $1\frac{1}{2}$ to 2 hours. Add bell pepper and continue to simmer until vegetables are tender, 5 to 8 minutes. Stir in basil. Taste and adjust seasoning.

Mustard

The word comes to us from the grandeur that was Rome — specifically a Roman mix of seeds from the *Sinapis* plant ground with unfermented grape juice, or must (from *Mustum ardens*, burning wine). Voilà, mustard, or as the French prefer it, *moutarde*. The plant itself belongs, like a bastard sibling, to the same family as the self-consciously healthy broccoli, kale and collards, but the hot yellow-brown powder that results offers digestive, antiseptic and laxative benefits of its own. For today's cook, it is second only to peppercorns among North American spices.

Mustard's heat varies greatly with seed type, preparation, and other ingredients such as water, vinegar or wine. Hottest of the seeds is the **black**, used in German *senfs* made around Düsseldorf, Germany's mustard capital, but elsewhere largely displaced, for economic reasons, by the **brown** (popular for pickling). The **white** is a larger seed, and milder. The white and the brown join forces for most English and French mustards. Mustard's pungency is reduced by heat, so if you add it during cooking much of its point will be lost. If bite is what you're after, add late.

At least 20 other cultures make their own mustard varieties, among them Amharic, Hindi, Hebrew, Arabic, Swahili, as well as Russian and Greek.

Mustard as medicine: Heap several tablespoons of powdered mustard into a bowl of boiling water, mix well, bend head over, inhale. Unfailingly clears the sinuses, and often colds as well. From empirical evidence, it really cuts the mustard.

In the Kitchen

English: Synonymous with the trade names Colman's and Keen's, and often in powdered (not prepared) form. Very hot when freshly made; an essential ingredient of the eggs-and-bacon English breakfast. Jeremiah Colman, founder of the company in 1814, once famously explained that it was the mustard people left on their plates that had made him such a wealthy man.

French: Commonly bought as **Dijon** (and in North America as Grey Poupon), after the capital of Burgundy, where the first mustard companies originated in the 14th century. Made with red and white wine, it is milder (and more flavorful) than the English variant (made with vinegar), and despite its name not genetically speaking very French: 90 percent of the seeds in Dijon mustards are imported from Canada, which then pays specialty prices for the product on return.

American: Made from white mustard seed with added sugar and turmeric, giving it its violent yellow hue. Sweeter than most varieties, it is the archetypal **ballpark mustard**. What would a hotdog be without it?

Chinese: Hotter than most, but with the distinctive heat that hits with fission force, and almost as quickly fades away. This is exciting mustard, often found in packages in take-outs. Not to be confused with similarly pungent wasabi, which is Japanese and a form of horseradish.

Honey (aka **Russian**): A blend, often 50/50, of mustard seeds and honey. Wonderful as a sandwich spread, as a dip for finger foods, and as a salad dressing, added to olive oil.

Mustard greens: The peppery dark green leaves of the *Sinapis* plant, right up there with collards as a favorite ingredient of soul food. Steamed, simmered or sautéed, they make a (typically) assertive vegetable side dish, stiff with vitamins A, B and C.

Bison Burgers

MAKES 4 BURGERS

Bison is a very lean and tender meat. We add juiciness to these burgers by inserting a little smoked cheese into the center of each patty.

Tip

The American bison, or buffalo, was near extinction by the late 1890s and a valuable source of sustenance was close to being lost. Today bison is farmed, or bred with beef, and is becoming available in butcher's shops. Bison is similar to beef and may be substituted in most beef recipes. Few folks will recognize the slightly gamy flavor; they will be happy enjoying really flavorful beef.

Variation

Mini Bison Burgers: Form the bison mixture into 12 to 16 mini patties (about 2 inches/5 cm wide and ½ inch/1 cm thick). Reduce grilling time to about 6 minutes, turning once. Brush with warm barbecue sauce. Serve on warm small buns to make a crowd-pleasing party snack.

- **Indoor grill or barbecue, lightly oiled**
- **Preheat grill to medium-high**
- **Instant-read thermometer**

1 lb	ground bison (see Tip, left)	500 g
1	clove garlic, minced	1
2 tsp	Dijon mustard	10 mL
1 tsp	grated fresh horseradish or drained prepared	5 mL
½ tsp	hot pepper sauce	2 mL
	Salt and freshly ground black pepper	
4 tbsp	coarsely shredded smoked Cheddar, Gouda or Mozzarella cheese, divided	60 mL
½ cup	Down-Home Barbecue Sauce (page 159) or your favorite barbecue sauce	125 mL
4	buns, warmed	4

1. In a large bowl, combine ground bison with garlic, mustard, horseradish, hot sauce and salt and pepper to taste. Form mixture into 4 patties, about 1 inch (2.5 cm) thick. Make a hole in each patty and insert 1 tbsp (15 mL) of grated cheese into the center. Press the meat together to enclose the cheese.

2. Grill burgers on preheated prepared grill. Cook for 3 to 4 minutes. Turn and cook until nicely browned and cooked through, 3 to 4 minutes more. An instant-read thermometer should register 160°F (71°C). Brush with warm barbecue sauce and serve on warm buns.

Down-Home Barbecue Sauce

**MAKES ABOUT
4 CUPS (1 L)**

*This basic barbecue sauce
is a family favorite and
used frequently in our
kitchen to glaze sides of
spareribs, chicken wings
and chicken pieces.
Adjust the amount of heat
to your taste with hot
pepper flakes or a dash or
two of hot sauce.*

1 tbsp	vegetable oil	15 mL
1	onion, finely chopped	1
2	cloves garlic, finely chopped	2
½ to 1 tsp	hot pepper flakes	2 to 5 mL
1 tbsp	tomato paste	15 mL
1½ cups	tomato ketchup	375 mL
1 cup	cider vinegar	250 mL
½ cup	packed brown sugar	125 mL
½ cup	light (fancy) molasses	125 mL
¼ cup	Dijon or prepared mustard	50 mL
	Salt and freshly ground pepper	
	Hot pepper sauce, optional	

1. In a saucepan, heat oil over medium heat. Add
   onion and sauté until softened but not browned, 4 to
   5 minutes. Add garlic and hot pepper flakes to taste
   and sauté, 1 to 2 minutes. Add tomato paste and cook,
   stirring, 1 to 2 minutes.

2. Add tomato ketchup, vinegar, brown sugar, molasses,
   mustard, 1 tsp (5 mL) salt and ¼ tsp (1 mL) pepper.
   Stir over medium heat while sugar melts. Reduce heat
   to low and simmer, stirring occasionally, until sauce is
   smooth and thickened to desired consistency, 40 to
   45 minutes. Taste and adjust seasoning. Add a dash or
   two of your favorite hot sauce, if you like.

3. Remove from heat. Let cool and store in covered
   container in the refrigerator for up to 1 month.

Veal Parmigiana

Tender slices of veal in a golden crust of seasoned crumbs is a perennial favorite with our customers. We offer it unadorned with a lemon slice or topped with tomato sauce and cheese, sometimes a slice of provolone or mozzarella and sometimes shaved Parmigiano-Reggiano. As a main dish, accompany with Rosemary Roasted Potatoes (page 297) and Broccoli Rabe with Garlic (page 280), or enjoy a glorious messy sandwich of veal Parmigiana on a crusty bun.

Tip

It is one of our chefs' mantras when breading or coating foods to arrange the breading ingredients in order of use at the "prep" station — dry, wet, dry (e.g. flour, egg, bread crumbs)

Variation

Breaded Pork Cutlets: Use the method in the recipe but substitute thin cutlets of pork for the veal. Increase the baking time until pork is tender and just a hint of pink remains inside, 6 to 8 minutes.

- **Preheat oven to 375°F (190°C)**
- **Baking sheet, lined with parchment paper**

1½ cups	all-purpose flour	375 mL
	Salt and freshly ground black pepper	
5	eggs	5
1½ cups	dry white bread crumbs	375 mL
1 cup	grated Parmesan cheese, preferably Parmigiano-Reggiano	250 mL
¼ cup	coarsely chopped flat-leaf parsley	50 mL
1 tbsp	coarsely chopped oregano	15 mL
1 tbsp	finely chopped rosemary	15 mL
6	slices veal scallopini, pounded thin (each about 5 oz/150 g)	6
1 cup	olive oil, divided	250 mL
2 cups	Chunky Tomato Sauce (page 133) or store-bought	500 mL
⅔ cup	shaved Parmesan cheese, preferably Parmigiano-Reggiano	150 mL

1. On a large platter, combine flour with 1 tbsp (15 mL) salt and ½ tsp (2 mL) pepper. In a large bowl, beat eggs. On another large platter, combine bread crumbs, 1 cup (250 mL) grated cheese, parsley, oregano, rosemary, 1 tbsp (15 mL) salt and ½ tsp (2 mL) pepper. Arrange items in front of you on the counter from left to right in order of flour, eggs, bread crumb mixture (see Tip, left).

2. Working with one veal scallopini at a time, coat in flour and then dip into beaten egg and let any excess drip back into bowl. Cover veal with seasoned bread crumbs, pressing crumbs in place to form a crust. Transfer to a rack. Repeat with the rest of the veal scallopini. Discard any excess flour, egg and bread crumb mixtures.

3. Heat a large skillet over medium-high heat. Add $\frac{1}{4}$ cup (50 mL) of the olive oil. When the oil starts to shimmer, add 1 or 2 veal scallopini to the pan. Cook until the bottom is golden brown, 2 to 3 minutes. Turn veal over and cook until golden on the other side, 3 to 4 minutes. Add more oil to the pan as needed. Transfer browned veal to prepared baking sheet. Repeat with browning the rest of the scallopini.

4. Bake in preheated oven until veal is cooked through and tender when tested, 5 to 7 minutes.

5. Serve hot with Chunky Tomato Sauce and shaved Parmigiano-Reggiano.

Osso Buco with Gremolata

Veal shanks braised in a rich tomato and onion sauce is a classic dish, originating in Milan. Ask your butcher for center shanks, cut about 1½ inches (4 cm) thick with nice nuggets of meat attached — ones that will provide delicious bites of bone marrow to enrich the sauce.

The traditional final touch to the dish is a garnish of Gremolata — finely chopped fresh garlic, lemon zest and parsley. Serve over creamy polenta. Use also to add instant fresh flavor to vegetable soups or simply grilled vegetables such as green beans or asparagus.

Variation

Bison Osso Buco: Follow the recipe but prepare with meaty center cuts of bison shank in place of veal. Cooking time will be the same.

● 8-quart (8 L) heavy pot

¼ cup	all-purpose flour	50 mL
	Salt and freshly ground black pepper	
6	meaty veal shank slices, 1½ inches (4 cm) thick	6
5 tbsp	olive oil, divided	75 mL
8 cups	Chicken Stock (page 54) or ready-to-use broth, divided	2 L
1	carrot, quartered	1
2	cloves garlic	2
1	onion, quartered	1
2	stalks celery, quartered	2
1	leek, quartered	1
12	sprigs flat-leaf parsley	12
6	sprigs thyme	6
3	bay leaves	3
1 tsp	black peppercorns	5 mL
1	shallot, minced	1
1	clove garlic, minced	1
2 tbsp	tomato paste	15 mL
½ cup	red wine	125 mL
1 tbsp	butter	15 mL
	Creamy Polenta (Variation, page 308)	
	Gremolata (page 163)	

1. On a large platter, combine flour with 1 tsp (5 mL) salt and ¼ tsp (1 mL) pepper. Toss veal shanks in seasoned flour. Sieve to remove excess, discarding excess flour.

2. In a large skillet, heat ¼ cup (50 mL) of the oil over medium-high heat. Add veal shanks, a few at a time, and sear on all sides until golden. Remove and set aside. Discard excess fat from pan and deglaze with ½ cup (125 mL) of the chicken stock, scraping up browned bits on the bottom.

3. Place veal shanks in a large pot with carrot, whole garlic, onion, celery, leek, parsley, thyme, bay leaves, peppercorns, remaining chicken stock and 1 tsp (5 mL) salt and a pinch of pepper. Bring to a boil over medium heat. Reduce heat to low. Cover pot and simmer until veal is very tender, $1\frac{1}{2}$ to 2 hours. Check pot occasionally and adjust heat so that meat braises at gentle pace.

4. Carefully remove veal from pot with a slotted spoon. Set aside. Strain braising liquid into a large bowl and reserve. Discard vegetables.

5. In same large pot, heat remaining oil over medium heat. Add shallot and minced garlic and sauté until softened, 2 to 3 minutes. Add tomato paste and cook, stirring, for 30 seconds. Deglaze pan with wine, scraping up browned bits on the bottom, and boil and reduce to a syrupy glaze. Add reserved braising liquid. Increase heat to medium-high and simmer sauce until reduced and slightly thickened. Taste and adjust seasoning. Whisk in butter. Reheat veal gently in the sauce. Serve each veal shank in a large deep bowl over polenta, add a ladle-full of sauce and a generous sprinkling of Gremolata.

Gremolata

Makes 3 tbsp (45 mL)

$\frac{1}{2}$	lemon	$\frac{1}{2}$
3	sprigs flat-leaf parsley	3
2	cloves garlic	2

1. Using a vegetable peeler, remove yellow zest from lemon. Slice peel into very thin strips and chop strips into very fine pieces. Set aside. Trim leaves from parsley and chop finely. Finely chop garlic.

2. Combine zest, parsley and garlic and chop all together until very fine.

Veal Medallions with Orange Mustard Sauce

Tender slices of veal with a sweet, fruity glaze are excellent served with roasted fingerling potatoes and grilled asparagus. This dish is prepared in minutes and is at its best when hot from the pan.

Variation

Blood oranges, navel oranges, tangerines, lemons all have wonderful distinct flavors, and their sweetness changes throughout the season. Vary the flavor of the sauce by using different varieties and combinations of citrus.

1½ lbs	veal tenderloin, cut into 6 medallions	750 g
	Salt and freshly ground black pepper	
3 tbsp	butter, divided	45 mL
¼ cup	minced shallots	50 mL
2 tbsp	cognac or brandy	25 mL
¼ cup	freshly squeezed orange juice	50 mL
2 tbsp	grainy Dijon mustard	25 mL
¼ cup	Chicken Stock (page 54) or ready-to-use broth	50 mL
2 tbsp	finely chopped flat-leaf parsley	25 mL

1. Season veal lightly with salt and pepper.
2. Place a large skillet over medium-high heat. Add 2 tbsp (25 mL) of the butter and heat until melted and foam subsides. Add veal, in batches if necessary, and sear until golden brown, 3 to 4 minutes. Do not crowd pan. Turn veal over and brown the other side, 2 to 3 minutes more. Set aside on a warm platter, loosely covered with foil.
3. Add remaining butter to pan. Add shallots and sauté until softened, 2 minutes. Deglaze pan with cognac — either flambé or cook briskly until liquid reduces slightly. Add orange juice. Stir in mustard and chicken stock. Simmer until sauce coats the back of a spoon, 3 to 4 minutes (see Tip, page 174). Add parsley. Taste and adjust seasoning. Drizzle sauce over veal medallions.

Pork and Lamb

Roast Pork Loin with Fresh Herb Spiral

A simple pork roast is made special by the spiral of fresh herbs coiled through the center. Serve with Brussels Sprouts with Pancetta and Cream (page 284) and crispy Rosemary Roasted Potatoes (page 297). It's delicious thinly sliced and served cold and makes a dynamite sandwich.

Variation

Roast Pork Loin with Chèvre and Sun-Dried Tomato Spiral: Follow the recipe but substitute the Chèvre and Sun-Dried Tomato stuffing (page 102) for the fresh herb mixture.

- **Preheat oven to 325°F (160°C)**
- **Butcher's string**
- **Large roasting pan**
- **Instant-read thermometer**

3 lbs	boneless pork loin roast	1.5 kg
½ cup	coarsely chopped flat-leaf parsley	125 mL
¼ cup	toasted pine nuts	50 mL
2 tbsp	grated lemon zest	25 mL
4 tsp	coarsely chopped thyme	20 mL
2 tsp	minced garlic	10 mL
	Salt and freshly ground black pepper	
4 tbsp	olive oil, divided	60 mL
1½ tsp	freshly ground black pepper, divided	7 mL

1. Lay pork loin on a cutting board perpendicular to your body. Take a very sharp chef's knife and make an incision in the loin about ½ inch (1 cm) from the cutting board along the length of the loin. Using long fluid cuts continue slicing into the loin carefully maintaining the same thickness all the while, unrolling the loin as you cut to create a flat piece of meat.

2. In a small bowl, combine parsley, pine nuts, lemon zest, thyme, garlic and 1 tsp (5 mL) of the salt and ½ tsp (2 mL) of the pepper. Add 2 tbsp (25 mL) of the oil and mix to a paste consistency.

3. Spread an even layer of herb mixture over the pork. Roll the loin back to its original shape, creating a spiral of herbs throughout the meat. Use butcher's string to tie the loin into a neat package (see Techniques, page 18).

4. In a large skillet, heat remaining oil over medium-high heat. Add pork loin, fat side down, and sear, turning often, until golden brown on all sides, 3 to 4 minutes per side. Transfer to a roasting pan and season lightly. Roast in preheated oven until pork is tender and an instant-read thermometer inserted into the thickest part of the meat registers 155°F (68°F) for medium, about $1\frac{1}{4}$ hours. Temperature will increase during resting period to recommended 160°F (71°C). Continue to roast longer, if necessary. Let roast stand, tented with foil, for 8 to 10 minutes before carving.

Roast Pork with Apricot-Walnut Stuffing

SERVES 6

This roast of pork is given special treatment with a tasty fruit and nut stuffing and a light, fruity glaze. This is family celebration fare. Serve with crisp Rosemary Roasted Potatoes (page 297) and Broccoli Rabe with Garlic (page 280). The stuffed loin can be prepared ahead and refrigerated for a day, or you could, of course, ask your friendly butcher to do it for you!

- **Preheat oven to 400°F (200°C)**
- **Butcher's string**
- **Instant-read thermometer**

3 lbs	boneless pork loin roast	1.5 kg
	Salt and freshly ground black pepper	
	Apricot-Walnut Stuffing (page 169)	

Apricot Glaze

3 tbsp	apricot jam	45 mL
1 tbsp	freshly squeezed lemon juice	15 mL
2 tbsp	olive oil	25 mL
½ cup	dry white wine	125 mL
½ cup	Vegetable or Chicken Stock (pages 56 and 54) or ready-to-use broth	125 mL

1. With a chef's knife, cut lines in the fat layer covering the meat at an angle all the way along the loin up to about ¼ inch (0.5 cm) of the flesh. Cut lines perpendicular to the first cuts at the same depth all the way along the loin to create a cross-hatch pattern. This helps to release the fat and assist in browning.

2. Place meat, fat side down, on a cutting board perpendicular to your body. Cut down the centre of the loin, halfway through the flesh. Cut from the center to the right of the loin through the flesh to within 1 inch (2.5 cm) of the edge. Repeat from the center to the left side. Open out the cut pork and press lightly to flatten. Season with salt and pepper.

3. Arrange Apricot-Walnut Stuffing down center of pork loin. Carefully bring both sides up and over stuffing and overlap to make a neat roll. Tie securely with string (see Techniques, page 18).

4. *Apricot Glaze:* In a small saucepan over low heat, combine apricot jam, lemon juice and 1 tbsp (15 mL) water. Set aside and keep warm.

5. In a large ovenproof skillet, heat oil over high heat. Add loin, fat side down, and sear undisturbed until the fat is golden brown, about 2 minutes. Turn and brown on all sides.

6. Transfer pan to preheated oven. Reduce heat to 325°F (160°C). After about 30 minutes, brush meat with warm Apricot Glaze and pan juices. Continue to roast pork, basting occasionally with Apricot Glaze, until an instant-read thermometer registers 155°F (68°C) for medium, about 1¼ hours. Temperature will increase during resting period to recommended 160°F (71°C) Transfer to a platter and let stand, loosely tented with foil, 8 to 10 minutes before carving.

7. Pour off and discard fat in roasting pan. Add white wine and deglaze pan, scraping up browned bits on bottom. Add stock and any juices collected from the meat on the platter. Bring to a boil, stirring constantly, 1 to 2 minutes. Season with salt and pepper to taste. Strain pan juices through a small sieve, if you like, and serve with the roast loin.

Apricot-Walnut Stuffing

Makes 1½ cups (375 mL)

3 tbsp	butter	45 mL
¼ cup	coarsely chopped shallots	50 mL
2 tbsp	finely diced celery	25 mL
1	clove garlic, minced	1
½ cup	dried apricots, diced	125 mL
½ cup	lightly toasted walnuts, chopped	125 mL
½ cup	diced day-old bread	125 mL
1 tbsp	coarsely chopped thyme	15 mL
1 tbsp	grated lemon zest	15 mL
1½ tsp	kosher or sea salt	7 mL
½ tsp	freshly ground black pepper	2 mL

1. In a large skillet, melt butter over medium heat. Add shallots, celery and garlic and sauté until softened but not browned, 4 to 5 minutes. Let cool briefly. Stir in apricots, walnuts, bread, thyme, lemon zest, salt and pepper.

Pork Chops with Apples and Onions

SERVES 4

This dish will bring comfort when chilly winds blow. Pork is particularly good when cooked on the bone and benefits from diligent basting in a fruity sauce. Serve with fluffy roasted garlic mashed potatoes and simple steamed Brussels sprouts or green beans.

2 tbsp	butter	25 mL
1 tbsp	olive oil	15 mL
4	pork loin chops, bone-in, each about 1 inch (2.5 cm) thick	4
	Salt and freshly ground black pepper	
1	clove garlic, finely chopped	1
2	sprigs thyme	2
1 cup	medium-dry white wine or unsweetened cider	250 mL
1	Vidalia or Spanish onion, thinly sliced	1
1	large apple, sliced in wedges	1
½ cup	whipping (35%) cream	125 mL
2 tbsp	chopped flat-leaf parsley	25 mL

1. In a large skillet, heat butter and oil over medium-high heat. Add pork chops, in batches, if necessary. Do not crowd the pan. Sprinkle with a pinch of salt and pepper and brown evenly on both sides, about 10 minutes. Add garlic, thyme and wine.

2. Add onion and apple slices and toss in the savory juices. Cover, reduce heat and cook at a gentle simmer until chops are tender and just a hint of pink remains inside, 10 to 15 minutes.

3. Transfer pork chops, apples and onions to a platter. Increase heat and boil cooking juices until reduced to about 1 cup (250 mL). Reduce heat to medium. Slowly stir in cream and simmer until sauce is thickened. Taste and adjust seasoning. Return pork, apples and onions to the pan and coat with sauce. Garnish with chopped parsley.

Pork with Chile Verde Sauce

SERVES 6

A robust stew with south-of-the-border flavors. Serve with rice and beans and Cornbread (page 383) or wrap in a wheat tortilla or Socca (chickpea flour crêpe) (page 243).

3½ lbs	pork shoulder or pork butt	1.75 kg
	Salt and freshly ground black pepper	
2 tbsp	vegetable oil	25 mL
1 lb	tomatillos (see Tips, left)	500 g
1	onion, chopped	1
1 tbsp	minced garlic	15 mL
3	jalapeño peppers, seeded and minced	3
1	green bell pepper, chopped	1
5	pieces cilantro root, scrubbed and coarsely chopped (see Tips, left)	5
2 cups	Chicken Stock (page 54) or ready-to-use broth	500 mL
2 cups	coarsely chopped cilantro	500 mL

Tips

A tomatillo looks like a small green tomato, wrapped in a papery husk. It is harvested when still green and tart. It was originally cultivated by the Aztecs and is used to add sharp flavor to Mexican stews and salsas. You'll find it fresh at produce markets and preserved in cans. When using fresh tomatillos in salsas and dressings, remove husks and simmer in water until they soften and turn olive green, then roughly chop or purée.

Cilantro, or fresh coriander, is the leafy herb with distinctive aroma and flavor used extensively in Mexican, Asian and Indian cooking. It is available in big bunches at the market, often with small root attached. You either love it, or you hate it. There are some who can detect and reject even the smallest pinch! There is no substitute. If you are among the rejecters, use flat-leaf parsley to add color and fresh taste, but the resulting dish will be different. Coriander is the seed of the plant, available in whole seed form and as a ground spice used extensively in curries.

1. Trim pork and cut into 1-inch (2.5 cm) pieces. Lightly season with salt and pepper.

2. In a heavy pot, heat oil over medium-high heat. Add pork, in batches, and sear on all sides until golden brown. Do not crowd the pot. Remove pork and set aside. Reserve 2 tbsp (25 mL) fat in pot, discarding the rest.

3. Remove outer papery skin from tomatillos and cut in half or quarters, depending on size.

4. Add onion to the pot and sauté in reserved fat for 4 to 5 minutes. Add tomatillos, garlic, jalapeños, bell pepper, cilantro root and salt and pepper to taste and sauté for 1 to 2 minutes. Stir in chicken stock and deglaze pot, scraping up the browned bits on the bottom. Return pork to the pot with all the collected juices.

5. Bring to a gentle simmer and cook, partially covered, until pork is tender, 25 to 30 minutes. Remove from heat. Taste and adjust seasoning. Serve garnished with chopped cilantro.

Grilled Pork Kebabs with Tzatziki

MAKES 6 KEBABS

A short period in a simple marinade of lemon and herbs does wonders for pork. We like to use dried leaf oregano imported from Greece in rubs and marinades. It has a flavor all its own — especially if you find a market that imports it in season.

The summery cucumber-yogurt dip is the perfect accompaniment. Enjoy it with grilled pork, chicken or lamb and serve as part of a Mediterranean dip selection with kalamata olives and warm grilled pita breads.

- **Barbecue grill or indoor grill**
- **Six 8-inch (20 cm) bamboo skewers, soaked in water for 30 minutes**

½ cup	olive oil	125 mL
2 tbsp	freshly squeezed lemon juice	25 mL
1 tsp	dried oregano	5 mL
½ tsp	freshly ground black pepper	2 mL
2	cloves garlic, minced	2
1¼ lbs	pork tenderloin, trimmed and cut into 1-inch (2.5 cm) cubes	625 g
	Salt and freshly ground black pepper	
	Tzatziki (see below)	

1. In a large bowl, mix together oil, lemon juice, oregano, black pepper and garlic. Add pork and toss to combine. Refrigerate, covered, at least for 2 hours or overnight.

2. Preheat barbecue grill to medium-high and lightly oil the grill.

3. Arrange pork pieces evenly on skewers, discarding marinade, and season lightly with salt and pepper. Set aside.

4. Arrange kebabs on grill. Grill for 2 minutes without moving so that the underside sears and does not stick. Turn and grill until all sides are nicely caramelized and pork is tender, 6 to 8 minutes. Serve hot with Tzatziki on the side.

Tzatziki

Makes about 2 cups (500 mL)

2 cups	plain yogurt	500 mL
½	English cucumber	½
	Kosher or sea salt	
2	cloves garlic, minced	2
1 tbsp	minced shallot	15 mL
1 tbsp	finely chopped dill	15 mL
1 tbsp	finely chopped mint	15 mL
2 tsp	freshly squeezed lemon juice	10 mL

1. Line a sieve with a damp coffee filter or cheesecloth and set over a small bowl. Spoon yogurt into sieve, cover and let drain in the refrigerator, 2 to 3 hours or overnight. Discard the whey.

2. Peel cucumber, cut lengthwise and scoop out seeds. Finely chop or grate. Sprinkle with $\frac{1}{4}$ tsp (1 mL) salt and set aside for 1 hour. Squeeze out and discard excess liquid.

3. In a bowl, combine yogurt, cucumber, garlic, shallot, dill, mint and lemon juice. Refrigerate for several hours for flavors to blend. Taste and adjust seasoning. Serve chilled.

Yogurt Tips

One of my most memorable taste experiences was in a hotel in Porta Carras in Northern Greece. I was participating in a conference orchestrated by Oldways (a healthy food educational and advocacy group founded in Boston) to celebrate the food and social customs of Greece. The breakfast buffet included giant bowls filled with creamy, thick, unbelievably pure-tasting yogurt, bowls of thyme-scented honey and honey sweet apricots. I was in heaven!

Yogurt in our markets suffers the fate of mass production. Many varieties are stuffed with stabilizers, thickeners and sweeteners. You will find the fat content ranges anywhere from 0 to 10%. Seek out small dairies that make natural yogurt the traditional way — just pure milk and natural cultures. Both whole-milk and low-fat yogurt have a sweet natural flavor, delicious to enjoy as is or to use in sauces and to garnish soups. Non-fat yogurt tends to be thin and bitter; flavor and consistency improves if you place it in a sieve overnight to drain off the whey. Enrich hot stews, curries and sauces by adding yogurt at the end of the cooking period over low heat to prevent it from separating; do not boil.

Pork Medallions with Dijon Cream Sauce

Tip

"The spoon test" is a chef's way to judge the thickening of a sauce or a reduction. If sauce runs off the back of a spoon it is still too thin. If sauce clings to the back of a spoon so that when you run your finger through the sauce it holds its shape, then it has reached light sauce consistency.

Variation

Omit mustard in the Dijon Cream Sauce and season to serve in a variety of dishes. Add chopped dill to serve with fish. Add chopped tarragon to serve with roast chicken. Add a pinch of saffron to serve with shellfish.

1 lb	pork tenderloin	500 g
2 tbsp	extra virgin olive oil	25 mL
	Salt and freshly ground black pepper	
	Dijon Cream Sauce (see below)	

1. Trim tenderloin of any fat or silverskin. Cut into 12 equal pieces, about $\frac{1}{2}$ inch (1 cm) thick. Place the pieces between plastic wrap and pound to a thickness of $\frac{1}{4}$ inch (0.5 cm).

2. In a large skillet, heat oil over medium-high heat. Add pork, a few slices at a time, and sauté until golden, 2 to 3 minutes per side. Season with a little salt and pepper while cooking. Serve with Dijon Cream Sauce.

Dijon Cream Sauce

Makes 1$\frac{2}{3}$ cups (400 mL)

2 tsp	vegetable oil	10 mL
$\frac{1}{2}$	onion, roughly chopped	$\frac{1}{2}$
1	clove garlic, smashed	1
1	sprig thyme	1
5 to 6	black peppercorns	5 to 6
$\frac{1}{2}$ cup	dry white wine	125 mL
2 cups	whipping (35%) cream	500 mL
	Salt	
2 tbsp	Dijon mustard	25 mL
1 tsp	chopped thyme	5 mL

1. In a saucepan, heat oil over medium heat. Add onion, garlic, thyme and peppercorns and sauté until onions are softened but not browned, 4 to 5 minutes. Add wine and boil until reduced to 2 to 3 tbsp (25 to 45 mL) of syrupy glaze.

2. Stir in cream. Reduce heat and simmer gently until cream is lightly thickened, 20 to 25 minutes (see Tip, left). Strain.

3. Add mustard and chopped thyme. Taste and adjust seasoning.

Sausage with Fennel and Potato

Here's a tasty, quick skillet supper. Include sweet or hot sausage according to your preference. Serve with warm crusty bread or Cornbread (page 383).

4 tbsp	olive oil, divided	60 mL
4 to 5	Italian sausages, 1¼ lbs (625 g)	4 to 5
1	red onion, thinly sliced	1
1	bulb fennel, thinly sliced	1
3	cloves garlic, minced	3
2	large tomatoes, seeded and cut into ¼-inch (0.5 cm) slices	2
2	Yukon Gold potatoes, diced (about 2 cups/500 mL)	2
1 tsp	fennel seeds	5 mL
	Salt and freshly ground black pepper	
⅔ cup	dry white wine	150 mL
⅔ cup	Chicken Stock (page 54) or ready-to-use broth or water	150 mL
¼ cup	coarsely chopped flat-leaf parsley	50 mL

1. In a large skillet, heat 1 tbsp (15 mL) of the oil over medium-high heat. Add sausages and cook until golden on all sides, 5 to 10 minutes. Remove from pan and set aside.

2. Add remaining oil to pan and reduce heat to medium. Add red onion and fennel and sauté until beginning to soften and color, 5 to 6 minutes. Add garlic and sauté for 1 minute. Add tomatoes, potatoes, fennel seeds, 1 tsp (5 mL) salt and ¼ tsp (1 mL) pepper. Add white wine and deglaze pan, scraping up browned bits on the bottom. Stir in stock.

3. Return browned sausages to pan. Reduce heat to low. Cover and simmer until sausages and vegetables are cooked through and tender, 25 to 35 minutes. Taste and adjust seasoning. Garnish with parsley.

Pork Tenderloin with Apple Fennel Chutney

SERVES 6

Pork tenderloin is a tender, fast-cooking cut of pork. It is also very low in fat. There is a problem however cooking the whole tenderloin — the thin pointed end gets dry and overcooked before the thicker portion is ready. One simple solution is to make an incision across the tenderloin at the thinner tip and tuck it underneath and tie with butcher's string.

As with all chutneys, this apple and fennel one is best made ahead so that flavors have time to blend. It is a delicious condiment to serve with pork or duck and dynamite when paired with aged Cheddar cheese.

- Preheat oven to 400°F (200°C)
- Butcher's string
- Large ovenproof skillet
- Instant-read thermometer

2	pork tenderloins (each 12 oz to 1 lb/375 to 500 g)	2
2 tbsp	olive oil	25 mL
1 tbsp	butter	15 mL
	Salt and freshly ground black pepper	
	Apple and Fennel Chutney (page 177)	

1. Trim tenderloins of any fat or silverskin. Lay on a cutting board. Make a shallow incision across the tenderloin at the point where the meat flares into the thickest part, tuck the thin end underneath and tie with butcher's string.

2. In large ovenproof skillet, heat oil and butter over medium-high heat. Lightly season pork on all sides with salt and pepper and add to pan, one at a time, if necessary. Do not crowd pan. Cook, undisturbed, to develop a good crust, for 2 minutes. Turn pork over to sear on all sides.

3. Transfer pan to preheated oven. Roast until an instant-read thermometer registers 155°F (68°C), about 5 minutes. (The internal temperature will rise 5° to 10°F/3° to 6°C during the resting period to the recommended 160°F/71°C). Let stand, loosely covered with foil, before slicing, about 5 minutes. Serve warm, cut on the diagonal into ½-inch (1 cm) slices and accompanied by warm Apple and Fennel Chutney.

Apple and Fennel Chutney

Makes 3 cups (750 mL)

¼ cup	apple cider vinegar	50 mL
¼ cup	natural rice vinegar	50 mL
1¼ cups	packed brown sugar	300 mL
1	bulb fennel, finely chopped	1
3	shallots, minced	3
2	cloves garlic, minced	2
½ tsp	ground cinnamon	2 mL
½ tsp	paprika, hot or sweet	2 mL
½ tsp	Chinese five-spice powder (see below)	2 mL
¼ tsp	fennel seeds	1 mL
	Salt and freshly ground black pepper	
3	apples, cut into ½-inch (1 cm) cubes	3

1. In a large heavy-bottomed pot over medium-low heat, combine apple and rice vinegars and brown sugar, stirring until sugar dissolves. Add fennel, shallots, garlic, cinnamon, paprika, five-spice powder, fennel seeds, 1 tsp (5 mL) salt and ¼ tsp (1 mL) pepper. Bring gently to a boil. Reduce heat and simmer for 20 minutes.

2. Add apples and simmer over low heat until apples are tender, about 25 minutes. Taste and adjust seasoning. Set aside and let cool. Store in a covered container in the refrigerator for up to 2 weeks. For longer storage, pour hot chutney into sterilized jars and seal. Serve warm or at room temperature.

Five-Spice Powder

Spread 1 tbsp (15 mL) Szechwan peppers, 8 star anise, 6 whole cloves, 1 piece (2 inches/5 cm) cinnamon stick, crushed, and 1 tbsp (15 mL) fennel seeds on a baking sheet. Toast in 250°F (120°C) oven until aromas are released, about 20 minutes. Let cool. In a spice mill, combine spices and 1 tsp (5 mL) black peppercorns and grind to a fine powder. Store in a covered container in a cool spot for up to 6 months. Makes ¼ cup (50 mL).

Baked Ham with Citrus Glaze

SERVES 12 TO 14

We are fortunate that we live close to a rural area where local small producers supply us with hams of outstanding flavor and texture, prepared and smoked following traditional custom. A ham is a taste treat that is part of many a joyful gathering. Serve it warm, accompanied by Potato Gratin with Leek and Double-Smoked Bacon (page 298) and platters of grilled asparagus, or serve at room temperature with an array of salads such as Grilled Corn and Lima Bean Salad (page 83), Tuscan Pepper and Tomato Salad (page 61) or Spanish Grilled Potato Salad (page 70).

- Preheat oven to 325°F (160°C)
- Large roasting pan
- Pastry brush
- Instant-read thermometer

1	bone-in cooked ham (about 12 lbs/5 kg)	1
15	whole cloves (approx.)	15
	Citrus Glaze (page 179)	

1. If the ham has a rough, leathery skin on the surface, shave it off using a sharp knife until the layer of white fat is exposed. Score the fat to within about $1/2$ inch (1 cm) of the flesh, making even strokes all in one direction in lines about $3/4$ inch (2 cm) apart. Repeat making strokes perpendicular to the first cuts to form a pattern of squares. Press a whole clove into the fat in the center of each square.

2. Place ham in a large roasting pan and add 2 cups (500 mL) water. Bake in preheated oven for about 15 minutes per pound (500 g) or until an instant-read thermometer registers 140°F (60°C), about 3 hours. Begin basting liberally with Citrus Glaze after 2 hours and baste every 15 minutes or so until done. Rotate the roasting pan to ensure even coloring. Let stand for 10 minutes before carving.

> **Pork Notes**
> Most commercially raised pigs today are bred and fed to grow and put on weight quickly. They produce very lean meat from large lean muscles with only a thin layer of fat. Today's pork tends to dry out very quickly during cooking and hams have to be given all kinds of flavor boosts to have any taste at all! Cook over medium heat and do not overcook. Seek out butchers who provide pork from local farmers who raise pigs on a smaller scale. Such prized breeds as Berkshire produce pork with a fine-grain marbling of fat so that the meat stays moist, juicy and flavorful. Every mouthful is succulent and tasty. You will be amazed and delighted.

Citus Glaze

Makes 1²⁄₃ cups (400 mL)

1 tbsp	minced gingerroot	15 mL
1 tbsp	grated orange zest	15 mL
2 tsp	grated lemon zest	10 mL
2 tsp	grated lime zest	10 mL
1 tbsp	minced shallots	15 mL
	Juice of 3 oranges (about ¾ cup/175 mL)	
	Juice of 2 lemons (about ½ cup/125 mL)	
	Juice of 2 limes (about ¼ cup/50 mL)	
1 cup	packed brown sugar	250 mL
3 tbsp	grainy Dijon mustard	45 mL
1 tsp	kosher or sea salt	5 mL
½ tsp	freshly ground black pepper	2 mL
2 tbsp	bourbon or rum, optional	25 mL

1. In a small saucepan over medium-high heat, combine ginger, orange, lemon and lime zests, shallots and orange, lemon and lime juices. Bring to a boil. Reduce heat and simmer until juices are reduced by one-third, about 1 cup (250 mL).

2. Stir in brown sugar, mustard, salt and pepper. Heat briefly to dissolve sugar. Stir in bourbon, if using.

Barbecued Pulled Pork

The secret to great pulled pork is slow cooking in a knock-your-socks-off sauce until pork is tender and juicy. Use the shredded seasoned pork in sandwiches, burritos or with hash browns or rice and beans.

Tip

Have the makings of a great sandwich on hand. Cool shredded pork and store in a covered container in the refrigerator for up to 3 days or freeze for up to 1 month for longer storage. Store the tangy sauce in a separate container and refrigerate up to 1 month. Combine and reheat before serving.

Variation

Barbecued Pulled Pork Sandwich: Slice crusty rolls in half. Pile shredded pork on bottom half of each roll and top with a slice of smoked Cheddar cheese. Press top half of roll in place. Arrange on a baking sheet and bake in preheated 325°F (160°C) oven until cheese is melted. Serve hot with lots of napkins.

1 tbsp	olive oil	15 mL
2 tsp	minced garlic	10 mL
1½ tsp	ground cumin	7 mL
1½ tsp	ground coriander	7 mL
1 tsp	ground cinnamon	5 mL
½ tsp	ground allspice	2 mL
4 lbs	boneless pork shoulder blade (butt)	2 kg
1 cup	Chipotle Barbecue Sauce (page 181) or your favorite barbecue sauce	250 mL
1½ cups	natural rice vinegar	375 mL
1 cup	apple cider vinegar	250 mL
1 cup	canned tomatoes with juice, chopped	250 mL
1 tbsp	kosher or sea salt	15 mL
1½ tsp	freshly ground black pepper	7 mL

1. In a small bowl, mix together oil, garlic, cumin, coriander, cinnamon and allspice. Rub spice mix all over pork and set aside, covered, in the refrigerator for at least 1 hour or overnight.

2. Preheat oven to 325°F (160°C).

3. In a bowl, combine barbecue sauce, 1½ cups (375 mL) water, rice and cider vinegars, tomatoes with juice, salt and black pepper.

4. Place marinated pork in a large heavy-bottomed pot and add barbecue sauce mixture. Bring to a simmer over medium-high heat. Cover and bake in preheated oven, basting every 15 to 20 minutes with spicy cooking liquid, removing lid after first hour, until pork is very tender, 2½ to 3 hours. Do not let the sauce bubble too vigorously during cooking. Reduce heat to 300°F (150°C), if necessary. Remove pork from pot and, when cool enough to handle, shred into bite-size pieces. Set aside.

5. Meanwhile, skim off fat from braising liquid and place over medium-high heat. Boil until reduced to barbecue sauce consistency, about 45 minutes, stirring often as the sauce gets thick. Combine shredded pork with reduced braising liquid. Taste and adjust seasoning.

Chipotle Barbecue Sauce

*Use this sauce when
you're wanting to add a
touch of heat and sweet,
spicy undertones to your
grilled or roasted chicken
or pork.*

2 tbsp	olive oil	25 mL
1	onion, finely chopped	1
2	cloves garlic, finely chopped	2
½ tsp	ground coriander	2 mL
¼ tsp	ground cloves	1 mL
¼ cup	tomato paste	50 mL
2	canned chipotle peppers in adobo sauce, drained and finely chopped	2
1 to 2 tbsp	adobo sauce from chipotles	15 to 25 mL
1 cup	beer	250 mL
¾ cup	natural rice vinegar	175 mL
½ cup	packed brown sugar	125 mL
½ cup	light (fancy) molasses	125 mL
	Salt and freshly ground pepper	

1. In a saucepan, heat oil over medium heat. Add onion and sauté until softened but not browned, 4 to 5 minutes. Add garlic, coriander and cloves and sauté, 1 to 2 minutes. Add tomato paste, chipotles and adobo sauce to taste and cook, stirring, 1 to 2 minutes.

2. Add beer, vinegar, brown sugar, molasses, 1 cup (250 mL) water, 1 tsp (5 mL) salt and ¼ tsp (1 mL) pepper. Stir over medium heat while sugar melts. Reduce heat to low and simmer, stirring occasionally, until sauce is smooth and thickened to desired consistency, 40 to 45 minutes. Taste and adjust seasoning.

3. Remove from heat. Let cool and store in covered container in the refrigerator for up to 1 month.

Hoisin-Glazed Pork Back Ribs

Tip

When are ribs ready? Ribs with meat falling off the bone are overdone! Cook until meat shrinks from the ends of the bones and easily pulls away from the bone but with some resistance left. A tip from a grill-meister: Use two sets of tongs and grab the rib rack at each end. Gently bend it: if it splits easily in two, the ribs are ready.

Variations

Roasted Pork Ribs: Follow Step 1, then arrange cooked ribs in a single layer in one or two roasting pans. Brush ribs on both sides with barbecue sauce. Bake in 350°F (180°C) oven for 15 minutes. Remove from oven and baste both sides again with sauce. Continue baking until ribs are moist, tender and nicely glazed, about 10 minutes more. Let ribs stand, loosely covered with foil, for 5 minutes. In a small saucepan, heat remaining barbecue sauce to serve alongside.

Other good glazes for ribs are Spicy Orange Sauce (page 187) and Chipotle Barbecue Sauce (page 181).

- **Large roasting pan**
- **Preheat oven to 300°F (150°C)**
- **Barbecue grill or indoor grill**

6 lbs	pork back ribs	3 kg
1	onion, quartered	1
4	stalks celery, halved	4
2	carrots, cut into thirds	2
4	bay leaves	4
¼ cup	coarsely chopped thyme	50 mL
2 tbsp	coarse sea salt	25 mL
1 tbsp	black peppercorns	15 mL
1 tsp	whole cloves	5 mL
2 cups	Hoisin Barbecue Sauce, divided (page 183)	500 mL

1. Arrange ribs in a large roasting pan and scatter onion, celery, carrots, bay leaves, thyme, salt, peppercorns and cloves over top. Cover with foil and roast in preheated oven until meat is just beginning to shrink from the ends of the bones and is fork tender, about 2 hours. Remove ribs, wipe off seasoning vegetables and spices and discard. Let cool. Cover and refrigerate until needed, for up to 3 days.

2. When ready to serve, preheat barbecue grill to medium-high heat and lightly oil grill. Return ribs to room temperature.

3. Sear ribs on both sides for 2 to 3 minutes. Brush with barbecue sauce and close barbecue lid. Turn and baste several times until ribs are tender, moist and nicely glazed, about 30 minutes. In a small saucepan, heat remaining barbecue sauce to serve alongside.

Hoisin Barbecue Sauce

**MAKES 2 CUPS
(500 ML)**

Sweet Asian flavors combine to make a sauce that is particularly delicious to glaze pork and spareribs.

1 tbsp	vegetable oil	15 mL
3	cloves garlic, finely chopped	3
½ tsp	hot pepper flakes	2 mL
1½ tsp	tomato paste	7 mL
2 cups	hoisin sauce	500 mL
1 tbsp	brown sugar	15 mL
1 tbsp	freshly squeezed lemon juice	15 mL

1. In a saucepan, heat oil over medium-low heat. Add garlic and hot pepper flakes and sauté until garlic is softened but not browned, 1 to 2 minutes. Add tomato paste and cook, stirring, 1 to 2 minutes.

2. Add hoisin sauce, brown sugar, lemon juice and ⅓ cup (75 mL) water, stirring while sugar melts. Reduce heat to low and simmer, stirring occasionally, until sauce is thickened to desired consistency and flavors are developed, about 15 minutes.

3. Remove from heat. Let cool and store in covered container in the refrigerator for up to 1 month.

The "Low Down" on Pork Ribs

Back ribs are cut from the loin. They have a good meat-to-bone ratio and are naturally more tender than side ribs. Side ribs, also known as spareribs, are longer and cut from farther down the side of the pig. Look for fresh-looking racks of ribs that have a good ratio of meat to bone. Juicy glazed ribs are not "fast food"! They need slow, careful cooking. The classic down-south grilling technique is long and slow with diligent "mopping" over indirect heat in a barbecue aromatic with fragrant wood smoke for 2 to 3 hours. We like to season ribs with a spice rub or marinade for a day or so and pre-roast them in a slow oven for 2 hours before finishing on the grill over direct heat.

Braised Red Cabbage with Bacon and Farmer's Sausage

This meal-in-a-dish is heart-warming fare for a winter weekend. The flavor is enhanced when the dish is prepared ahead and gently reheated at serving time. Offer a selection of good country mustards at the table and have warm crusty sourdough bread to serve alongside.

Variations

Braised cabbage makes a great side dish. Here are two versions for it:

Braised Cabbage 1: Proceed with recipe but omit sausages and pork hock.

Braised Cabbage 2: Omit bacon, sausages and pork hock. Proceed with recipe from Step 3. Brown onion in 2 tbsp (25 mL) vegetable oil and use vegetable stock instead of chicken.

8 oz	double-smoked bacon, cut into ½-inch (1 cm) cubes	250 g
6	pork sausages	6
1	onion, thinly sliced	1
3	cloves garlic, minced	3
2 tsp	brown sugar	10 mL
½ tsp	caraway seeds	2 mL
½ tsp	yellow mustard seeds	2 mL
½ tsp	fennel seeds	2 mL
¼ tsp	ground allspice	1 mL
¼ tsp	ground cinnamon	1 mL
	Salt and freshly ground black pepper	
¾ cup	apple cider vinegar	175 mL
½ to 1 cup	Chicken Stock (page 54) or ready-to-use broth or water	125 to 250 mL
1	small head red cabbage, cut into 8 pieces, cored and thinly sliced	1
2	tart apples, peeled and thinly sliced	2
8 oz	smoked pork hock, optional	250 g

1. Place bacon in a large cold pot over medium-high heat to render the fat. When fat has released to coat the bottom of the pot, reduce heat to medium and cook, stirring, until outside of bacon is crispy, 5 to 6 minutes. Transfer bacon to a plate lined with paper towel and set aside. Pour off all but ¼ cup (50 mL) of fat from pot, reserving any excess fat. Set aside.

2. Add sausages to pot and cook until golden brown on all sides, about 5 minutes. Transfer to plate with bacon and set aside.

3. Add onion to pot and sauté over medium heat until softened and lightly browned, 5 to 7 minutes. Add more fat, if needed. Add garlic and sauté for 2 to 3 minutes. Stir in brown sugar, caraway, mustard and fennel seeds, allspice, cinnamon, 1 tsp (5 mL) salt and ¼ tsp (1 mL) pepper and sauté for 1 to 2 minutes.

4. Add vinegar and deglaze pot, scraping up browned bits on the bottom. Add ½ cup (125 mL) chicken stock, cabbage, apples and pork hock, if using. Return bacon and sausage to the pot.

5. Reduce heat to low. Cover pot and simmer, stirring occasionally, until sausage is cooked through and cabbage is tender, about 25 minutes. Add a little more stock to keep the cabbage moist, if necessary. Remove pork hock and, when cool enough to handle, pull off pieces of lean meat and return them to the pot. Discard fat, trim and bone. Taste and adjust seasoning. Reheat over low heat before serving.

Pork Stir-Fry with Spicy Orange Sauce

When stir-frying, take the time to gather and prepare all your ingredients ready at hand at the stove. Stir-frying is a fast-cooking technique that requires constant movement of ingredients over very high heat. Include your favorite fast-cooking vegetables, all sliced or slivered in pieces so they cook evenly in the same time. Serve accompanied by steamed rice or lo mein noodles.

● **Large wok or large skillet**

¼ cup	soy sauce	50 mL
2 tbsp	brown sugar	25 mL
2	cloves garlic, coarsely chopped	2
2 tbsp	coarsely chopped gingerroot	25 mL
1 lb	pork blade or shoulder, thinly sliced	500 g
¼ cup	vegetable oil, divided	50 mL
1 tbsp	julienned gingerroot (½ inch/1 cm long)	15 mL
2	cloves garlic, thinly sliced	2
1	small red onion, thinly sliced	1
1	red bell pepper, julienned	1
1	yellow bell pepper, julienned	1
1½ cups	small broccoli florets	375 mL
4 oz	oyster mushrooms, pulled in half	125 g
12	asparagus spears, cut into thirds then halved lengthwise	12
	Spicy Orange Sauce (page 187)	
	Steamed rice or noodles	
2	green onions, thinly sliced on the diagonal	2

1. In a large bowl, combine soy sauce, brown sugar, garlic and chopped ginger. Add pork. Marinate, covered, in the refrigerator for 2 hours or overnight.

2. When ready to cook, remove pork from marinade and pat dry. Discard marinade.

3. Heat wok over high heat until almost smoking. Add 2 tbsp (25 mL) of the oil and heat until it starts to ripple. Add pork and stir-fry for 3 to 4 minutes. Remove pork from wok and set aside.

4. Return wok to high heat. Add 2 tbsp (25 mL) of oil and heat until it starts to ripple. Add julienned ginger and garlic and stir-fry for about 30 seconds. Add red onion, red and yellow bell peppers, broccoli and mushrooms. Stir-fry for 2 to 3 minutes. Add asparagus and cooked pork and toss together for 1 to 2 minutes. Transfer to a large warm bowl.

5. Return wok to heat. Add Spicy Orange Sauce and boil, stirring, until reduced by about one-third, 1 to 2 minutes. Return pork and vegetables to wok and toss together for 30 seconds. Serve with steamed rice or noodles garnished with green onions.

Spicy Orange Sauce

Makes about 1 cup (250 mL)

	Zest of 1 orange	
½ cup	freshly squeezed orange juice	125 rnL
¼ cup	soy sauce	50 mL
2 tbsp	natural rice vinegar	25 mL
2 tbsp	brown sugar	25 mL
1 tbsp	oyster sauce (see Tips, right)	15 mL
1 tbsp	hoisin sauce (see Tips, right)	15 mL
1 tbsp	Asian hot chile sauce, or to taste	15 mL

1. In a bowl, combine orange zest and juice, soy sauce, rice vinegar, brown sugar, oyster sauce, hoisin sauce and chile sauce.

Tips

Oyster sauce is a thick, grayish-brown sauce made from a concentrate of oysters, soy sauce and brine. It is used in Chinese cooking as a flavor enhancer and to add smooth richness to sauces and stir-fried dishes. It's available in cans, jars and bottles. Look for a reliable imported brand. Stored in a covered jar, it will keep for months in the refrigerator.

Hoisin sauce is a thick, sweet and spicy, dark brownish-red sauce made from soybeans, garlic, chile and spices. Used as a seasoning for pork, duck and shellfish in Chinese cooking. It's available in cans, jars and bottles. Look for a reliable imported brand. Stored in a covered jar in the refrigerator, it will keep for months.

Maple-Brined Pork Chops

A period in a spicy brine adds moisture and flavor to lean pork chops. You can also use the brining technique for large cuts of pork or turkey. Salt penetrates the meat over time, encourages the muscle fibers to absorb water and breaks down connective tissues. It also acts on the protein so that moisture is retained in the meat during cooking. Plan your meal two to three days ahead — you need time to make and chill brine and to brine the pork. Brine small cuts no longer than 18 hours; brine larger cuts for one to two days.

The Maple Brine makes enough brine to cover approximately 2 to 3 lbs (1 to 1.5 kg) meat. Double the amount to brine a large roast or a small turkey.

- **Large ovenproof skillet**
- **Instant-read thermometer**

	Maple Brine (page 189)	
6	pork rib or loin chops, bone-in, cut 1 inch (2.5 cm) thick, chilled	6
2 tbsp	olive oil	25 mL
	Salt and freshly ground black pepper	
	Caramelized Apples (page 190)	

1. Add chilled pork chops to cold brine, making sure that the meat is completely submerged at least 2 inches (5 cm) below the surface. You may need to weigh them down. (A plate, weighted down with a can of beans does the trick.) Cover and refrigerate for at least 6 hours or for up to 18 hours.

2. Preheat oven 350°F (180°C).

3. Drain pork and pat dry. Discard brine. In a large ovenproof skillet, heat oil over medium-high heat. Season pork chops with salt and pepper. Brown chops in batches, 3 to 4 minutes per side. Do not crowd the pan.

4. Transfer skillet to oven and roast in preheated oven until an instant-read thermometer registers 160°F (71°C) for medium, 10 to 15 minutes. Let pork chops rest, loosely covered in foil, 3 to 4 minutes, before serving with Caramelized Apples.

Maple Brine

Makes 8 cups (2 L)

8 cups	water	2 L
½ cup	kosher salt	125 mL
½ cup	packed brown sugar	125 mL
½ cup	pure maple syrup	125 mL
2	bay leaves	2
4	cloves garlic, coarsely chopped	4
¼ cup	whole allspice, crushed (see Tip, right)	50 mL
2	whole nutmegs, crushed	2
1 tbsp	fennel seeds	15 mL
2 tsp	black peppercorns, crushed	10 mL

1. In a large saucepan over medium heat, combine water, salt, brown sugar, maple syrup, bay leaves, garlic, allspice, nutmeg, fennel seeds and peppercorns. Bring to a boil, stirring until salt and sugar are dissolved. Reduce heat and simmer for 5 minutes. Pour into a large deep bowl and set aside to cool. Cover and refrigerate until cold.

Tip

Softer whole spices, such as allspice berries, whole peppercorns and cloves can be roughly crushed in a mortar and pestle or with the bottom of a small bowl. Harder whole spices, like nutmeg, can be broken into rough small pieces with a quick smack of a rolling pin or a meat tenderizing mallet.

Caramelized Apples

Here's a sweet-tart condiment to serve with brined pork chops, or indeed many other roasted or grilled pork dishes. Try them also as dessert with a topping of crème fraîche or spooned over strained yogurt.

Tips

Cook apples over medium-high to high heat to ensure that the sugar in the fruit caramelizes. At lower heat apples will steam in their juices rather than becoming a delicious caramel.

Use firm tart apples like Granny Smiths that hold their shape during cooking. Feel free to experiment with different varieties to experience different distinct flavors.

3 tbsp	butter, divided	45 mL
3	tart apples, peeled and sliced into $\frac{1}{4}$-inch (0.5 cm) wedges (see Tips, left)	3
2 tbsp	brown sugar	25 mL
2 tbsp	rum	25 mL
$\frac{1}{2}$ tsp	grated lemon zest	2 mL
2 to 3 tbsp	freshly squeezed lemon juice	25 to 45 mL
$\frac{1}{4}$ tsp	coarsely chopped thyme	1 mL
	Kosher or sea salt	

1. Heat a large skillet over high heat. Add 2 tbsp (25 mL) of the butter and heat until melting and starting to brown. Add apples and toss to coat. Spread apples in a single layer and cook, undisturbed, for 1 minute. Turn apple slices over to brown the other side, 1 to 2 minutes.

2. Reduce heat to medium-high and continue to cook apples, turning often, until they are fork tender and deeply browned, 3 to 4 minutes.

3. Increase heat to high. Add remaining butter and brown sugar. Toss to melt and coat apples with syrupy glaze, about 1 minute. At this point, be attentive: the apples can burn in a flash! Add rum and flambé, or let the alcohol reduce for 1 minute.

4. Remove from heat. Stir in lemon zest and juice to taste, thyme and salt.

Pork

All but the squeal: it's an old line but true enough. Just about everything else that the friendly, generous and cruelly mocked pig offers us is put to our advantage. Skin for leather, bristles for brushes; heart, liver, kidneys, lungs, sweetbreads, teats and testicles for various and varied international stews and fry-ups hymned in song and story; jowl, feet, tail and whatever's left for sausages; not much is remaindered. In these inventive days why is it nobody has been able to do anything with the squeal?

Domesticated from the wild boar, probably first in China about 7,000 years ago, the pig was always a pushover. It adapted anywhere and in most climates, it ate everything, it wasn't fussy about living arrangements (but fussier about personal sanitation than it has usually been allowed to show). By its flesh, of course, we know it best: cured, as in bacon and ham, and fresh, as in pork. The European Union (27 countries) leads consumption with (rounded figures) 97 lbs (44 kg) per capita a year, followed by China with 88 lbs (40 kg), the U.S. with 64 lbs (29 kg), Canada with 48 lbs (22 kg), Japan with 44 lbs (20 kg). Rich in thiamin, the B_1 vitamin that converts carbohydrates into energy, it is the most widely eaten meat in the world (outside Islam, Judaism and Seventh-day Adventists), accounting for almost 40 percent of the world's meat production. And in an era of demand for ever leaner meats, none has met the demand more selflessly than the pig. Thirty years ago a full-grown pig commonly weighed more than 300 lbs (136 kg). Today, a comparative Kate Moss, it weighs about 240 lbs (109 kg), and a 4-oz (125 g) serving of tenderloin contains no more saturated fat or calories than the same amount of skinless chicken breast.

Some would say that leaner pork has lost some of its old, juicier flavor. The so-called **Heritage** pigs are now being raised to meet the lack: fatter, darker meat from old breeds such as **Berkshire**, **Duroc**, **Gloucester Old Spot**, **Tamworth** and **Large Black**. There is also the international favorite **suckling** pig, aged 2 to 6 weeks (20 to 30 lbs/9 to 14 kg), fed only on its mother's milk, and roasted whole.

In the Kitchen

The four principal cuts of pork are loin, shoulder, leg and belly.

Loin, the most popular, can be divided into roasts, back ribs, cutlets and chops; cured, it gives us back (or Canadian) bacon.

Shoulder can have the bone removed and rolled for a roast and is great for stews, curries and such. (Despite its name, pork butt also comes from the shoulder and is now called blade).

Leg (**rump**, **center**, **shank**) is usually used for roasting, bone in; it is also where hams come from.

Belly (aka **side**) pork supplies fattier meat and may be rolled for roasting, cured to make streaky bacon, or chopped to kick any stir-fry up a notch.

Trichinosis, once associated with undercooked pork, is now rare thanks to improved feeding methods, both ours and the pig's. It remains unwise to gamble. One should wash anything that has contact with raw pork (hands, knives, cutting boards) — and cook it to an internal temperature of 160°F (71°C). The result will be slightly pink, juicy and tender (and safe). Above 170°F (77°C) and the pork will be dryer, tougher, and about as interesting as an overcooked metaphor.

Tourtière

SERVES 4 TO 6

Winter in Canada would not be complete without a taste of this classic savory Quebec pie. Serve with chili sauce or chutney, and a tossed green salad at brunch, lunch or supper. Make Mini Tourtières (see Variation, below) — they're a great standby when friends drop in over the holidays.

Variation

Mini Tourtières: Line mini tart pans with pastry. Spoon about 1 tbsp (15 mL) pork filling into each tartlet and top with a small pastry circle. Brush pastry circles with egg wash. Bake in 400°F (200°C) oven for 5 minutes. Reduce heat to 350°F (180°C) and continue to bake until filling is hot and pastry is golden, about 10 minutes more. Makes about 72 mini tarts.

8-inch (20 cm) metal pie plate

3 tbsp	vegetable oil, divided	45 mL
1½ lbs	lean ground pork	750 g
1	onion, chopped	1
2	cloves garlic, minced	2
1	large potato, peeled and cut into ¼-inch (0.5 cm) cubes	1
1 tbsp	coarsely chopped thyme	15 mL
1	bay leaf	1
	Salt and freshly ground black pepper	
½ tsp	ground cinnamon	2 mL
¼ tsp	ground cloves	1 mL
¼ tsp	ground allspice	1 mL
½ cup	Chicken Stock (page 54) or ready-to-use broth	125 mL
	Tourtière Pastry (page 193)	
1	egg, lightly beaten with 1 tsp (5 mL) water	1

1. In a large skillet, heat 1 tbsp (15 mL) of the oil over medium-high heat. Add pork and brown lightly, breaking up the meat as it browns, about 10 minutes. Remove meat from skillet with a slotted spoon and set aside in a bowl. Pour off and discard fat.

2. In the same skillet, heat 2 tbsp (25 mL) of oil over medium heat. Add onion and garlic and sauté until tender, 3 to 4 minutes. Add pork, potato, thyme, bay leaf, 1 tsp (5 mL) salt, ¼ tsp (1 mL) pepper, cinnamon, cloves and allspice and stir to combine.

3. Add chicken stock and deglaze skillet, scraping up browned bits on the bottom. Reduce heat to low. Cover and cook until potato is tender, 8 to 10 minutes. Season to taste with salt and pepper. Let cool and refrigerate until needed for up to 3 days.

4. Preheat oven 400°F (200°C). Line pie plate with half of pastry and fill with cooled pork filling. Top with another pastry layer and crimp edges to seal (see Techniques, page 22). Brush top with egg wash and cut 2 slits in top pastry to let steam escape while baking. A sprinkling of coarse salt and freshly ground black pepper on top adds extra flavor and interest to the appearance.

5. Bake in preheated oven for 15 minutes. Reduce temperature to 350°F (180°C) and continue baking until pastry is cooked and nicely browned, 25 to 35 minutes more. Let stand for 5 minutes before slicing.

Tourtière Pastry

Makes one 8-inch (20 cm) pie

● **Food processor**

½ cup	shortening	125 mL
¼ cup	butter	50 mL
2 cups	all-purpose flour (approx.)	500 mL
1 tsp	kosher salt	5 mL
1 tsp	coarsely chopped thyme	5 mL
6 tbsp	ice cold water	90 mL

1. Place shortening and butter in the freezer for 30 minutes.

2. In a food processor, combine shortening, butter, flour, salt and thyme. Process until shortening and butter are cut into pea-size pieces.

3. Transfer flour mixture to a bowl and sprinkle with ice water. Toss with a fork and gather into a ball. Divide the ball into 2 equal disks and wrap with plastic wrap. Set dough aside to rest for 30 minutes in the refrigerator before rolling. Keep well wrapped in refrigerator for up to 3 days or freezer for up to 6 weeks, if making ahead.

4. Roll out dough (see Techniques, page 21).

Sausage Lasagna

Of all the lasagna we make, this one, with layers of spicy sausage, creamy spinach sauce and noodles is my personal favorite. It's a great dish for family gatherings and, as with all lasagnas, the work can be spread out over several days if necessary. Serve a tossed salad with lots of bitter greens (radicchio, frisée, endive) in a lemony dressing to complement the richness of the pasta and thick slices of warm crusty bread.

Tip

Frozen vegetables do not play a big role in our kitchens. However, frozen leaf spinach, corn or peas are just the thing in some dishes. A 10-oz (300 g) package of frozen leaf spinach, thawed, squeezed dry and chopped, yields 1 cup (250 mL) spinach — useful to have on hand to add to dips and fillings. This equals about 1 lb (500 g) fresh spinach. When time permits choose fresh, young spinach. Being a purist, I consider the benefit of bright, fresh flavor in fresh spinach is worth the effort.

Variation

Enjoy the sausage mix as a sauce for penne. Add vegetable or chicken stock to increase sauciness as desired.

- Preheat oven to 350°F (180°C)
- 13- by 9-inch (3 L) glass baking dish, lightly oiled

1 lb	hot Italian-style sausage	500 g
1 lb	sweet Italian-style sausage	500 g
1	onion, finely chopped	1
1	red bell pepper, diced	1
1	green bell pepper, diced	1
2 tbsp	tomato paste	25 mL
	Salt and freshly ground black pepper	
1	can (28 oz/796 mL) plum tomatoes with juice, chopped	1
12	lasagna noodles, about 12 oz (375 g)	12
	Olive oil	
	Spinach Béchamel (page 195)	
3 cups	shredded Mozzarella cheese	750 mL

1. Remove sausage meat from casings and break up into chunks. In a large skillet over medium-high heat, cook sausage meat, breaking up the meat with a wooden spoon, until brown, 5 to 10 minutes. Using a slotted spoon, transfer browned meat to a dish. Set aside. Reserve 2 tbsp (25 mL) fat in pan, discarding any excess.

2. Reduce heat to medium. In the same skillet, add onion and red and green bell peppers and cook, stirring often, until soft, 10 to 12 minutes. Add tomato paste and sauté for 1 to 2 minutes. Return sausage to the pan. Season with $\frac{1}{2}$ tsp (2 mL) salt and $\frac{1}{4}$ tsp (1 mL) pepper. Stir in tomatoes with juice. Bring to a boil. Reduce heat, partially cover and simmer until sauce is thick and well seasoned, 35 to 40 minutes. Taste and adjust seasoning. Set aside.

3. In a large pot of boiling lightly salted water, cook lasagna noodles until just al dente. You may need to do this in 2 batches. Lift noodles from water. Drain and lay flat. Brush lightly with olive oil.

4. *To assemble the lasagna:* Spread a thin layer of Spinach Béchamel on the bottom of prepared dish. Lay 4 lasagna noodles over top. Add a layer of half the sausage mixture, sprinkle with one-third of the cheese and top with 4 lasagna noodles. Repeat the layers of sausage mixture, cheese and noodles. Finish with a layer of béchamel and cheese.

5. Cover with foil and place on a large baking sheet. Bake in preheated oven until heated through and bubbling, 45 to 50 minutes. Remove foil. Increase temperature to 450°F (230°C) and cook until top is nicely golden, 6 to 8 minutes (or set briefly under the broiler). Let stand for 10 minutes before slicing to serve.

Spinach Béchamel

Makes about 2¹/₂ cups (625 mL)

2 cups	milk	500 mL
¼ cup	butter	50 mL
¼ cup	all-purpose flour	50 mL
½ cup	blanched spinach, squeezed dry (see Tip, left)	125 mL
	Salt and freshly ground black pepper	

1. In a small saucepan, bring milk just to a simmer over medium heat,

2. In another saucepan, melt butter over medium-low heat. Stir in flour and cook, stirring, 2 to 3 minutes. Do not brown. Slowly whisk hot milk into flour mixture. Stir diligently until all liquid is incorporated and sauce is smooth. Stir while sauce comes to a slow rolling simmer and thickens, 5 to 10 minutes. Remove from heat. Stir in spinach. Season with salt and pepper to taste.

Roast Leg of Lamb
with Charmoula Sauce

A glistening, browned leg of lamb cooked to tender, juicy perfection and aromatic with garlic and fresh herbs is a feast fit for a king. For summer parties we like to grill boned, marinated legs of lamb over charcoal or in seasoned wood smoke (see Variation), which adds wonderful flavor to the meat. Ask your butcher to prepare boned and butterflied legs of lamb ready for the barbecue. They are easy to carve so serving a crowd is a breeze!

Variation

Grilled Boned Leg of Lamb: Trim and marinate 2 to 3 lbs (1 to 1.5 kg) boneless lamb as in Step 1. Preheat barbecue to high. Place lamb on grill and sear on each side, 5 to 10 minutes. Reduce heat to medium and continue to cook lamb over indirect heat (either turn off middle or side burner, depending on barbecue instructions) with lid down. In a bowl, separate a few tablespoons (25 mL) of herb-flavored oil from the Charmoula Sauce and use this to baste lamb every 15 to 20 minutes until meat is slightly resistant to touch, juices run rosy red and instant-read thermometer registers 135°F (57°C) for rare, about 1½ hours. Continue with Step 4.

- **Roasting pan**
- **Instant-read thermometer**

1	leg of spring lamb, bone-in (about 6 lbs/3 kg)	1
	Charmoula Marinade and Sauce, divided (page 197)	
2 tbsp	extra virgin olive oil	25 mL
	Salt and freshly ground black pepper	

1. Trim lamb to remove tough outer membrane and excess fat. Place in a large baking dish or heavy-duty plastic bag and coat on all sides with ¼ cup (50 mL) Charmoula Sauce. Cover and marinate in the refrigerator for 4 hours or overnight.

2. Preheat oven 450°F (230°C).

3. Wipe lamb dry. Place in roasting pan and brush with oil and season lightly with salt and pepper. Place in upper third of preheated oven. Turn and baste with pan juices every 5 minutes until outside of meat is nicely seared, 15 to 20 minutes. Reduce temperature to 350°F (180°C). Place roasting pan on middle rack and continue roasting until meat is slightly resistant to the touch, the juices run rosy red and an instant-read thermometer registers 135°F (57°C) for rare, about 1 hour.

4. Transfer lamb to a warm platter and brush with 2 to 3 tbsp (25 to 45 mL) Charmoula Sauce. Cover loosely with foil and let stand for 15 to 20 minutes before carving to let surface juices retreat back into the meat. Serve remaining sauce on the side.

Charmoula Marinade and Sauce

MAKES 1¼ CUPS (300 ML)

This fragrant marinade is wonderful for lamb and also excellent for fish, scallops and shrimp.

1 tbsp	ground cumin	15 mL
1 tbsp	ground coriander	15 mL
1 tbsp	paprika	15 mL
2 tsp	cayenne pepper	10 mL
¼ cup	finely chopped mint	50 mL
3 tbsp	freshly squeezed lemon juice	45 mL
2 tbsp	finely chopped flat-leaf parsley	25 mL
2 tbsp	finely chopped cilantro	25 mL
1 tbsp	minced garlic	15 mL
2 tsp	kosher or sea salt	10 mL
1 cup	extra virgin olive oil	250 mL

1. In a small dry skillet over medium heat, toast cumin, coriander, paprika and cayenne, stirring constantly, until fragrant, 2 to 3 minutes.
2. In a bowl, combine toasted spices with mint, lemon juice, parsley, cilantro, garlic and salt. Whisk in olive oil. Set aside for 15 minutes for flavors to blend.

Marinated Lamb Kebabs with Feta Mint Sauce

These tender morsels of lamb are grilled to perfection with a colorful selection of vegetables and accompanied by a tangy Feta Mint Sauce. For authentic flavor seek out imported Greek or Bulgarian feta cheese. Close your eyes and you could be dining on the shores of the Aegean.

Tips

Add, subtract or substitute the selection of vegetables on the skewer. Just cut them in appropriate-size pieces so that everything cooks in the same length of time.

Allow a little space on the skewers between pieces of meat and vegetables so that heat can penetrate and elements cook evenly. If too closely packed, the vegetables will still be raw when the lamb is done. To avoid that possibility altogether, assemble and grill separate skewers of lamb and vegetables.

- Barbecue grill or indoor grill
- Twelve 8-inch (20 cm) bamboo skewers, soaked in water for 30 minutes

2 lbs	boneless lamb shoulder or leg	1 kg
¼ cup	olive oil	50 mL
1 tbsp	freshly squeezed lemon juice	15 mL
2 tsp	minced garlic	10 mL
1 tsp	ground cumin	5 mL
1 tsp	ground coriander	5 mL
½ tsp	cayenne pepper	2 mL
½ tsp	freshly ground black pepper	2 mL
12	small mushrooms, trimmed	12
1	red bell pepper, cut into 1-inch (2.5 cm) pieces	1
1	yellow bell pepper, cut into 1-inch (2.5 cm) pieces	1
1	red onion, cut into small wedges	1
12	cherry tomatoes	12
	Kosher or sea salt	
	Feta Mint Sauce (page 199)	

1. Trim lamb and cut into cubes, about 1½ inches (4 cm). In a small bowl, combine olive oil, lemon juice, garlic, cumin, coriander, cayenne pepper and black pepper. Pour three-quarters of the lemon mixture over lamb. Cover and marinate in the refrigerator for at least 1 hour or overnight. Reserve the remaining marinade to brush over lamb in last few minutes of grilling.

2. Preheat barbecue grill to medium-high and lightly oil grill.

3. Arrange separate bowls on your counter containing mushrooms, red and yellow bell peppers, onion wedges, tomatoes and marinated lamb. Alternate vegetables and lamb on skewers to make a colorful arrangement. Season with salt.

4. Grill kebabs until nicely browned and cooked to your liking, about 6 to 7 minutes per side for medium-rare. Serve hot with Feta Mint Sauce.

Feta Mint Sauce

Makes 2 cups (500 mL)

- **Food processor or blender**

12 oz	feta cheese	375 g
¾ cup	plain yogurt	175 mL
2 tbsp	freshly squeezed lemon juice	25 mL
2 tbsp	olive oil	25 mL
2 tsp	minced garlic	10 mL
½ tsp	kosher salt or sea salt	2 mL
¼ tsp	freshly ground black pepper	1 mL
2 tbsp	coarsely chopped mint	25 mL

1. In a food processor, combine feta, yogurt, lemon juice, olive oil, garlic, salt and pepper. Process in short bursts until smooth, scraping down the sides of the food processor bowl as needed.
2. Stir in mint. Taste and adjust seasoning.

Moroccan Lamb Tagine
with Onions and Tomatoes

This rich, wonderfully aromatic braise of lamb features the favorite spices used in North African cuisine. It is delicious served over couscous seasoned with a hint of fresh mint. The flavor intensifies if the dish is made a day ahead and then reheated gently in the oven before serving.

- Preheat oven to 350°F (180°C)
- Large shallow overproof casserole dish

3 lbs	boneless lamb shoulder	1.5 kg
3 tbsp	vegetable oil	45 mL
	Salt and freshly ground black pepper	
½ cup	chopped onion	125 mL
1 tsp	ras el hanout (page 201)	5 mL
1 tsp	ground ginger	5 mL
8 cups	Chicken Stock (page 54) or ready-to-use broth or water, divided	2 L
2	bay leaves	2
2 lbs	large Spanish onions, sliced	1 kg
2 tbsp	liquid honey	25 mL
1 tsp	ground cinnamon, divided	5 mL
Pinch	saffron	Pinch
1 lb	tomatoes (about 4 large), thickly sliced	500 g
¼ cup	chopped cilantro	50 mL
	Couscous	

1. Trim lamb and cut into cubes, about 1 inch (2.5 cm). In a large heavy-bottomed pot, heat oil over medium-high heat. Lightly season lamb pieces with salt and pepper and brown, in batches, on all sides. Do not crowd the pot. Return lamb to pot with any accumulated juices. Add chopped onion, ras el hanout and ginger and cook, stirring, 2 to 3 minutes. Add 4 cups (1 L) of the stock and bay leaves. Bring gently to a boil. Reduce heat to low. Cover and simmer until lamb is almost tender, about 1½ hours.

2. Meanwhile, arrange sliced onions in a large roasting pan. Sprinkle with honey, ½ tsp (2 mL) of the cinnamon, saffron and salt and pepper to taste. Add remaining 4 cups (1 L) of stock. Cover pan with foil and bake in preheated oven, about 1 hour. Arrange layer of tomato slices over onions. Sprinkle with remaining cinnamon.

Cover, return to oven and bake until vegetables are tender, about 30 minutes. Strain off cooking liquid from onions and tomatoes and pour into the lamb pot. Return roasting pan to oven for about 15 to 20 minutes longer to dry and slightly caramelize the vegetables.

3. *To assemble and finish the dish*: Transfer lamb from pot with a slotted spoon to casserole. Bring liquids to a rapid boil over medium-high heat and reduce until sauce is thickened to coat the back of a spoon, about 30 minutes. Taste and adjust seasoning.

4. Arrange a layer of onions and tomatoes on top of the lamb. Pour spicy sweet sauce over top. Bake in preheated oven for about 30 minutes. Garnish with chopped cilantro and serve hot over couscous.

Ras el Hanout

This is a version of Paula Wolfert's ras el hanout, the spice blend so popular in North African cuisine that we make in our kitchen.

In a small dry skillet over medium heat, toast 6 whole allspice, 4 whole cloves, $1\frac{1}{2}$ tsp (7 mL) coriander seeds and 1 tsp (5 mL) cumin seeds, stirring constantly, just until the spicy aromas are released, 2 to 3 minutes. In spice mill, combine toasted spices, $1\frac{1}{2}$ tsp (7 mL) peppercorns, $1\frac{1}{2}$ tsp (7 mL) cinnamon, 1 tsp (5 mL) ground ginger and $\frac{1}{4}$ tsp (1 mL) cayenne and process until finely ground. Store spice mix in a covered container in a cool cupboard and use whenever a touch of sweet/spiciness is needed.
    Makes about $2\frac{1}{2}$ tbsp (32 mL).

Lamb and White Bean Ragoût

Here we have tender lamb and white beans in a rich wine sauce flavored with rosemary. This classic lamb stew is a favorite with our customers. It improves in flavor when made ahead and reheats beautifully. Serve with steamed haricots verts and chunks of warm grilled garlic bread.

Variation

For speed and convenience, replace dried beans with 1 can (14 to 19 oz/398 to 540 mL) navy beans, rinsed and drained.

2 lbs	boneless lamb shoulder	1 kg
1 cup	red wine	250 mL
3	sprigs rosemary	3
1 cup	dried navy beans	250 mL
1	bay leaf	1
	Salt and freshly ground black pepper	
4 tbsp	olive oil, divided	60 mL
1	onion, chopped	1
2	cloves garlic, finely chopped	2
2 tbsp	all-purpose flour	25 mL
5 cups	Chicken Stock (page 54) or ready-to-use broth	1.25 L
1 tbsp	coarsely chopped thyme	15 mL
1 tbsp	Worcestershire sauce	15 mL
2 tsp	finely chopped rosemary	10 mL
1	sweet potato, cut into ½-inch (1 cm) cubes	1
¼ cup	coarsely chopped flat-leaf parsley	50 mL

1. Trim lamb and cut into cubes, about 1 inch (2.5 cm). In a large bowl or heavy-duty plastic bag, combine lamb, wine and rosemary sprigs. Cover and marinate in the refrigerator for 4 hours or overnight.

2. Meanwhile, rinse and pick over dried beans. Soak in 4 cups (1 L) cold water in refrigerator overnight.

3. The next day, rinse and drain beans. In a saucepan, combine beans with 6 cups (1.5 L) cold water and bay leaf. Bring to a boil. Reduce heat, partially cover and simmer until beans are tender to the bite, 40 to 45 minutes. Remove from heat and add ½ tsp (2 mL) salt. Set aside for 5 minutes. Drain and set aside.

4. Drain lamb, reserving marinade, and pat dry. Discard rosemary from marinade. In a large heavy pot, heat 2 tbsp (25 mL) of the oil over medium-high heat. Lightly season lamb with salt and pepper. Sear lamb, in batches, on all sides until nicely browned. Do not crowd the pot. Transfer lamb to a bowl and set aside. Pour off and discard excess fat.

5. In the same pot, heat remaining oil over medium heat. Add onion and garlic and sauté until softened and lightly browned, 4 to 6 minutes. Stir in flour and cook, stirring, 2 to 3 minutes. Stir in reserved marinade, scraping up all the browned bits on the bottom of the pot and whisk until smooth. Add chicken stock, thyme, Worcestershire sauce, chopped rosemary and browned lamb with any collected juices. Bring gently to a boil. Reduce heat to low and simmer, covered, until lamb is tender, 1 to $1\frac{1}{2}$ hours. Add beans and sweet potato and cook until sweet potato is tender, 10 to 15 minutes. Remove from heat. Stir in parsley. Taste and adjust seasoning.

Beer-Braised Lamb Shank

The secret to a delicious lamb shank lies in slow, gentle braising of the meat and the rich full-bodied sauce that accompanies it. Serve in warm deep bowls over Creamy Polenta (Variation, page 308).

- Preheat oven to 325°F (160°C)
- Large heavy-bottomed ovenproof pot

½ cup	all-purpose flour	125 mL
	Salt and freshly ground black pepper	
6	lamb shanks (about 6 lbs/3 kg total)	6
6 tbsp	olive oil, divided	90 mL
1	large onion, quartered	1
2	carrots, quartered	2
2	stalks celery, cut in half	2
6	cloves garlic, chopped	6
10 to 12 cups	Chicken Stock (page 54) or ready-to-use broth	2.5 to 3 L
2 cups	canned plum tomatoes with juice, roughly chopped	500 mL
1	bottle (12 oz/341 mL) beer, ale or lager, divided	1
3	bay leaves	3
¼ cup	chopped thyme	50 mL
¼ cup	minced shallots	50 mL
2 tbsp	tomato paste	25 mL

1. On a platter or in a heavy-duty plastic bag, combine flour with 1 tsp (5 mL) salt and ½ tsp (2 mL) pepper. Pat lamb shanks dry with paper towel. Dredge each lamb shank in seasoned flour and set aside. Discard any excess flour.

2. In large skillet, heat 3 tbsp (45 mL) of the oil over medium-high heat. Add lamb shanks, in batches if necessary, and sear on all sides until golden brown. Do not crowd the pan. Transfer lamb shanks to a large ovenproof pot. Pour off and discard excess fat.

3. Add 2 tbsp (25 mL) of oil to the skillet. Add onion, carrots, celery and garlic and sauté for 2 to 3 minutes. Add to lamb shanks. Add 1 cup (250 mL) of the chicken stock and deglaze skillet, scraping up browned bits on bottom of pan, and pour over lamb and vegetables. Add tomatoes, beer (reserving ½ cup/125 mL), bay leaves, thyme, 1 tsp (5 mL) salt and ½ tsp (2 mL) pepper and stock to cover. Bring to a simmer. Cover and transfer to preheated oven and braise lamb shanks for 35 to

45 minutes. Check to ensure that braising liquid is just at simmering point. If sauce is bubbling too vigorously, reduce heat to 300°F (150°C). Cook for 2 to 2½ hours. With the tip of a small knife, test for doneness — the meat should be very tender and come away from the bone easily.

4. Remove lamb shanks from pot and set aside. Strain braising liquid into a large bowl, pressing down on the vegetables to gather all the good juices; discard solids. Set aside.

5. In the same pot, heat remaining oil over medium heat. Add shallots and sauté until soft, 2 to 3 minutes. Add tomato paste and cook, stirring, for 1 minute. Add reserved beer and deglaze pan, scraping up browned bits on bottom of pan, and boil and reduce to a syrupy glaze. Stir in reserved braising liquid. Increase heat to medium-high and reduce sauce until nicely thickened, 15 to 20 minutes. Taste and adjust seasoning. Return lamb shanks to the pot and coat with sauce. If making ahead, set aside until cool, cover and refrigerate for up to 3 days. Reheat over medium-low heat or in 325°F (160°C) oven until heated through, about 1 hour when taken straight from the refrigerator.

Pots and Pans

Essential among your kitchen equipment is a large heavy-bottomed ovenproof Dutch oven or casserole in which to cook stews and braises. In our commercial kitchen, the workhorse pots are large heavy aluminum rondeaux, ranging in diameter from 18 inches (45 cm) to 36 inches (90 cm) with sides about 8 inches (20 cm) high. Frequently you'll see a large heavy baking sheet, partially or totally covering the top and acting as a lid. In my home kitchen, my prized pot is an oval, cast-iron 6-quart (6 L) casserole. It has a good surface for browning meats and vegetables on top of the stove, high sides to accommodate vegetables and liquids and a well-fitting lid. It's just about indestructible. I've probably used it at least once a week for more than 20 years!

Lamb Curry

Gentle cooking of the meat in lots of aromatic spices is essential for making a great curry. Serve with steamed basmati rice and sautéed spinach.

Tip

Add more liquid during the long slow cooking time, if needed. If at the end of the cooking process there is an excess of liquid, remove lamb from the pot with a slotted spoon and set aside. Reduce the sauce over medium-high heat until desired consistency is achieved.

3 lbs	boneless lamb shoulder	1.5 kg
2 tbsp	Garam Masala (page 117) or store-bought	25 mL
6 tbsp	vegetable oil, divided	90 mL
	Salt and freshly ground black pepper	
4 cups	Chicken Stock (page 54) or ready-to-use broth or water, divided	1 L
6	green cardamom pods	6
1½ tsp	coriander seeds	7 mL
1	piece (4 inches/10 cm) cinnamon stick, broken	1
1	onion, thinly sliced	1
2 tbsp	each minced garlic and gingerroot	25 mL
1½ to 2 tbsp	Curry Spice Blend (page 207) or your favorite curry powder	22 to 25 mL
1½ cups	canned plum tomatoes with juice, chopped	375 mL
1	can (14 oz/400 mL) coconut milk	1

1. Trim lamb and cut into 1-inch (2.5 cm) cubes. In large bowl, toss lamb with garam masala and 2 tbsp (25 mL) oil. Cover and marinate in refrigerator 2 hours or overnight.

2. In a large pot, heat 2 tbsp (25 mL) oil over medium-high heat. Lightly season lamb with salt and pepper. Sear lamb, in batches, on all sides until nicely browned, adding more oil as needed. Do not crowd the pot. Transfer to bowl and set aside. Discard excess fat. Add ½ cup (125 mL) stock and deglaze pot, scraping up browned bits on the bottom. Pour over lamb.

3. In the same pot, heat 2 tbsp (25 mL) of oil over medium heat. Add cardamom pods, coriander seeds and cinnamon and sauté until cardamom pods start to swell and aromas are released, about 5 minutes. Add onion and sauté until softened and deeply browned, 8 to 10 minutes. Add garlic and ginger and sauté until softened, 3 to 4 minutes. Add spice blend and salt and pepper to taste and cook, stirring, 1 to 2 minutes.

4. Stir in tomatoes with juice, coconut milk and remaining stock. Return lamb with any collected juices to pot. Gently bring to a boil. Reduce heat to low and simmer, covered, until lamb is very tender, 1 to 1½ hours. Taste and adjust seasoning.

Curry Spice Blend

MAKES ABOUT
2 TBSP (25 ML)

Our word "curry" comes from "kari," the South Indian word for "sauce" that refers to a blend of spices used to flavor meat and vegetable stews. Indian cooks do not use a prepared blend, but instead roast and grind individual spices to suit a particular dish. Commercial curry powder usually includes cayenne, cinnamon, coriander, cloves, cumin, fennel seeds, fenugreek, ground mustard, turmeric and black pepper. The distinct color comes from yellow turmeric. The level of heat varies from mild to very hot, depending upon how much red pepper is included in the mix. As with all ground spices, the fresher they are, the better the flavor and aroma. Always sauté raw spices in oil for a minute or two before use to bring the flavors to life.

Spice mill or mortar and pestle

6	green cardamom pods or ½ tsp (2 mL) green cardamom seeds	6
2 tsp	cumin seeds	10 mL
1½ tsp	coriander seeds	7 mL
½ tsp	fennel seeds	2 mL
1	piece (4 inches/10 cm) stick cinnamon, crumbled	1
1 tsp	ground fenugreek	5 mL
1 tsp	freshly ground black pepper	5 mL
½ tsp	ground turmeric	2 mL

1. In a heavy-bottomed dry skillet over medium heat, toast cardamom pods, cumin, coriander and fennel seeds and cinnamon. Stir spices until aromas are released, about 10 minutes.

2. Crush the cardamom pods. Save the small green seeds and discard the shells.

3. Use a spice mill to grind spices to a fine powder. You may need to grind spices in several batches. Sieve, if necessary, to remove any remaining chunky pieces.

4. Combine toasted spices with fenugreek, pepper and turmeric. Store in a covered jar in a cool cupboard and use within 6 months for best flavor.

Sweet and Hot Peppers

Sweet

Sweet peppers sail, at best, under a flag of convenience. Peppers they are, technically, since they belong, like the chile, to the *Capsicum* family. But the addition of pepper (pimento) to the name — by Christopher Columbus is misleading since we all know, from the crib, what pepper means: hot stuff, and in varying degrees more than enough to make us sneeze, cry or turn into a raging, molten furnace.

Not so the sweet variety, most popular of which are the **bell peppers**, named for their shape. They are everywhere and come in a rich variety of colors — starting out a rich bright green when young, moving through yellow and orange to purple, blue and brown (and sometimes a mix of several) to red. The **reds** are simply the end product of the **greens**, ripened on the vine, and generally the sweetest of the lot.

Studies have shown that bell peppers help prevent blood clots, reduce the risk of heart attacks and strokes, and protect against cataracts. They all carry vitamins C (more in a cup, chopped, than an orange) and B_6, thiamine, beta-carotene and folic acid; but the reds, thanks to all the extra time on the vine, have significantly more of all of them — plus lycopene, the carotene that fights cancer and heart disease.

In the Kitchen

Roasting peppers, particularly the reds, deepens and concentrates the flavor. This can be done in the oven or on a gas stove, but works at its best on a grill over charcoal. Once blackened and cooled, the skins may be scraped or peeled, and the results make a revelation of soups, pizzas, salads, pastas, and every sandwich known to man, woman and child. Unroasted, but hollowed out and with their tops sliced off, all the bells make excellent stuffers, or stuffees, for almost any filling that strikes the fancy, served salad cold or oven hot.

Among the sweet varieties are the **Aristotle**, **Boyton Bell**, **Paladin**, **King Arthur** and **Merlin**, variations on the theme; in taste not much to choose between. There is also the **Sweet Chocolate**, so called because it stops at brown, but is every bit as sweet as the red. The **Sweet Banana**, **Cubanelle**, **Bull's Horn** and **Gypsy** varieties are smaller than the bells, not as sweet, but particularly good for frying and pickling. Where bells are plump and full-figured, these are slim, tapered, and could easily be taken for a variety of jalapeños. Don't be taken — unless you thrive on surprise.

Also in the mild sweet variety is the fleshy **poblano**, which when dried becomes the dark red **ancho** and is related to the chocolate-brown **mulato** — a touch hotter. Both these milder dried chiles and also the small purplish-black **pasilla**, are used in Mexican cooking to add depth of sweet fruity flavor to salsas, stews and mole. Colorful **Hungarian (banana)** peppers, ranging from mild to piquant are available pickled and the sweet **pimento** is roasted and preserved in jars and cans — useful for dips, salads and pizza toppings.

Wash dried chiles in water. Remove stems, seeds and veins and tear into pieces. Cover with hot water (about 1 cup/250 mL for 6 large chiles) and set aside to soak for 1 hour. Purée chiles in a blender with soaking liquid to make a smooth paste. Use the purée to flavor soups, stews and chilies.

Hot

Between the sweet and the hot a deep gulf is fixed, psychologically as much as by flavor. It is the difference between driving Jennifer Aniston (or Keanu Reeves) home to meet the parents in the old Volvo — or calling for the limo to escort you and George Clooney (or Sharon Stone) on the same mission. And having the limo wait.

Peppers, the true ones, the hotties containing the fiery compound capsaicin, are the chiles, originating in what is now South America and enlivening the human diet for about 10,000 years. To the north, and east as far as Africa, we have Diego Álvarez Chanca, a doctor on Columbus's second voyage to the West Indies in 1493, to thank for them: while Columbus was boasting how close he was to China and killing and enslaving many thousands of Taíno Indians, Álvarez Chanca was making a study of chiles and their fiery seeds, and was the first to write about their medicinal virtues the following year.

These are many, not all yet proven for *Homo sapiens*. Chile's nutritional content, gram for gram, is more potent than that of sweet peppers; since we are able to eat far more bell peppers than, say, jalapeños, this evens out. Still, studies have shown, variously, that capsaicin, the vital element in the chile seeds, kills cancer cells in rats, and fights diabetes and obesity in mice, thereby giving hope to human sufferers; has a protective effect fighting ulcers; cleanses the stomach and produces good digestive acid; and helps control microbial contamination of food in countries with little or no refrigeration. (The body's perspiration during consumption of hot-spiced food is a cooling mechanism of its own.)

In the Kitchen

Handle hot peppers with care and gloves, if you are sensitive. Even a trace of hot pepper juice near lips or eyes is very painful.

Naturally, not all chiles are created equal. Some are hotter than others, many within the same cultivars. Relative heat is measured in **Scoville units**, named after American chemist Wilbur Scoville who devised them in 1912. Thus the **sweet peppers** rate

0 Scoville Heat Units (SHU); the **poblano/ancho**, 1,000–2,000; the **jalapeño**, 2,500–8,000; the **chipotle**, 5,000-8,000; the **serrano**, 8,000–22,000; the **tabasco** and **cayenne**, 30,000–50,000; the **datil**, up to 300,000; the **Scotch bonnet**, 150,000–325,000; the **habaneros**, 150,000–575,000.

Many of these hot varieties are available in other forms other than fresh. The **jalapeño**, named **chipotle** when dried and smoked, is available preserved in cans in a tomato-based sauce (chipotle pepper in adobo sauce). Much of the heat is released into the sauce over time, so add with caution. Smoky chipotle, milder **ancho** and familiar **cayenne** are also found in powdered form. 1 tbsp (15 mL) ground ancho chile is approximately equal to 1 whole chile when substituted in recipes. $\frac{1}{8}$ tsp (0.5 mL) cayenne equals one tiny hot fresh or dried whole hot pepper as in **cayenne**, tiny **pequín** or **cascabel**.

Top of the scorch list, verified in 2007 by Guinness World Records, is the truly fearsome **naga jolokia**, native to Assam, northeast India. This little bundle of fury packs from 800,000 SHU to the record 1,041,000, meaning that for most of us, eating one seed of a naga will produce intense mouth pain for about half an hour. We should raise a thoughtful glass to Assam's own Anandita Dutta Tamuly, 26, who on April 9, 2009, while watched with stunned astonishment by the celebrity chef Gordon Ramsay, ate 51 naga jolokia peppers in two minutes. Over to you, Guinness.

What to do when capsaicin consumption exceeds common sense, unless you are Assamese? Drinking water will be useless (capsaicin is not water soluble). Cold beer will be better than useless but not much. Best SOS will come from milk and ice cream. Milk contains casein, which will wash away the capsaicin molecules the way soap dissolves grease.

Lamb Sosaties

SERVES 4

Recipes come into our repertoire in many ways. This tasty curried lamb skewer came from the South African grandmother of one of our brides, whose wedding we were catering. She wanted to include a favorite family dish in her bridal buffet. Delicious served over herb-flavored couscous.

The spicy Curried Apricot Glaze is also good with pork kebabs, pork tenderloin, spareribs, chicken wings or even scallops.

Tip

To create a smooth glaze, press apricot mixture through a fine sieve.

● **Eight 8-inch (20 cm) bamboo skewers, soaked in water for 30 minutes**

1 tbsp	vegetable oil	15 mL
1	clove garlic, finely chopped	1
1 tsp	curry powder	5 mL
1½ lbs	boneless lamb shoulder	750 g
24	dried apricots	24
	Boiling water	
½	red onion, cut into small wedges	½
	Salt and freshly ground black pepper	
	Curried Apricot Glaze, divided (page 211),	
1 tbsp	coarsely chopped cilantro or flat-leaf parsley	15 mL

1. In a small skillet, heat oil over medium-low heat. Add garlic and sauté until soft, 1 to 2 minutes. Stir in curry powder and cook, stirring, 1 to 2 minutes.

2. Trim lamb, cut into cubes, about 1 inch (2.5 cm), and place in a bowl. Add garlic mixture and toss to combine. Cover and marinate in the refrigerator for several hours or overnight.

3. Preheat barbecue grill to medium-high and lightly oil grill.

4. Place apricots in a small bowl and add boiling water to cover. Let soak until soft, about 20 minutes. Drain and set aside. Arrange separate bowls on your counter containing apricots, onion wedges and marinated lamb. Alternate lamb, onion and apricots on skewers, beginning and ending with lamb. Season with salt and pepper. Divide Curried Apricot Glaze into 2 small bowls. Use one bowl for glazing meat during grilling and reserve the other for brushing on cooked lamb or to serve at the table. Set aside.

5. Grill lamb skewers until nicely browned and cooked to your liking, 3 to 4 minutes each side for medium-rare. While grilling, turn diligently and brush occasionally with glaze. Remove from grill, brush with glaze and garnish with chopped cilantro.

Curried Apricot Glaze

Makes ²/₃ cup (150 mL)

1 tbsp	vegetable oil	15 mL
½	onion, finely chopped	½
1	clove garlic, finely chopped	1
1 tsp	curry powder	5 mL
1	bay leaf	1
½ cup	apricot jam	125 mL
2 tbsp	water	25 mL
1 tbsp	brown sugar	15 mL
1 tbsp	white wine vinegar	15 mL
	Salt and freshly ground black pepper	
1 tbsp	freshly squeezed lemon juice	15 mL

1. In a saucepan, heat oil over medium heat. Add onion and sauté until softened but not browned, 5 minutes. Add garlic, curry powder and bay leaf and sauté for 1 to 2 minutes. Stir in jam, water, brown sugar, vinegar, and a pinch each of salt and pepper. Reduce heat to low and simmer, stirring occasionally, for 5 minutes. Stir in lemon juice. Taste and adjust seasoning.

Lamb Bisteeya

This Moroccan-style lamb pie is prepared in several steps. Marinate lamb overnight. The next day, cook filling. Cool and refrigerate. At your leisure, prepare and bake the pie or assemble small cocktail pies.

Tip

Depending on the size of your phyllo sheets, you may be able to cut 2 circles from each sheet. If so, stack 2 sheets of phyllo at a time, using a total of 8 sheets, and cut 2 circles each time (you'll get one extra circle — just discard it or use it for something else).

Variation

Lamb Bisteeya Phyllo Triangles: Use the spicy lamb mixture to make tasty party snacks. Follow method described on page 214 for creating phyllo triangles.

- **Large ovenproof pot**
- **9-inch (23 cm) springform pan**
- **Baking sheet, lined with parchment paper**

3 lbs	boneless lamb shoulder, trimmed and diced	1.5 kg
	Moroccan Spice Blend, divided	
6 tbsp	vegetable oil, divided	90 mL
	Salt and freshly ground black pepper	
1	onion, chopped	1
2	cloves garlic, chopped	2
1 cup	chicken stock or water	250 mL
1 cup	chopped fresh or canned tomatoes	250 mL
¾ cup	dried apricots, halved	175 mL
1 tsp	hot pepper flakes	5 mL
½ tsp	saffron threads	2 mL
1 cup	toasted sliced almonds	250 mL
¼ cup	coarsely chopped mint	50 mL
¼ cup	coarsely chopped cilantro	50 mL
15	sheets phyllo pastry (see Tip, left)	15
⅓ cup	melted butter	75 mL
1 tsp	confectioner's (icing) sugar, sifted	5 mL
½ tsp	ground cinnamon	2 mL

1. In a large bowl, combine lamb, 1 tbsp (15 mL) of the Moroccan Spice Blend and 2 tbsp (25 mL) of the oil. Cover and marinate in the refrigerator overnight.

2. Preheat oven to 350°F (180°C). In large ovenproof pot, heat 2 tbsp (25 mL) of oil over medium-high. Lightly season lamb with salt and pepper and brown, in batches, on all sides. Do not crowd pot. Transfer to bowl and set aside. Drain and discard excess fat.

3. In same pot, heat 2 tbsp (25 mL) of oil over medium heat. Add onion and sauté until softened and deeply browned, 7 to 8 minutes. Add garlic and sauté until softened, about 2 minutes. Stir in remaining Moroccan Spice Blend and sauté for 30 seconds. Add stock and deglaze pot, scraping up browned bits on bottom. Return lamb to pot with any collected juices. Add tomatoes, apricots, hot pepper flakes, saffron and salt and pepper to taste.

4. Cover pot and transfer to preheated oven. Bake until lamb is very tender, $1\frac{1}{2}$ to 2 hours. Let cool. Add almonds, mint and cilantro. Taste and adjust seasoning.

5. *To assemble bistyeea:* Preheat oven to 350°F (180°C), if necessary. Remove bottom from springform pan. Use the bottom as a template around which to cut pastry circles. Place the springform ring on a parchment-lined baking sheet and use it as the mold in which to assemble the pie.

6. Carefully unroll phyllo pastry. Spread phyllo on top of a cutting board in stacks of 3. Place bottom of the springform pan (to use as a template) on top of the phyllo pastry and cut out 15 circles using a small knife.

7. Cover 3 circles with a damp cloth. Working quickly, brush each of the 12 remaining circles with butter, then drape them over the ring of the springform pan. Be sure the circle covers about 1 inch (2.5 cm) of the bottom of the pie, circles should overlap slightly to create a double layer of phyllo all the way around the edge of the pie.

8. Brush each of the remaining 3 circles with butter and place flat in the bottom of the ring.

9. Add lamb filling and smooth out the surface. Pull up one section at a time of the overhanging phyllo to cover the filling; work your way around the pie overlapping the pieces as you pull them up to cover the filling.

10. Carefully lift the springform pan ring from around the pie. Brush the sides and top of the pie with butter. Bake in preheated oven until golden brown, about 30 minutes. Sprinkle with icing sugar and cinnamon to serve.

Moroccan Spice Blend
In a small bowl, combine $1\frac{1}{2}$ tsp (7 mL) ground coriander, 1 tsp (5 mL) ground cumin, 1 tsp (5 mL) paprika, 1 tsp (5 mL) ground black pepper, $\frac{1}{2}$ tsp (2 mL) ground ginger, $\frac{1}{2}$ tsp (2 mL) ground cinnamon, $\frac{1}{2}$ tsp (2 mL) cayenne and $\frac{1}{4}$ tsp (1 mL) ground cloves.
    Makes 2 tbsp (25 mL).

Working with Phyllo Pastry

Wafer-thin sheets of this light-textured pasty are used to make dozens of hors d'oeuvres and sweet and savory pastries. Fillings of lamb and chicken and vegetable mixtures including spinach or mushrooms and feta cheese are very popular, as are sweet versions that include nuts and honey.

If your city has a vibrant Greek community, as we have in Toronto, you will likely find packages of handmade phyllo for sale in small Greek bakeries. A real treat, since to make your own is quite a challenge and, I suspect, requires generations of practice. Packages of phyllo sheets are also available in the freezer at the supermarket.

Let frozen phyllo thaw in the package overnight in the refrigerator, or for about 5 hours at room temperature. Do not remove from package until you are ready to get to work. Phyllo sheets dry out and become brittle very quickly. Cover the phyllo sheets you are going to use with a damp cloth as you work. Keep any extra phyllo sheets securely wrapped in plastic wrap and refrigerate: refreeze at once or keep in refrigerator and use within 2 to 3 days.

Phyllo Bundles

Have at hand a small bowl of melted butter and a pastry brush. Using 2 sheets of phyllo, lay one sheet on work surface and brush with melted butter. Lay the other sheet on top. Cut the pastry rectangle lengthwise into 3 and across into 3, to make 9 squares. Place about 1 tbsp (15 mL) of the filling in the center of each square. Bring up edges of pastry over filling and pinch together. Brush lightly with butter. Place bundles on a lightly greased baking sheet. Bake in preheated 375°F (190°C) oven until golden, 10 to 15 minutes.

Phyllo Triangles

Have at hand a small bowl of melted butter and a pastry brush. Using 2 phyllo sheets, lay one sheet on work surface and brush with melted butter. Lay the other sheet on top. Cut the pastry rectangle lengthwise into 4 strips. Place about 1 tbsp (15 mL) of the filling about 1 inch (2.5 cm) from the bottom of each strip. Lift bottom right corner of strip up and over the filling, lining up with edge of pastry on the left to make a triangle. Continue to fold triangle over from left to right up the strip. Brush lightly with butter. Place triangles on a lightly greased baking sheet. Bake in preheated 375°F (190°C) oven until golden, 10 to 15 minutes.

Phyllo Rolls

Have at hand a small bowl of melted butter and a pastry brush. Using 2 phyllo sheets, lay one sheet on work surface and brush with melted butter. Lay the other sheet on top. Cut the pastry rectangle lengthwise into 4 strips. Place about 1 tbsp (15 mL) of the filling about 1/2 inch (1 cm) from the bottom of each strip. Fold pastry up over filling and fold over each edge, 1/2 inch (1 cm) to enclose filling. Brush edges with melted butter. Roll up each strip halfway and brush again with melted butter. Continue rolling up the strip into a cylinder. Brush top and sides lightly with butter. Place rolls, seam side down, on a lightly greased baking sheet. Bake in preheated 375°F (190°C) oven until golden, 10 to 15 minutes.

Lamb Navarin

SERVES 6

A classic bistro-style lamb and vegetable stew — a delicious one-pot dish that improves in flavor when made ahead. Warm Cheddar 'n' Chive Scones (page 379) would make a tasty accompaniment.

2 lbs	boneless lamb shoulder	1 kg
4 tbsp	olive oil, divided	60 mL
	Salt and freshly ground black pepper	
2	onions, chopped	2
2	cloves garlic, minced	2
2 tbsp	all-purpose flour	25 mL
1 cup	red wine	250 mL
5 cups	Chicken Stock (page 54) or ready-to-use broth	1.25 L
2 cups	chopped tomatoes, fresh or canned with juice	500 mL
1 tbsp	finely chopped rosemary	15 mL
2	bay leaves	2
8 oz	pearl onions	250 g
1 lb	mini white-skinned potatoes, halved	500 g
8 oz	carrots, cut into ½-inch (1 cm) pieces	250 g
¼ cup	coarsely chopped flat-leaf parsley	50 mL

1. Trim lamb and cut into cubes, about 1 inch (2.5 cm). In a large heavy pot, heat 2 tbsp (25 mL) of the oil over medium-high heat. Lightly season lamb with salt and pepper. Sear lamb, in batches, on all sides until nicely browned. Do not crowd the pot. Transfer to a bowl and set aside. Pour off and discard excess fat.

2. In the same pot, heat 2 tbsp (25 mL) of oil over medium heat. Add chopped onions and garlic and sauté until softened and lightly browned, 4 to 6 minutes. Stir in flour and cook, stirring, 2 to 3 minutes. Stir in wine and deglaze pot, scraping up all the browned bits from the bottom. Whisk until smooth. Add chicken stock, tomatoes, rosemary, bay leaves and browned lamb with collected juices. Bring gently to a boil. Reduce heat, cover and simmer for about 1 hour. Add pearl onions and cook for 10 minutes. Add potatoes and carrots and cook until vegetables and lamb are tender, 10 to 15 minutes. Remove from heat. Stir in parsley. Taste and adjust seasoning.

Herb-Crusted Rack of Lamb

Fresh spring lamb is always a treat. The rack of small rib chops, coated with fresh herbs and simply roasted, is truly an elegant and delicious main course.

- Preheat oven to 400°F (200°C)
- Roasting pan
- Instant-read thermometer

2 tbsp	olive oil, divided	25 mL
2	racks of lamb, 8-rib (each about 1½ lbs/750 g)	2
½ tsp	kosher or sea salt	2 mL
¼ tsp	freshly ground black pepper	1 mL
1 cup	fine fresh bread crumbs	250 mL
¼ cup	chopped flat-leaf parsley	50 mL
2 tbsp	chopped thyme	25 mL
1 tbsp	chopped mint	15 mL
1 tbsp	chopped rosemary	15 mL
2	cloves garlic, finely chopped	2
2 tbsp	Dijon mustard	25 mL

1. In a large skillet, heat 1 tbsp (15 mL) of the olive oil over medium-high heat. Lightly season lamb with salt and pepper. Brown lamb, one rack at a time, 2 to 3 minutes per side. Transfer to roasting pan fat side up.

2. In a small bowl, toss bread crumbs with parsley, thyme, mint, rosemary, garlic and remaining oil. Brush tops of racks with mustard and coat with bread crumb-herb mixture.

3. Roast in preheated oven until an instant-read thermometer inserted in the meaty portion, not touching the bone, registers 135°F (57°C) for rare, 8 to 10 minutes. Transfer to a cutting board and let stand loosely covered with foil, for 10 minutes. Slice into 2-rack portions to serve.

Fish and Seafood

Saffron-Roasted Halibut with Cherry Tomatoes and Herbs

For this dish, choose Pacific halibut and avoid Atlantic halibut, which is overfished with stocks vastly depleted.

Statistics tell us that it takes 14,000 stigmas taken from the Crocus Sativus *to make 1 ounce (28 g) saffron, making this spice the most expensive in the world! Its heady aroma and golden color suggest luxury, and the musky flavor is marvelous with mild white fish and seafood.*

Tip

Nobody likes to deal with a mouthful of bones! Run your fingers over the surface of the filleted fish to locate any stray bones. Keep tweezers in your kitchen utensil jar to quickly remove bones from fish portions before cooking.

- Preheat oven to 400°F (200°C)
- 13- by 9-inch (3 L) shallow baking dish or large ovenproof skillet

2 cups	cherry tomatoes	500 mL
2 tbsp	olive oil, divided	25 mL
	Salt and freshly ground black pepper	
1 tbsp	chopped cilantro	15 mL
1 tbsp	chopped basil	15 mL
2	green onions, thinly sliced	2
1 tbsp	balsamic vinegar	15 mL
6	skinless Pacific halibut fillets (each about 6 oz/175 g)	6
½ tsp	saffron threads	2 mL
½ cup	Fish Stock (page 229), water or clam juice	125 mL

1. In a bowl, toss tomatoes with 1 tbsp (15 mL) of the oil. Season lightly with salt and pepper and spread on a baking sheet in a single layer. Roast in preheated oven until beginning to split and soften, 6 to 8 minutes. Keep warm.

2. Meanwhile, in a small bowl, combine cilantro, basil, green onions, remaining oil and vinegar. Place halibut fillets in a baking dish. Spread mixture over top of halibut fillets and set aside for 10 minutes. Soften saffron in fish stock and set aside.

3. Season fish lightly and sprinkle with saffron/stock mixture. Roast in oven until fish flakes easily when tested with the tip of a sharp knife (see Tip, page 219), 10 to 15 minutes, depending on the thickness of the fillets. Serve each portion of fish garnished with roasted tomatoes and spoonfuls of the saffron-scented broth.

Herb-Roasted Salmon

This is a favorite treatment for salmon that results in very moist flavorful fish, equally delicious to serve warm or at room temperature. Combine any leftovers with mayonnaise to make a very tasty sandwich.

Tip

When is fish cooked? Insert the tip of a small sharp knife into the thickest part of the fillet. When cooked, the flesh is resilient to the touch and uniformly opaque. The flesh of a flaky fish separates into soft flakes. A noteworthy fish-cooking rule: Allow approximately 10 minutes of cooking time per 1-inch (2.5 cm) thickness of fish, as measured at the thickest part.

Grilling Variation

Grill salmon, flat side down, on a lightly oiled barbecue over medium-high heat. Cook with lid down for 8 to 10 minutes, depending on the thickness of the fillets.

- **Preheat oven to 400°F (200°C)**
- **Baking sheet, lightly oiled**

⅓ cup	finely chopped cilantro or flat-leaf parsley	75 mL
⅓ cup	finely chopped dill	75 mL
⅓ cup	finely chopped green onions	75 mL
2 tbsp	vegetable oil	25 mL
1 tbsp	white wine vinegar	15 mL
1 tbsp	grainy Dijon mustard	15 mL
	Salt and freshly ground black pepper	
6	salmon fillets (each approx. 6 oz/175 g), skin removed	6

1. In a small bowl, combine cilantro, dill, green onions, oil, vinegar, mustard and a pinch of pepper.

2. Sprinkle salmon fillets with a little salt and coat each fillet evenly with herb mixture. Arrange herb-topped fillets on prepared baking sheet.

3. Roast in preheated oven until fish flakes easily when tested with the tip of a sharp knife (see Tip, left), 10 to 15 minutes, depending on the thickness of the fillets.

Grilled Cedar-Planked Arctic Char with Maple Glaze

Variation

Cedar-Planked Salmon: Replace Arctic char with individual center-cut salmon fillets.

- **2 untreated cedar boards, approx. 8 by 16 by ¾ inch (20 by 40 by 2 cm)**
- **Barbecue grill**

¼ cup	pure maple syrup	50 mL
2 tbsp	grainy Dijon-style mustard	25 mL
1 tbsp	extra virgin olive oil	15 mL
2 tsp	kosher or sea salt	10 mL
½ tsp	freshly ground black pepper	2 mL
2	skinless sides Arctic char (each about 12 oz/375 g)	2

1. Place cedar boards in a large pan or sink and cover with water. Let soak for 30 minutes.
2. Preheat barbecue grill to high.
3. In a small bowl, combine maple syrup, mustard, oil, salt and pepper. Mix well.
4. Remove boards from water. Place one side of fish, flat side down, on each board. Spread maple mixture over the surface of the fish. Loosely cover fish with foil and place boards directly on grill. Close lid, reduce heat to medium-high and cook until fish flakes easily when tested with the tip of a sharp knife (see Tip, page 219), about 10 minutes.

Fish

Time was, and not so long ago, when eating seafood in much of the Western world was a bit of a penance — either religiously, on fish Fridays or during Lent, or by happenstance, as the fallback option when the meat money had run out. Food matters have changed, of course: Religion, pragmatic when it has to be, saw that scarfing down lobster thermidor on a Friday constituted penance of a specialized kind, and the fallback option, recognized at last as the healthy one, has now increasingly become the option of first choice. Today's North Americans are consuming 70 percent more seafood — fish and shellfish — than they did a generation ago; seafood sales in the United Kingdom swam past poultry for the first time in 2005; and seafood worldwide has become a $70-billion-a-year industry.

So it hardly seems fair that just when we're realizing how good fish is for us that media gloomsayers start issuing jeremiads about how bad some of those good fish can be. Thus delicious fish such as salmon, tuna, swordfish, shark and halibut have plenty of those omega-3 polyunsaturates so fine for our hearts and cholesterol levels but have also been found to contain dangerous levels of carcinogens and mercury (bad for everything else, encouraging dementia and death before our time). And the bigger, fattier and older the fish, the worse for us since the 3s may stay the same but the bad stuff accumulates and concentrates. What to do?

Use common sense, is the short answer. *The Journal of the American Medical Association* and Health Canada both agree: Eating fish is good for us, even if it has a bit of mercury in it — just let's not go overboard. Researchers at the Harvard School of Public Health have found that eating fish moderately (80 g of farmed salmon, for instance, or 160 g of mackerel a week) reduced the risk of premature death from heart disease by 36 percent and from any cause by 17 percent. In short, the benefits far outweigh the risks.

According to the Food and Agriculture Organization of the United Nations, more than 70 percent of the world's fish species are either fully exploited or seriously depleted. The North Atlantic in particular has been so egregiously overfished that populations of cod, hake, haddock and flounder — once sufficiently plentiful that they impeded the progress of John Cabot's ships off Newfoundland — have fallen by as much as 95 percent over the last 20 years. Perhaps the most arresting statistic (from the FAO) is that one in four of the fish caught in trawlers' fishing gear dies as "bycatch" — whether too small, too young or just not the right kind, all unwanted, unintentional and discarded. The waste truly shocks.

In the Kitchen

That under our belts, what does the concerned consumer avoid or choose? **Avoid:** *Bluefin tuna, Atlantic cod* and *halibut, Chilean sea bass, grouper, monkfish, orange roughy, shark, Atlantic sole, flounder* and *plaice*. **Choose** (with care, aiming for some 280 g/week): *Arctic char, catfish* (farmed, from the southern states), *Pacific cod* and *halibut, herring, mackerel, mahi-mahi* (*dorado*)*, pickerel* (*walleye*)*, pollock* (often used as crab substitute, without credit)*, sablefish, salmon* from B.C. and Alaska, *sardines, sea bass* (U.S. Pacific)*, swordfish* (from North American waters)*, trout, tuna* (*albacore*) caught in North American waters by pole or troll.

For further information: *Bottomfeeder*, by Taras Grescoe (HarperCollins), a well researched, witty, encouraging yet profoundly sobering account of where global fishery is today, what we have done to it and how we can help. See also www.seachoice.org.

Fish with Capers and Lemon

This is a simple and delicious treatment for almost any fresh fish — salmon, Pacific halibut, black cod. Choose what looks fresh at the market and remember to check your "sustainable fish" list (see Fish, page 221 or visit www.seachoice.org).

Tip

If you don't have a large enough skillet, the searing process can be done in batches and the fish transferred to a parchment paper-lined baking sheet for the oven.

● **Preheat oven to 375°F (190°C)**
● **Large ovenproof skillet**

6	fish fillets (each approx. 5 oz/150 g)	6
	Salt and freshly ground black pepper	
6 tbsp	butter, divided	90 mL
2 tbsp	finely chopped shallots	25 mL
½ cup	white wine	125 mL
2 tbsp	capers, coarsely chopped	25 mL
2 tbsp	coarsely chopped flat-leaf parsley	25 mL
	Juice of ½ lemon	

1. Pat fillets dry and season with salt and pepper.
2. Place large ovenproof skillet over medium-high heat for 1 minute. Add 2 tbsp (25 mL) of the butter and swirl in pan until melted and hot. Add fish fillets, in batches, skin side up, and add more butter, if necessary. Do not crowd pan. Reduce heat to medium and cook fish until golden brown, 3 to 4 minutes.
3. Carefully turn fillets over and transfer pan to preheated oven. Bake until fish flakes easily when tested with the tip of a sharp knife (see Tip, page 219), 5 to 6 minutes. Transfer fish to a warm serving platter.
4. Return skillet to stovetop over medium heat. Add butter, as required, to make about 2 tbsp (25 mL) fat. Add shallots and sauté for 30 seconds. Add white wine and deglaze pan, scraping up browned bits on bottom. Add capers, parsley and lemon juice. Stir to combine and heat through. Whisk in 2 tbsp (25 mL) butter and pour over fish. Serve at once.

Prosciutto-Wrapped Mahi-Mahi with Blood Orange Relish

This dish combines firm-fleshed mild mahi-mahi with salty prosciutto and tart blood oranges. Blood oranges have a too-short season in January and February. For the rest of the year, substitute navel oranges and sharpen the flavor by adding lemon or lime juice to the relish.

Tip

If you don't have a large enough skillet, the searing process can be done in batches and the fish transferred to a parchment paper-lined baking sheet for the oven.

- Preheat oven to 375°F (190°C)
- Large ovenproof skillet

6	mahi-mahi fillets (each approx. 5 oz/150 g)	6
	Salt and freshly ground black pepper	
6	large slices prosciutto	6
1 tbsp	olive oil	15 mL
	Blood Orange Relish (see below)	

1. Season fillets with salt and pepper.
2. Wrap each piece of fish with one piece of prosciutto. Tuck the ends in on the bottom of each fillet and secure with a toothpick.
3. Place a large ovenproof skillet over medium-heat for 1 minute. Add oil. Add wrapped fillets, with edges down to seal the prosciutto, and cook on each side until golden brown, about 2 minutes per side.
4. Transfer pan to preheated oven and bake until fish is opaque and tender when tested with a sharp knife, about 10 minutes. Serve hot with Blood Orange Relish.

Blood Orange Relish

Makes 1¼ cups (300 mL)

3	blood oranges	3
½ cup	finely diced red onion	125 mL
½ cup	coarsely chopped cilantro	125 mL
3 tbsp	extra virgin olive oil	45 mL
1 tbsp	natural rice vinegar	15 mL
	Salt and freshly ground black pepper	

1. Working over a bowl, remove peel and pith from oranges and cut between membranes into segments (save the juices).
2. Combine orange segments and juice, red onion, cilantro, oil, vinegar and salt. Stir gently. Add pepper to taste. Make at least 2 hours ahead of serving to allow flavors to develop. Enjoy the same day for freshest flavor.

Poached Salmon

SERVES 6

Salmon, with delicate pink flesh and mild flavor, is by far the most popular fish in our repertoire, especially in summer months. A whole salmon, simply poached in a light broth and handsomely garnished, may be part of a festive summer buffet.

Tips

Charmoula Marinade Sauce (page 197) is good to serve with warm poached salmon.

To accompany cold poached salmon, try Aïoli (Variation, page 96) or Dill and Garlic Dip (page 316).

Variation

Poached Shrimp: Bring Court Bouillon to a simmer. Add 2 lbs (1 kg) shrimp in shell. Bring back to a simmer and cook until pink and just firm to the touch when pinched, 3 to 5 minutes for medium-size shrimp. When cool enough to handle, remove shell and devein.

- **Preheat oven to 350°F (180°C)**
- **Large ovenproof baking dish or large sauté pan**

7 to 8 cups	Court Bouillon (page 225)	1.75 to 2 L
6	salmon fillets (each approx. 6 oz/175 g), skin removed	6
6	small sprigs dill	6
1	lemon, thinly sliced	1

1. In a large sauté pan, heat Court Bouillon over medium heat until simmering. Arrange salmon in bouillon in a single layer.

2. Bake in preheated oven or simmer on the stovetop until fish flakes easily when tested with the tip of a sharp knife (see Tip, page 219), 10 to 15 minutes. Lift salmon fillets from poaching broth with a slotted spoon and transfer to a cooling rack to remove excess liquid. Serve warm or chilled and garnish with dill and lemon.

Poaching a Whole Salmon

Bring Court Bouillon to a simmer in a fish poacher. Carefully lower whole salmon, usually 6 to 7 lbs (3 to 3.5 kg), into hot liquid. Simmer on stovetop or in a 350°F (180°C) oven. Time is counted from when the poaching liquid begins to bubble and depends upon the thickness of the fish. Allow 10 minutes of cooking time for each 1 inch (2.5 cm) of fish measured at the thickest part. If you do not have a fish poacher, season whole fish with aromatics, such as a splash of white wine, lemon, parsley and green onions, and season with salt and pepper. Wrap fish securely in heavy-duty foil. Place on a baking sheet and bake in a 350°F (180°C) oven. Allow the same 10 minutes cooking time for each 1 inch (2.5 cm) of fish and an additional 5 minutes to account for the time it takes for heat to penetrate the foil. Unwrap fish and lift onto a rack to drain. Carefully peel away skin. Serve warm or chilled with appropriate sauces and garnish.

Court Bouillon

Makes 7 to 8 cups (1.75 to 2 L)

8 cups	water	2 L
½ cup	dry white wine or ¼ cup (50 mL) Pernod	125 mL
½	lemon, thinly sliced	½
2	shallots, sliced, or ½ onion, sliced	2
1	bay leaf	1
4	sprigs flat-leaf parsley	4
8	black peppercorns	8
1 tsp	fennel seeds	5 mL
1 tsp	sea salt	5 mL

1. In a large pot over medium-high heat, combine water, wine, lemon, shallots, bay leaf, parsley, peppercorns, fennel seeds and salt. Bring to a boil. Reduce heat to low and simmer for 20 minutes. Strain and let cool. Use at once or freeze for later use. Store in a covered container in the refrigerator and use within 2 days or freeze for up to 6 months.

Tip

Use this flavorful broth to poach fish or seafood. Use it also to poach vegetables such as mushrooms, leeks or shallots that you plan to serve cold. Remove the cooked fish or vegetables from the broth and reduce to make a flavorful glaze, if you like.

Salmon and Leek Strudel

Each bite of crisp buttery pastry and lemony dill-scented salmon and leeks is a delight — perfect for brunch, lunch or a light springtime supper. This recipe makes two strudels. Cut each on the diagonal into four pieces to create serving portions.

Tip

Phyllo pastry sheets are widely available and usually found in the freezer section of the supermarket. Follow instructions on the package and let thaw in the refrigerator the day before you plan to use them. You have to work quickly since the sheets dry out quickly. Keep stack of phyllo sheets covered with a damp tea towel while you work. See Working with Phyllo Pastry, page 214.

- Preheat oven to 350°F (180°C)
- Large baking sheet, lightly oiled

6 tbsp	butter, divided	90 mL
2	leeks, white and tender green parts only, finely chopped (see Tip, page 44)	2
	Salt and freshly ground black pepper	
1 lb	salmon fillets, skin removed, cut into 1-inch (2.5 cm) pieces	500 g
2 tbsp	fresh bread crumbs	25 mL
2 tbsp	chopped dill	25 mL
1 tsp	grated lemon zest	5 mL
6	sheets phyllo pastry (see Tip, left)	6

1. In a large skillet, melt 2 tbsp (25 mL) of the butter over medium heat. Add leeks and sauté until tender, 7 to 10 minutes. Season with salt and pepper to taste.

2. In a bowl, combine leeks, salmon, bread crumbs, dill and lemon zest. Season lightly and set aside.

3. In a small saucepan, melt remaining butter and place it beside you on your work surface. Lay out one phyllo sheet on the work surface with shorter side towards you, brush lightly with butter and lay another phyllo sheet on top. Brush second sheet of phyllo with butter and top with a third phyllo sheet to make 3 layers. Arrange half the salmon mixture in a rectangle parallel with the bottom edge, approximately 3 inches (7.5 cm) from the edge and leaving about 2 inches (5 cm) uncovered at each side. Bring the bottom of the phyllo sheet up and over the filling and gently roll up two more times. Fold in each side of the phyllo sheet to seal the ends of the roll and continue rolling to make a neat parcel. Repeat the process with the remaining 3 phyllo sheets and salmon mixture.

4. Arrange salmon and leek packages on prepared baking sheet, seam side down, and brush tops with melted butter. Bake in preheated oven until pastry is nicely golden and salmon is cooked, 25 to 30 minutes. To serve, cut each salmon package into 4 equal pieces and serve 2 per person.

Shellfish

Mostly, we use the term shellfish for *crustaceans*, such as crabs, crayfish, lobster and shrimp, and *mollusks*, such as clams, mussels, scallops and oysters. These are the exoskeletons, wearing their "bones" on the outside. Less common on our tables are the octopus and the squid, cephalopods of the mollusk species, where what remains of their shells have been internalized. (Not all of us can enjoy them since about two percent of North Americans have a shellfish allergy, often severe; not only do they miss out on some of the great nutritional treats of the last few million years, but they have to suffer the pity of the 98 percent of the rest of us.)

In the Kitchen

Shrimp: An imprecise word, embracing both the larger prawns (10 to 15 per pound) and the baby salad ones (51 to 60 per pound). Sometimes the word scampi is used in restaurants, meaning they feel they can charge more for them. Many of the shrimp available here are white shrimp from the Caribbean and the Gulf of Mexico; freshness is all. Recently overtook tuna as the most popular restaurant seafood in the U.S. Good source of calcium and phosphorus; once thought high in cholesterol but new studies show a 3-oz (90 g) serving of shrimp contains half the cholesterol in one chicken egg.

Scallops: Bay and **Sea**. The bays are small, the seas three to four times larger. Some claim that there's little difference in taste and buy only the bays since they cost less. Others know that the extra expense of sea scallops is repaid many times by their extra sweetness, firmness and delicacy of taste. Atlantic sea scallops harvested off the northern U.S. and Canadian seaboards are the most widely sold. Most bay scallops sold in North America come from China's Bohai Bay, southeast of Beijing; Nantucket's, though from a minor market, are highly prized. When cooking, always undercook.

Oysters: "He was a brave man who first ate an oyster," noted the 18th-century satirist Jonathan Swift. Recent evidence of scallop shell remains in a South African cave suggests there were plenty of brave people there 164,000 years ago. The best oysters, eaten fresh, are often the ones we've eaten last; but oysters from Prince Edward Island, Louisiana and Washington (recently surpassing Louisiana as the largest oyster-producing state) always rank high.

Octopus: Of the same family as the increasingly popular **squid** (or **calamari**) and **cuttlefish**. All distinctively chewy, filled with flavor and nutrients; cuttlefish is the most delicate, octopus not at all. General rule: Cook them short or cook them long, nothing in between (it makes all of them tougher). Most squid (not a name to love) are no more than 24 inches (60 cm) long, but a **Colossal squid** (*Mesonychoteuthis hamiltoni*), netted off Antarctica in 2007, was 33 feet (10 m) long and weighed 1,091 pounds (495 kg), making it the largest invertebrate ever caught. It had eyes the size of dinner plates. If carved up for calamari rings, the rings would have been the size of tractor tires, and just as tender. And scientists say it may well have been a youngster. Octopuses are the most intelligent of their order — they can solve problems and escape from one aquarium to another in search of food; none of it learned from their parents, who disregard them after birth. Some humans keep them as pets…but they should keep a sharp eye on them.

Tuscan Shrimp and Beans

One taste of these spicy garlic shrimp, combined with fresh tomatoes and herbs and perfectly cooked white beans, and you are transported to sunny Italy. Serve with Broccoli Rabe with Garlic (page 280) and a wedge of crusty Italian bread.

Tip

Do not add salt when soaking or cooking dried beans because it prevents the beans from becoming tender.

Variation

For speed and convenience, replace dried beans with 2 cans (14 to 19 oz/398 to 540 mL) white beans, rinsed and drained.

1½ cups	dried white beans (see Tip, left)	375 mL
2	bay leaves, divided	2
	Kosher or sea salt	
¼ cup	extra virgin olive oil	50 mL
4	cloves garlic, finely chopped	4
Pinch	hot pepper flakes	Pinch
6	ripe Roma (plum) tomatoes, seeded and diced	6
1 lb	large shrimp, peeled and deveined	500 g
2 tbsp	basil chiffonade	25 mL
2 tbsp	finely chopped flat-leaf parsley	25 mL
	Freshly ground black pepper	

1. Soak beans in water to cover overnight. Drain beans and place in a large saucepan with 6 cups (1.5 L) fresh water and 1 bay leaf. Bring to a boil. Reduce heat and simmer, partially covered, until beans are tender, 40 to 45 minutes. Remove from heat. Add a pinch of salt and let stand for 5 minutes. Drain and set aside.

2. In a large sauté pan, heat oil over medium heat. Add garlic and hot pepper flakes and sauté for 1 to 2 minutes. Add beans, tomatoes and bay leaf and cook, stirring, 4 to 5 minutes. Add shrimp and stir diligently until pink and opaque, 4 to 5 minutes.

3. Remove from heat and stir in basil and parsley. Season with pepper to taste.

Fish Stock

**MAKES 7 TO 8 CUPS
(1.75 TO 2 L)**

*Here's a basic preparation
that's useful to have in
your freezer for fish and
shellfish soups, stews
and sauces.*

Tip

Instant fish stock in a pinch:
Bottled clam juice is readily
available at the market. Have
it on hand to use in fish soups
and stews. Taste for saltiness
and adjust recipe accordingly.
Add additional flavor by
simmering clam juice with
wine and aromatic herbs.

2 lbs	white fish heads and bones, rinsed and drained	1 kg
6 cups	cold water	1.5 L
1	onion, sliced	1
8	black peppercorns	8
6	sprigs parsley	6
4	sprigs thyme	4
1	bay leaf	1

1. In a large stockpot, combine fish heads, bones, water, onion and peppercorns. Tie parsley sprigs, thyme and bay leaf together with kitchen string and toss them in the pot.
2. Slowly bring to a boil over medium heat. Reduce heat to low and simmer, frequently skimming away foam that gathers on the surface, for 20 minutes.
3. Strain fish stock, discarding heads and bones. Let cool. Store in a covered container in the refrigerator and use within 2 days or freeze for up to 6 months. The stock captures the essence of the fish. Add salt to taste when incorporating stock in recipes.

Miso-Glazed Black Cod

Black cod, or sablefish, has a firm sweet flesh that responds well to the robust salty flavors of miso and soy. It is delicious either roasted in the oven or cooked on the barbecue.

The Miso Glaze is also good on other fish, such as tuna or salmon, and also with chicken and pork.

Tips

Miso is a pungent, savory paste made from cooked and fermented grain, most commonly rice or barley, cooked soybeans and salt. You will find several varieties — white, yellow and red — in Asian markets. Use yellow or white miso to add complex, rich flavor to marinades, dressings, soups and sauces. Red miso is sweeter and most frequently used in condiments for dishes that are served cold.

Palm sugar adds a special delicate sweetness with undertones of caramel to Asian dishes. Available in pressed cones at Asian markets. Shred or grate as needed.

Grilling Variation

Place miso-glazed black cod fillets, flat side down, on a lightly oiled barbecue grill over medium-high heat. Cook with barbecue lid down for 5 minutes. Brush with Miso Glaze again and grill for 3 to 5 minutes, depending on the thickness of the fillets.

- **Preheat oven to 400°F (200°C)**
- **Baking dish, lightly oiled**

4	black cod fillets (each approx. 6 oz/175 g), skin removed	4
1 tsp	sesame oil	5 mL
	Miso Glaze (see below)	

1. Arrange black cod fillets, flat side down, in prepared baking dish. Brush lightly with sesame oil and 2 tbsp (25 mL) of the Miso Glaze. Set aside for 10 minutes.
2. Roast in preheated oven for 5 minutes. Lightly brush with Miso Glaze again and roast until fish flakes easily when tested with the tip of a sharp knife (see Tip, page 219), 5 to 10 minutes, depending on the thickness of the fillets. Not all the glaze will be used.

Miso Glaze

Makes ²/₃ cup (150 mL)

¼ cup	mirin	50 mL
¼ cup	sake	50 mL
2 tbsp	white miso paste (see Tips, left)	25 mL
1 tbsp	soy sauce	15 mL
1 tsp	brown sugar or palm sugar (see Tips, left)	5 mL

1. In a bowl, combine mirin, sake, miso, soy sauce and brown sugar and whisk together until smooth. Store in a covered container in the refrigerator for up to 1 month.

Herb-Crusted Halibut with Pineapple Salsa

A fruit relish adds a pleasing tart-sweet dimension to roasted or grilled white firm-fleshed fish. Try it also with pork.

Tip

Fresh pineapple: Remove outer skin and eyes from pineapple. On a large plate, to catch all the juice, slice pineapple lengthwise into quarters and remove core. Cut into small dice.

● **Preheat oven to 350°F (180°C)**
● **Baking sheet, oiled**

½ cup	panko or fresh bread crumbs	125 mL
½ cup	coarsely chopped flat-leaf parsley	125 mL
¼ cup	coarsely chopped chives	50 mL
6	Pacific halibut fillets (each approx. 5 oz/150 g)	6
¼ cup	melted butter	50 mL
1 tsp	kosher or sea salt	5 mL
½ tsp	freshly ground black pepper	2 mL
	Pineapple Salsa (see below)	

1. In a food processor, combine bread crumbs, parsley and chives and pulse until finely chopped.
2. Place fish fillets on prepared baking sheet. Brush with melted butter and season lightly with salt and pepper. Press bread crumb mixture onto fillets.
3. Bake in preheated oven until fish flakes easily when tested with the tip of a sharp knife, 12 to 16 minutes. Serve hot with Pineapple Salsa on the side.

Pineapple Salsa

Makes 2¼ cups (550 mL)

2 cups	finely diced ripe pineapple (see Tip, left)	500 mL
¼ cup	finely diced red bell pepper	50 mL
¼ cup	finely diced red onion	50 mL
2	green onions, thinly sliced on the diagonal	2
1 tbsp	natural rice vinegar	15 mL
1 tsp	grated lime zest	5 mL
1 to 2 tbsp	lime juice	15 to 25 mL
	Kosher or sea salt	
	Brown or palm sugar	

1. In a bowl, combine pineapple, pepper and onions. Season with vinegar, lime zest and juice and salt. Set aside to allow flavors to develop, about 30 minutes. Taste and adjust flavor with a pinch of brown sugar or dash of lime juice.

Marmita-kua (Baked Fish and Potato Casserole)

SERVES 3 TO 4

This is a rustic dish of Portuguese origin. Substitute other firm fish for the Arctic char — tuna is excellent. Serve hot from the oven with steamed green beans and fresh crusty bread for mopping up the fragrant cooking juices.

- Preheat oven to 350°F (180°C)
- 11- by 7-inch (2 L) baking dish

½ cup	extra virgin olive oil, divided	125 mL
	Salt and freshly ground black pepper	
2	large Yukon Gold potatoes, cut into ⅛-inch (3 mm) slices	2
½ tsp	paprika	2 mL
2	cloves garlic, thinly sliced	2
1	onion, thinly sliced	1
2	large ripe tomatoes, cut into ⅛-inch (3 mm) slices	2
1	whole fillet Arctic char, skin removed (about 12 oz/375 g)	1
¼ cup	dry white wine	50 mL
2 tbsp	coarsely chopped flat-leaf parsley	25 mL
1	lemon, cut into wedges	1

1. Drizzle bottom of baking dish with 2 tbsp (25 mL) of the olive oil and sprinkle lightly with salt and pepper.

2. Arrange potatoes in dish, overlapping slices slightly, to cover the entire bottom in an even layer. Sprinkle with paprika and distribute garlic and onion evenly over the potato layer. Drizzle with ¼ cup (50 mL) of oil and season with ½ tsp (2 mL) salt and ¼ tsp (1 mL) pepper.

3. Arrange tomatoes over top of potatoes in the same way, drizzle with remaining oil and season lightly with salt and pepper.

4. Bake in preheated oven until potatoes are fork tender, 30 to 35 minutes.

5. Place fish, flat side down, over top of tomatoes and pour in wine. Baste fish and tomato layer with fragrant wine mixture and season with salt and pepper.

6. Return to oven and continue baking until fish flakes easily when tested with the tip of a sharp knife (see Tip, page 219), 8 to 10 minutes. Garnish with parsley and serve hot with lemon wedges on the side.

Beer-Steamed Mussels with Chorizo

We steam mussels in a beer broth seasoned with spicy sausage for a quick, easy and heart-warming lunch or supper.

2 tbsp	extra virgin olive oil	25 mL
1	leek, white and tender green parts only, julienned (see Tip, page 44)	1
2	cooked chorizo sausages, about 1 lb (500 g) sliced	2
1 tbsp	garlic, finely chopped	15 mL
1	bottle beer, ale or wheat beer	1
5 lbs	mussels, cleaned	2.5 kg
	Salt and freshly ground black pepper	
2 tbsp	finely chopped flat-leaf parsley	25 mL
	Crusty country-style bread	

1. Heat a large pot over medium-high heat. Add oil. Add leek and cook until softened, 3 to 4 minutes. Add sausage and sauté until lightly browned, about 5 minutes. Add garlic and cook, stirring occasionally, 1 to 2 minutes.

2. Stir in beer. Increase heat to high and deglaze pot, scraping up all the browned bits on the bottom.

3. Add mussels and cover pot. Cook mussels, shaking pot occasionally, until all mussels are open. Discard any that do not open.

4. Divide mussels into warm serving bowls. Taste sauce, bring to a boil and reduce to intensify flavor, if desired. Season with salt and pepper to taste. Pour sauce over mussels and sprinkle with parsley. Serve with plentiful chunks of crusty country-style bread.

Thai Lobster Curry

Richly flavored lobster, whether the spiny/rock lobster or the blue-black northern lobster, is always a treat. They are equally delicious boiled, steamed, grilled or broiled with lots of melted butter, or added to bisques, stir-fries and curries. If using uncooked lobster in the curry you must prepare yourself to deal with a live lobster (see Techniques, page 20).

Tips

You will need 1 lobster, 1 to 1½ lbs (500 to 750 g) per serving. A 3-lb (1.5 kg) lobster serves 2.

Boiling a Live Lobster: Bring a large pot of salted water to the boil, adding 1 tbsp (15 mL) salt per 1 quart (1 L) water. Or use Court Bouillon (page 225). When the liquid is at a rolling boil add the lobster, head first. Reduce heat to medium and simmer, allowing 5 minutes for the first pound (500 g) lobster and about 3 minutes for each additional pound (500 g). Lift from water at once. Drain and cool.

Variation

Use uncooked lobster meat. Simmer pieces of lobster in the sauce until opaque, about 5 minutes. Add any accumulated juices to the sauce.

3 tbsp	vegetable oil	45 mL
1	leek, white and tender green parts only, thinly sliced	1
¼ cup	minced shallots	50 mL
2 tbsp	minced gingerroot	25 mL
2 tbsp	minced lemongrass	25 mL
2 tsp	minced garlic	10 mL
4 oz	shiitake mushrooms, stemmed and thinly sliced	125 g
1 tsp	Thai red curry paste	5 mL
½ tsp	ground coriander	2 mL
Pinch	ground turmeric	Pinch
	Salt and freshly ground pepper	
1 cup	tomato juice	250 mL
1	can (14 oz/400 mL) coconut milk	1
½ cup	snow peas, trimmed and sliced on the diagonal	125 mL
½	red bell pepper, thinly sliced	½
1 tsp	fish sauce	5 mL
2 cups	cooked lobster meat, cut into bite-size pieces	500 mL
1 tbsp	freshly squeezed lime juice	15 mL
½ cup	coarsely chopped cilantro	125 mL
	Asian noodles or steamed rice	

1. Heat a large pot over medium heat. Add oil. Add leek, shallots, ginger, lemongrass and garlic. Cook, stirring occasionally, until leeks are soft and translucent, 4 to 5 minutes. Add mushrooms and sauté 1 to 2 minutes.

2. Add red curry paste, coriander, turmeric and 1 tsp (5 mL) salt and ½ tsp (2 mL) pepper and cook for 1 minute. Add tomato juice and deglaze pot, scraping up the browned bits on the bottom.

3. Stir in coconut milk and 1 cup (250 mL) water and bring to a simmer. Add snow peas, red pepper and fish sauce and simmer until pepper is just tender, about 5 minutes.

4. Stir in lobster meat and any accumulated juices and heat through. Add lime juice and ¼ cup (50 mL) cilantro. Season with salt and pepper to taste.

5. Serve in warm bowls over your favorite Asian noodles or steamed rice garnished with remaining cilantro.

Shrimp and Scallop Kebabs with Lime Chile Glaze

Tip
If you prefer less heat, remove seeds and ribs from chiles.

- Barbecue grill or indoor grill
- Six 8-inch (20 cm) bamboo skewers, soaked in water for 30 minutes

18	large shrimp, peeled and deveined	18
12	sea scallops	12
	Lime Chile Glaze (see below)	
	Salt and freshly ground black pepper	

1. Toss shrimp and scallops with half of the Lime Chile Glaze. Set aside to marinate for 15 to 20 minutes. Reserve remaining glaze. Meanwhile, preheat barbecue grill to medium-high and lightly oil grill.
2. Alternate 3 shrimp and 2 scallops on each skewer. Season with salt and pepper.
3. Grill skewers, turning once, until seafood is nicely glazed and cooked, 3 to 4 minutes per side. Remove from grill and brush with remaining glaze before serving.

Lime Chile Glaze

Makes 1 cup (250 mL)

2 tbsp	vegetable oil	25 mL
4	cloves garlic, chopped	4
½ cup	minced shallots	125 mL
2 tbsp	minced gingerroot	25 mL
2	bird's eye (Thai) chiles, minced	2
¾ cup	packed brown sugar	175 mL
2 tbsp	grated lime zest	25 mL
½ cup	freshly squeezed lime juice	125 mL
¼ cup	freshly squeezed orange juice	50 mL
2 tbsp	natural rice vinegar	25 mL

1. In a small skillet, heat oil over medium heat. Add garlic, shallots and ginger and sauté until softened but not browned, 4 to 5 minutes.
2. In a small bowl, combine garlic mixture with chiles, brown sugar, lime zest and juice, orange juice and vinegar, stirring until sugar is dissolved.

Seafood Gratin

SERVES 6

You'll find countless ways to use this luxurious seafood mixture, from baking in a casserole as part of a buffet or serving in individual gratin dishes as a starter for a special dinner party. You can also top it with a flaky puff pastry to make a wonderful pie, or use as a filling for savory crêpes, cannelloni or lasagna. This dish is not fast food! Each component is prepared separately and comes together for a one-dish extravaganza. The joy is that all the work can be done up to a day ahead.

Tips

If you plan to make the Cream Sauce a few hours or up to 1 day ahead, place in a bowl in the refrigerator with a layer of plastic wrap placed on the surface of the sauce to prevent a skin from forming. The sauce will thicken when cold. Gently reheat before using and thin with extra stock if necessary.

Cream Sauce can be used for any fish dish. Use Fish Stock (page 229) or clam juice instead of the poaching liquid

Variation

Create your own favorite seafood combinations. Replace scallops with crab or lobster. Substitute other lean white fish for the halibut.

- **Preheat oven to 350°F (180°C)**
- **13- by 9-inch (3 L) baking dish, lightly buttered**

4 to 6 cups	Fish Stock (page 229) or clam juice	1 to 1.5 L
1 lb	sea scallops	500 g
1 lb	Pacific halibut, skin and bones removed, cut into 1-inch (2.5 cm) pieces	500 g
8 oz	large shrimp, peeled and deveined	250 g

Cream Sauce

5 tbsp	butter, divided	75 mL
3 tbsp	all-purpose flour	45 mL
2 cups	fish poaching liquid	500 mL
1 cup	milk	250 mL
¼ cup	whipping (35%) cream	50 mL
	Salt and freshly ground white pepper	

2	leeks, white and tender green parts only, finely chopped (se Tip, page 44)	2
	Salt and freshly ground black pepper	
1 tbsp	olive oil	15 mL
2	shallots, finely chopped	2
2 cups	sliced mushrooms	500 mL
1½ cups	sliced king oyster mushrooms	375 mL
1 tsp	chopped thyme	5 mL
2 tbsp	finely chopped flat-leaf parsley	25 mL
	Parsley Crumb Topping (page 237)	

1. In a large sauté pan, heat fish stock over medium heat until simmering. Add scallops and cook gently until opaque, 1 to 2 minutes. Lift out of liquid with a slotted spoon and transfer to a large bowl. Repeat with halibut and shrimp, reheating stock as necessary between batches, and transfer to bowl with scallops. Strain and reserve 2 cups (500 mL) of the poaching liquid to include in sauce (refrigerate or freeze extra for another use).

2. *Cream Sauce:* In a medium saucepan, melt 3 tbsp (45 mL) butter over medium-low heat. Add flour and cook, stirring constantly, 1 to 2 minutes.

3. Gradually add reserved poaching liquid, $\frac{1}{4}$ cup (50 mL) at a time, whisking until smooth after each addition. Stir in milk and bring to a simmer. Cook, stirring often, until sauce is smooth and nicely thickened, 4 to 5 minutes. Stir in cream and season with salt and pepper to taste. Set aside.

4. In a large skillet, melt 2 tbsp (25 mL) butter over medium heat. Add leeks. Season lightly with salt and pepper and sauté until tender, 7 to 10 minutes. Add to bowl of prepared seafood. Set aside.

5. Add oil to the same pan. Increase heat to medium-high and add shallots and mushrooms and sauté until mushrooms begin to release their moisture, about 5 minutes. Add thyme and season with salt and pepper. Add to bowl of prepared seafood and leeks. Set aside.

6. Add Cream Sauce and parsley to bowl of prepared seafood, leeks and mushrooms. Mix all together gently but thoroughly. Taste and adjust seasoning.

7. Spoon seafood mixture into prepared baking dish and sprinkle Parsley Crump Topping evenly over top.

8. Bake in preheated oven until sauce is gently bubbling, 25 to 30 minutes. To obtain a golden, crunchy top, place dish under the broiler for 1 to 2 minutes. Serve hot.

Parsley Crumb Topping

Makes 1½ cups (375 mL)

1½ cups	fresh coarse white bread crumbs	375 mL
2 tbsp	chopped flat-leaf parsley	25 mL
	Salt and freshly ground pepper	
Pinch	cayenne pepper, optional	Pinch
3 tbsp	butter, melted	45 mL

1. In a bowl, combine bread crumbs and parsley and season lightly with salt, pepper and cayenne, if using. Pour melted butter over crumb mixture and toss with a fork to ensure crumbs are evenly coated with butter.

Chicken, Shrimp and Mussel Paella

SERVES 6 TO 8

This glorious, one-pot dish of Spanish origin may be simple or as exotic as you wish. The essentials are rice, saffron and paprika. In our version we combine chicken, pork and spicy chorizo sausage in an aromatic broth and add shrimp, mussels and clams. Accompany with crusty country bread and a salad of tangy greens.

Tip

If you do not have a paellera and it looks as though all of the ingredients will not fit in your skillet in Step 4, don't despair! Use a slotted spoon to remove some of the chicken, sausage and vegetables (leave the pork pieces in the pan), before adding the rice and shellfish. Keep it warm and mix back into the rice mixture before serving.

- **14-inch (35 cm) paella pan or skillet with lid**

2	fresh chorizo sausages	2
¼ cup	olive oil, divided	50 mL
8	skinless boneless chicken thighs, cut into 1-inch (2.5 cm) pieces	8
	Salt and freshly ground black pepper	
2 tsp	sweet paprika, divided	10 mL
8 oz	lean pork shoulder, cut into 1-inch (2.5 cm) pieces	250 g
1	onion, chopped	1
1	red bell pepper, thinly sliced	1
4	cloves garlic, minced	4
2	ripe Roma (plum) tomatoes, peeled, seeded and chopped	2
2	bay leaves	2
½ tsp	saffron threads	2 mL
½ tsp	dried oregano	2 mL
½ tsp	dried thyme	2 mL
½ cup	dry white wine	125 mL
4 cups	Chicken Stock (page 54) or ready-to-use broth, divided	1 L
2 cups	short-grain rice	500 mL
12 oz	large shrimp, peeled and deveined	375 g
1 cup	frozen peas	250 mL
24	mussels and/or clams, scrubbed and debearded	24
¼ cup	coarsely chopped flat-leaf parsley	50 mL
1	lemon, cut into wedges	1

1. Place sausages in a saucepan. Cover with cold water and bring to a boil over high heat. Reduce heat to medium and simmer for 5 minutes. Drain and cut into ¼-inch (0.5 cm) slices. Set aside.

2. In a paella pan or heavy skillet, heat 2 tbsp (25 mL) of the oil over medium-high heat. Season chicken lightly with salt, pepper and ½ tsp (2 mL) of the paprika. Add to pan and sauté until golden brown on all sides, about 5 minutes. Transfer to a platter and set aside.

3. Heat remaining oil in pan until it shimmers. Add pork and sausage and sauté until lightly browned. Add onion and bell pepper and sauté until softened and beginning to brown, 6 to 8 minutes. Add garlic, tomatoes, bay leaves, saffron, $1\frac{1}{2}$ tsp (7 mL) of paprika, oregano and thyme and cook, stirring, for 2 minutes. Add wine and $\frac{1}{2}$ cup (125 mL) of the chicken stock and deglaze pan, scraping up browned bits on bottom. Return chicken pieces to pan, cover and reduce heat to low and simmer until chicken is just cooked, about 15 minutes. Taste and adjust seasoning. Dish may be prepared a few hours or for up to 3 days ahead to this point. Let cool, cover and refrigerate.

4. About a half hour before serving, add remaining stock to pan and bring to a boil over medium heat. Sprinkle in rice, pushing it down into the liquid and oil, 4 to 5 minutes. Scatter shrimp and peas on top of the rice. Push mussels, hinged end down, gently into the liquid. Do not stir.

5. Cook, uncovered and undisturbed, until most of the liquid is absorbed and rice grains are tender, but not too soft, shrimp are pink and opaque and mussels and/ or clams are open (discard any that do not open), 10 to 15 minutes.

6. Remove from heat, cover loosely with foil and let stand for 5 minutes before serving. Serve hot from the pan, garnished with parsley and lemon.

Variation

Paellas out-of-doors:
Paellas were first cooked out-of-doors over wood fires. Try cooking paella over a charcoal fire — it makes a fabulous al fresco feast. Prepare the dish in two parts; cook the aromatic mix of meat and vegetables in the kitchen first and prepare the seafood and other ingredients to be added later. Follow recipe, taking everything outside to cook on the barbecue instead of on the stove. Time everything so that it is perfectly cooked when the rice is done.

Paella

Paella is named from the traditional pan in which it is cooked and served; a black round shallow metal pan with handles on both sides called a "paellera," usually about 14 inches (35 cm) in diameter and about $2\frac{1}{2}$ inches (6 cm) deep. Use a deep skillet, at least 14 inches (35 cm) in diameter, or flameproof casserole if you do not own a paella pan.

In a successful paella, rice must be perfectly cooked with grains separate and slightly al dente. A Spanish cook uses short-grained, grayish rice from the Levante region. It cooks to perfect consistency in an open pot in about 15 minutes. You'll find it, usually packaged in cloth bags, in Spanish markets. Short-grained Italian rice or converted long-grain rice may be substituted.

Bouillabaisse

In Marseille, the home of this celebrated fish stew, the varieties of fish to be included are sacrosanct and native to the Mediterranean. Our version uses firm lean white fish and shellfish native to our northern oceans. We use whatever is fresh at the market — the more variety, the better the flavor. Pacific halibut, cod and haddock are all good and a cracked lobster cut up into serving portions is a tasty addition. A spicy, garlicky pepper mayonnaise is the classic condiment to serve alongside.

Tip

Time-saving tip for fish stews: Prepare the cooking broth (Steps 1 and 2) several hours ahead or up to 1 day. Let cool, cover and refrigerate. Prepare fish and shellfish and set aside, covered, in a bowl in the refrigerator until needed, for up to 4 hours ahead.

6 tbsp	olive oil	90 mL
1	onion, finely chopped	1
3	cloves garlic, finely chopped	3
2 cups	chopped seeded tomatoes	500 mL
1 cup	finely chopped fennel	250 mL
½ cup	dry white wine	125 mL
	Salt and freshly ground black pepper	
4 cups	Fish Stock (page 229) or clam juice	1 L
1 tsp	coarsely chopped thyme	5 mL
½ tsp	saffron threads	2 mL
2	bay leaves	2
2 lbs	lean white fish, skin removed and cut into 1-inch (2.5 cm) pieces	1 kg
3	squid, bodies cut into ¼-inch (0.5 cm) rings, heads cut in half	3
12 oz	shrimp, peeled and deveined	375 g
12 oz	mussels, scrubbed and debearded	375 g
12 oz	clams, scrubbed	375 g
8 oz	scallops	250 g
12 to 16	Crostini (page 320)	12 to 16
¼ cup	coarsely chopped flat-leaf parsley	50 mL
	Roasted Red Pepper Mayonnaise (page 241), optional	

1. In a large heavy-bottomed pot, heat oil over medium heat. Add onion and sauté until softened but not browned, 4 to 5 minutes. Add garlic and cook, stirring, 1 to 2 minutes.

2. Add tomatoes, fennel, wine, 1 tsp (5 mL) salt and ¼ tsp (1 mL) pepper. Bring to a boil. Reduce heat to low and simmer for 2 to 3 minutes. Add stock, thyme, saffron, and bay leaves and cook, about 5 minutes.

3. Add fish and squid and simmer for 5 minutes. Add shrimp, mussels, clams and scallops. Simmer until mussels and clams open, 4 to 5 minutes. Remove and discard any mussels or clams that do not open.

4. Taste and adjust seasoning. Place 2 crostini in the bottom of each large warm bowl. With a slotted spoon, arrange a portion of fish and shellfish over top. Ladle the fragrant broth over all and garnish with parsley. Serve with Roasted Red Pepper Mayonnaise, if you wish.

Roasted Red Pepper Mayonnaise

This spicy sauce is a delicious condiment with just about any grilled or poached fish.

Tips

This recipe contains raw egg yolks. If you are concerned about the safety of using raw eggs, use pasteurized eggs in the shell or ¼ cup (50 mL) pasteurized liquid whole eggs, instead. Because of the egg yolks, this dressing does not store well. Make it fresh and use it right away.

Flavor of olive oils rests on the variety of olive, or the blend of a variety of olives, used in production. We recommend a smooth, buttery extra virgin olive oil with a light, pleasant "fruity" olive flavor for making mayonnaise, such as those from Liguria, in the Italian Riviera or from Catalonia, in Spain. These oils are particularly fine for cooking fish. Earthy peppery olive oils, for example those from Tuscany, can overwhelm delicate flavors.

Add fresh herbs to complement your dish. Add 1 tsp (5 mL) chopped fresh thyme, oregano or dill, or a chiffonade of fresh basil.

Variation

If you prefer to further lighten the flavor and texture of the sauce, you can replace olive oil with ¾ cup (175 mL) vegetable oil and whisk in 2 to 3 tbsp (25 to 45 mL) extra virgin olive oil at the end.

2 to 3	cloves garlic, minced	2 to 3
½ cup	chopped roasted red bell pepper or chopped canned pimento, drained	125 mL
Pinch	cayenne pepper	Pinch
	Kosher or sea salt	
1	egg yolk (see Tips, left)	1
1 tsp	Dijon mustard	5 mL
1 cup	light-flavored extra virgin olive oil (see Tips, left)	250 mL
	Freshly squeezed lemon juice	

1. In a bowl, crush garlic, roasted pepper, cayenne and salt to make a fine paste. Add egg yolk and mustard.

2. Gradually whisk in oil, a few drops at a time, until egg yolk begins to thicken. Continue to add oil in a steady stream, whisking diligently until sauce is thick and smooth. Taste and adjust seasoning with salt, cayenne pepper and lemon juice. Add herbs to complement your dish if you like (see Tips, left). Mayonnaise is best enjoyed at once or within a few hours.

Socca with Shrimp Provençal

SERVES 8 TO 10

Socca are thin, moist-on-the-inside, crispy-on-the-outside crêpes made of chickpea flour, olive oil and salt and baked in huge pizza pans in wood burning ovens on the streets of Nice in Provence. They are a hugely popular street food and snack to eat out of hand.

These hearty crêpes can be filled with mixtures of spicy vegetables, seafood or chicken. Here we fill socca with a quick sauté of Mediterranean vegetables and shrimp to make a light, yet satisfying, lunch or supper.

Variation

Socca with Curried Vegetables: Substitute ½ tsp (2 mL) toasted black cumin seeds for the thyme in the Socca. Stuff with curried vegetables, as in Gobi Masala (page 283).

- **Preheat oven to 350°F (180°C)**
- **Baking sheet, lined with parchment paper**

¼ cup	olive oil, divided	50 mL
½	red onion, chopped	½
2	cloves garlic, minced	2
1	red bell pepper, cut into ½-inch (1 cm) cubes	1
1	yellow bell peppers, cut into ½-inch (1 cm) cubes	1
½	small bulb fennel, diced	½
	Salt and freshly ground black pepper	
1	zucchini, cut into ½-inch (1 cm) cubes	1
2 cups	seeded and chopped Roma (plum) tomatoes	500 mL
2 tbsp	basil chiffonade, divided	25 mL
12 to 16	shrimp, peeled, deveined and cut in half lengthwise	12 to 16
8 to 10	Socca (chickpea flour crêpes) (page 243)	8 to 10

1. In a large skillet, heat 2 tbsp (25 mL) of the oil over medium heat. Add red onion and sauté until softened but not browned, 4 to 5 minutes. Add garlic and sauté for 1 to 2 minutes. Add remaining oil to the skillet with red and yellow bell peppers and fennel, ½ tsp (2 mL) salt and ¼ tsp (1 mL) pepper and sauté for 3 to 5 minutes. Stir in zucchini, tomatoes and half of the basil. Cook, stirring, until vegetables are just tender, 5 to 7 minutes.

2. Add shrimp and cook, stirring, until pink and opaque, 3 to 4 minutes. Taste and adjust seasoning. Set aside. Filling may be prepared ahead. Let cool and refrigerate until needed or for up to 1 day. Reheat over medium heat before filling socca.

3. Spread crêpes on a work surface. Divide vegetable filling into 8 to 10 portions. Arrange filling across bottom third of each crêpe. Sprinkle with remaining basil. Lift lower end of crêpe up and over the filling. Fold in each side to enclose the filling and roll up. Set aside, seam side down, on prepared baking sheet. Cover with foil. Heat in preheated oven, 10 to 15 minutes.

Socca

Makes eight to ten 8-inch (20 cm) crêpes

- **8-inch (20 cm) crêpe pan or nonstick skillet**
- **Baking sheet, lined with parchment paper**

1½ cups	chickpea flour (see Tips, right)	375 mL
1 tsp	kosher or sea salt	5 mL
1 tsp	finely chopped thyme	5 mL
¼ tsp	freshly ground black pepper	1 mL
⅔ cups	extra virgin olive oil	150 mL
¼ cup	vegetable oil	50 mL

1. Sift chickpea flour and salt into a large bowl. Add thyme and pepper. Whisk in olive oil and 1¼ cups (300 mL) water and mix until smooth. Let batter stand, covered, in the refrigerator for 1 hour. Batter should be smooth and quite thin; add a little more water, if necessary.

2. Heat crêpe pan over medium heat. Dip a pastry brush in vegetable oil and lightly brush crêpe pan.

3. Stir crêpe batter. Scoop up a scant ⅓ cup (75 mL) batter, using a small ladle or measuring cup.

4. Hold the pan just off of the heat and pour batter into pan. Immediately tilt and move pan in a circular direction so that the batter spreads to the edges of the pan in a thin even layer. Return pan to heat and cook until the lacy edges of the crêpe begin to brown, about 2 minutes. Use a spatula or your fingers, lift crêpe and flip it over to cook for 1 minute on the underside. Slide the crêpe onto prepared baking sheet. Repeat with remaining batter. Overlap crêpes slightly on the baking sheet or stack with a square of parchment paper in between. Crêpes can be made 1 day ahead. Let cool. Wrap in plastic wrap and refrigerate.

Tips

You'll find chickpea flour in most health food stores and markets that specialize in providing ingredients for Middle Eastern and Indian cooking.

The first crêpe is always a test. Now you can judge the heat of the pan and the amount of batter needed to create the thickness of the crêpe you desire.

Udon Noodle Pot

If we were to feast on a version of this noodle pot every day, we would likely all be superbly healthy and thin! Pieces of lean white fish and fresh vegetables are cooked in simmering broth with noodles. We use half fish stock and half dashi for the broth and have extra soy sauce and sesame oil available for seasoning.

Variation

Vegetarian Noodle Pot: Omit seafood and dashi. Use vegetable stock and include 1 cup (250 mL) diced tofu with the vegetables.

8 oz	skinless firm white fish, cut into 1-inch (2.5 cm) pieces	250 g
8 oz	sea scallops	250 g
1 tsp	finely chopped gingerroot, divided	5 mL
	Kosher or sea salt	
6 cups	dashi (page 44) or Fish Stock (page 229) or clam juice	1.5 L
2 tbsp	soy sauce	25 mL
2 tbsp	mirin	25 mL
1	carrot, halved lengthwise and sliced thinly on the diagonal	1
1	package (14 oz /400 g) cooked udon noodles	1
4 oz	shiitake mushroom caps, halved	125 g
2 oz	snow peas, trimmed and halved on the diagonal	60 g
1 cup	napa cabbage, coarsely chopped	250 mL
2	green onions, thinly sliced on the diagonal	2
1 tsp	sesame oil	5 mL

1. In a bowl, combine fish and scallops with $\frac{1}{2}$ tsp (2 mL) of the ginger and a pinch of salt. Set aside.

2. In a saucepan over medium heat, combine dashi, remaining ginger, soy sauce and mirin. Bring to a boil. Add carrot and cook for 3 to 4 minutes.

3. In a large pot, combine noodles, shiitake, snow peas, and cabbage. Pour in hot dashi with carrots. Cover pot and return to a boil over medium heat. Reduce heat and simmer for 5 minutes. Add fish and scallops and cook until opaque, 2 to 3 minutes. Stir in green onions and sesame oil. Divide noodles, vegetables and seafood into warm bowls with tongs or a slotted spoon and pour cooking broth over top.

Southwest Ceviche

Serve this zesty seafood salad chilled as a light lunch or starter. Arrange portions in small glass bowls, or serve on a bed of frisée or radicchio.

Tip

Chipotles in adobo sauce: Chipotle peppers, smoked jalapeño peppers, are available in small cans, preserved in a fiery, tomato-based sauce. They're devilishly hot so use with caution. They add five-alarm flavor to sauces, stews and marinades. To store unused chiles from the can, spoon into an ice cube tray and freeze. Pop into a small freezer bag and they're on hand ready to use.

Variation

Include sea scallops, cut in half horizontally, instead of, or in addition to, shrimp.

1 lb	shrimp, peeled and deveined	500 g
4	tomatillos, paper-thin skin removed, finely diced (about 1 cup/250 mL)	4
1	jalapeño pepper, halved lengthwise, seeds removed and thinly sliced	1
¼ cup	coarsely chopped cilantro	50 mL
2 tbsp	finely diced red bell pepper	25 mL
2 tbsp	finely diced yellow bell pepper	25 mL
1 tbsp	finely grated lime zest	15 mL
1 cup	freshly squeezed lime juice	250 mL
2 tbsp	extra virgin olive oil	25 mL
4 tsp	minced chipotle peppers in adobo sauce, or to taste (see Tip, left)	20 mL
1 tsp	kosher or sea salt	5 mL
½ tsp	freshly ground black pepper	2 mL

1. Slice shrimp in half lengthwise.
2. In a glass or other nonreactive bowl, mix together tomatillos, jalapeño, cilantro, red and yellow peppers, lime zest and juice, oil, chipotle peppers, salt and pepper.
3. Add shrimp, cover and refrigerate until the flesh of the shrimp is opaque, about 1½ hours or for up to 3 hours. Do not leave longer than this in the acidic marinade or the seafood will "overcook" and no longer be tender and juicy.

Grilled Calamari and Citrus Salad

Serve this salad of tender grilled squid tossed in a tangy citrus dressing as a delicious addition to a summer buffet or as part of a seafood antipasto plate.

Tips

Successful calamari grilling: Make sure calamari is very dry before cooking to ensure that it grills and doesn't steam when introduced to heat. Line a baking tray with several layers of paper towels, lay the calamari bodies and tentacles down on the tray and cover with more layers of paper towel. Press down firmly to soak up as much liquid as possible.

Use tangy blood oranges when in season.

- Barbecue grill or indoor grill
- Preheat barbecue grill to high

2 lbs	calamari, bodies and tentacles separated	1 kg
2 tbsp	olive oil	25 mL
	Salt and freshly ground black pepper	
1	red grapefruit	1
2	navel oranges	2
1	lemon	1
3	green onions, thinly sliced	3
¼	bulb fennel, very thinly sliced	¼
4	red radishes, thinly sliced into half moons	4
¼ cup	mint chiffonade	50 mL
¼ cup	basil chiffonade	50 mL
¼ cup	cilantro leaves, thinly sliced	50 mL
1 tbsp	sherry vinegar	15 mL
	Granulated sugar to taste	
2 to 4 tbsp	extra virgin olive oil, divided	25 to 60 mL

1. Place calamari bodies on a cutting board. Using a very sharp knife score across the body about halfway through, about ½ inch (1 cm) apart. Cut the body in half across the width.

2. Dry calamari thoroughly. Place in a bowl and toss with olive oil and salt and pepper to taste.

3. Grill calamari, in batches. This is a very fast cooking process. Turn over when grill marks appear on the under side and remove from grill when both sides are marked, 4 to 5 minutes in total. Let cool.

4. Remove peel and outer white pith from grapefruit, oranges and lemon. Holding fruit over a small bowl, cut between membranes into segments. Reserve citrus juices for the dressing. Roughly chop fruit segments. In a small bowl, combine fruit with green onions, fennel, radishes, mint, basil and cilantro. Toss with calamari.

5. To make the dressing, whisk together citrus juices, vinegar, salt, pepper and sugar to taste and drizzle in extra virgin olive oil to combine. Set aside.

6. Toss calamari with the citrus dressing just before serving.

Vegetarian Mains

Macaroni and Cheese

Creamy cheese sauce and pasta must be the ultimate comfort food. Make the dish tangy or mild depending on the amount and quality of the cheese you include. We use a two-year-old Ontario Cheddar, which gives just the right bite without overwhelming. Add Parsley Crumb Topping, if you like.

- **Preheat oven to 350°F (180°C)**
- **11- by 7-inch (2 L) shallow baking dish, lightly oiled**

2 cups	dried macaroni	500 mL
¼ cup	butter	50 mL
½	onion, finely chopped	½
1	clove garlic, chopped	1
¼ cup	all-purpose flour	50 mL
Pinch	cayenne pepper	Pinch
	Salt and freshly ground pepper	
4 cups	milk	1 L
2 cups	shredded Cheddar cheese	500 mL
2 tbsp	grated Parmesan cheese	25 mL
	Parsley Crumb Topping, optional (page 237)	

1. In a large pot of boiling lightly salted water, cook pasta until tender, but not too soft, 10 to 13 minutes or according to package directions. Drain, rinse in cold water, drain again and set aside in a large bowl.

2. In a large saucepan, melt butter over medium heat. Add onion and sauté until soft, but not colored, 4 to 5 minutes. Add garlic, flour, cayenne, ½ tsp (2 mL) salt and pinch of pepper and sauté for 2 to 3 minutes.

3. In a small saucepan, heat milk over medium heat until steaming. Slowly add hot milk to flour mixture, whisking briskly until all milk is incorporated and sauce is smooth. Reduce heat and cook sauce gently, stirring, for 5 minutes. Remove from heat and stir in Cheddar and Parmesan cheeses. Pour cheese sauce over cooked macaroni and stir gently to combine. Taste and adjust seasoning.

4. Pour macaroni into prepared baking dish. Sprinkle Parsley Crumb Topping over top, if using. Bake in preheated oven until sauce is bubbling, 20 to 25 minutes. Broil briefly to lightly brown the top. Let stand for 5 to 10 minutes before serving.

Roasted Pepper and Goat's Cheese Quiche

SERVES 4 TO 6

Every day our chefs prepare four or five flavors of freshly baked quiche. They are a favorite for lunch and make a quick, easy supper when time is short. This roasted pepper and goat's cheese quiche is one of our most popular.

Tip
Freeze unused egg whites and save for making meringues.

Quiche Variations
Spinach and Mushroom Quiche: Add 1 cup (250 mL) blanched spinach (squeezed dry), ½ cup (125 mL) sautéed sliced mushrooms and ¾ cup (175 mL) shredded Gruyère cheese in place of the roasted peppers and goat's cheese.

Cocktail Quiches: Use quiche fillings to fill small tartlet shells (see Chèvre Tartlets, page 354).

Non-Vegetarian Quiche Variations
Crab and Leek Quiche: Add 1 cup (250 mL) sliced leeks sautéed in butter until soft, 1 cup (250 mL) chopped crab meat and ¾ cup (175 mL) shredded Gruyère cheese in place of the roasted peppers and goat's cheese.

Ham and Green Onion Quiche: Add ¾ cup (175 mL) slivered country-style ham, ¾ cup (175 mL) grated Gruyère cheese and 3 tbsp (45 mL) finely sliced green onions in place of the roasted peppers and goat's cheese.

Preheat oven to 350°F (180°C)

2	eggs	2
2	egg yolks (see Tip, left)	2
1½ cups	half-and-half (10%) cream	375 mL
½ tsp	kosher or sea salt	2 mL
Pinch	freshly ground black pepper	Pinch
Pinch	cayenne pepper	Pinch
Pinch	freshly grated nutmeg	Pinch
	9-inch (23 cm) partially baked Flaky Pie Pastry Shell (page 409) or store-bought	
1 tsp	Dijon mustard	5 mL
1 cup	roasted bell peppers, red, yellow and green, sliced	250 mL
⅔ cup	crumbled fresh goat's cheese	150 mL
1 tsp	soft butter	5 mL

1. In a large bowl, whisk together eggs, egg yolks, cream, salt, pepper, cayenne and nutmeg.
2. Place pie dish with pastry on a baking sheet. Brush partially baked pie shell bottom and sides with a light coating of mustard. Scatter an even layer of peppers and goat's cheese in bottom of pastry shell and gently pour in egg mixture to fill quiches about three-quarters full.
3. Place in preheated oven. Pour in remaining quiche filling and dot with soft butter for better browning. Bake until filling is puffed and lightly browned, 45 to 50 minutes. Let stand for 5 minutes before slicing.

Braised Butternut Squash and Tofu with Sesame Seeds

SERVES 4 TO 6

The addition of Asian flavors turns reliable butternut squash into a satisfying and tasty dish.

Tip

Cutting up squash is always a hand-numbing experience. We trim stem and blossom ends from butternut squash and cut into crosswise slices, about 1 inch (2.5 cm) wide. It is then easy to peel and remove seeds.

6 tbsp	soy sauce	90 mL
1 tbsp	mirin	15 mL
½ tsp	granulated sugar	2 mL
1½ cups	water	375 mL
2 tbsp	minced shallot	25 mL
2 tbsp	vegetable oil	25 mL
1	butternut squash (approx. 2 lbs/1 kg), peeled and cut into 1-inch (2.5 cm) pieces	1
12 oz	firm tofu, cut into 1-inch (2.5 cm) pieces	375 g
1	small bird's eye (Thai) red chile, seeded and minced	1
3	baby bok choy, halved lengthwise and thinly sliced	3
¼ cup	toasted sesame seeds, divided	50 mL
	Kosher or sea salt	

1. In a small bowl, combine soy sauce, mirin, sugar and water. Set aside.
2. Heat a large sauté pan over medium heat. Add oil. Add shallots and stir-fry until softened, 2 to 3 minutes. Add butternut squash and cook, stirring, 2 to 3 minutes. Add tofu, chile and soy sauce mixture.
3. Cover pan and cook over low heat until squash is just tender, about 15 minutes. Add bok choy and cook, stirring, 2 to 3 minutes.
4. Remove from heat and toss with 3 tbsp (45 mL) of the sesame seeds. Add salt to taste. Serve garnished with remaining sesame seeds.

Moroccan Vegetable Stew

*This warming mix of
vegetables is sustaining
enough to serve as a main
dish. Accompany with
grilled pita breads.*

1	sweet potato	1
1	carrot	1
1/2	rutabaga	1/2
1	zucchini	1
6 to 8	button mushrooms	6 to 8
1/4 cup	olive oil	50 mL
1/2	onion, chopped	1/2
2 tsp	minced garlic	10 mL
2 tsp	minced gingerroot	10 mL
1/2 tsp	ground cinnamon	2 mL
1/2 tsp	ground cumin	2 mL
1/2 tsp	ground turmeric	2 mL
	Salt and freshly ground pepper	
1/3 cup	sultana raisins	75 mL
2 cups	tomato juice	500 mL
1 cup	water	250 mL
1	can (14 to 19 oz/398 to 540 mL) chickpeas, rinsed and drained	1

1. Peel sweet potato, carrot and rutabaga and cut into
   1/2-inch (1 cm) pieces. Cut zucchini into 1/2-inch (1 cm)
   pieces and quarter or halve mushrooms, depending on
   size. Set aside.

2. In a large pot, heat oil over medium-high heat. Add
   onion, garlic and ginger and sauté until softened, 3 to
   4 minutes. Stir in cinnamon, cumin, turmeric and salt
   and pepper to taste and sauté for 2 to 3 minutes. Add
   prepared vegetables and raisins.

3. Deglaze pot with tomato juice and water, scraping up
   browned bits on the bottom. Reduce heat and simmer
   until vegetables are tender, 15 to 20 minutes. Add
   chickpeas and heat through. Taste and adjust seasoning.

Torta Rustica

MAKES 1 PIE
SERVES 6

This impressive multilayered pie is delicious for brunch, lunch or supper. The preparation of each vegetable layer and the assembly of the pie takes time, so when you are in the mood to create a special dish, put on some good cooking music and have fun. Serve with a light Roasted Tomato Coulis. This simple sauce is also delicious to accompany many light vegetable, pasta and fish dishes.

- Preheat oven to 400°F (200°C)
- 6- by 3-inch (15 by 7.5 cm) springform pan, greased, then bottom and sides lined with parchment paper

1	potato	1
1 tbsp	butter	15 mL
1	onion, chopped	1
1½ cups	cooked spinach, squeezed dry	375 mL
2 tbsp	freshly grated Parmesan cheese, preferably Parmigiano-Reggiano	25 mL
1 tbsp	fresh bread crumbs	15 mL
2	eggs	2
	Salt and freshly ground pepper	
	Flaky Pie Pastry (page 409) or pastry for a 9-inch (23 cm) double-crust pie	
2	roasted red bell peppers, peeled, seeded and chopped	2
9	slices provolone cheese	9
	Roasted Tomato Coulis, optional (page 253)	

1. Boil potato in a pot of lightly salted water to cover until tender, about 30 minutes. Let cool. Peel and slice ¼ inch (0.5 cm) thick. Set aside.

2. In a medium skillet, heat butter over medium heat. Add onion and sauté until soft, 4 to 5 minutes. Add spinach and cook, stirring, until moisture is evaporated. Transfer to a bowl and stir in Parmesan, bread crumbs and 1 beaten egg. Season with salt and pepper to taste. Set aside.

3. Roll two-thirds of the pastry into a large circle, about 12 inches (30 cm) in diameter. Roll out the remaining pastry to make a circle about 7 inches (18 cm) in diameter. Carefully ease the large pastry circle into the springform pan, allowing the pastry to hang over the edge of the pan by 1 inch (2.5 cm) or so (see Techniques, page 22). Layer one-third of the spinach mixture evenly on the bottom. Arrange one-third of potato slices in a layer over top. Season lightly. Sprinkle with one-third of the bell peppers and add a layer of provolone cheese. Repeat layers two more times.

4. Beat remaining egg with 1 tsp (5 mL) water to make an egg wash and brush edge of the pastry. Lay smaller pastry circle over top. Trim away excess pastry. Lift up the edges and crimp to form a decorative stand-up edge and brush top of pie with egg wash. Make small slit in pastry top to allow steam to escape.

5. Place pie on a baking sheet and bake in preheated oven for 30 minutes. Reduce heat to 350°F (180°C) and continue to bake until pastry on top and sides is golden, 15 to 30 minutes more. To check whether the pastry sides are cooked, remove the pie from the oven, release the clasp of the springform pan and gently raise the sides. The pastry should be a light golden color and be firm to the touch. Let cool in pan. Serve warm or at room temperature with Roasted Tomato Coulis, if you like.

Roasted Tomato Coulis

Makes 1 cup (250 mL)

- **Preheat oven to 450°F (230°C)**
- **Large rimmed baking sheet**
- **Food processor or blender**

12 oz	ripe Roma (plum) tomatoes (about 9), cut in half lengthwise	375 g
2 tbsp	extra virgin olive oil	25 mL
	Kosher or sea salt	
1 tsp	balsamic vinegar	5 mL
2 tbsp	basil chiffonade	25 mL
	Freshly ground black pepper	

1. Toss tomatoes with olive oil.
2. Arrange, cut side down, in a single layer on baking sheet. Roast in preheated oven until tomatoes are soft and beginning to char, about 20 minutes.
3. Transfer to a food processor. Add about $\frac{1}{4}$ tsp (1 mL) salt and vinegar and process briefly until smooth. For a finer smoother sauce, press tomatoes through a sieve to remove seeds. Stir in basil. Season with salt and pepper to taste. Sauce may be made up to 1 day ahead. Add basil just before using. Cover and keep chilled.

Vegetable Chili

SERVES 6

This chili is a winner with heaps of fresh vegetables, and bulgur and beans added for extra nourishment. It's a customer favorite and a constant item on our weekly menu. Spice it up with the addition of a little smoky chipotle, if you wish. Add a topping of shredded old Cheddar cheese and a spoonful of sour cream and serve with warm Cornbread (page 383). Delicious!

Tips

Bulgur is wheat that has been steamed whole, dried and cracked into small flakes. It does not require further cooking but may be cooked and served hot in combination with rice and other ingredients in stews, soups or side dishes. Taste test after soaking period. If bulgur is still not tender, add more hot water and soak for a bit longer. Bulgur is available in fine, medium and coarse flakes. Fine bulgur is used to make the popular Middle Eastern salad, tabbouleh. Coarse bulgur is particularly good in pilafs.

For the vegetables use a combination of carrots, celery, red and green bell peppers, mushrooms and zucchini.

½ cup	fine bulgur (see Tips, left)	125 mL
	Hot water	
2 tbsp	vegetable oil	25 mL
1	onion, chopped	1
3	cloves garlic, chopped	3
6 cups	vegetables, cut into 1-inch (2.5 cm) pieces (see Tips, left)	1.5 L
1 tbsp	Mexican chili powder	15 mL
1 tsp	ground cumin	5 mL
½ tsp	cayenne pepper	2 mL
	Salt and freshly ground pepper	
1	can (28 oz/769 mL) plum tomatoes with juice, chopped	1
1	can (14 to 19 oz/395 to 540 mL) kidney beans, drained and rinsed	1

1. In a small bowl, soak bulgur in hot water to cover for 5 to 7 minutes. Drain and set aside.

2. In a large heavy-bottomed pot, heat oil over medium heat. Add onion, garlic and vegetables and sauté for 4 to 5 minutes. Stir in chili powder, cumin, cayenne, 1 tsp (5 mL) salt and ¼ tsp (1 mL) pepper. Toss all together over the heat for 2 to 3 minutes.

3. Add tomatoes with juice and bring to a boil. Reduce heat, partially cover and simmer until vegetables are tender, 25 to 30 minutes. Stir in bulgur and beans. Heat through and taste and adjust seasoning.

Chili Powder

The chili powder commonly found on market shelves is a blended spice that combines ground hot red chile peppers, ground cumin, oregano and garlic powder. Some brands include paprika, cayenne pepper, black pepper, salt and sometimes coriander and cloves. We suggest that you read the label and find a quality brand that suits your taste — preferably one that has the fewest additions. You can always have fun and create your own blend, combining ground chili powders made from a variety of chiles, such as New Mexican, ancho or chipotle. Most important: don't keep your chili powder hanging around in the cupboard too long — once opened, aroma and flavor quickly fades.

Spinach and Feta Pie

Pies made with well-seasoned meat and vegetable fillings baked in a light phyllo crust are classic fare in the eastern Mediterranean. Spanakopita, spinach and feta pie, is delicious as a light lunch, and small spanakopitas are among our most popular cocktail bites.

Tips

If using frozen spinach, squeeze out excess moisture from thawed spinach. Add to onions and cook, stirring, for 2 to 3 minutes.

Take the spice sniff test! Sniff ground nutmeg in the jar in your cupboard and then sniff freshly grated nutmeg. The difference in taste and aroma is astounding. You may never buy ground nutmeg again!

Variation

Individual Spinach and Feta Pies: To make about 60 bite-size triangles, follow the tips in Working with Phyllo Pastry (page 214). Each phyllo sheet is divided into 4 strips, so you will need to repeat the process using 15 sheets of phyllo. Remember to keep unused phyllo sheets covered with a damp cloth while you work.

Preheat oven to 350°F (180°C)
13- by 9-inch (3 L) glass baking dish

¼ cup	olive oil	50 mL
½	onion, chopped	½
4	green onions, thinly sliced	4
2 lbs	fresh spinach, trimmed, or 2 packages (each 10 oz/300 g) frozen leaf spinach, thawed (see Tips, left)	1 kg
	Salt and freshly ground pepper	
1 tbsp	coarsely chopped flat-leaf parsley	15 mL
1 tbsp	chopped dill	15 mL
¼ tsp	freshly grated nutmeg (see Tips, left)	1 mL
1 cup	crumbled Greek or Bulgarian feta cheese	250 mL
1 cup	ricotta cheese	250 mL
2	egg yolks, lightly beaten	2
¼ cup	butter, melted	50 mL
12	sheets phyllo pastry (see page 214)	12

1. In a large skillet, heat oil over medium heat. Add onion and green onions and sauté until soft, but not browned, 4 to 5 minutes. Stir in spinach. Cover and cook for 3 to 4 minutes. Remove lid and continue to cook until spinach is wilted and most of the moisture has evaporated, 2 to 3 minutes more. Sprinkle with a ½ tsp (5 mL) salt and ¼ tsp (1 mL) pepper. Stir in parsley, dill and nutmeg and let cool.

2. In a large bowl, combine feta and ricotta. Stir in spinach mixture and egg yolks. Set aside.

3. Lightly brush baking dish with some of the melted butter. Lay one sheet of phyllo in dish with pastry overhanging the edges. Brush lightly with melted butter. Repeat to make 6 layers of phyllo. Spread spinach filling in dish in an even layer. Top with 6 layers of phyllo, brushing each layer with melted butter. Carefully roll and tuck pastry around the edge of the dish, making sure to enclose filling. Brush top with remaining butter.

4. Bake in preheated oven until pie is cooked through and pastry is crisp and golden brown, 40 to 45 minutes. Let stand for 5 to 10 minutes before slicing into serving portions.

Legumes

Like many things legume sounds better in French, where it gains an accent and means vegetable. In English it has come to mean something both narrower and broader, which may explain why many people who know their way around their kitchens seem not quite sure what it means at all. Mostly the word is an umbrella for forage plants such as alfalfa and clover, grown for livestock grazing; and for foods such as lentils, peanuts, peas and beans in all their manifold varieties, grown for people who know their kitchens more than they graze their livestock. These are the pulses — the "pods," which commonly open along the sides and in cinematic form are the terrifying vehicles for *Invasion of the Body Snatchers* — and are among the basic building blocks of human civilization: staples in Europe, Asia and the Americas by 6,000 BC, essential suppliers of protein when meat has been in short supply. The generous legume can also lower a farmer's fertilizer costs, when used in rotation by replenishing the nitrogen content in overused soil. Not only does it feed humanity and help keep it healthy, but it does the same for the soil from which it comes. All told, we owe it a lot.

In sum, all beans punch far above their weight in the nutrition ring. Long derided in song and story for weight-encouraging carbs (in fact their carbs are of the complex variety, which do not add poundage), as well as their production of intestinal gas, beans are now recognized as some of the greatest fighters in the wars against diabetes, heart disease, obesity and cancer. Also sources of quick energy, powerful antioxidants, and stiff, particularly lentils, with the B-vitamin folate (highly recommended for drinkers, smokers and users of birth-control pills), as well as B_6, calcium, potassium and alpha-linolenic acid. A bit of gas is a small price to pay.

In the Kitchen

Some of the more popular varieties among the 13,000 species of legumes:

Beans: There are many kinds available in a variety of colors and sizes. Found all around the world and a staple food in the area where they originated and are still grown. **Black turtle beans** (a staple food in the Caribbean, Mexico and South America). **Broad beans** (aka **fava**), lightly cooked when young and tender, perhaps the most delicious legume on its own. Greeks eat them in a dish called *koukia* (meaning broad beans), a stew with artichokes, the beans cooked fresh in their pods. In Egypt, *ful medames* — broad beans cooked with lemon, parsley, cumin, olive oil and don't spare the garlic, and commonly eaten at breakfast, with onions on the side — is considered the Egyptian national dish. **Cannellini** (aka **white kidney beans**). **Kidney beans**, available red and white, pink and striped, kidney-shaped. **Red kidney beans** (aka **Mexican reds**) are large with a strong flavor; traditional for "rice and beans," chilies and Creole dishes. They can hold their own. **Lima beans**, fruit of an herbaceous vine. **Mung beans**, small dark green beans, whole or split, widely used in China and India. **Navy beans**, small, white, oval, mild in flavor, often used in stews and soups, and commonly used for canned baked beans. So named by being a staple of the U.S. Navy in the early 20th century. Despite their unassertive demeanor, they are among the most nutritious of the leguminous tribe. **Pinto beans**, medium-size ovals, with a spotty brown/beige color, turning completely brown when cooked. The favorite ingredient for refried beans and other Mexican bean dishes.

Peas: Grow in pods on vines, probably originating in Persia. Available green, yellow, whole or split. **Black-eyed peas**, medium-size, oval, cream-colored, with distinguishing black dot. Tart in flavor, often used as a side dish. (Black-eyed peas and chickpeas, although they are members of the pea family, are treated like beans when whole and dried). **Chickpeas** (aka **garbanzo beans**) are round, small, beige, nutty in taste, popular in Indian dishes, Middle Eastern hummus dips and fried falafel balls. The chickpea falafel of the Levant battles it out with Egypt's broad-bean version for taste points and national pride.

Lentils (aka **dal** or **pulse**): Flat seeds of annual plant originating in central Asia. Available brown, black, yellow, pink, green and red. **Red lentils** are particularly popular in dals and soups. **Le Puy lentils** from France are excellent for side dishes and salads because they hold their shape and have more distinct flavor.

Basic Legume Cooking

- Rinse legumes well and pick over carefully to remove any stray grit.
- Beans and whole peas (chickpeas and black-eyed peas) have thick skins and must be soaked to shorten cooking time. They absorb about four times their volume of water and swell to $2\frac{1}{2}$ to 3 times in size. Soak beans, covered in cold water by about 2 inches (5 cm) in the refrigerator, for 4 hours or overnight. Or use the "quick soak" method: Bring beans to a boil in water, using ratio of 1 cup (250 mL) beans to 4 cups (1 L) water. Remove from heat and set aside covered for 1 hour. Drain. Cover beans by about 2 inches (5 cm) with fresh water and

bring to a boil for 5 minutes. Skim off any foamy particles that come to the surface. Reduce heat, partially cover, and simmer until tender.

- Cooking times will be longer due to several factors — the variety and age of the beans, hardness of water and altitude. (Beans that have been stored for too long take longer to cook; they are best eaten within a year of harvest.) When cooked, beans are soft and creamy with skins intact. Start testing after 45 minutes, but cooking time may take as long as $1\frac{1}{2}$ to 2 hours. Add seasonings such as a whole onion, bay leaf, herb sprigs or whole spices to cooking water, if you wish, but do not add salt or acidic ingredients until the beans are tender or the skins will never soften. Drain, discard flavorings and reserve the cooking water, if you like; add to soups, stews or sauces.
- If using cooked chickpeas for a purée: Cover with water in a bowl and gently swish them around and rub between your fingers to release the skins. Pour away water and skins. Repeat if necessary.
- Lentils and split peas do not need soaking. Combine lentils with cold water to cover (about 2 cups/500 mL water to 1 cup/250 mL lentils), add salt and bring to a boil. Reduce heat, partially cover pot, and cook until tender, about 25 minutes. When cooked, lentils become a coarse purée. For a fine purée, force through a sieve. They are particularly good seasoned with browned butter and Indian spices.
- For convenience, canned beans and lentils are a boon. We find that some organic brands are indeed quite good. Always drain and rinse before using.

Vegetable Tortilla Casserole

This tasty casserole includes layers of salsa, corn tortillas, vegetables and cheese baked together to make a popular family feast. All the work can be done up to a day ahead. Serve a crisp romaine salad on the side.

Tip

To save time, you may wish to substitute a store-bought salsa. Choose a basic chunky tomato one. If using store-bought salsa, decrease the amount of salt to ½ tsp (2 mL).

- Preheat oven to 375°F (190°C)
- 13- by 9-inch (3 L) glass baking dish
- Parchment paper

3 cups	diced zucchini	750 mL
2 cups	frozen corn kernels	500 mL
2 tbsp	vegetable oil	25 mL
2 tsp	ground cumin, divided	10 mL
1 tsp	kosher or sea salt	5 mL
½ tsp	freshly ground black pepper	2 mL
2	red bell peppers, roasted, seeded and chopped	2
12 oz	Cheddar cheese, shredded (about 3½ cups/875 mL)	375 g
1 cup	ricotta cheese	250 mL
4	green onions, thinly sliced	4
1 cup	coarsely chopped cilantro	250 mL
3 cups	Salsa Roja (page 318) or store-bought (see Tip, left)	750 mL
18	6-inch (15 cm) corn tortillas (see Tip, right)	18
2 cups	sour cream	500 mL

1. In a large bowl, combine zucchini, corn, oil, 1 tsp (5 mL) cumin, salt and pepper. Spread on baking sheet and roast in preheated oven until vegetables are tender, 8 to 10 minutes. Add roasted peppers and set aside.

2. In another bowl, mix together 2½ cups (625 mL) shredded Cheddar, ricotta, remaining cumin, green onions and cilantro.

3. Reduce oven temperature to 350°F (180°C).

4. *To assemble the casserole:* Spread ¼ cup (50 mL) of the salsa on bottom of baking dish. Lay 6 tortillas over the salsa, coming slightly up the sides and ends of the dish. Spread half the vegetable mixture over the tortilla shells and spread half the ricotta mixture over the vegetables. Cover with a layer of salsa, about 1 cup (250 mL). Repeat the layers of tortillas, vegetables, cheese and salsa. Lay remaining tortillas over top. Cover completely with remaining salsa and shredded Cheddar cheese.

5. Cut a piece of parchment to fit the dish and lay it over top of the cheese. Cover the whole dish with foil. (The parchment prevents the cheese from sticking to the foil.)

6. Bake in preheated oven for 50 minutes. Remove foil and parchment and continue to bake until bubbling and nicely browned, about 20 minutes more. Let casserole stand for 10 minutes before slicing into serving portions. Serve with sour cream.

Tip

If corn tortillas are hard to find in your neighborhood, substitute readily available flour tortillas. They will work nicely.

Corn and Whole Wheat Tortillas

Delicate, round, thin, unleavened breads made from cornmeal have been an essential food in Mexico for the past many centuries, as they are still today. The best corn tortillas are freshly made in the home kitchen by practiced hands, but they may be purchased either fresh from a local commercial tortilla-maker or frozen at the supermarket. Use them as a scoop (totopos) or as a plate (tostadas) or wrap them around savory fillings to enjoy enchiladas, quesadillas and tacos.

Soft, large 6- to 8-inch (15 to 20 cm) tortillas made from wheat or whole wheat flour, sometimes flavored with spinach, herbs or tomato, are also available in packages at the market. These are folded and served warm as a bread, rolled around a savory filling and served warm in a sauce as in burritos, or served cold as a sandwich wrap. They make excellent scoops for dips when cut into wedges and strips and toasted until crisp in a hot oven.

Mediterranean Pizza

Pizzas with a variety of delicious toppings are popular with all ages for supper or a snack. They also serve as a hot party bite, cut into small wedges or decorative shapes.

Variations

Here are three pizzas you can make with a 10-inch (25 cm) pizza crust. Follow recipe to bake.

Three-Cheese Pizza: Spread dough with ½ cup (125 mL) tomato sauce, ½ cup (125 mL) shredded mozzarella, ¼ cup (50 mL) shredded orange Cheddar and ½ cup (125 mL) grated Parmigiano-Reggiano cheese over crust. Drizzle with 1 tbsp (15 mL) olive oil. For non-vegetarians, add thin slices of pepperoni or crumbled cooked sausage meat over top of mozzarella.

Margherita Pizza: Spread ½ cup (125 mL) tomato sauce over dough. Arrange 1 sliced mozzarella di bufala or 6 slices small fresh mozzarella, 1 tbsp (15 mL) olive oil, 6 to 8 fresh basil leaves over top.

Roasted Peppers and Mascarpone Pizza: Spread ¼ cup (50 mL) mascarpone cheese over the dough. Arrange ½ cup (125 mL) sliced roasted red peppers, ½ cup (125 mL) shredded mozzarella, and 2 tsp (10 mL) coarsely chopped thyme over top. For non-vegetarians, add 4 slices bacon, cut ⅛-inch (3 mm) thick.

- **Preheat oven to 450°F (230°C)**
- **10-inch (25 cm) pizza tray or preheated pizza stone**

1 tbsp	cornmeal	15 mL
1	disk Basic Pizza Dough (page 261) or about 10 oz (300 g) store-bought	1
¼ cup	black olive tapenade	50 mL
½ cup	slivered roasted red bell peppers	125 mL
½ cup	drained oil-marinated artichokes, quartered	125 mL
½ cup	crumbled soft goat's cheese	125 mL
1 tbsp	olive oil	15 mL
6 to 8	basil leaves	6 to 8

1. Sprinkle pizza tray or stone with cornmeal.
2. Turn out dough onto a floured board. With floured fingers, gently lift and stretch dough into a circle, 10 inches (25 cm) in diameter. Lift dough onto prepared tray or onto a rimless baking sheet, if you are baking on a pizza stone.
3. Spread an even layer of tapenade over dough, leaving about ½-inch (1 cm) border. Sprinkle bell peppers, artichokes and goat's cheese over top. Drizzle oil over all. If using pizza stone, slide pizza from baking sheet onto stone. Bake in preheated oven, turning pizza around after 10 minutes, until crust is cooked and goat's cheese is melted and lightly browned, 15 to 20 minutes. Top with basil leaves.

Basic Pizza Dough

Makes 1¼ lbs (625 g), enough for two 10-inch (25 cm) round pizzas

1 cup	lukewarm water	250 mL
1 tbsp	active dry yeast (see Tips, right)	15 mL
Pinch	granulated sugar	Pinch
2½ to 3 cups	all-purpose flour	625 to 750 mL
1 tsp	kosher or sea salt	5 mL
	Olive oil	

1. Pour water into a small bowl or measuring cup. Sprinkle yeast on the surface of the water and stir to combine. Stir in sugar. Let mixture stand for about 5 minutes. Mixture will bubble and froth, which indicates that the yeast is active.

2. In a large bowl, combine 2½ cups (625 mL) of the flour and salt. Make a well in the center of the flour and pour in 2 tbsp (25 mL) olive oil and yeast mixture. Using fingertips or a fork, gradually incorporate the flour into the liquid. Form the dough into a ball and knead it in the bowl until smooth and elastic, 3 to 4 minutes. If dough sticks to the bowl knead in a little more flour. If dough seems a little dry, pour a little oil on to your hands and knead it into the dough.

3. Place dough in a clean bowl. Lightly oil the entire surface of the dough ball with olive oil and cover loosely with plastic wrap. Let rise in a warm, draft-free spot until doubled in bulk, 1½ hours. Uncover and gently press to deflate dough. Cover again with plastic wrap and set aside to double in size, about 30 minutes. Deflate dough again and divide into 2 disks.

Tips

Always keep packages and jars of yeast in the refrigerator and check expiry dates.

For a light puffy pizza crust: Form dough into a round. Dust a piece of plastic wrap with flour and lay it loosely over the dough. Let stand for 10 minutes or so before topping and baking.

Fast and easy pizza: Great for kids and spur-of-the-moment snacks. Toast flour tortillas on the barbecue grill or on a grill pan for 1 to 2 minutes. Spread pizza toppings on toasted tortillas and bake in preheated 450°F (230°C) oven until cheese is bubbling and edges of tortillas are beginning to brown, about 5 minutes.

To store dough: After the first rise in Step 3, gently deflate dough and divide into 2 disks. Wrap each securely in plastic wrap and wrap again in foil or seal in a freezer bag. Dough may be stored for up to 2 days in the refrigerator or for 1 month in the freezer. Let pizza dough thaw in original packaging in the refrigerator before using.

Roast Vegetable Lasagna

Lasagna is family comfort food at its best and a perennial favorite with our customers: layers of sauce, cheese, chunky vegetables and noodles. A great lasagna takes time. However, the good thing is that all the work can be done ahead. At dinnertime all you have to do is put the lasagna in the oven, toss up a fresh green salad and warm up some crusty country bread.

Tip

If making ahead, assemble the lasagna and store, covered, in the refrigerator for several hours or for up to 1 day. Remove lasagna from refrigerator and let stand at room temperature for 30 minutes before baking as in Step 6.

- **Preheat oven to 350°F (180°C)**
- **13- by 9-inch (3 L) glass baking dish, lightly oiled**
- **Large baking sheet**

12	lasagna noodles	12
2 tbsp	olive oil, divided	25 mL
2	red onions, diced	2
2	red bell peppers, diced	2
2	green bell peppers, diced	2
2	zucchini, diced	2
	Salt and freshly ground pepper	
1 lb	ricotta cheese	500 g
3 cups	shredded mozzarella cheese (about 10 oz/300 g), divided	750 mL
	Alfredo Sauce (page 263) or store-bought, divided	
2 tbsp	coarsely chopped basil	25 mL
	Chunky Tomato Sauce (page 133)	
2 tbsp	grated Parmesan cheese, preferably Parmigiano-Reggiano	25 mL

1. Bring a large pot of lightly salted water to a boil. Add noodles and cook until just al dente. You may need to do this in 2 batches. Lift noodles from water. Drain. Lay flat and brush with 1 tbsp (15 mL) oil. Set aside.

2. In a large bowl, toss red onions, red and green bell peppers and zucchini with 1 tbsp (15 mL) of the oil and a pinch of salt. Spread on baking sheet and roast in preheated oven until vegetables are tender and onions are beginning to brown, 25 to 30 minutes. Remove from pan. Let cool slightly.

3. In a large bowl, combine ricotta, 2 cups (500 mL) of the mozzarella, roasted vegetables, ¾ cup (175 mL) of the Alfredo Sauce and basil. Taste and adjust seasoning.

4. *To assemble the lasagna:* Spread a layer of Chunky Tomato Sauce in the bottom of prepared baking dish and top with 4 lasagna noodles. Add a layer of half the ricotta mixture and half of the remaining tomato sauce. Repeat the layers of noodles, ricotta mixture and tomato sauce. Finish with another layer of noodles, Alfredo Sauce, remaining mozzarella and Parmesan cheese.

5. Lay a piece of parchment paper on top of lasagna. Cover with foil. This prevents the cheese from sticking to the foil.

6. Place dish on a baking sheet and bake in preheated oven until heated through and bubbling, 45 to 50 minutes. Remove foil and parchment and broil briefly until top is nicely browned, 5 to 6 minutes. Let stand for 10 minutes before slicing to serve.

Alfredo Sauce

Makes 4 cups (1 L)

4 cups	whipping (35%) cream or 2 cups (500 mL) each whipping (35%) cream and milk	1 L
2 tbsp	butter	25 mL
1	clove garlic, finely minced, optional	1
2 tbsp	all-purpose flour	25 mL
¼ cup	grated Parmesan cheese, preferably Parmigiano-Reggiano	50 mL
¼ tsp	freshly grated nutmeg	1 mL
	Salt and freshly ground white pepper	

1. In a small saucepan, bring cream just to a simmer over medium heat.

2. In another saucepan, melt butter over medium-low heat. Add garlic, if using, and sauté for 1 to 2 minutes. Stir in flour and cook, stirring, without letting it brown, 2 to 3 minutes.

3. Slowly whisk hot cream into flour mixture. Stir diligently until all cream is incorporated and sauce is smooth. Simmer, stirring occasionally while sauce thickens, 5 to 10 minutes.

4. Remove from heat. Stir in Parmesan and nutmeg. Season with salt and pepper to taste. If you plan to make the sauce a few hours ahead, pour a little extra cream over the surface to prevent a skin from forming (stir in just before using). Use immediately or let cool, cover and refrigerate for up to 1 day.

Tip

This basic creamy Alfredo sauce has many applications. It's a building block for many pasta dishes. We use whipping cream to make a sublimely rich sauce, but you can lighten it up by substituting half cream, half milk, or, indeed, use only milk.

Three-Mushroom Lasagna

When word got out that this cookbook was in the works, our customers began to put in requests! This lasagna was at the top of the list. The mushrooms give the lasagna a rich, meaty flavor. Essential to the success of the dish is flavorful Swiss cheese. We recommend nutty imported Emmental or a mix of half Emmental and half Gruyère.

Tip

If making ahead, assemble the lasagna and store, covered, in the refrigerator for several hours or for up to 1 day. Remove lasagna from refrigerator and let stand at room temperature for 30 minutes before baking as in Step 6.

- Preheat oven to 350°F (180°C)
- 13- by 9-inch (3 L) glass baking dish, lightly oiled
- Large baking sheet
- Parchment paper

Cheese (Mornay) Sauce

3 cups	milk	750 mL
7 tbsp	butter, divided	105 mL
1/3 cup	all-purpose flour	75 mL
1/3 cup	dry white wine	75 mL
1/4 cup	grated Grana Padano or Parmesan cheese	50 mL
1/4 tsp	freshly grated nutmeg	1 mL
	Salt and freshly ground pepper	
12	lasagna noodles	12
	Olive oil	
3	cloves garlic, finely chopped	3
1	shallot, finely chopped	1
1 lb	portobello mushrooms, sliced	500 g
1 lb	button mushrooms, sliced	500 g
4 oz	shiitake mushrooms, sliced	125 g
2 tbsp	chopped thyme	25 mL
1 tsp	chopped rosemary	5 mL
1 tsp	chopped sage	5 mL
2 tbsp	freshly squeezed lemon juice	25 mL
3 cups	shredded Swiss cheese (about 10 oz/300 g), divided	750 mL

1. *Cheese (Mornay) Sauce:* In a small saucepan over medium heat, bring milk just to a simmer. In another saucepan, melt 5 tbsp (75 mL) of the butter over medium-low heat. Stir in flour and cook, stirring, without letting it brown, 2 to 3 minutes. Slowly whisk hot milk and wine into flour mixture. Stir diligently until all liquid is incorporated and sauce is smooth. Simmer, stirring occasionally while sauce thickens, 5 to 10 minutes. Remove from heat. Stir in cheese and nutmeg. Season with salt and pepper to taste. Set aside.

2. Bring a large pot of lightly salted water to a boil. Add lasagna noodles and cook until just al dente. You may need to do this in 2 batches. Lift noodles from water. Drain. Lay flat and brush with a little oil. Set aside.

3. In a large skillet, melt remaining butter over medium heat. Add garlic and shallot and sauté until shallot is soft, 2 to 3 minutes. Add portobello, button and shiitake mushrooms and sauté until they have released their liquid and are beginning to brown, about 5 minutes. Add thyme, rosemary, sage and lemon juice. Season lightly with salt and pepper and cook for 2 to 3 minutes. Transfer mushrooms to a sieve set over a bowl to drain away any excess liquid. Let cool.

4. In a large bowl, combine cooled mushrooms, 2 cups (500 mL) of the Swiss cheese and 2 cups (500 mL) of the cheese sauce.

5. *To assemble the lasagna:* Spread a thin layer of remaining cheese sauce on the bottom of the prepared baking dish and lay 4 lasagna noodles over top. Add a layer of half the mushroom mixture and top with 4 lasagna noodles. Repeat the layers of mushroom mixture and noodles. Finish with remaining cheese sauce and Swiss cheese. Lay a piece of parchment paper over top and cover with foil.

6. Place dish on a baking sheet and bake in preheated oven until heated through and bubbling, 45 to 50 minutes. Remove foil and parchment and broil briefly until top is nicely browned, 5 to 6 minutes. Let stand for 10 minutes before slicing to serve.

Three-Cheese Crespelles

Tender, savory crêpes make delicate wraps for a variety of fillings. They're delicious to serve for a light lunch or supper. The filling can be as simple or luxurious as you choose, from a mix of cheeses to creamy Seafood Gratin (page 236). The dish can be assembled several hours ahead. The crêpes and sauces can be made a day or more ahead.

- **Preheat oven to 375°F (190°C)**
- **13- by 9-inch (3 L) glass baking dish, lightly oiled**

1 tbsp	olive oil	15 mL
2	shallots or green onions, finely chopped	2
1	clove garlic, finely chopped	1
1 lb	ricotta cheese	500 g
1 cup	shredded mozzarella cheese	250 mL
½ cup	grated Parmesan cheese, preferably Parmigiano-Reggiano, divided	125 mL
2 tbsp	coarsely chopped basil, divided	25 mL
	Salt and freshly ground pepper	
2	eggs, beaten	2
2 cups	Alfredo Sauce (page 263) or store-bought	500 mL
12	Savory Crêpes (page 267)	12
2 cups	Chunky Tomato Sauce (page 133) or store-bought	500 mL

1. In a skillet, heat oil over medium heat. Add shallots and garlic and cook until soft, but not browned, 2 to 3 minutes. Remove from heat.

2. In a large bowl, combine ricotta, mozzarella, ¼ cup (50 mL) of the Parmesan and 1 tbsp (15 mL) of the basil. Add shallot mixture. Season with salt and pepper to taste. Add eggs. Mix well and set aside.

3. Stir remaining basil into Alfredo Sauce. Set aside.

4. Spread about ¼ cup (50 mL) of the cheese filling across bottom third of each crêpe and roll up.

5. Spread Chunky Tomato Sauce on the bottom of prepared baking dish and arrange crêpes over top, seam side down, in a single layer. Pour Alfredo Sauce across the top of the crêpes and sprinkle with remaining Parmesan. Cover dish with foil and bake in preheated oven for 30 minutes. Remove foil and broil briefly until top is lightly browned.

Savory Crêpes

Makes 12 crêpes

● **Crêpe pan or 8-inch (20 cm) nonstick skillet**

¾ cup	all-purpose flour	175 mL
½ tsp	kosher or sea salt	2 mL
2	eggs	2
½ cup	milk	125 mL
½ cup	cold water	125 mL
3 tbsp	melted butter, divided	45 mL

1. In a large bowl, combine flour and salt. Make a well in the center. In a small bowl, combine eggs, milk and water. Pour into the middle of the flour and stir briskly from the center, gradually incorporating the flour and making a smooth batter. Cover bowl with plastic wrap and set aside in refrigerator for 1 to 2 hours.

2. When ready to cook, stir in 2 tbsp (25 mL) of the melted butter. Place remaining butter in a small bowl at the stove with a pastry brush at hand.

3. Place crêpe pan over medium-high heat. Brush lightly with melted butter. Lift hot pan just off heat and add ¼ cup (50 mL) of the batter. Quickly rotate the pan to swirl batter into a thin even layer on the bottom of the pan. (If there is excess batter, pour it back into the batter bowl.) Place pan over heat for 1 minute. Lift up edge of crêpe with fingers or a spatula and take a peek. When the bottom is a nice light brown, flip the crêpe over to brown the other side for 20 to 40 seconds. Repeat with the remaining batter. The underside of the crêpe only browns in spots and is used as the inside when rolled or folded. Stack cooked crêpes on a plate with squares of parchment or wax paper between. If not used immediately, wrap in plastic wrap and refrigerate for up to 2 days.

Variation

Savory Herb Crêpes: When ready to cook crêpes, stir 1 tbsp (15 mL) fresh chopped herbs into the batter. Chives, dill and tarragon are particularly compatible with eggs.

Cannelloni with Peppers and Olives

Rolls of fresh pasta stuffed with a variety of fillings is a popular lunch or light supper.

Tip

Fresh pasta sheets, cut into pieces about 10 by 6 inches (25 by 15 cm), are available in packages in the refrigerator at many markets. A package of 6 sheets, approx. 12 oz (375 g) is enough to make 12 cannelloni or 1 lasagna.

Variation

Spinach Ricotta Cannelloni: For filling, combine 2 shallots, chopped and cooked until soft in 1 tbsp (15 mL) oil, 1 lb (500 g) ricotta cheese, 1 cup (250 mL) cooked spinach, ½ cup (125 mL) shredded mozzarella, ½ cup (125 mL) grated Parmesan cheese, 2 tbsp (25 mL) chopped flat-leaf parsley, 3 beaten eggs and salt and pepper to taste. Continue with Step 3.

- Preheat oven to 350°F (180°C)
- 13- by 9-inch (3 L) glass baking dish, lightly oiled

1 tbsp	olive oil	15 mL
1	leek, white and tender green parts only, halved lengthwise and sliced	1
1	green bell pepper, diced	1
1	red bell pepper, diced	1
1	yellow bell pepper, diced	1
1	clove garlic, chopped	1
	Salt and freshly ground pepper	
1 lb	ricotta cheese	500 g
6 tbsp	grated Parmesan cheese, preferably Parmigiano-Reggiano, divided	90 mL
6 tbsp	chopped pitted green olives, divided	90 mL
6 tbsp	chopped pitted kalamata olives, divided	90 mL
2 tbsp	chopped basil	25 mL
2	eggs, beaten	2
6	sheets fresh pasta (see Tip, left)	6
4 cups	Chunky Tomato Sauce, divided (page 133) or store-bought	1 L

1. In a large skillet, heat oil over medium heat. Add leek, bell peppers and garlic and cook, stirring occasionally, until vegetables are tender, 10 to 15 minutes. Season with salt and pepper to taste. Remove from heat.

2. In a large bowl, combine ricotta, 4 tbsp (60 mL) of the Parmesan, 4 tbsp (60 mL) each of the green and black olives, basil and cooked leek and peppers. Taste and adjust seasoning. Stir in eggs. Set aside.

3. Soak pasta sheets in water according to manufacturer's directions. Drain and pat dry. Cut each fresh pasta sheet in half to make 12 strips. Place a scant ½ cup (125 mL) of filling across the bottom of each pasta strip and roll up.

4. Spread 2 cups (500 mL) of the Chunky Tomato Sauce on the bottom of prepared baking dish and arrange cannelloni on top, seam side down, in a single layer. Combine the rest of the olives with the remaining sauce and spread evenly across the top and between cannelloni. Sprinkle with remaining Parmesan. Cover dish with foil and bake in preheated oven until noodles are tender, sauce is bubbling and filling is hot, 30 to 35 minutes. Remove foil and broil briefly until top is lightly browned.

Grains

Mesopotamia — roughly present-day Syria, Iraq, Israel, Kuwait, Jordan, southeastern Turkey and much of Iran — is recognized as the cradle of civilization, the birthplace, some 6,000 years ago, of writing and the wheel. The area is also blessed with rich earth (hence its secondary name, Fertile Crescent) where the unlettered, no-wheel-drive natives cultivated grains — barley, flax and wheat, the founding grassy fathers — two or three thousand years before they could write about it. Rice, part of the wheat family, came later, being grown in Thailand about the same time as the wheel started rolling; similarly corn, thanks to the Aztecs in what are now Mexico and Guatemala. Fast-forward, and how would the world now get through its day without some bread, rice or pasta? In one form or another, grains have become a sustenance for us all.

How much of a sustenance depends on whether we choose whole grains or refined grains — and do we know the difference, read the labels, or care? Simply put, refined grains offer convenience, speed in cooking and digestion; whole grains, no part of "instant" foods, take longer to get our heads around, usually longer to prepare and longer to work their way through our systems. But whole grains are by any measure better for us — they contain the bran, the germ and the endosperm, while the refined variety retains, after milling, only the endosperm, the starchy white inner core.

The bran is grain's protective outer layer, high in fiber and rich in protein. The germ is the part of the seed that sprouts, and is rich in minerals, essential fatty acids and vitamins. Minus both, the refined grain's endosperm has only a fraction of its parent's original nutrition, lacking iron and many B vitamins as well as the fiber. It forms the structure for white bread and white flour products, so

omnipresent (and financially successful) in the marketplace, but its deficiency is betrayed by how often one reads the word "enriched" on its packaging. Adding a few synthetic nutrients to the mix hardly makes up for the mass of natural plant nutrients displaced in the milling — primarily fiber, so vital for intestinal health.

Studies have shown that diets rich in whole grains help reduce risks of cardiovascular disease, type 2 diabetes, various cancers, from mouth to stomach to colon, and in the simple prevention of constipation. Three servings daily are recommended as a minimum. Sample single servings: 1 slice whole-grain bread; half a whole-grain bagel or muffin; 1 oz (30 g) whole-grain cereal; $\frac{1}{2}$ cup (125 mL) oatmeal, brown rice, or whole wheat pasta; 5 to 6 whole wheat crackers; 3 cups (750 mL) popcorn.

To be sure you get a whole-grain product, check that one of these whole-grain ingredients is listed first: whole wheat, brown rice, bulgur, graham flour, oatmeal, whole-grain corn, whole oats, whole rye, wild rice. Common refined-grain products include: white bread, white flour, white rice, degermed cornmeal, hominy and pasta (but whole-grain pastas are available). Beware the weasel words: seven-grain, 100% wheat, stone-ground, cracked wheat or bran. They are usually not whole grain. And color doesn't always tell the truth: bread may be brown because molasses has been added.

In the Kitchen

When cooking, it's important to use either whole-grain or refined. Don't mix the two. They fight each other and the result tends to be ugly. Cook highly processed grains (often labeled "instant") according to package directions. Cooking time is influenced by the quality and freshness of the grain. The flavor of most grains is enhanced if lightly toasted in a skillet with a little butter or olive oil before proceeding with preparation.

Basic Cooking for Popular Grains

Bulgur: Rinse and drain. In a large bowl, pour 2 cups (500 mL) boiling water over 1 cup (250 mL) fine bulgur and let stand, covered tightly with plastic wrap, for 15 minutes. Drain and press to remove excess water. Fluff with a fork and add seasonings. For coarse bulgur, increase boiling water to $2\frac{1}{2}$ cups (625 mL) and let stand for 20 minutes. May also be sautéed for a minute in butter or oil and cooked for 10 minutes with stock and vegetables as in a pilaf. Yields about 3 cups (750 mL) cooked.

Couscous: In a large bowl, pour $1\frac{1}{2}$ cups (375 mL) boiling water over 1 cup (250 mL) instant couscous and let stand for 5 minutes. Fluff with a fork and add olive oil or butter, herbs and seasonings as desired. Couscous becomes extra light and fluffy when cooked as in North Africa in a couscousière, or in a colander over about 3 inches (7.5 cm) simmering water. The process takes longer and is accomplished in two stages. First steam rinsed couscous for about 20 minutes. Then spread out on a tray, sprinkle with about $\frac{1}{2}$ cup (125 mL) water and $\frac{1}{2}$ tsp (2 mL) salt and separate the grains with lightly oiled fingers. Let cool and dry. Return couscous to steamer and steam, uncovered, for about 20 minutes more. Israeli couscous (pearl pasta) is cooked like pasta in a large amount of boiling salted water until tender, about 10 minutes. Yields about 3 cups (750 mL) cooked.

Pearl barley: In a large saucepan of boiling, salted water, cook 1 cup (250 mL) barley over medium heat until tender, 25 to 30 minutes. Drain and season with salt and pepper. Yields about 2 cups (500 mL) cooked.

Quinoa: Rinse in a bowl with four to five changes of water. Drain. In a saucepan, combine 1 cup (250 mL) quinoa with 2 cups (500 mL) boiling water. Simmer over low heat, covered, 12 to 15 minutes. Remove from heat and let stand, covered, for 5 minutes. Steamed quinoa: In a large saucepan of boiling salted water, cook quinoa for 10 minutes. Drain and rinse under cold water. Set quinoa in a sieve, or a cheesecloth-lined colander, over a saucepan containing about $1\frac{1}{2}$ inches (4 cm) simmering water. Cover sieve with a cloth and a lid. Steam quinoa until the grains are fluffy and separate, 10 to 12 minutes. Toss in a bowl with oil and seasonings. Yields about 3 cups (750 mL) cooked.

Rice (see page 304)

Wheat berries: In a large saucepan, add 1 cup (250 mL) wheat berries and cover with water. Bring to a boil, reduce heat, cover pan and simmer until tender, about 1 hour. Test often and do not add salt until berries soften. Combine with herbs, vegetables, nuts and seasonings as desired. (Soft wheat berries will take about 10 minutes less time to cook than hard wheat berries.)

If time allows, soak wheat berries in cold water to cover overnight in the refrigerator. Once soaked, they cook in about 15 minutes less time and are easier to digest. Yields about 4 cups (1 L) cooked.

Nasi Goreng

SERVES 6

Whenever this spicy Indonesian Fried Rice dish is on the menu, it's a sellout! Enjoy alone as a nutritious main dish and garnish with extra stir-fried or grilled tofu, or for non-vegetarians shrimp or chicken.

Tips

Fish sauce (*nam pla, nuoc nam*) is an essential seasoning used in Southeast Asian cooking made from the liquid of salted fermented fish. To make a dish more strictly vegetarian, seek out Vietnamese vegetarian fish sauce (*nuoc mam an chay*) or add a dash more soy.

Sambal oelek is a paste of crushed red chiles that originated in Southeast Asia. It has a clean fresh taste and is very easy to use. It adds instant heat to stir-fries, sauces and dressings. Widely available in jars. Keep in refrigerator after opening.

● **Large wok or nonstick skillet**

1½ cups	long-grain white rice	375 mL
6	eggs	6
2 tbsp	soy sauce	25 mL
1 tbsp	vegetarian fish sauce (see Tips, left)	15 mL
3 tbsp	vegetable oil	45 mL
2	shallots, finely chopped	2
3	cloves garlic, finely chopped	3
1 tbsp	minced gingerroot	15 mL
1 tbsp	minced lemongrass	15 mL
1 cup	diced firm tofu	250 mL
½ cup	frozen peas	125 mL
½	red bell pepper, finely chopped	½
1 tbsp	sambal oelek (see Tips, left)	15 mL
	Salt and freshly ground black pepper	
1 cup	cilantro leaves	250 mL
3	green onions, thinly sliced on the diagonal	3

1. In a large saucepan of boiling lightly salted water, cook rice until tender, 14 to 15 minutes. Drain and spread out in a shallow dish so rice will cool and dry quickly. Cook rice the day ahead if possible — the drier the rice, the better the dish. Cover rice and refrigerate.

2. In a small bowl, lightly beat eggs with soy sauce and fish sauce. Set aside.

3. Heat wok over medium-high heat. Add oil. Add shallots, garlic, ginger and lemongrass and cook, stirring constantly to prevent scorching and sticking, 1 to 2 minutes. Add tofu, peas, bell pepper and sambal oelek. Cook, stirring diligently to prevent scorching and sticking, until peas are hot and there is no liquid in the pan, 2 to 3 minutes. Add egg mixture and stir until egg has just set, about 30 seconds.

4. Stir in rice and heat through, stirring often, 2 to 3 minutes.

5. Taste and season with salt and pepper to taste. Toss in cilantro and green onions.

Vegetable Noodle Stir-Fry

Tip
Precooked chunky Miki wheat noodles are often available packaged in the refrigerator section of the supermarket. They need less than 1 minute to reheat in stir-fries and soups. They can also be used in Asian salads.

Non-Vegetarian Variation
Chicken Vegetable Stir-Fry: Stir-fry 8 oz (250 g) thinly sliced skinless boneless chicken breasts in oil for 2 to 3 minutes in Step 2. Remove and set aside. Proceed with recipe. You may need to add 1 tbsp (15 mL) more oil. Return chicken to wok after heating the noodles.

Large wok or skillet

2 tbsp	vegetable oil	25 mL
1	clove garlic, chopped	1
3	shiitake mushroom caps, thinly sliced	3
1	red bell pepper, cubed	1
1	carrot, thinly sliced on the diagonal	1
1	small head broccoli, cut into small florets	1
4 oz	snow peas, trimmed and halved on the diagonal	125 g
2	baby bok choy, roughly chopped	2
1 tbsp	dry sherry	15 mL
1	package (14 oz/400 g) Miki noodles (see Tip, left)	1
½ cup	Vegetable Stock (page 56) or ready-to-use broth	125 mL
2 to 3 tbsp	soy sauce	25 to 45 mL
2 tbsp	sesame oil	25 mL
½ to 1 tsp	sambal oelek, optional (see Tips, page 272)	2 to 5 mL
2	green onions, thinly sliced on the diagonal	2

1. In a wok, heat oil over medium-high heat until oil shimmers. Add garlic, mushrooms, bell pepper, carrot and broccoli and stir-fry for 3 to 4 minutes. Add snow peas, bok choy and sherry and stir-fry for 2 to 3 minutes.

2. Stir in noodles and heat through, tossing gently, 3 to 4 minutes. Reduce heat to medium-low. Stir in vegetable stock, 2 tbsp (25 mL) soy sauce, ½ tsp (2 mL) sambal oelek, if using, and sesame oil. Toss over heat for a minute to blend flavors. Taste and season with a dash more soy sauce, sambal oelek or sesame oil to taste. Garnish with green onions.

Thai Vegetable Curry

This quick and easy curry is tasty and versatile. It's a delicious vegetarian dish served over rice, and for non-vegetarians add a stir-fry of chicken, fish or seafood.

Tips

For the assorted vegetables I suggest Japanese eggplant, sliced carrot, red and green bell peppers, zucchini and sliced onion.

Green curry paste is a blend of Thai flavorings. The authentic blends usually include green chiles, garlic, lime leaves, galangal (Thai ginger), coriander and lemongrass and are used in chicken, fish and vegetable dishes.

The lime leaf so popular in Indonesian cooking is the leaf of the aromatic and beautiful thorny wild lime tree. You may find them in some Asian markets, often frozen. Its flavor is distinct from the cultivated lime tree. For convenience, wild lime leaves can be stored well-wrapped in the freezer.

2 tbsp	vegetable oil	25 mL
6 cups	assorted vegetables, cubed (see Tips, left)	1.5 L
2 tbsp	Thai green curry paste (see Tips, left)	25 mL
1	can (14 oz/400 mL) coconut milk	1
2 tbsp	fish sauce	25 mL
1	wild lime leaf (see Tips, left)	1
1 tbsp	chopped Thai basil	15 mL
	Salt and freshly ground pepper	
2 tbsp	chopped cilantro	25 mL
1	lime, sliced	1
	Cooked rice	

1. In a large skillet, heat oil over medium-high heat. Add vegetables and stir-fry for 2 to 3 minutes. Add curry paste and stir-fry for 1 minute.

2. Stir coconut milk and add to vegetables with fish sauce, lime leaf and basil. Reduce heat and simmer until vegetables are tender, 5 to 10 minutes. Season with salt and pepper to taste. Serve garnished with cilantro and lime over steamed fragrant rice.

Sides

Grilled Asparagus with Shallots and Lemon

Asparagus is particularly delicious when grilled or roasted. Choose medium to thick stalks — thin ones do not remain juicy when cooked in this way.

Tips

To trim firm thin asparagus stalks: Hold the tough root end of the stalk with one hand and grasp the stalk with the other hand, about 2 inches (5 cm) away. Gently bend the stalk until it snaps at the natural point where the tough end stops and the tender part begins.

To trim fat asparagus stalks: Cut across the stalk where you see the color of the tough root end changes from whitish green to green. If the stem end still seems a little tough, make another cut a bit higher up the stalk. Peel about two-thirds of the way up the stalk, if you wish. A swivel potato peeler is perfect for the job.

Variation

Grilled Asparagus with Prosciutto: Cut 2 slices of prosciutto into slivers. In a small skillet, heat 1 tsp (5 mL) olive oil. Add prosciutto and sauté until lightly browned and crisp, 2 to 3 minutes. Sprinkle on top of grilled asparagus with extra virgin olive oil, chopped shallots and lemon zest and juice.

Preheat barbecue or indoor grill to medium-high

2 lbs	asparagus, trimmed (see Tips, left)	1 kg
2 tbsp	olive oil	25 mL
	Salt and freshly ground black pepper	
1 tsp	extra virgin olive oil	5 mL
1	shallot, finely chopped	1
1 tsp	grated lemon zest	5 mL
	Freshly squeezed lemon juice to taste	

1. Toss asparagus stalks with olive oil and season lightly with salt and pepper. Grill until tender, turning every 3 to 4 minutes to cook and brown evenly, 6 to 10 minutes, depending on the thickness of the stalks.
2. Transfer to a warm platter. Drizzle with extra virgin olive oil and sprinkle with shallot and lemon zest. Season with pepper and a squeeze of lemon juice to taste.

Ginger-Glazed Carrots and Parsnips

The flesh of the parsnip has a sweet, distinctive flavor. The cream-colored carrot-shaped tapered root vegetable is often overlooked. It is available from fall through to early summer. Alone or in combination with other root vegetables, parsnips can be boiled, roasted or puréed and make excellent soups.

Tip

When sautéing, add food item to hot oil and leave untouched for 2 minutes or so to allow time to brown the under surface of the food. Turn to brown the other side. If the oil is not hot enough, or you move the food around in the pan in the first minute, the food is likely to stick.

2 tbsp	butter, softened	25 mL
2 tsp	finely chopped gingerroot	10 mL
4	parsnips	4
3	carrots	3
2 tbsp	vegetable oil (approx.)	25 mL
	Salt and freshly ground black pepper	
½ cup	vegetable stock or water	125 mL
1 tbsp	finely chopped flat-leaf parsley	15 mL

1. In a small bowl, mash together butter and ginger with a fork. Set aside.
2. Cut parsnips and carrots down the center lengthwise. Slice on the diagonal about ¼ inch (0.5 cm) thick.
3. Heat large skillet over medium-high heat. Add vegetable oil. Add parsnips and carrots and sauté until lightly browned, 2 to 3 minutes. Add more oil if the vegetables seem to be sticking. Season with salt and pepper. Reduce heat to medium. Add stock. Cover and cook until just tender, 5 to 6 minutes.
4. Remove lid and increase heat to bring liquid to a boil; boil, reducing liquid until about 1 tbsp (15 mL) remains. Add ginger-butter mixture. Let it melt in the pan and toss to glaze vegetables. Toss with parsley and serve hot.

Beet Green Gratin

SERVES 4

Bunches of leafy beet greens with bright purple stalks are in markets from fall through spring. Like chard and spinach, beet greens cook quickly and have a sweetish flavor. This simple, luscious gratin is delicious served with roast pork, chicken or grilled fish.

Tip

Beet greens, kale, chard, curly leaf spinach, collards and some other leafy greens have tough stalks that have to be removed before cooking. Grab the bottom of the stalk in one hand and pull away the tender part of the leaves with the other, or use a sharp chef's knife to make an inverted "v" cut down each side of the stalk. Discard tough stalks.

- **Preheat oven to 375°F (190°C)**
- **8-inch (20 cm) small casserole, lightly buttered**

1 lb	beet greens, thick stalk removed (about 4 bunches) (see Tip, left)	500 g
3 tbsp	olive oil	45 mL
2	shallots, minced	2
2 to 3	cloves garlic, minced	2 to 3
1 cup	half-and-half (10%) cream	250 mL
	Salt and freshly ground black pepper	
½ cup	bread crumbs, divided	125 mL

1. Cut trimmed beet greens into ¼-inch (0.5) slivers. Set aside.

2. In large skillet, heat oil over medium heat. Add shallots and garlic to taste and sauté until just softened, 1 to 2 minutes. Add beet greens and toss until wilted, 2 to 3 minutes. Stir in cream and season with ½ tsp (2 mL) salt and ¼ tsp (1 mL) pepper. Gently bring to a boil. Remove from heat. Stir in ¼ cup (50 mL) of the bread crumbs. Taste and adjust seasoning.

3. Transfer beet greens to prepared casserole. Sprinkle top with remaining bread crumbs. Bake in preheated oven until gently bubbling and bread crumbs are golden brown, 15 to 20 minutes.

Green Beans Gremolata

Freshly picked green and yellow beans at the height of the season have fantastic flavor. Simply blanch and toss with a little butter, pepper and fresh dill — that's it. Sometimes just beyond the season, or when they have had to travel too far to market, beans need a little help. Beans are universally popular and add bright color to just about every main course.

Variation

Green Beans with Roasted Pepper and Toasted Almonds: Prepare recipe up to end of Step 2. Omit lemon zest, parsley and cheese. Add 1 roasted red pepper, cut into slivers. Toss pepper slices with garlicky beans, season with salt and pepper to taste and garnish with 2 tbsp (25 mL) slivered toasted almonds and 2 tbsp (25 mL) julienned basil.

1 lb	green beans, trimmed	500 g
2 tbsp	extra virgin olive oil	25 mL
2	cloves garlic, minced	2
1/4 cup	chopped flat-leaf parsley	50 mL
2 tbsp	grated Parmesan cheese, preferably Parmigiano-Reggiano	25 mL
2 tsp	grated lemon zest	10 mL
	Salt and freshly ground black pepper	

1. Bring a saucepan of lightly salted water to a boil. Add beans and cook until just tender, 3 to 5 minutes. Drain and keep warm.

2. In a small skillet, heat oil over medium-low heat. Add garlic and sauté for 1 to 2 minutes. Transfer to a warm large bowl.

3. Stir parsley, cheese and lemon zest into garlic. Add beans and toss to coat in flavorings. Season with salt and pepper to taste. Serve hot as soon as possible; the bright color and fresh flavor fades over time and with reheating.

Balsamic Green Beans and Portobellos

Tip

Our chefs sometimes scrape away the soft brown gills under the cap of large portobello mushrooms with the sharp edge of a spoon. The mushrooms don't release as much moisture during sautéing and any loose brown bits do not cloud the sauce or cling to other ingredients.

1 lb	green beans, trimmed	500 g
1 tbsp	extra virgin olive oil	15 mL
2	shallots, sliced	2
2	portobello mushrooms, caps only, sliced (see Tip, left)	2
	Salt and freshly ground black pepper	
2 tbsp	balsamic vinegar	25 mL
1 tsp	chopped thyme	5 mL

1. Bring a saucepan of lightly salted water to a boil. Add beans and cook until just tender, 3 to 5 minutes. Drain and keep warm.
2. In a skillet, heat oil over medium heat. Add shallots and mushrooms and sauté until soft and lightly browned, 3 to 4 minutes. Season with 1 tsp (5 mL) salt and a pinch of pepper. Stir in vinegar. Add beans and thyme and toss together. Heat through. Taste and adjust seasoning. Serve hot as soon as possible because the bright color and fresh flavor fade over time and with reheating.

Broccoli Rabe with Garlic

Variation

Broccoli Rabe and Beans: Follow Step 1. In Step 2, add a pinch of hot pepper flakes with the garlic and add 1 can (14 to 19 oz/398 to 540 mL) white beans, rinsed and drained.

1	bunch broccoli rabe (about 1½ lbs/750 g)	1
2 tbsp	olive oil	25 mL
3	cloves garlic, thinly sliced	3
1 tbsp	freshly squeezed lemon juice	15 mL
	Kosher or sea salt	

1. Remove tough ends of stalks of broccoli rabe. Bring a saucepan of lightly salted water to a boil. Add broccoli rabe and cook until just tender, about 5 minutes. Drain and set aside.
2. In a large skillet, heat oil over medium-low heat. Add garlic and sauté until soft and just beginning to color, 5 to 7 minutes. Add broccoli rabe, toss to coat in garlicky oil and heat through, 5 minutes. Add lemon juice. Add salt to taste. Serve hot as soon as possible.

Butternut Squash and Carrot Purée with Maple Syrup

Butternut squash is a prized winter vegetable in our kitchen. It's used in a wide range of soups, stews, gratins and purées and is included in the daily roasted root vegetable medley. It's easier to peel than most winter squashes, but you still may have some blisters remaining after the holiday season, when this purée is most popular served with the festive bird.

Food processor or blender

¼ cup	butter	50 mL
1	onion, chopped	1
1	butternut squash, diced	1
3	carrots, sliced	3
½ tsp	grated orange zest	2 mL
1 cup	freshly squeezed orange juice	250 mL
	Salt and freshly ground black pepper	
2 to 3 tbsp	pure maple syrup	25 to 45 mL

1. In a large pot, melt butter over medium heat. Add onion and sauté until soft and just starting to brown, 5 to 6 minutes. Add squash, carrots, orange juice and ½ tsp (2 mL) salt and pepper. Bring to a boil. Reduce heat, cover and simmer until vegetables are tender and liquid is reduced to a glaze, about 25 minutes.

2. Remove from heat and stir in maple syrup to taste and orange zest. Let cool slightly.

3. Using a food processor, purée vegetables in batches. Return to pot and heat through, stirring occasionally, over medium-low heat. Taste and adjust seasoning.

Braised Pearl Onions

Tip

Make the job of peeling small onions fast and easy! Blanch them in boiling water for 1 to 2 minutes. Drain. Trim the root end with a small sharp knife and slip the outer skins off.

Variations

Instead of pearl onions, use the same method to cook small flat-topped cipollinis or shallots.

You can use dry red wine in place of half of the stock, if you prefer.

1 tbsp	olive oil	15 mL
1 tbsp	butter	15 mL
8 oz	pearl onions, peeled	250 g
½ cup	Chicken or Beef Stock (pages 54 and 55) or ready-to-use broth	125 mL
2	sprigs thyme	2
2	sprigs parsley	2
1	bay leaf	1
	Salt and freshly ground black pepper	

1. In a medium saucepan, heat oil and butter over medium-high heat. Add onions and sauté, rolling the onions around so that they brown on all sides, about 10 minutes,

2. Add stock, thyme, parsley, bay leaf and salt and pepper to taste. Cover, reduce heat and simmer until onions are tender, about 30 minutes. Set aside until needed.

Shallots and Cipollinis

Shallots belong to the onion family yet are quite different. They have a subtle yet intense flavor that is beloved by chefs, particularly in France and Southeast Asia. There are hundreds of varieties but in our markets you will most often find oval ones with a brown skin and small globe-shaped ones with a papery skin ranging in color from golden brown to grayish and rosy red. The firm-textured off-white flesh is tinged with dark red or green. Use raw finely chopped in salads, marinades and vinaigrettes and cooked as an aromatic in sauces and as a garnish. Whole shallots may be braised or roasted and are delicious pickled. Cook chopped shallots over gentle heat until soft; they burn and become bitter very quickly.

Cipollinis are small flat onions grown from Italian seed that are milder and richer in taste than smaller pearl onions. (Cipollini means "small onion" in Italian.) They are sometimes hard to find fresh but you will find them preserved in olive oil or pickled in balsamic vinegar and are a nice addition to an antipasto plate.

Gobi Masala

SERVES 4 TO 6

Here's an aromatic side dish to serve as part of a meal featuring foods prepared with Indian spices.

1 tbsp	vegetable oil	15 mL
1 tsp	mustard seeds	5 mL
1 tsp	ground coriander	5 mL
1 tsp	ground turmeric	5 mL
½ tsp	cayenne pepper	2 mL
1	head cauliflower, cut into florets	1
	Kosher or sea salt	
2 tbsp	chickpea flour	25 mL
1 cup	coconut milk (approx.)	250 mL
½ cup	water (approx.)	125 mL
8 oz	green beans, trimmed and cut in half	250 g

1. In a large skillet, heat oil over medium-high heat. Add mustard seeds, coriander, turmeric and cayenne and cook, stirring, until spices begin to sizzle, about 30 seconds. Add cauliflower, stir to coat with spices and add ½ tsp (2 mL) salt.
2. Sprinkle in chickpea flour and cook, stirring, for 1 minute. Stir in coconut milk and water. Reduce heat to medium, cover and cook for 5 minutes.
3. Stir in green beans. Cover and cook until vegetables are tender, about 10 minutes. Lift lid and stir vegetables occasionally, adding a little more coconut milk and water if pot gets too dry before the vegetables are cooked to your liking. Taste and adjust seasoning.

Brussels Sprouts with Pancetta and Cream

In our experience Brussels sprouts are sadly mistreated and usually overcooked. Simply blanch until just resistant to the bite and toss with butter, salt and pepper, or combine with smoky bacon and cream to make this delectable side dish for roasted or grilled meats.

2 lbs	Brussels sprouts, trimmed and cut in half lengthwise	1 kg
3 oz	pancetta, cut into thin strips	90 g
1 cup	whipping (35%) cream	250 mL
1 tbsp	butter	15 mL
¼ tsp	freshly grated nutmeg	1 mL
¼ tsp	cayenne pepper	1 mL
	Salt and freshly ground black pepper	
¼ cup	toasted pine nuts, optional	50 mL

1. In a large pot of boiling lightly salted water, cook Brussels sprouts until al dente, 4 to 5 minutes. Drain and set aside.

2. In a large skillet over medium heat, sauté pancetta until crisp and lightly browned. Transfer with a slotted spoon to paper towels to drain and set aside. Discard all but 1 tbsp (15 mL) fat from the pan.

3. Meanwhile, in a small saucepan, heat cream over low heat. Simmer gently until reduced to about ¾ cup (175 mL) and lightly thickened.

4. In the skillet, add butter to reserved fat and heat over medium heat. Add Brussels sprouts, in batches, and brown lightly, 2 to 3 minutes. Return all sprouts to the skillet. Season with nutmeg and cayenne. Stir in reserved pancetta and cream reduction and heat through. Season with salt and pepper to taste. Serve hot garnished with pine nuts, if desired.

Sesame-Glazed Baby Bok Choy

Bok choy is a mild member of the cabbage family that comes in bunches of soft white stems and green leaves. It is most familiar used in stir-fries. The large bunches are usually cut in half or chopped. Baby bok choy are delicious cooked whole and glazed to complement dishes of Asian flavors.

Tip

Be sure to wash boy choy carefully, paying attention to root ends.

Bamboo steamer, optional

1 tbsp	vegetable oil	15 mL
1	clove garlic, finely chopped	1
1 tsp	finely chopped gingerroot	5 mL
1 tbsp	brown sugar	15 mL
1 tbsp	soy sauce	15 mL
1 tsp	grated lime zest	5 mL
2 tbsp	freshly squeezed lime juice	25 mL
1 tsp	sesame oil	5 mL
6 to 8	small bok choy (see Tip, left)	6 to 8
	Kosher or sea salt	
1 tsp	black sesame seeds, optional	5 mL

1. In a small saucepan, heat oil over medium heat. Add garlic and ginger and sauté until fragrant but not browned, 1 to 2 minutes. Stir in brown sugar, soy sauce, and lime zest and simmer, stirring, while sugar melts. Remove from heat and add lime juice and sesame oil. Set aside.

2. Slice bok choy in half lengthwise if large. Steam in a bamboo steamer over simmering water, or place in a shallow skillet in $1/2$ inch (2 mL) lightly salted water and cook, covered, until tender, 3 to 4 minutes. Drain.

3. Toss steamed bok choy with soy glaze. Add salt or a dash of sesame oil to taste. Serve hot, garnished with black sesame seeds, if using.

Mushroom Ragoût

This elegant mix of mushrooms in a richly flavored sauce is a favorite for vegetarians when accompanied by grilled polenta or tucked into an omelet. It's also a delicious side dish to serve with roast beef or turkey. Careful sautéing of the different varieties of mushrooms captures their essential flavor and texture.

Tips

A soft bristle pastry brush is a handy tool for gently brushing dirt from mushrooms.

You can rinse off the shiitake stems and save them to add to stock.

8 oz	cremini mushrooms	250 g
8 oz	king oyster mushrooms	250 g
8 oz	shiitake mushrooms	250 g
½ cup	olive oil, divided	125 mL
	Salt and freshly ground black pepper	
½ cup	minced shallots	125 mL
2	cloves garlic, minced	2
2½ cups	Vegetable Stock (page 56) or ready-to-use broth	625 mL
2 tsp	chopped thyme	10 mL
1 tsp	balsamic vinegar	5 mL
2 tbsp	butter	25 mL
¼ cup	coarsely chopped flat-leaf parsley	50 mL

1. Trim off cremini stems and thinly slice caps. Set aside.
2. Trim off bottom of king oyster stems and separate top from bottom. Thinly slice the mushroom tops. Cut the stem in half and slice into half moons. Set aside.
3. Remove shiitake stems and discard (or rinse with water and save for stock). Thinly slice mushroom caps. Set aside.
4. In a large skillet, heat 2 tbsp (25 mL) of the oil over medium-high heat and swirl to completely coat pan. Add cremini mushrooms in a single layer. Let them sit for 1 minute, then stir. Let them sit for another minute. Season lightly with salt and pepper and stir until mushrooms brown, 2 to 3 minutes. Transfer mushrooms to a large bowl. Repeat the same cooking method with king oyster and shiitake mushrooms. Set aside.
5. In the same skillet, heat remaining oil over medium heat. Add shallots and garlic and sauté for 1 minute. Return cooked mushrooms to the pan with the cooking juices collected in the bowl. Add vegetable stock, thyme, 1 tsp (5 mL) salt and ½ tsp (2 mL) pepper.
6. Reduce heat to medium-low and simmer mushroom mixture until liquid is reduced and slightly thickened, 5 to 6 minutes.
7. Add balsamic vinegar and stir in butter to lightly thicken and add sheen to the sauce. Toss with parsley and taste for seasoning.

Mushrooms

Easy to grow, easy to pick, easy to love when edible, dead easy to fear when not, the mysterious mushroom has us in thrall. Small wonder, when the genus *Amanita* embraces some 600 species of fungus, from the inescapably delicious to the hallucinogenic to some of the most inescapably toxic mushrooms in the world. For millennia they have been remembered in song, story and 4,500-year-old Egyptian hieroglyphics for their association with both life and death. Pharaohs thought eating them ensured immortality. Five thousand years later, 11th-century Normans fed a pound of them to the groom on his wedding day to ensure continuity of his bloodline.

Today the mushrooms everyone knows, since they take bully place on vegetable shelves, are the white buttons: mushroom arithmetic. Wild mushrooms offer the trigonometry, the most flavor and variety.

The common cultivated mushroom offers: Zero fat, zero cholesterol, low in calories and carbohydrates, good source of the B vitamins, notably riboflavin (B_2), niacin (B_3) and pantothenic acid (B_5), plus selenium, copper, potassium, phosphorus and folate.

In the Kitchen

To clean mushrooms, brush off any dirt or rinse them briefly. Although mushrooms won't absorb water as commonly thought, rinsing can discolor them.

Chanterelle, prized by chefs for its strong woodsy tones and a faintly peppery taste.

Cremini, immature portobello (see right), closely related to the common white mushroom, with a light brown color, firmer texture and fuller flavor.

Enoki come in thin white bunches with long stems and tiny brown shiny caps; mild in taste, very good eaten raw in sandwiches and salads; add to a cooked dish only at the last or they will toughen.

Morel is the same species as the truffle (see below) but infinitely cheaper; tan to dark brown, greatly prized for its strong earthy flavor; at their best when simply sautéed in a bit of butter.

Oyster, whitish beige, and so named because of its shape when spread; often found in tree trunks; strong flavor when eaten raw, milder when cooked.

Porcini, aka **cepe**, are among the great fungus treasures of the wild; pale brown. Fresh, it has a smooth texture and an unforgettably pungent, woodsy flavor. Often sold dried; one ounce (30 g) used in soups and stews will be enough for four.

Portobello, mature cremini, flavorful with a dark meaty texture; can grow as large as 5 inches (12.5 cm); good for grilling.

Shiitake, dark brown caps, from 3 to 10 inches (7.5 to 25 cm) in diameter; firm texture, woodsy flavor; add the caps to stews and stir-fries, save the stems for sauces and stocks.

Truffle, wildly expensive, intensely aromatic and musky, often shaved into omelets and risottos. Found in the winter among the roots of oaks from the south of France to northern Italy, Spain and Portugal, and snuffled out by trained dogs and pigs. Most prized is the black variety (aka black diamond), followed closely by the white, which has a creamy beige exterior.

Ratatouille

Many years ago I spent a stint learning from Roger Vergé at his restaurant Moulin de Mougins in the little town of Mougins, just north of Nice, France. When ratatouille is cooking, the aromas that fill the kitchen take me back to that time and the abundance of wonderful vegetables and fruits in the markets in Provence in late summer. This vegetable dish is a celebration of the abundance that we, too, enjoy, if for a shorter season. Careful cooking of each vegetable and a long gentle simmer of the mélange of vegetables is the secret to success. Serve warm or at room temperature as a side dish or part of an antipasto plate.

Tips

You can substitute 1 can (28 oz/796 mL) plum tomatoes, drained and roughly chopped, for the fresh tomatoes.

If time allows, set dish aside for 1 hour or so to let flavors develop. Ratatouille tastes even better the next day.

● **4- to 6-quart (4 to 6 L) casserole with lid**

2	zucchini	2
1	eggplant	1
	Salt and freshly ground black pepper	
6 tbsp	extra virgin olive oil, divided	90 mL
1	onion, sliced	1
1	red bell pepper, sliced	1
1	green bell pepper, sliced	1
1 lb	ripe Roma (plum) tomatoes, seeded and chopped (see Tips, left)	500 g
2 to 3	cloves garlic, chopped	2 to 3
1 tbsp	chopped flat-leaf parsley, divided	15 mL
1 tbsp	basil chiffonade, divided	15 mL
1 tsp	chopped thyme	5 mL

1. Cut zucchini and eggplant into pieces roughly 3 by 1 inch (7.5 by 2.5 cm). Place in a colander and sprinkle with salt. Set aside for 30 minutes. Drain and pat dry.
2. Meanwhile, preheat oven to 325°F (160°C).
3. In a large skillet, heat 3 tbsp (45 mL) of the oil over medium-high heat. Add zucchini and eggplant, in batches, and cook until browned on all sides. Add oil as needed. Sprinkle with salt and pepper and set aside.
4. In same pan, heat 2 tbsp (25 mL) of oil. Reduce heat to medium. Add onion and red and green peppers and sauté until soft and starting to brown, about 10 minutes. Stir in tomatoes, garlic to taste, half the parsley and basil, and thyme. Season lightly with salt and pepper and cook for 5 minutes.
5. In casserole, arrange half of the tomato mixture on the bottom, add a layer of browned zucchini and eggplant, and top with the remaining tomato mixture. Cover casserole tightly with foil and a lid. Bake in preheated oven for 20 to 25 minutes. Raise lid and baste the vegetables with the fragrant cooking juices. Continue to bake until vegetables are tender and juices are reduced, about 10 minutes more. Taste and adjust seasoning. Serve hot or at room temperature garnished with remaining parsley and basil.

The Best Pork 'n' Beans

A great make-ahead meal and a favorite side dish for family cookouts and barbecues at all times of year. Serve with lots of freshly baked Cornbread (page 383). The beans taste even better when gently reheated in the oven the following day.

Variation

Vegetarian Baked Beans: Omit pork hock. Add 1 tbsp (15 mL) ground coffee to molasses mixture for added depth of flavor.

Large casserole with lid

2 cups	dried navy beans	500 mL
1	bay leaf	1
	Salt and freshly ground black pepper	
2 tbsp	vegetable oil	25 mL
1	onion, coarsely chopped	1
2	cloves garlic, minced	2
1 cup	ketchup	250 mL
¼ cup	light (fancy) molasses	50 mL
¼ cup	packed brown sugar	50 mL
2 tbsp	Worcestershire sauce	25 mL
12 oz	smoked pork hock	375 g

1. Soak beans in water to cover overnight in the refrigerator.
2. Drain beans. In a saucepan, cover beans with 8 cups (2 L) fresh water and add bay leaf. Bring to a boil over medium-high heat. Reduce heat and simmer, partially covered, until beans are tender, 35 to 45 minutes. Remove from heat and add 1 tsp (5 mL) salt. Let stand for 5 minutes. Drain and set aside.
3. Meanwhile, preheat oven to 325°F (160°C).
4. In a large skillet, heat oil over medium heat. Add onion and sauté until soft, 4 to 5 minutes. Add garlic and sauté for 1 to 2 minutes. Set aside.
5. In a bowl, combine ketchup, ½ cup (125 mL) water, molasses, brown sugar, Worcestershire sauce, 1 tsp (5 mL) salt and ¼ tsp (1 mL) pepper. Set aside
6. In casserole, combine beans, onion mixture, molasses mixture and pork hock. Stir to mix everything together well. Cover casserole and bake in preheated oven until beans are very tender, 1¾ to 2 hours. Remove pork hock and, when cool enough to handle, pull off pieces of lean meat, discarding fat, trim and bone, and return meat to the pot. Taste and adjust seasoning.

Channa Masala

Nicely spiced and not too hot, this chickpea curry may be part of a meal or enjoyed as a complete main course when served with steamed Basmati rice.

Tips

Tamarind is the dark brown pod of the tamarind tree and contains a sour fleshy pulp that is an important ingredient in Indian cooking. Tamarind pulp is available in packages or jars in Asian and Indian markets.

To obtain tamarind juice: Soak 1 tsp (5 mL) tamarind in 2 tbsp (25 mL) boiling water. Break up the paste with a fork and set aside until soft, 5 to 10 minutes. Press through a sieve to extract juice and discard seeds, fibers and skin.

If 14-oz (398 mL) cans of chickpeas are not available in your market, substitute two 19-oz (540 mL) cans.

¼ cup	vegetable oil	50 mL
1 cup	coarsely chopped onion	250 mL
2 tsp	minced garlic	10 mL
2 tbsp	Garam Masala (page 117) or store-bought	25 mL
1 tbsp	tamarind juice or 1 tsp (5 mL) freshly squeezed lemon juice (see Tips, left)	15 mL
2 tsp	granulated sugar	10 mL
1½ tsp	kosher or sea salt	7 mL
½ tsp	freshly ground black pepper	2 mL
1 cup	canned plum tomatoes with juice	250 mL
3	cans (14 oz/398 mL) chickpeas, rinsed and drained (see Tips, left)	3
¼ cup	coarsely chopped cilantro	50 mL

1. In a large skillet, heat oil over medium-high heat. Add onion and garlic and sauté for 3 to 4 minutes. Add garam masala, tamarind, sugar, salt and pepper and cook, stirring diligently, for 1 minute. Add tomatoes and 1 cup (250 mL) water, scraping up any browned bits on the bottom. Add chickpeas.

2. Bring to a boil. Reduce heat and simmer until flavors are blended and sauce is slightly thickened, 15 to 20 minutes. Taste and adjust seasoning. Serve hot, garnished with cilantro.

Masur Dal

In Indian cuisine all kinds of legumes, fresh and dried, are used with great ingenuity to create very tasty dishes. Serve this simple dish of red lentils, browned onions and spices with a vegetable curry and basmati rice for a completely nourishing vegetarian meal.

1 cup	red lentils (masur dal)	250 mL
1	piece (1½ inches/4 cm) gingerroot, sliced	1
1 tsp	ground turmeric	5 mL
1 tsp	kosher or sea salt	5 mL
¼ tsp	cayenne pepper	1 mL
3 to 4 tbsp	ghee, clarified butter or vegetable oil (see Tips, left)	45 to 60 mL
1	onion, cut lengthwise in half and sliced lengthwise in fine slivers	1
2	cloves garlic, finely chopped	2
1 tsp	cumin seeds	5 mL
2 tbsp	chopped cilantro	25 mL

Tips

To make ghee: In a small heavy saucepan, heat chunks of unsalted butter over low heat until melted. Leave undisturbed over very low heat until a crust has formed on top and milk solids on bottom are golden brown, about 35 minutes. Carefully skim off crust and spoon clear nutty-flavored butter from pan through a sieve lined with cheesecloth or a coffee filter. Store in a covered jar in refrigerator; it keeps indefinitely. Prepared ghee is available in jars at Indian markets.

To make clarified butter: In a small heavy saucepan, heat chunks of butter over low heat until melted. Skim foam from top and carefully strain out milk solids. It keeps indefinitely in the refrigerator and is the best thing in the world to sauté potatoes. For variety, add bay leaf, sprigs of rosemary or thyme, saffron or cumin seeds to the melting butter. Strain before storing.

1. Pick over lentils, discarding any discolored pieces or unwanted bits. Rinse in a bowl of cold water, changing the water a couple of times. In a large pot, combine 2 cups (500 mL) water, lentils, ginger, turmeric, salt and cayenne. Bring to a boil over medium heat. Reduce heat to low and simmer, partially covered, until lentils are tender, about 30 minutes. Discard ginger and set lentils aside.

2. In a skillet, heat 3 tbsp (45 mL) of the ghee over medium-high heat. Add onion, garlic and cumin seeds. Reduce heat to medium-low and sauté until onions are soft and nicely browned, 6 to 8 minutes.

3. Add lentils to the skillet with the browned onions. Stir over low heat to blend flavors, 1 to 2 minutes. Taste and adjust seasoning. Serve hot and garnish with a swirl of ghee or clarified butter and chopped cilantro.

Potatoes

The humble potato — often so called, though the most popular vegetable in the world has little to be humble about — contains multitudes and many zeroes. It took its time emigrating from the Andean highlands (Sir Walter Raleigh is said to have introduced it to Europe by planting it on his Irish estate in the late 1580s), but as soon as the rest of the world got over the fact that it is a member of the deadly nightshade family (as also the eggplant and the tomato) it wasted no time.

Today it supplies a worldwide production of some 350 million tons from at least 5,000 varieties, 3,000 of them in the Andes, where it has been cultivated for about 6,000 years; and its historical failure (from late blight, 1845-52, but by no means eradicated today) wracked Europe and ravaged Ireland, where the resultant famine killed one million people and caused another million to emigrate (for a total of one in four of the total population). The potato would rather forget this, naturally, and concentrate on what it does best, being the kitchen helpmate par excellence.

It can do the obvious things, like be boiled, baked, fried, roasted or mashed. It can also do the less obvious ones, like act as a binder, because of its starch content, in the making of breads, cakes, gratins, and as a thickener for soups, gravies and other sauces. It is also used in the making of many vodkas — particularly in Poland, where they take the tuber seriously and harvest 7 pounds (3.5 kg) of podlasie potatoes to make one bottle of premium Chopin.

In the Kitchen

In North America the potato may be divided into four basic groups: **Round white**, **round red**, **long white**, and **russet** (aka **baking** and **Idaho**, for its rough skin). The round white and round red are similar and contain less starch and more moisture than the Idaho and long white; this makes them excellent for boiling, mashing, frying, not so good for baking, where the Idaho shines. The long white, a bit starchier, may be baked as well as boiled and fried. The small thin long whites are called **fingerlings**, and have the sweet flavor of generic new potatoes.

Two Canadian varieties are widely prized: potatoes from **Prince Edward Island**, where the island's rich red soil has nurtured them for more than 200 years, and the **Yukon Gold** that has buttery yellow flesh and a nutty flavor, and is a standout baked, boiled, mashed or sliced for a gratin.

Old wives' tale: Potatoes are fattening. *Fact:* A medium-size potato contains no fat, no cholesterol and 110 calories. (How you cook them and what you add to them once cooked is your business, not the potato's). *OWT:* Not very nutritious. *Fact:* Potatoes are rich in fiber, vitamins C and B_6, contain antioxidants, and are stiff with potassium, which helps maintain blood pressure; they rank highest for potassium content among the top 20 most consumed vegetables and fruits. *OWT:* Just a bundle of simple, fattening carbohydrates. *Fact:* The majority of carbs in a potato are complex — the type that fuels body and brain, and are the body's main energy source.

Storage

Store in a cool, dark spot. Prolonged exposure to light can cause potatoes to turn green. Cut away any green parts. They taste bitter and may contain an alkaloid called solanine, which can be toxic if eaten in quantity.

Chèvre Sage Mashed Potatoes

Mashed potatoes, the ultimate comfort food, are given a lift with creamy goat's cheese and fresh sage. They're particularly good served with roast pork or chicken.

Tip

Take the potato taste test! Compare a potato boiled in the skin, peeled and mashed, and a potato that has been peeled, cut up and cooked. The difference in taste is astonishing. However in this and other recipes for mashed potatoes, peel and cook potatoes if you find it more convenient.

Potato masher

2 lbs	Russet or Yukon Gold potatoes	1 kg
4	cloves garlic	4
	Kosher or sea salt	
½ cup	milk	125 mL
½ cup	chèvre (fresh goat's cheese)	125 mL
¼ cup	butter	50 mL
1 to 2 tbsp	chopped fresh sage	15 to 25 mL
	Freshly ground black pepper	

1. Place potatoes in a large pot with lightly salted cold water to cover. Add garlic cloves and 1 tsp (5 mL) salt. Bring to a boil over high heat. Reduce heat and boil gently until potatoes are tender, about 30 minutes. Drain potatoes and peel away skin. (Hold potatoes in a dry tea towel and peel away the skin with a paring knife. The skin will slip off easily.) Return peeled potatoes and garlic to the pot.

2. Add milk, chèvre and butter and mash until smooth and light. Stir in sage and heat through over medium heat. Season with salt and pepper to taste.

Sweet Potato Ginger Mash

At your local farmer's markets you are likely to discover many varieties of sweet potato — each with their own distinctive flavor and texture. These are the moist, sweet-fleshed kind, and not yam, which is a drier tropical vegetable. Sweet potatoes are wonderful simply baked in their skins or roasted, and they make excellent purées. Enjoy these gingery sweet potatoes with grilled fish seasoned Asian-style.

Variation

Add variety to the sweet potato purée by using different combinations of root vegetables. Replace one sweet potato with a regular potato. Replace 2 sweet potatoes with 2 parsnips and 1 potato.

● **Potato masher**

2 lbs	sweet potatoes, peeled and cubed	1 kg
⅓ cup	butter	75 mL
1 tbsp	grated gingerroot	15 mL
1 cup	milk	250 mL
	Kosher or sea salt	
2	green onions, thinly sliced or 1 tbsp (15 mL) chopped cilantro	2

1. Place potatoes in a large pot with lightly salted cold water to cover. Bring to a boil over medium-high heat. Reduce heat and boil gently until potatoes are tender, 10 to 15 minutes. Drain. Return to saucepan and keep warm.

2. In a small skillet, melt butter over medium heat. Add ginger and sauté until soft but not browned, for 1 minute.

3. Mash sweet potatoes with butter-ginger mixture, milk and salt to taste. Heat through over medium heat. Stir in green onions.

Fresh Herb Mashed Potatoes

Add fresh herbs to mashed potatoes to complement the flavors on the plate. Soft herb leaves such as chervil, chives or tarragon blend beautifully with potatoes, as do lightly wilted leaves of spinach, arugula, green onions or watercress.

Variation

Potato Celeriac Mash: Replace 1 lb (500 g) potatoes with 1 celeriac, peeled and cut into cubes. Cover and boil celeriac in lightly salted water until tender, about 10 minutes. Drain and combine with potatoes in Step 2. Replace tarragon with thyme.

Potato masher

2 lbs	Russet or Yukon Gold potatoes	1 kg
4	cloves garlic	4
⅔ cup	buttermilk or milk	150 mL
⅓ cup	whipping (35%) cream	75 mL
2 tbsp	butter	25 mL
2 tbsp	chopped flat-leaf parsley	25 mL
1 tbsp	chopped chives	15 mL
2 tsp	chopped tarragon	10 mL
	Kosher or sea salt	

1. Place potatoes in a large pot with lightly salted cold water to cover. Add garlic cloves. Bring to a boil over high heat. Reduce heat and boil gently until potatoes are tender, about 30 minutes. Drain potatoes and peel away skin. (Hold them in a dry tea towel and peel away the skin with a paring knife. It will slip off easily.) Return peeled potatoes and garlic to the pot and keep warm.

2. Add buttermilk, cream and butter and mash until smooth. Heat through over medium heat. Stir in parsley, chives and tarragon. Season with salt to taste.

Potato Latkes

Always popular, these crispy brown potato cakes that are traditionally served at Hanukkah can be served as a side dish to roasted meats. We make many variations, sometimes including grated carrot, sweet potato, minced green onions or herbs. They also appear in bite-size portions at cocktail parties with a topping of sour cream and caramelized onions or duck confit.

1½ cups	grated potato	375 mL
1 cup	grated parsnip (about 1 medium)	250 mL
½ cup	grated onion	125 mL
1	egg, beaten	1
3 tbsp	all-purpose flour	45 mL
1½ tsp	kosher or sea salt	7 mL
¼ tsp	freshly ground black pepper	1 mL
2 to 3 tbsp	vegetable oil or clarified butter	25 to 45 mL

1. In a large sieve, combine grated potato, parsnip and onion. Drain off excess moisture and squeeze dry.

2. In a large bowl, combine grated vegetables with egg, flour, salt and pepper.

3. In a large skillet, heat 2 tbsp (25 mL) of the oil over medium heat. Fill ¼ cup (50 mL) measuring cup with vegetable mixture. Tip mixture into your hand and form into a small patty. Slip patty into hot oil and brown one side, about 4 minutes. Turn and cook the other side until golden, about 3 minutes more. Place latkes on a warm platter lined with paper towel. Repeat with remaining vegetable mixture, adding more oil to pan as needed.

Rosemary Roasted Potatoes

We roast many pans of assorted vegetables for our customers every day, seasoning them in various ways to suit the featured roast meat of the day — rosemary, thyme, fennel, paprika, lemon, garlic — there are infinite options. For variety, roast mini yellow or red-skinned potatoes or little oval fingerlings.

Variations

Roasted Root Vegetables: Sweet potatoes, onions, turnips, squash are all delicious when roasted. Roast them alongside the potatoes. Parsnips are good, too, but roast them in a separate pan because they cook in a shorter time.

Roast Potato or Sweet Potato Skins: Slice baked potatoes or baked sweet potatoes into long slices and scoop out most of the flesh. (Reserve the flesh to make mashed potatoes.) Brush skins with olive oil, season with smoked paprika, salt and pepper and roast in 450°F (230°C) oven until browned and crisp, about 15 minutes.

Roasted Summer Vegetables: Add a slivered garlic clove to the olive oil and set aside for 10 minutes. Prepare a colorful mix of roasted summer vegetables following Step 1. Include uniform cut pieces of red, yellow and green peppers, summer squash, Japanese eggplant and red onion.

- **Preheat oven to 425°F (220°C)**
- **Large roasting pan**

1½ lbs	potatoes, cut into uniform chunks, about 1½ inches (4 cm)	750 g
2 tbsp	olive oil	25 mL
2	sprigs fresh rosemary, broken in half	2
1 tsp	kosher or sea salt	5 mL
½ tsp	freshly ground black pepper	2 mL

1. Toss potatoes with oil and rosemary and season with salt and pepper. Spread in a single layer in large roasting pan and roast in preheated oven, stirring a few times so they brown evenly, until tender and nicely browned, about 20 minutes.

Potato Gratin with Leeks and Double-Smoked Bacon

This is a luxurious potato dish, delicious to serve with baked ham.

Variation

Substitute half-and-half (10%) cream, if you like for the whipping cream.

- Preheat oven to 350°F (180°C)
- 10-cup (2.5 L) shallow baking dish, lightly oiled

1 cup	diced double-smoked bacon	250 mL
2 tbsp	butter, divided	25 mL
3	leeks, white and tender green parts only, sliced (see Tip, page 44)	3
3	cloves garlic, chopped	3
2 tbsp	chopped thyme	25 mL
	Salt and freshly ground black pepper	
3½ lbs	potatoes, sliced ⅛ inch (3 mm) thick	1.75 kg
3 cups	whipping (35%) cream	750 mL

1. In a large skillet over medium heat, fry bacon until crisp and lightly browned. Remove with a slotted spoon and set aside on a plate lined with paper towels. Reserve 1 tbsp (15 mL) bacon fat in pan.

2. Add 1 tbsp (15 mL) butter to pan. Add leeks and sauté until softened but not browned, 5 to 7 minutes. Add garlic and thyme and sauté for 1 to 2 minutes. Season lightly with salt and pepper.

3. In prepared baking dish, arrange about one-quarter of the sliced potatoes in an even layer. Sprinkle with salt and pepper and top with one-third of the leeks and one-third of the bacon. Repeat the layers two more times. Finish with a layer of potatoes. Pour cream into the dish, season lightly and dot with remaining butter. Cover dish with foil and bake in preheated oven, 1¼ to 1½ hours. Remove foil and continue to bake until potatoes are tender, cream is absorbed and top is lightly browned, 5 to 10 minutes. Serve hot.

Fragrant Basmati Rice

**MAKES 3 CUPS
(750 ML)**

*In India, a new bride
must demonstrate to her
husband's family her
ability to cook aromatic
long-grained basmati
rice to perfection. We
learned the necessary
steps from a long-time
friend and talented
cooking teacher Arvinda
Chauhan. Arvinda adds
a pinch of garam masala
to her basmati rice before
serving. It's a finishing
touch that you might like,
too. Arvinda has also
perfected a line of fragrant
masalas that we often
use in our kitchen.
To learn more, visit
www.arvindas.com.*

Tip

To check whether rice
is cooked, pinch a grain
between your thumb and
finger. If rice is not fully cooked
after 15 minutes, sprinkle
with a little extra water,
cover and cook for about
5 minutes more.

Variation

Add ½ cup (125 mL) frozen
peas with rice in Step 2.

1 cup	basmati rice	250 mL
1 tbsp	ghee, clarified butter or oil (see Tips, page 291)	15 mL
½ tsp	whole cumin seeds	2 mL
1 tsp	kosher or sea salt	5 mL
1½ to 1¾ cups	cold water (see Tip, left)	375 to 425 mL
1 tbsp	chopped cilantro	15 mL

1. Pick through rice and rinse in a bowl of lukewarm water. Change the water several times and swish the rice grains gently with your fingers. Soak for 10 minutes. (Soaking encourages the rice to lengthen into long fine grains, releases excess starch and slightly reduces the cooking time.) Gently wash rice again until the water is clear. Drain rice well.

2. In a saucepan over medium heat, melt ghee. Add cumin seeds and sauté until fragrant, about 1 minute. Add drained rice and salt. Stir to coat rice grains with melted ghee. Add 1½ cups (375 mL) cold water and bring to a boil. Cover pan with a tight-fitting lid, reduce heat to low and cook until water is absorbed, about 15 minutes. Remove from heat and let stand, undisturbed, for 5 minutes. Remove lid and fluff grains with a fork. Serve garnished with cilantro.

Basmati Rice Pilaf with Fresh Herbs

This is a side dish with infinite possibilities. Stir in fresh herbs, such as chopped flat-leaf parsley, tarragon, basil or cilantro, or add spices and flavorings to complement your main dish.

Variations

Saffron Rice Pilaf: Proceed with recipe and add ½ tsp (2 mL) saffron threads to the cooking water in Step 2.

Brown Rice Pilaf: Use short-grain brown rice instead of basmati. Rinse rice, but do not soak. Proceed with Step 2 and add an extra ½ cup (125 mL) water and increase gentle cooking time to 40 to 45 minutes.

1 cup	basmati rice	250 mL
1 tbsp	butter	15 mL
1	onion, finely chopped	1
1 tsp	kosher or sea salt	5 mL
1½ to 1¾ cups	cold water (see Tip, page 299)	375 to 425 mL
2 tbsp	chopped flat-leaf parsley	25 mL
1 tbsp	chopped cilantro, optional	15 mL
1	green onion, finely chopped	1

1. Pick through rice and rinse in a bowl of lukewarm water. Change the water several times and swish the rice grains gently with your fingers. Soak for 10 minutes. (Soaking encourages the rice to lengthen into long fine grains, releases excess starch and slightly reduces the cooking time.) Gently wash rice again until the water is clear. Drain rice well.

2. In a saucepan, melt butter over medium heat. Add onion and sauté until softened but not browned, 4 to 5 minutes. Add drained rice and salt and stir to coat with buttery onions. Add 1½ cups (375 mL) cold water and bring to a boil. Cover pan with a tight-fitting lid, reduce heat to low and cook until water is absorbed, about 15 minutes. Remove from heat and let stand, undisturbed, for 5 minutes. Stir in parsley, cilantro, if using, and green onions and fluff grains with a fork. Taste and adjust seasoning.

Wild Rice and Cranberry Pilaf

Earthy, crunchy grains of wild rice combine with mushrooms and dried cranberries to provide a festive side dish to serve with roast turkey or Cornish hen. The pilaf also makes a tasty stuffing for turkey or pork.

1 cup	wild rice	250 mL
2 tbsp	butter	25 mL
1	onion, chopped	1
8 oz	cremini mushrooms, sliced	250 g
1 cup	long-grain white rice	250 mL
¼ cup	dry sherry	50 mL
2 cups	water, Vegetable or Chicken Stock (pages 56 and 55) or ready-to-use broth	500 mL
¼ cup	dried cranberries	50 mL
	Salt and freshly ground black pepper	
¼ cup	pepitas (toasted green pumpkin seeds)	50 mL
2 tbsp	coarsely chopped flat-leaf parsley	25 mL

1. In a bowl, cover wild rice with cold water. Scoop off any bits of chaff and dust that float to the surface and drain. Add wild rice to a large saucepan of lightly salted water. Bring to a boil and cook until grains are almost tender and the husks are beginning to crack, 25 to 30 minutes. Drain and set aside.

2. In a large saucepan or ovenproof pot, heat butter over medium heat. Add onion and mushrooms and sauté until soft and just beginning to brown, 5 to 6 minutes. Stir in white rice, wild rice and sherry and toss to coat grains in buttery juices. Add water, cranberries, 1 tsp (5 mL) salt and ¼ tsp (1 mL) pepper. Bring to a boil. Reduce heat to low and cover pan with tight-fitting lid. Cook gently until rice is tender and liquid is absorbed, 20 to 25 minutes (or transfer to a 375°F/190°C oven and bake). Taste and adjust seasoning. Serve garnished with pepitas and parsley.

Risotto

*A creamy risotto is
included in our weekly
menu throughout the year.
The flavor changes with
the season — asparagus
in the spring, tomato and
basil in the summer and
wild mushroom in the fall
are among the favorites.*

Tip

If you like a creamy risotto,
add a little more stock. If your
risotto is too creamy for your
taste, add a spoonful more
cheese, cover and let it stand
off the heat for a few minutes.

8 cups	chicken stock	2 L
¼ cup	olive oil	50 mL
1	onion, finely chopped	1
½ cup	dry white wine	125 mL
2 cups	Arborio rice	500 mL
	Salt and freshly ground black pepper	
½ cup	grated Parmesan cheese, preferably Parmigiano-Reggiano	125 mL
2 tbsp	butter	25 mL

1. In a small saucepan, heat chicken stock over medium heat until steaming and keep hot.

2. In a large saucepan, heat oil over medium heat. Add onion and sauté until softened but not browned, 4 to 5 minutes. Add wine, increase heat to medium-high and reduce until syrupy, 2 to 3 minutes. Add rice and cook, stirring to coat rice grains with flavorful juices, for 1 minute. Add ½ tsp (2 mL) salt and ¼ tsp (1 mL) pepper.

3. Reduce heat to medium-low. Gradually add 1 to 2 cups (250 to 500 mL) warm stock and cook, stirring, until liquid is absorbed, 12 to 15 minutes. Add stock, about 1 cup (250 mL) at a time and continue to cook and stir until liquid is absorbed, 10 to 12 minutes. Continue to add stock in small ½ cup (125 mL) amounts. Taste rice after each addition and add stock and cook until rice is perfectly al dente.

4. Stir in cheese and butter. Taste and adjust seasoning.

Risotto Variations

We usually sauté the flavoring vegetables separately and add to the rice when it is perfectly cooked al dente before stirring in cheese and final seasoning. It is easier then to control both the texture of the rice and the fresh flavor and texture of the vegetables.

Vegetarian Risotto: Replace chicken stock with vegetable stock.

Saffron Risotto: Add $\frac{1}{2}$ tsp (2 mL) saffron to the stock for delicious golden color and fragrance — perfect to accompany fish and seafood.

Gremolata: Season risotto with gremolata at the end. Mix together 1 tbsp (15 mL) finely chopped parsley, 1 clove minced garlic and grated zest of $\frac{1}{2}$ lemon.

Mushroom Risotto: Add 8 oz (250 g) sliced wild mushrooms sautéed in butter.

Squash Risotto: Add 1 cup (250 mL) roasted diced butternut squash and 1 tsp (5 mL) chopped thyme.

Asparagus Risotto: Add 8 oz (250 g) trimmed blanched asparagus, tips and stalks cut into 1-inch (2.5 cm) pieces, 2 tbsp (25 mL) chopped parsley and 2 tsp (10 mL) lemon zest.

Leek Risotto: Add 1 cup (250 mL) sautéed leeks and 1 tsp (5 mL) chopped thyme.

Tomato and Basil Risotto: Add 1 cup (250 mL) seeded and diced ripe tomato and 2 tbsp (25 mL) slivered basil.

Creamy Risotto: Replace Parmesan with another cheese, such as creamy goat's cheese or Gorgonzola.

Rice

In China rice has been found in sealed pots that are almost 8,000 years old. No word on whether it was still edible, but one has to have doubts. No doubt, though, that it is now grown on every continent except Antarctica — anywhere with unrationed supplies of water, heat and mosquitoes — and has fed and nourished more people in more countries over more eons than any other crop. Corn? More of it is grown but less of it is eaten, much being diverted to other jobs. Aside from its use in sake and a few niche milks and beers, rice is what it is: a storehouse of protein, starch, minerals, B vitamins and fiber, excellent for bowel health, stabilizing blood-sugar levels, and for giving a boost of fast energy. Also easily digested.

Anyone who has watched people at work in rice paddies, and surely even the people working them, may be struck by the evident rightness of the enterprise. No giant threshers or combines thundering their might to the suffering sky, just a gentle quiet peaceability.

Yes, but. For all rice's proven virtues over millennia, its halo is a bit crooked. For one thing, rice is a water hog, needing much more of it than any other grain. In some areas where surface water is rapidly drying up, farmers bore ever deeper for diminishing groundwater, thus ensuring a riceless future down the road.

For another, rice plants and the paddies they grow in are unrighteous producers of methane gas; bigger even than cows. For years it was thought that carbon dioxide (produced in quantity by those threshers and carbines) was the prime suspect in global warming from the Greenhouse Effect. Not so. It is now recognized that molecule for molecule, methane traps 20 times more energy than CO_2. Between them, the paddies where the methane bacteria grow, and the plants that act as gas vents, are suspected of pumping 115 million tons of methane into the atmosphere each year.

All energy except wind power comes with a price, and with rice it's clearly something we're willing to pay. Currently it feeds half the world's population, and since 1960 production has more than tripled and per capita consumption has gone up by about 50 percent.

In the Kitchen

Rice is commercially classified by size — long-, medium-, or short-grain. **Long:** Four to five times its width, produces light dry grains that separate easily. **Medium:** Moister, fluffy after cooking, but clumps quickly as it cools. Starchier than Long, but not as starchy as **Short**, which is moist and sticky when cooked, a big enabler of chopsticks and thus the preferred rice in the Orient.

Generically: Brown whole-grain rice — most nutritious, milled to remove only outer husk, leaving bran layer intact; chewy, distinct nutty flavor. **White rice** — milled to remove husks, then polished. Milder. **Converted (parboiled) rice** — soaked, steamed under pressure, and dried before milling. This forces nutrients into the endosperm to preserve them when milled and polished. **Enriched rice** — nutrients are added, but lacks brown rice's fiber. **Instant rice** — precooked, dehydrated, cooked again. Convenient, foolproof, flavorless.

Arborio: Italian short-grain with high starch content. Cooked, it retains a slightly al dente firmness, and the starch creates the creaminess that makes the best risottos so distinctive. **Carnaroli** and **Vialone Nano** are other Italian short-grains prized for the dish.

Basmati: Long-grain, the most fragrant of rice, from the Punjab province in the

Himalayan foothills: Aged to reduce moisture content and increase taste. Excellent for pilafs, and to accompany curries.

Forbidden: Short-grain, dark purple when cooked, nutty flavor. Forbidden either because it was reserved, as so much else, for emperors in ancient China; or because it was banned by the Greeks, who suspected their enemies of using it to strengthen their slaying arms; or because marketers have come up with it as a sales ploy.

Jasmine: Long-grain from Thailand, smooth texture, nutty taste, fragrant.

Patna: Long-grain, firm, grown in the Ganges plains; similar to basmati, less aromatic. First rice imported to South Carolina (aka **Carolina rice**).

Sticky (Glutenous, Sweet): Short-grain, sticky when cooked, thus chopstick friendly and most prized wherever they are used.

Texmati: Grown mainly in Texas, a cross between American long-grain and basmati; more aromatic than the first, less than the second.

Wehani: Long-grain, unmilled, red-brown, nutty, chewy, delicious in pilafs and salads.

Wild: Any of four species of grass (*zizania*) that grow in shallow waters and streams, and not a true rice. It's chewy, earthy, nutty. Native to the Canadian prairies and Minnesota. Can be cooked together with true rice in a ratio of about 1 to 4.

Rice Cooking Basics

Rinse rice only if it looks dusty. Do not rinse enriched, converted or instant rice. Also do not rinse, or boil and drain Italian and Spanish short-grain rice or the creaminess is lost. Basmati rice is soaked to soften and lengthen the grains. Wehani rice is soaked to soften and swell the grains.

If rice is not tender when all cooking liquid is absorbed, sprinkle 1 to 2 tbsp (15 to 25 mL) water over rice, cover and return to heat for 5 minutes. If there is still some moisture remaining and rice is tender, remove from heat and set aside covered for a few minutes and the liquid will be absorbed. If way too much water remains, strain.

Boiled rice: Add rice to a large saucepan of boiling lightly salted water (a ratio of 1:4 rice to water). Cook, until tender, 12 to 15 minutes for white and 25 to 30 minutes for brown. Drain and spread on trays to cool.

Steamed white or brown rice: Add rice to boiling lightly salted water. (Measure $1\frac{3}{4}$ cups/425 mL water for each cup/ 250 mL white rice; $2\frac{1}{4}$ cups/550 mL for brown.) Reduce heat to low, cover and cook until water is absorbed, 15 to 20 minutes for white; 40 to 50 minutes for brown. Add 1 tbsp (15 mL) butter to cooking liquid if you like. Fluff grains with a fork before serving. Yields about 3 cups (750 mL) cooked white rice; $2\frac{1}{2}$ cups (625 mL) brown.

Basmati rice: Rinse rice in a bowl with several changes of water until water is clear. Soak for 30 minutes. Drain. In a saucepan, combine 1 cup (250 mL) rice with $1\frac{3}{4}$ cups (425 mL) water and $\frac{1}{2}$ tsp (2 mL) salt. Bring to a boil, reduce heat to low, cover and cook for 20 minutes. Remove from heat and set aside for 10 minutes. Fluff with a fork. Yields about 3 cups (750 mL).

Wild rice: Rinse grains in a bowl with several changes of water. In a saucepan, bring 4 cups (1 L) water to a boil with $\frac{1}{2}$ tsp (2 mL) salt. Add 1 cup (250 mL) rice. Reduce heat to low, cover and cook until tender but with a little crunch, 45 to 50 minutes. Cover and let stand for 5 minutes. Fluff with a fork and add salt, pepper and a little butter to taste. Yields about 3 cups (750 mL).

Couscous with Apricots and Almonds

SERVES 4

One of the joys of couscous is that a delicious side dish can be ready in minutes with a minimum of fuss. This dish, seasoned with fruit and sweet spices, complements grilled lamb, pork or chicken.

Tip

Couscous is a small granular pasta made from semolina, most frequently associated with the cuisine of the Middle East and North Africa. Traditionally couscous is steamed in a couscoussière, a steaming unit that sits on top of the pot in which a tasty stew, or tagine, is slowly braising. It cooks up light and fluffy with delicate separate grains. Packaged couscous, familiar in our markets, is an "instant" variety. Just pour on hot liquid, let it stand for a few minutes, fluff with a fork and add seasonings to taste. Toasting couscous in oil before adding liquids adds flavor and helps to keep couscous grains separate.

1 tbsp	olive oil	15 mL
1/2	red onion, finely chopped	1/2
1 tsp	finely chopped gingerroot	5 mL
1	piece (3 inches/7.5 cm) cinnamon stick	1
1 cup	couscous	250 mL
1/4 cup	dried apricots, quartered	50 mL
2 tbsp	currants	25 mL
1 tbsp	raisins	15 mL
1 cup	orange juice	250 mL
1/2 tsp	kosher or sea salt	2 mL
1 tbsp	freshly squeezed lemon juice	15 mL
2 tbsp	toasted slivered almonds	25 mL

1. In a large pot, heat oil over medium heat. Add red onion and sauté until soft, 4 to 5 minutes. Add ginger and cinnamon stick and sauté for 1 to 2 minutes. Stir in couscous, apricots, currants and raisins and cook, stirring, 1 to 2 minutes.

2. Meanwhile, in a small pot over medium-high heat, bring orange juice, 1/2 cup (125 mL) water and salt to a boil. Pour hot liquid over couscous mixture. Cover and set aside until liquid is absorbed, 6 to 8 minutes. Fluff with a fork and sprinkle with lemon juice and a little more hot water if needed. Let stand for 5 minutes. Taste and adjust seasoning. Garnish with toasted almonds.

Currants and Raisins

Currants and raisins are dried grapes with size and flavor distinctions depending on variety and processing. Currants, dried Zante grapes, small and purplish-black with sweet tart flavor are among the most popular dried fruits in the world for use in both sweet and savory dishes. Slightly larger, dark brown Thompson raisins, naturally sun-dried, develop a rich sweetness. Seedless golden raisins are artificially dried and preserved with sulfur dioxide to prevent darkening. Sultana raisins, a small greenish-gold grape, have a distinct flavor. Muscat raisins are large, fleshy dried grapes with a sweet sugary crunch — delicious for snacking on with cheeses.

Couscous with Olives and Lemon

Enjoy this couscous either warm or at room temperature. Crumble a little firm goat's cheese or feta on top to turn the dish into a main course to please vegetarians in the group.

1 tbsp	olive oil	15 mL
½	onion, finely chopped	½
1 cup	couscous	250 mL
¼ tsp	ground turmeric	1 mL
	Kosher or sea salt	
1½ cups	Vegetable Stock (page 56) or ready-to-use broth	375 mL
2 tbsp	freshly squeezed lemon juice	25 mL
¼ cup	pitted dry-cured ripe olives, halved	50 mL
1 tbsp	basil chiffonade	15 mL
1 tbsp	mint chiffonade	15 mL

1. In a large pot, heat oil over medium heat. Add onion and sauté until soft, 4 to 5 minutes. Add couscous, turmeric, and ½ tsp (2 mL) salt and cook, stirring, 1 to 2 minutes.

2. Meanwhile, in a small pot, bring stock to a boil over medium-high heat. Pour hot liquid over couscous mixture. Cover and set aside until liquid is absorbed, 6 to 8 minutes. Fluff with a fork and sprinkle with lemon juice. Add olives, basil and mint. Let stand for 5 minutes. Taste and adjust seasoning, adding a splash more olive oil and lemon juice if needed.

Polenta Cakes

Genuine Italian polenta is a creamy corn pudding that requires gentle cooking and about 30 minutes of diligent stirring to develop full corn flavor. Excellent Italian brands of quick-cooking cornmeal are available, reducing cooking time to about 10 minutes — just follow package directions.

Tip

Use a lightly oiled spatula to make a smooth, even layer of polenta.

Variations

Creamy Polenta: To serve creamy polenta as a side dish for braised dishes, such as Osso Buco (page 162), add ½ to 1 cup (125 to 250 mL) more liquid and serve hot from the pot at the end of Step 2.

Grilled Polenta Cakes: Brush polenta cakes on both sides with a little olive oil and grill over medium-high heat until hot and nicely marked.

Replace instant polenta with cornmeal, stirring vigorously. Increase cooking time to 30 minutes.

13- by 9-inch (3 L) baking dish

1¼ cups	milk	300 mL
1 tbsp	kosher or sea salt	15 mL
¼ tsp	freshly ground black pepper	1 mL
1 cup	instant polenta	250 mL
2 tbsp	finely chopped shallots	25 mL
1 tbsp	grated lemon zest	15 mL
2 tsp	coarsely chopped thyme	10 mL
¼ cup	grated Parmesan cheese, preferably Parmigiano-Reggiano	50 mL
1 tbsp	butter	15 mL
1 to 2 tbsp	olive oil, as needed	15 to 25 mL
	Mushroom Ragoût (page 286)	

1. Line baking dish with plastic wrap. Press the plastic wrap on the bottom of the dish, smoothing out any wrinkles, to ensure a smooth surface for the polenta.

2. In a large pot over medium heat, combine milk, 1 cup (250 mL) water, salt and pepper and bring to a boil. Slowly sprinkle polenta on the surface of the liquid, stirring vigorously with a whisk to prevent lumps from forming. Cook, stirring diligently to prevent sticking and burning, 6 to 8 minutes. Stir in shallots, lemon zest, thyme, Parmesan and butter.

3. Pour hot polenta into baking dish and spread in an even layer. Cover loosely and refrigerate until completely cool, about 1 hour, or wrap securely when cool and make up to 1 day ahead.

4. Turn out cooled polenta onto a cutting board. Discard plastic wrap. Cut polenta into 9 to 12 even pieces.

5. Shortly before serving, heat oil in a large, preferably nonstick, skillet over medium-high heat. Place 2 to 3 polenta cakes in skillet, smooth side down. Sauté until bottom of polenta cakes develop a lovely golden crust, 2 minutes. Turn and brown the other side. Repeat with the remaining cakes, adding extra oil as needed. Serve hot topped with Mushroom Ragoût.

Party Fare

Guacamole

This avocado mix is a popular party snack and an essential condiment with many south-of-the-border dishes. Our version has texture, but if you like smooth guacamole use quick pulses of the food processor to combine ingredients.

Tips

Avocados loose their vibrant fresh color very quickly. Add a spoonful or two of sour cream to the mix if you need to keep guacamole for more than a day. Press plastic wrap directly on the top of the dip and refrigerate.

Remove the pit from avocados with a dessert spoon and use the spoon to release the flesh quickly and easily from the skin.

Do not attempt to make guacamole with under-ripe avocados.

Variation

Papaya Guacamole: Add a fruit and spice twist to traditional guacamole to make an unusual and delicious condiment. It's particularly tasty with Deep-Fried Corn Chips (see right). Add 1 ripe papaya with the avocado and ½ finely minced jalapeño pepper, ½ tsp (2 mL) ground cumin and a pinch of freshly ground black pepper and your favorite hot sauce. Rinse some papaya seeds and use as garnish; they add a pleasing crunch.

- **Potato masher**

1	tomato, finely diced	1
1	shallot, finely diced	1
1	clove garlic, minced	1
1 tbsp	chopped cilantro	15 mL
1 tbsp	freshly squeezed lime juice	15 mL
	Kosher or sea salt	
2	avocados (see Tips, left)	2

1. In a small bowl, combine tomato, shallot, garlic, cilantro, lime juice and salt. Set aside.

2. In a large bowl, using a potato masher or a fork, mash avocados until almost smooth. Stir in two-thirds of the tomato mixture. Taste and adjust seasoning.

3. Transfer guacamole to a serving bowl and garnish with the rest of the tomato mixture. Set aside for 1 hour for flavors to develop. Best enjoyed the day it is made.

Deep-Fried Corn Chips

When we first made our own deep-fried corn chips and served them with Papaya Guacamole at a party, we caused quite a stir: guests kept coming back for more! Slice corn tortillas to make 6 wedges. Deep-fry in hot corn oil at about 375°F (190°C) until crisp and the edges are beginning to brown, 1 to 2 minutes. Sprinkle with sea salt. Let cool on racks. The corn chips are at their best when freshly made. Sprinkle with other seasonings, such as cayenne pepper, chipotle powder, garlic powder or smoky paprika along with the salt, if you wish.

Roasted Red Pepper and Feta Dip

MAKES 1 CUP (250 ML)

This dip, without doubt, is a bestseller! There are countless commercial versions now available in the supermarkets but the flavor will be super-delicious when you make it fresh yourself with freshly roasted peppers and quality imported feta.

Food processor or blender

3 tbsp	olive oil	45 mL
2 to 3	cloves garlic, chopped	2 to 3
¼ tsp	hot pepper flakes	1 mL
1	roasted red bell pepper, peeled	1
½ cup	crumbled feta cheese	125 mL
	Kosher or sea salt	

1. In a small saucepan, heat oil over low heat. Add garlic to taste and hot pepper flakes and cook gently, stirring, until garlic is softened but not browned, 1 to 2 minutes. Let cool.

2. In a food processor, combine bell pepper and garlic-oil mixture and process until smooth. Add feta and process briefly just until combined. Season with salt to taste. Transfer to a serving bowl, cover and refrigerate for 1 hour before serving or for up to 3 days.

Baba Ghanoush

This creamy Middle Eastern eggplant purée is a favorite dip with grilled pita bread triangles. It is part of a popular party snack platter in combination with other Middle Eastern dips such as Tzatziki (page 172) and Hummus (page 313).

Tip

Tahini is a creamy paste made from ground sesame seeds and is available in jars in most markets. It is used in many Middle Eastern sauces and dressings to drizzle over legumes, vegetables and salads.

- Preheat oven to 400°F (200°C) or barbecue grill to medium
- Food processor or blender

1	eggplant (about 1 lb/500 g)	1
¼ cup	tahini (see Tip, left)	50 mL
1	clove garlic, minced	1
2 tbsp	extra virgin olive oil	25 mL
1 tbsp	freshly squeezed lemon juice	15 mL
	Salt and freshly ground black pepper	

1. Prick skin of eggplant a few times with a fork. Place on a baking sheet and roast in preheated oven or on a barbecue, turning occasionally, until soft, 45 to 50 minutes. Place roasted eggplant in a sieve set over a bowl and weigh down to extract excess liquid. Let cool. Peel and discard skin.

2. In a food processor, combine eggplant, tahini, garlic, oil and lemon juice and process until smooth. Season with salt and pepper to taste. Transfer to a serving bowl, cover and refrigerate for 1 hour for flavors to blend before serving or for up to 3 days.

Hummus

MAKES 2 CUPS (500 ML)

This classic Middle Eastern dip makes a great snack and a delicious, and healthy, condiment to tuck into a pita with grilled lamb and tabbouleh. We like to serve it on a shallow plate with a drizzle of fruity Greek olive oil and a light sprinkle of paprika, accompanied with lemon wedges, ripe olives and wedges of grilled pita bread.

Tip

If a 19-oz (540 mL) can of chickpeas isn't available, you'll need about 2 cups (500 mL) chickpeas.

Variations

Hummus is open to many variations. Increase the quantity of oil, lemon juice and water to create a sauce-like consistency to serve with grilled meats and salads. Add different flavors such as chopped dill, roasted garlic, roasted red bell peppers, green or black olives or a roasted jalapeño.

- **Food processor or blender**

1	can (19 oz/540 mL) chickpeas, rinsed and drained, or ½ cup (125 mL) dried chickpeas, soaked and cooked (see Tip, left)	1
¼ cup	tahini	50 mL
2 tsp	minced garlic	10 mL
¼ tsp	cayenne pepper	1 mL
3 tbsp	freshly squeezed lemon juice	45 mL
3 tbsp	olive oil, divided	45 mL
	Sea salt	
2 to 3 tbsp	water	25 to 45 mL

1. In a food processor, combine chickpeas, tahini, garlic, cayenne, lemon juice, olive oil and ½ tsp (2 mL) salt. With motor running, add water, 1 tbsp (15 mL) at a time, until smooth and desired consistency is reached. Taste and adjust seasoning. Transfer to a serving bowl, cover and refrigerate for 1 hour for flavors to blend before serving or for up to 3 days.

Cheese Melt

**MAKES 1½ CUPS
(375 ML)**

*We had to search back
through the bundles of
old, well-worn recipe
cards to find the original
recipe for this hot dip.
It has been a customer
favorite for more than
20 years!*

Variation

Seafood Melt: In a skillet, melt
1 tbsp (15 mL) butter over
medium heat. Add 1 cup
(250 mL) chopped cooked
crab, lobster or shrimp and
1 finely chopped green
onion and cook, stirring, 1 to
2 minutes. Add 2 tbsp (25 mL)
Pernod or dry sherry. Boil to
reduce liquid to a glaze and let
cool. Stir seafood mixture into
Cheese Melt in Step 2. Heat
and serve as directed.

● **Small ovenproof bowl**

2 tbsp	butter	25 mL
1	onion, finely chopped	1
1 cup	shredded old Cheddar cheese	250 mL
1 cup	mayonnaise	250 mL
	Salt and freshly ground white pepper	
	Corn chips or crisp breads	

1. In a saucepan, melt butter over medium-low heat. Add onion and cook, stirring, until very soft and just beginning to brown, 15 to 20 minutes. Let cool. Sieve to remove excess moisture if necessary.

2. In a bowl, combine onion, cheese and mayonnaise. Season with salt and pepper to taste. Transfer to a serving bowl, cover and refrigerate for 1 hour for flavors to blend before serving or for up to 3 days.

3. Preheat oven to 350°F (180°C). Transfer cheese mixture to ovenproof bowl and cover with foil. Just before serving, bake until cheese is bubbling, 5 to 7 minutes. Remove foil and lightly brown top under broiler, 1 to 2 minutes. Serve hot with corn chips or crisp breads for dipping.

Jalapeño Pepper Dip

MAKES 1¼ CUPS (300 ML)

This party dip sets the taste buds tingling. We suggest you add jalapeños with discretion at first — the dip gets hotter as it sits. Our customers tell us they use it in many ways — as a vegetable or chip dip, a sandwich spread or a condiment for grilled lamb kebabs.

½ tsp	Mexican chili powder	2 mL
¼ tsp	paprika	1 mL
¼ tsp	cayenne pepper	1 mL
¼	roasted red bell pepper, finely chopped	¼
½ to 1 tbsp	canned jalapeño peppers, drained and chopped	7 to 15 mL
1	clove garlic, chopped	1
1 cup	sour cream or strained yogurt	250 mL
	Kosher or sea salt	

1. In a small skillet over medium heat, toast chili powder, paprika and cayenne, stirring constantly, until fragrant, 30 seconds. Set aside.

2. In a bowl, or with mortar and pestle, combine bell pepper, and jalapeño peppers, to taste, garlic and toasted spices. Blend to make a smooth paste. Add sour cream or yogurt and blend briefly. Add salt to taste. Transfer to a serving bowl, cover and refrigerate for 1 hour for flavors to blend before serving or for up to 3 days.

Dill and Garlic Dip

**MAKES 1 CUP
(250 ML)**

Here's a dip that's so delicious and useful you'll never buy store-bought versions again! Use with crudités and potato chips as a dip. Serve with cold poached salmon, grilled scallops, shrimp or sliced cucumbers.

1	clove garlic, minced	1
$\frac{1}{2}$ tsp	kosher or sea salt	2 mL
1 cup	sour cream	250 mL
2 tbsp	thinly sliced green onions	25 mL
2 tbsp	chopped dill	25 mL

1. In a small bowl, mash garlic with salt to a fine paste. Add sour cream and stir in green onions and dill. Taste and adjust seasoning. Transfer to a serving bowl, cover and refrigerate for 1 hour for flavors to blend before serving or for up to 3 days.

Variation

Dill and Garlic Cream Cheese:
Add 1 cup (250 mL) deli-style cream cheese to $\frac{1}{2}$ cup (125 mL) Dill and Garlic Dip and combine well.

Crostini at Room Temperature
Create dozens of interesting savory bites using Crostini (page 320) with different toppings. (See also Crostini served Warm, page 321). Here are a few suggestions to try topping the crostini with:
- Bruschetta topping (page 317) garnished with basil chiffonade.
- Hummus (page 313) garnished with strips of roasted red bell pepper.
- Dill and Garlic Dip (above) blended with cream cheese and garnished with a fold of smoked salmon, smoked trout or a poached shrimp halved lengthwise. Season with the dill, caper lemon mix as for Herbed Crêpes with Smoked Salmon (page 327).
- A blend of creamy chèvre and cream cheese topped with Sun-Dried Tomato Pesto (page 321).
- Chicken Liver Mousse (page 330) with thin slices of cornichons.
- Duck Rilettes (page 129) with Shallot Port Marmalade (page 129).
- A mix of red and yellow grape tomatoes, halved lengthwise, and diced bocconcini tossed with Basil Pesto (page 320) and garnished with basil chiffonade.

Bruschetta

Some taste experiences are never forgotten. The most incredible bruschetta I have ever eaten was in an ancient hill town in Italy at Bagnoregio in Lazio province. (For film buffs, that was the location for La Strada.*) The town was accessed by a swaying foot bridge across a deep ravine; a heart-stopping experience as I recall! The soft-textured homemade bread was grilled over an open wood fire, rubbed with a garlic clove, topped with wonderful, ripe chopped tomatoes and drizzled with a superb local olive oil. Heaven in every bite!*

Variation

For variety, top with cheese such as crumbled feta, goat's cheese or fresh mozzarella.

● **Preheat barbecue grill to medium-high or broiler**

1	large ripe tomato, seeded and diced	1
2 tbsp	finely diced red onion	25 mL
6	slices soft Italian-style country bread, 1 inch (2.5 cm) thick	6
1	clove garlic, halved	1
	Kosher or sea salt	
2 tbsp	extra virgin olive oil	25 mL
1 tbsp	basil chiffonade	15 mL
1 tbsp	chopped oregano	15 mL

1. In a small bowl, combine tomato and onion.
2. Grill bread slices on preheated barbecue grill until nicely marked on both sides. Rub with cut sides of garlic.
3. Arrange tomato mixture on bread slices. Sprinkle with salt, drizzle lightly with oil and garnish with basil and oregano. Enjoy at once.

Salsa Roja

Our salsa is a simple mix of tomatoes and chiles. It's a very useful sauce to have on hand to serve with tacos, enchiladas, burritos, grilled fish or even just as a refreshing snack with corn chips. Cut back on the jalapeño to make it child-friendly. There are many excellent prepared salsas on the market, but somehow the one you make yourself with fresh ingredients tastes so much better.

Tips

Whole pickled jalapeño peppers imported from Mexico are available in small cans and are a useful item to have on hand on your pantry shelf. Transfer any unused peppers from the can into a covered container and keep in the refrigerator.

For the fresh tomatoes, you can substitute with 1 can (28 oz/796 mL) plum tomatoes, drained, seeded and chopped.

1 tbsp	vegetable oil	15 mL
1	onion, diced	1
2	cloves garlic, finely chopped	2
1	jalapeño pepper, seeded and chopped, or 2 tbsp (25 mL) chopped and drained canned jalapeño peppers (see Tips, left)	1
1 tsp	ground cumin	5 mL
½ tsp	dried oregano	2 mL
6	ripe Roma (plum) tomatoes, seeded and finely chopped (see Tips, left)	6
1 tbsp	apple cider vinegar	15 mL
	Kosher or sea salt	
1	green onion, finely chopped	1
2 tbsp	chopped cilantro	25 mL

1. In a saucepan, heat oil over medium heat. Add onion and sauté until softened but not browned, 4 to 5 minutes. Add garlic and jalapeño and sauté for 1 to 2 minutes. Stir in cumin and oregano and cook, stirring, 1 to 2 minutes.

2. Add tomatoes, vinegar and ½ tsp (2 mL) salt. Simmer until tomatoes are soft and excess liquid is reduced, about 15 minutes. Stir in green onion and cilantro. Heat through. Taste and adjust seasoning. Let cool. Use immediately or cover and keep in the refrigerator for up to 1 week. Serve chilled or reheat gently, if required.

Spicy Bean Dip

MAKES 2 CUPS (500 ML)

Made with red kidney beans, black beans or pinto beans, this bean purée is a popular addition to south-of-the-border-style snacks.

Tip

Use ½ cup (125 mL) dried beans, soaked and cooked (see page 257) instead of canned beans. Reserve about ½ cup (125 mL) of the bean cooking liquid to add to the puréed beans as required.

Variation

Hot Spicy Bean Dip: Add 1 cup (250 mL) shredded Monterey Jack or mild Cheddar cheese to bean purée. Transfer mixture to a small ovenproof bowl and cover with foil. Before serving, bake in a preheated 350°F (180°C) oven until beans are bubbling, 5 to 10 minutes. Brown top lightly under the broiler. Serve hot with corn chips or crisp breads for dipping.

- **Food processor**

1 tbsp	vegetable oil	15 mL
1	onion, finely chopped	1
1	clove garlic, minced	1
1 tsp	chili powder	5 mL
1	jalapeño pepper, seeded and finely chopped	1
1	can (14 to 19 oz/398 to 540 mL) red kidney beans (see Tip, left)	1
	Salt and freshly ground black pepper	
¼ to ½ cup	water	50 to 125 mL

1. In a large skillet, heat oil over medium heat. Add onion and sauté until softened and nicely browned, 8 to 10 minutes. Add garlic, chili powder and jalapeño and sauté for 1 to 2 minutes. Set aside.

2. In a food processor, purée beans until almost smooth. Add beans to onion mixture and season lightly with salt and pepper. Add ¼ cup (50 mL) water and cook, stirring diligently, for 5 minutes. Add more water, if needed, until beans are heated through and of good spreading consistency — not too runny and not too stiff. Transfer to a serving bowl and serve hot or cover and keep in the refrigerator for up to 1 week. Reheat gently, as required.

Basil Pesto

Make this renowned Genovese sauce in quantity when fresh basil is at its peak. Use a spoonful to add zip to a tomato sauce, summer vegetables or a vegetable soup. Team it with soft goat cheese on a crostini as a snack. Basil pesto is a delight with tomatoes, grilled chicken, on a pizza and tossed with pasta.

Tips

Don't overprocess the mixture or you'll end up with a mush. The paste should have some texture to it.

Pesto may be frozen. Follow recipe but omit cheese. Stir cheese into thawed pesto at serving time.

Variation

Cilantro Pesto: A fine condiment with fish, seafood and grilled lamb. Substitute slivered almonds for pine nuts and 4 cups (1 L) loosely packed trimmed cilantro for basil. Grated cheese may be part Parmesan and part pecorino Romano.

● **Food processor**

2	cloves garlic	2
3 tbsp	pine nuts	45 mL
1 tsp	kosher or sea salt	5 mL
¼ tsp	freshly ground black pepper	1 mL
3 cups	loosely packed basil leaves, trimmed	750 mL
½ cup	extra virgin olive oil (approx.)	125 mL
½ cup	grated Parmigiano-Reggiano cheese	125 mL

1. In a food processor with motor running, drop in garlic through the feed tube and chop. Add pine nuts, salt and pepper and process until finely chopped. Add basil. Drizzle in oil through the feed tube and pulse to combine until just smooth. Add cheese and process just to combine. Taste and adjust seasoning. Transfer pesto to a small container and cover surface with a little olive oil and seal tightly. Keep in the refrigerator for up to 1 week.

Crostini

Homemade crostini form the basis of many tasty snacks and appetizers. Serve them alongside soups, salads, dips and cheeses and create dozens of interesting savory bites using different toppings.

Cut a baguette or a long Calabrese-style bread into ½-inch (1 cm) slices on the diagonal. (The sharper the angle of your diagonal cut the larger your crostini will be: cut on a shallow angle for a crostini of 2 to 3 bites.) Peel and slice a clove of garlic and let it stand in ¼ cup (50 mL) olive oil for 15 minutes. Brush both sides of the bread slices lightly with garlic oil and place in a single layer on baking sheets. Bake in preheated 350°F (180°C) oven, turning once, for 7 to 10 minutes. Or grill the bread slices on the barbecue until nicely marked on both sides, 2 to 3 minutes per side.

Parmesan Crostini: Here's a savory crisp to serve on the side with soups or salads. Prepare the bread slices as above. After turning crostini over, bake for a couple of minutes then top each one with a layer of about 1 tsp (5 mL) grated Parmesan and a sprinkling of freshly ground black pepper. Continue baking until cheese is melted, 2 to 3 minutes. Serve warm. Use other good melting cheeses instead of Parmesan such as Gruyère, Fontina or smoked Cheddar.

Saffron-Roasted Halibut with Cherry Tomatoes and Herbs (page 218)

Chicken, Shrimp and Mussel Paella (page 238)

Torta Rustica (page 252)

Cannelloni with Peppers and Olives (page 268)

Grilled Asparagus with Shallots and Lemon (page 276)

Basil Pesto (page 320), Sun-Dried Tomato Pesto (page 321) and Tapenade (page 324)

Grilled Vegetable Bundles (page 326) and
Herbed Crêpes with Smoked Salmon (page 327)

Sweet Potato Latkes with Caramelized Onions and Stilton (page 348)
and Spicy Coconut Shrimp with Mango Salsa (page 350)

Rocky Road Cookies (page 358) and
Orange Cranberry Oat Cookies (page 361)

Fruit and Nut Bread (page 384)

Tiramisù (page 404)

Fresh Raspberry Tart (page 414)

Sun-Dried Tomato Pesto

MAKES 1 CUP (250 ML)

We use this full-flavored pesto in many combinations to make tasty party snacks — to garnish soft goat's cheese on a crostini or in a crisp endive leaf, combined with crumbled feta on a pizza and to add zip to a pasta salad. Add to deli-style cream cheese for a delicious spread for toasts or bagels.

Tip

The best sun-dried tomatoes are tender and juicy and packed in olive oil. They add intense flavor to pastas, salads and sauces, so it's best to add them to a dish in modest quantities, thinly slivered or finely chopped. Dry-packed sun-dried tomatoes should be softened in warm water then drained before using, or added to a saucy dish at the beginning of the cooking period.

Food processor

1 cup	oil-packed sun-dried tomatoes, drained (see Tip, left)	250 mL
1/4 cup	chopped toasted almonds	50 mL
1	clove garlic	1
2 tbsp	chopped basil	25 mL
2 tbsp	chopped flat-leaf parsley	25 mL
1 tsp	grated lemon zest	5 mL
1/2 tsp	kosher or sea salt	2 mL
1/4 tsp	freshly ground black pepper	1 mL
1/2 cup	extra virgin olive oil (approx.)	125 mL

1. In a food processor, combine sun-dried tomatoes, almonds and garlic and pulse to combine. Add basil, parsley, lemon zest, salt and pepper and process until finely chopped. Drizzle in oil through the feed tube and pulse to combine until just smooth. Taste and adjust seasoning. Transfer pesto to a small container and cover surface with a little olive oil and seal tightly. Keep in the refrigerator for up to 1 week.

Crostini Served Warm

Try these toppings with Crostini (page 320). Place crostini with topping under a preheated broiler for 2 to 5 minutes until crostini and topping is warm and cheese is melted and beginning to brown. (See also Crostini at Room Temperature, page 316.) Here are some toppings to try:

- A mix of creamy chèvre scented with fresh rosemary. Brush top with a little extra virgin olive oil.
- Sautéed mushrooms (page 151) chopped fine and topped with shavings of Gruyère cheese. Garnish each with a small sprig of thyme.
- Caramelized Onions (page 344) chopped finely and topped with crumbled Gorgonzola cheese or shaved Emmental. Garnish each with a small sprig of rosemary or thyme.

Planning a Party

Party Essentials

All The Best has catered hundreds of great parties over the years, so I asked our party-planning experts for advice. We all agree on the essentials: whether you're arranging a dinner for eight or a party for 80 you need to be well organized and make a plan. Since everyone has such busy schedules, it's wise to be realistic as to your time and your available resources.

Decide the number of guests and the time of day. Is to be a sit-down dinner, a buffet, brunch or cocktails at 6 p.m.? Do you plan to provide a full bar or keep it simple with just beer and wine? For large events and special celebrations send out your invitations two to three months ahead. If you think you may need a tent, rental glasses or wait staff put in your order well ahead of time, too, especially during popular entertaining times (May, June and December), since supplies of the best are quickly booked.

When you're planning food for a party, inquire about any dietary restrictions or allergies among your guests or, failing that, be sure to offer a selection of vegetarian options and dishes that do not include shellfish, pork and nuts.

Leave last minute chores to a minimum. For a large party plan your space. Arrange tables and seating. Choose table covers and napkins and arrange flowers. Check supplies of serving dishes (not forgetting ice bucket and tongs and pitchers for juice), dishware, cutlery and glasses. Pick up ice, lemons and limes for the bar. Chill the white wine, water (plain and sparkling) and mix or fruit juice. Do as much of the work as possible ahead of time so that you can relax and join in the fun. Remember if time is short you can always enlist the help of your trusty local deli!

Menus

The following party menu suggestions use recipes in this book that are easily multiplied to suit your occasion. They include many dishes that can be made ahead to make it easy on the cook.

Winter Cocktail Party

For a cocktail party over a couple of hours, offer a selection of 8 to 10 easy-to-handle tasty bites, allowing 6 to 8 bites per hour per person (i.e. for 20 guests from 6 to 8 p.m. prepare about 20 dozen bites, and since this is over the dinner hour include a few substantial choices). The selection might include 3 to 4 vegetarian and 3 to 4 meat or fish options divided between those to be served hot and cold. Add to the party fare with a display of antipasto items, charcuterie or cheese if desired.

Hot

Mini Bison Burgers (page 158)

Curried Scallop Cakes (page 342) with Red Pepper Mayonnaise (page 241)

Sweet Potato Latkes with Caramelized Onions and Stilton (page 348)

Mini Tourtières (Variation, page 192)

Cold

Duck Rillettes Crostini (page 129) with Shallot Port Marmalade (page 129)

Poached Shrimp (Variation, page 224) with Lemon Dill Mayonnaise (page 96)

Prosciutto-Wrapped Figs (page 325)

Grilled Vegetable Bundles (page 326)

A Spring Brunch

Salmon and Leek Strudel (page 226)

Roasted Pepper and Goat's Cheese Quiche (page 249)

French Potato Salad (page 69)

Cherry Tomato Basil Focaccia (page 385)

Mesclun Greens with Lemon Vinaigrette (page 90)

Cheese board (page 353)

Rhubarb Upside-Down Cake (page 425)

Spring Sit-Down Dinner

Select small bites to serve with drinks when guests arrive that are light and tasty to stimulate the appetite, not to spoil dinner. For a simpler dinner omit the soup and serve the salad at the start of the meal.

Appetizers with Drinks

Chèvre Tarts (page 354)

Chilled Octopus with Olive Tomato Antiboise (page 334)

Dinner

Spring Green Soup (page 48)

Herb-Crusted Rack of Lamb (page 26) with Grilled Asparagus (page 276)

Grilled red and yellow bell peppers and Rosemary Roasted Potatoes (page 297)

Baby arugula salad with mushrooms, shaved Parmigiano-Reggiano and Lemon Vinaigrette (page 90)

Cheese course, optional (page 352)

Lemon Mousse (page 398) with berries

South-of-the-Border Barbecue

Guacamole (page 310)

Gazpacho (page 34)

Grilled Boned Leg of Lamb with Charmoula Sauce (Variation, page 196)

Southwest Slaw (page 59)

Grilled Corn and Lima Bean Salad (page 83)

Cornbread (Variation, page 383)

Lime Mousse Cheesecake (page 424) with Raspberry Coulis (page 396)

Fall Buffet Dinner
Appetizers with Drinks

Pissaladiére (page 344)

Chicken Liver Mousse on whole wheat toast triangles (page 330) with cornichons

Sesame Ginger Cashews (page 338)

Lemon Rosemary Olives (page 336)

Dinner

Roast Beef Tenderloin with Madeira Pan Jus (page 138)

Mushroom Ragoût (page 286)

Broccoli Rabe with Garlic (page 280)

Potato Gratin with Leeks and Double-Smoked Bacon (page 298)

Mixed mesclun greens with beets, Gorgonzola with Lemon Vinaigrette (page 90)

Cheese course, optional (page 352)

Tiramisù (page 404)

Bridal Tea or Baby Shower

Chilled Zucchini Basil Soup (page 51) in shooter glasses with warm mini Cheddar 'n' Chive Scones (Variation, page 379)

Herbed Crêpes with Smoked Salmon (page 267)

Mini Ham and Green Onion Quiches (Variations, page 249)

Mushroom Pinwheels (page 339)

Crudités with Fresh Herb Dip (page 60)

Lemon Chiffon Cake (Variation, page 428)

Fresh Raspberry Tartlets (Variation, page 414)

Tapenade

**MAKES 1 CUP
(250 ML)**

This zesty olive paste has dozens of uses. Spread on crostini and top with goat's cheese, fresh mozzarella or Asiago. Team with tomatoes or roasted bell peppers on a bruschetta or pizza.

Variation

Taggiasca Tapenade: Purée ½ cup (125 mL) of the wonderful fruity taggiasca olives with 1 clove garlic, a splash of Balsamic vinegar and enough extra virgin olive oil to make a fine paste.

● **Food processor**

1	clove garlic	1
1	anchovy fillet, rinsed and dried	1
2 tbsp	chopped flat-leaf parsley	25 mL
1 tbsp	freshly squeezed lemon juice	15 mL
1 tbsp	red wine vinegar	15 mL
1 tsp	chopped oregano	5 mL
½	green bell pepper, roasted, peeled and seeded (see page 35)	½
½ cup	pitted kalamata olives, rinsed	125 mL
½ cup	pimento-stuffed manzanilla olives, rinsed	125 mL
¼ cup	olive oil (approx.)	50 mL
	Salt and freshly ground black pepper	

1. In a food processor, combine garlic, anchovy, parsley, lemon juice, vinegar and oregano and process until smooth. Add bell pepper and kalamata and manzanilla olives and process briefly, until olives are chopped but still retain some texture. Drizzle in oil through the feed tube and pulse to combine until just smooth. Taste and adjust seasoning. Transfer tapenade to a container and cover surface with a little olive oil and seal tightly. Keep in the refrigerator for up to 1 week.

Prosciutto-Wrapped Figs

MAKES 24

Sweet ripe figs complemented by creamy mascarpone cheese and salty prosciutto is a match made in heaven!

Tip

Lay out prosciutto slices on work counter and assemble the rolls 6 to 8 at a time. This makes the task quicker and easier than assembling them one at a time.

Variation

Mascarpone-Stuffed Dates: When sweet, soft dates are at their best, split them in half lengthwise, remove stone and stuff with creamy mascarpone. Top with a crisp toasted walnut half.

6	ripe figs	6
12	thin slices prosciutto	12
¼ cup	mascarpone cheese	50 mL
24	basil leaves	24

1. Cut each fig in quarters lengthwise. Cut each slice of prosciutto in half lengthwise.

2. Lay prosciutto slices on work counter. Spoon ½ tsp (2 mL) of the mascarpone on one end of each prosciutto slice. Place a basil leaf on the cheese with the tip extending slightly above one long side of the prosciutto and arrange a piece of fig on top of the basil. Roll up prosciutto to enclose the fig, keeping the bottom of the roll even, so that the prosciutto-wrapped fig stands up on the platter and the tip of the basil leaf peaks out the top. Repeat with remaining figs.

Grilled Vegetable Bundles

Matisse on a platter! These small vegetable bundles are almost too pretty to eat, but they taste so good that guests keep coming back for more.

Tip

Lay out zucchini slices on work counter and assemble the bundles 12 at a time. This makes the task quicker and easier than assembling them one at a time.

● **Preheat indoor grill or barbecue grill to medium-high**

2	zucchini	2
1/2	red onion	1/2
	Salt and freshly ground black pepper	
1/2	red bell pepper	1/2
1/2	yellow bell pepper	1/2
1/2 cup	soft goat's cheese	125 mL
24	small basil leaves	24
24	small mint leaves	24
24	baby arugula leaves	24

1. Slice zucchini lengthwise in thin slices, $1/8$ to $1/4$ inch (3 mm to 0.5 cm) thick. Remove outside 2 layers from the onion and save the rest to use later.

2. Lightly oil grill. Grill zucchini slices on preheated grill until nicely marked on one side only. Season lightly with salt and pepper and place between layers of paper towels to dry and cool. Grill red and yellow bell peppers and red onion until lightly charred on both sides. Transfer to a cutting board and season lightly. Cut into matchsticks, about $1\frac{1}{2}$ by $1/8$ inches (4 cm by 3 mm).

3. Lay zucchini slices on work counter, grill marks down. Spread about 1 tsp (5 mL) of soft goat's cheese down the center in a thin layer. Place one slice each of red and yellow pepper and onion with a leaf of basil, mint and arugula at one end lining up even with the bottom long edge of zucchini slice. Roll up so that the zucchini encloses a small neat bundle of vegetables and herbs that will stand up on a platter.

Herbed Crêpes with Smoked Salmon

MAKES 24 PIECES

Fill delicate small herb crêpes with a variety of savory combinations. Smoked salmon, poached shrimp and creamy lobster are the favorites, but smoked chicken and duck confit are excellent, too.

Tip

Party food must taste delicious and it also has to look spectacular. You need nimble fingers, patience and an interest in artistry in the kitchen to assemble some of the more intricate party snacks and platters. Don't be discouraged if first efforts are less than perfect. The steps are easily mastered and after a few tries you will be a pro.

2 tbsp	drained capers, roughly chopped	25 mL
2 tbsp	finely chopped dill	25 mL
1 tbsp	grated lemon zest	15 mL
12	Savory Herbed Crêpes, 6 inches (15 cm) (Variation, page 267)	12
1/2 cup	Dill and Garlic Dip (page 316)	125 mL
12	slices smoked salmon	12
1 tbsp	freshly squeezed lemon juice	15 mL
	Freshly ground black pepper	
24	small sprigs dill	24

1. In a small bowl, combine capers, chopped dill and lemon zest. Set aside.
2. Cut herbed crêpes in half. Spread each half with about 1 tsp (5 mL) of the Dill and Garlic Dip.
3. Cut each slice of salmon in half and sprinkle slices with 1/2 tsp (2 mL) caper mixture, a drizzle of lemon juice and season with pepper. Roll each salmon slice into a loose cylinder and place it horizontally across the crêpe with one end about 1/2 inch (1 cm) from the cut edge of the crêpe. Overlap the edges of the crêpe and form into a cone shape. Tuck a sprig of dill into the top of each crêpe cone as the finishing touch and arrange seam side down on a serving platter.

Caprese Skewers

The popular Caprese salad of sliced tomatoes, fresh mozzarella and basil appears as a fresh-tasting party bite when mini tomatoes and small bocconcini are threaded on skewers. A drizzle of Balsamic Reduction adds the finishing touch.

Tips

Use small fresh mozzarella about the size of a cherry tomato.

Balsamic Reduction: In a small saucepan over medium heat, combine 1 cup (250 mL) balsamic vinegar and 2 tbsp (25 mL) liquid honey. Stir while mixture comes to a boil. Reduce heat and simmer until liquid is reduced to desired thin syrup-like consistency. Flavoring may be added to the simmering vinegar — a sprig of rosemary or thyme, a slice of ginger or garlic — depending on how the reduction is to be used.

Variation

Watermelon Feta Skewers: Thread each small skewer with 1-inch (2.5 cm) cubes of peeled watermelon and top with ½-inch (0.5 cm) cube of Greek feta. Drizzle with Balsamic Reduction before serving.

Twenty-four 6-inch (15 cm) bamboo skewers

24	mini fresh mozzarella (see Tips, left)	24
24	basil leaves	24
24	mini heirloom tomatoes	24
	Kosher or sea salt	
	Balsamic Reduction (see Tips, left)	

1. Wrap each mini mozzarella in a basil leaf and thread on a skewer. Thread a tomato on top. Arrange on a serving platter. Sprinkle with a little salt and add a small drizzle of Balsamic Reduction.

Mozzarella

Today fresh mozzarella comes in many sizes: tiny balls that are the size of chickpeas called "pearls," small balls the size of a cherry tomato and larger ones about the size of a large walnut. The crème de la crème is mozzarella di bufula (made from milk of the water buffalo) and flown in fresh from Italy in season. They are found in the refrigerated cheese display in the supermarket, packaged in plastic containers and covered with water. Their shelf life is short so be sure to check "best before" dates and, once opened, rinse, cover with fresh cold water daily and enjoy within a day or two. All are delicious to use in light summery dishes and as a snack, especially when paired with fresh ripe tomatoes and fresh basil.

Parmesan Cups

**MAKES 12
COCKTAIL-SIZE CUPS**

We fill these crisp, lacy cups of toasted Parmesan cheese with a variety of tasty mixtures. A favorite with our customers is a miniature Caesar salad with all the ingredients finely slivered, or a salad of seedlings topped with finely diced ripe tomato or roasted red bell pepper.

Tip

If the cheese circles harden too fast on the tray, before you are able to shape them, place them back in the oven for a few seconds to soften.

- **Preheat oven to 350°F (180°C)**
- **2 baking sheets, lined with parchment paper**
- **Mini muffin tin**

¾ cup	freshly grated Parmesan cheese	175 mL
Pinch	freshly ground black pepper	Pinch

1. Scoop about 1 tbsp (15 mL) grated Parmesan and place in a mound on prepared baking sheet. Pat it down with your fingers and form into a circle. Sprinkle with pepper. Repeat with the rest of the cheese. We recommend preparing only 6 to 8 mounds on each tray to make things easier to manage when you come to form the cups.

2. Bake in preheated oven until cheese is bubbling and edges are lightly browned, 6 to 8 minutes.

3. Let stand for 10 seconds. Carefully lift each hot circle of cheese from baking sheet with a thin metal spatula. Drape over the small cup of an inverted muffin tin. Leave to cool for about 5 minutes. Lift off and set aside. Cups are fragile and best stored in a single layer in a covered container and used the same day. At serving time, fill Parmesan cups with filling of your choice.

Chicken Liver Mousse

**MAKES ABOUT
2 CUPS (500 ML)**

Here's a silken mixture of delicately spiced chicken livers, butter and brandy. A simple pre-dinner snack accompanied by slices of fresh baguette, multicolored mini tomatoes, olives and cornichons: the perfect picnic lunch, too.

Variation

Aspic-Coated Chicken Liver Mousse (page 331).

● **Food processor or blender**
● **Two 1-cup (250 mL) ramekins**

1 lb	chicken livers, trimmed	500 g
½ cup	brandy, divided	125 mL
1 cup	butter, softened, divided	250 mL
¼ cup	minced shallots	50 mL
1 tbsp	minced garlic	15 mL
1 tsp	whole allspice	5 mL
	Salt and freshly ground black pepper	
2 tbsp	balsamic vinegar	25 mL

1. In a bowl, marinate chicken livers in ¼ cup (50 mL) of the brandy for 1 hour. Drain, discarding liquid and set livers aside.

2. In a large skillet, melt 2 tbsp (25 mL) of the butter over medium-low heat. Add shallots and garlic and sauté until softened but not browned, about 5 minutes. Add chicken livers, allspice and season lightly with salt and pepper. Cook, stirring occasionally, until livers are no longer pink inside, about 15 minutes. Transfer chicken livers with a slotted spoon to a bowl and set aside.

3. Increase heat to high. Deglaze pan with vinegar and remaining brandy, scraping up the browned bits, and boil until reduced to about ¼ cup (50 mL).

4. In a food processor, combine chicken livers, pan juices and ¼ cup (50 mL) of the soft butter and pulse 3 or 4 times. Add remaining butter in small amounts, pulsing to combine until all the butter is incorporated and mixture is smooth. Press mixture through a sieve to obtain a super-smooth texture. Taste and adjust seasoning.

5. Spoon mixture into ramekins, smooth the surface and cover with plastic wrap. Refrigerate for at least 1 hour for flavors to develop and mousse to set.

To Prepare Aspic

In a bowl, place 2 tbsp (25 mL) cold water and sprinkle 1½ tsp (7 mL) unflavored powdered gelatin on top. Set aside for 5 minutes, without stirring, while gelatin swells and becomes spongy. Place the bowl in a saucepan of hot water so that the water comes halfway up the sides of the bowl. Place saucepan over low heat and warm gelatin until it is melted and clear, about 2 minutes. Do not stir. Remove bowl from saucepan and gently stir in 1 cup (250 mL) hot clear Chicken Stock (page 54) or ready-to-use broth. Set aside and chill until mixture is syrupy and just beginning to set, about 30 minutes. (For faster chilling, place the bowl over ice and stir mixture gently until just beginning to set.)

Aspic-Coated Chicken Liver Mousse: Lightly butter two ramekins or one 2-cup (500 mL) mold and line with plastic wrap, taking care to smooth out plastic wrap on bottom and sides to avoid marks on the finished mousse. Spoon mousse mixture into ramekins or molds and refrigerate for at least 1 hour.

Garnish top of chilled chicken mousse with ½ tsp (2 mL) cracked peppercorns or several leaves of thyme or tarragon. Brush a thin layer of aspic over top and chill until set, about 30 minutes, keeping remaining aspic at room temperature. Gently pour remaining aspic over top to make a layer about ¼ inch (0.5 cm) thick and chill until set. Cover loosely and refrigerate for up to 3 days.

Before serving, place bottom of ramekin or mold in hot water just long enough to loosen the plastic wrap lining. Gently lift the mousse from mold and place on a platter. Remove and discard plastic wrap.

Terimaki

In Japan the art of sushi-making is pursued with passion — the flavor and texture of the vinegared rice must be perfect and the toppings, usually raw fish and shellfish, must be exceptionally fresh and of the highest quality. Our party sushi are versions of the kyuri-maki, the popular cucumber sushi roll: A layer of vinegared rice surrounding one or two flavored ingredients enclosed in a circle of nori. They're very tasty and easy to eat.

Tip

When assembling sushi, moisten your fingers in *tezu* ("hand vinegar") to prevent the rice grains from sticking to your hands. In a small bowl, add 1 tbsp (15 mL) rice vinegar to ½ cup (125 mL) water.

- **Preheat indoor grill or barbecue grill to medium, if using**
- **Sushi rolling mat or small linen napkin**

1	skinless boneless chicken breast (about 8 oz/250 g)	1
2 tsp	vegetable oil, divided	10 mL
	Kosher or sea salt	
	Teriyaki Glaze, divided (page 333)	
1 tsp	sesame oil, divided	5 mL
2 oz	shiitake mushrooms, caps only, sliced ⅛ inch (3 mm)	60 g
2	squares nori	2
4 cups	cooked Sushi Rice (page 333)	1 L
1 cup	baby spinach leaves, trimmed	250 mL

1. Brush chicken breast lightly with 1 tsp (5 mL) of the oil and sprinkle with salt. Lightly oil grill. Cook on preheated grill or in a skillet over medium heat until lightly browned, 3 to 4 minutes. Turn chicken over and brush with Teriyaki Glaze. Continue to cook until chicken is no longer pink inside, 3 to 4 minutes more. Remove from heat and brush again with Teriyaki Glaze. Slice lengthwise into fine strips and let cool.

2. In a skillet, heat 1 tsp (5 mL) each vegetable and sesame oil over medium-high heat. Add mushrooms and sauté until tender and nicely browned, about 3 minutes. Set aside and let cool.

3. Toast nori by passing the shiny side of the sheets over a gas burner, or lay in a hot skillet for a few seconds.

4. Place one toasted nori sheet, shiny side down, on a sushi rolling mat. Using your fingers (see Tip, left), spread 2 cups (500 mL) Sushi Rice in a layer about ⅜ inch (0.75 cm) thick over the nori, leaving about 1½ inches (4 cm) uncovered at the top. Arrange a narrow strip of slivered teriyaki chicken across the center of the rice. Arrange slivers of shiitake mushrooms and baby spinach leaves on top of the chicken. Hold the ingredients in place in the center with your fingertips and use your thumbs to pick up and turn the rolling mat, lifting up the nori to meet at the top and enclose the rice. Gently but firmly press the mat around the roll to make a neat cylinder. Repeat with the other nori sheet.

5. Place the roll on a flat board, with the seam of the nori sheet on the bottom. Using a very sharp knife cut the roll in half and then cut each half in two pieces on the diagonal.

Teriyaki Glaze

1. In a small saucepan, combine 1 cup (250 mL) soy sauce, 3 tbsp (45 mL) honey, 2 tbsp (25 mL) mirin and ½ tsp (2 mL) each powdered garlic and ground ginger. Bring to a boil. Reduce heat and simmer until reduced to about ⅓ cup (75 mL) glaze.

Sushi Rice

Makes 4 cups (1 L)

● **Rimmed baking sheet, lined with parchment paper**

1½ cups	short-grain Sushi rice, rinsed	375 mL
	Kosher or sea salt	
3 tbsp	rice vinegar	45 mL
3 tbsp	granulated sugar	45 mL

1. In a heavy-bottomed saucepan, combine rice, water to cover by about ½ inch (1 cm), about 2 cups (500 mL), and ½ tsp (2 mL) salt. Cover and bring to a boil over medium heat and cook for 2 minutes. Reduce heat to low and continue to cook until rice is tender and all liquid has been absorbed, about 15 minutes. Remove from heat and let rice stand, still tightly covered, 10 to 15 minutes.

2. Meanwhile, in a small saucepan, combine vinegar, sugar and 1½ tsp (7 mL) salt. Stir over low heat until sugar and salt are dissolved. Let cool.

3. Spread cooked rice in a thin layer on prepared baking sheet. Toss grains lightly with a flat wooden spoon, or rice paddle, to cool and separate. Do not bruise and break the grains. Sprinkle rice with vinegar dressing as you toss the grains. You may not need all the dressing; use just enough to moisten and flavor the rice.

4. When rice is cool, cover with a damp cloth and set aside. Use the same day. Do not refrigerate.

Variation

Replace powdered garlic and ground ginger with 1 tsp (5 mL) each finely chopped fresh garlic and ginger. Strain after simmering.

Chilled Octopus with Olive Tomato Antiboise

Don't overlook octopus and squid when you are planning a marinated seafood antipasto selection. Bite-size slices of tender octopus, topped with a flavorful Mediterranean salsa is a delicious light snack.

Tip

Octopus are most commonly available vacuum-sealed and frozen. Thaw in the refrigerator overnight. Wash in many changes of cold water to remove any sand and grit and pay particular attention to the body sack, which contained the innards. Make sure that the hard "beak" in the middle of the underside has been removed (if it hasn't, just squeeze it out and discard).

Variations

Marinate cooked octopus pieces in a zesty Lemon Vinaigrette (page 90).

Toss cooked octopus in a little garlic-flavored oil and place over a hot grill, turning frequently, until nicely charred on all sides, about 5 minutes. Slice pieces and toss with additional vinaigrette.

8 cups	water	2 L
½ cup	dry white wine	125 mL
½	onion, sliced	½
1	head garlic, cut in half crosswise	1
2	pieces (each 3 inches/7.5 cm) cinnamon sticks	2
5	whole cloves	5
3	bay leaves	3
10	black peppercorns	10
1 tsp	sea salt	5 mL
1	octopus, about 2 lbs (1 kg), cleaned (see Tip, left)	1
	Salt and freshly ground black pepper	
	Olive Tomato Antiboise (page 335)	

1. In a large pot over medium-high heat, combine water, wine, onion, garlic, cinnamon sticks, cloves, bay leaves, peppercorns and salt. Add octopus and bring to the boil. Reduce heat to low and simmer until octopus is tender, 30 to 40 minutes.

2. Transfer octopus to a bowl, discarding cooking broth, and let cool slightly. When cool enough to handle, peel away any hanging soft outer skin. Remove tentacles from the body by making deep V-shaped cuts where the tentacles meet the body. Cut off sack above the eyes. Cut off and discard the part with the eyes. Cut tentacles into slices on the diagonal, about ⅜ inch (0.75 cm) thick. And cut the sack into slivers. Cover, set aside and refrigerate until serving for up to 2 days ahead.

3. Shortly before serving, season octopus slices lightly with salt and pepper and garnish with Olive Tomato Antiboise.

Olive Tomato Antiboise

Makes about 2 cups (500 mL)

½ cup	Niçoise olives, pitted and roughly chopped	125 mL
½ cup	Picholine olives, pitted and roughly chopped	125 mL
3	ripe Roma (plum) tomatoes, peeled and finely diced	3
2	shallots, finely diced	2
1	clove garlic, minced	1
1 tbsp	white wine vinegar	15 mL
1 tbsp	fruity extra virgin olive oil (see Tips, page 241)	15 mL
2 tbsp	basil chiffonade	25 mL
	Salt and freshly ground black pepper	

1. In a bowl, combine Niçoise and picholine olives, tomatoes, shallots and garlic. Add vinegar, oil, basil and salt and pepper to taste. Taste and adjust seasoning. Set aside for 1 hour for flavors to meld or for up to 2 days. If not serving on the same day, divide the basil and save some to be added at serving time.

Lemon Rosemary Olives

½ cup	kalamata olives	125 mL
½ cup	large green olives	125 mL
1 tbsp	chopped thyme	15 mL
1 tbsp	chopped rosemary	15 mL
½ tsp	grated lemon zest	2 mL
1 tbsp	freshly squeezed lemon juice	15 mL
1	clove garlic, thinly sliced	1
½ tsp	freshly ground black pepper	2 mL
1 tbsp	extra virgin olive oil	15 mL

1. Rinse kalamata and green olives to remove brine. Drain and pat dry.
2. In a bowl, combine olives, thyme, rosemary, lemon zest and juice, garlic and pepper. Add oil and mix well. Set aside for flavors to meld.

Spicy Olives

1 cup	green olives	250 mL
1 tsp	crumbled dried oregano, preferably Greek	5 mL
1	clove garlic, thinly sliced	1
½ tsp	hot pepper flakes	2 mL
1 tbsp	olive oil	15 mL

1. Rinse olives to remove brine. Drain and pat dry.
2. In a bowl, combine olives, oregano, garlic and hot pepper flakes. Add oil and mix well. Set aside for flavors to meld.

Olives

Everything about the olive is beautiful. The fruit, the color, the oil, the wood, the tree — Aldous Huxley once said that if he could only tear himself away from writing, he'd do nothing but paint olive trees for a few years: "What a wealth of variations upon a single theme!" The theme is Character, etched into the trees over centuries (and sometimes millennia, several, still producing, dating back to the time of Christ), gnarled, stupendously weathered, hard as truth, yet always generous with their fruit. The fruit, too, is not easy: impossibly bitter if eaten off the tree, unripe green or super-ripe black, it must be pickled, cured, or washed long in water to be made edible.

For the happy result, older than the written language, mythology tells us we can thank the ancient Egyptians of about 5,000 years ago (Isis, goddess of green fields and olives, and just about everything else) and the ancient Greeks (who borrowed many Egyptian customs and whose goddess Athena struck the ground with her spear and gave them the olive tree that resulted). Today, olive cultivation has more than tripled in area in the past 50 years, and fittingly the two countries leading the world in yield per hectare are mythology's onlie begetters, Greece and Egypt.

In the Kitchen

Olives come in a myriad of colors, shapes, sizes and flavors. From crisp green, picked when unripe and cured in brine, to soft black, picked when fully ripe, and dry-cured.

Italy: Black Ligurian olives, used for oil and eating, are among the best in the world. Prime among them are the **Taggiasche**, developed by Benedictine monks centuries ago, and traditionally cured in fresh water, changed daily, for 40 days; thereafter brined, and scented with thyme, rosemary and bay leaves. Delicate, mellow, perfect in tapenades, and eaten alone. **Gaeta:** Central Italian, purple brown, excellent for pizza. **Cerignola:** Southern Italian, big, crisp, green, make a statement on party platters.

France: Niçoise, one of the black jewels of the olive world, rich and nutty, akin to the neighboring Taggiasche, essential for regional dishes such as salade Niçoise, or the pissaladière. **Nyons**: Black, intense, dry-cured and aged in brine. **Picholine**: Green, crisp, with hints of anise; excellent in stews.

Spain: Manzanilla, green, often pitted and stuffed with garlic or pimento, thus popular for martinis. **Arbequina**, brown, very small, delicious eaten out of hand.

Greece: Kalamata, deep purple, harvested fully ripe, bracingly pungent, cracked and cured in a red wine vinegar brine. **Nafplion**: cracked green and crisp. **Amfissa**, black, soft, sweet, picked very ripe. Grown around Delphi, home of the legendary oracles. Eat enough and you will be able to explain what happens in 2012.

Portugal: Galega, which accounts for 80 percent of the country's cultivation, makes an excellent eating olive.

California: home of nearly all U.S. production. **Mission**, introduced by missionaries 250 years ago from Spain, black, mild, but lacking the flavor of the Europeans; often artificially ripened, canned and leached of much flavor. **Sevillano**, green, large and crisp, introduced in the mid-1880s.

Morocco: Moroccan, black, dry-cured intense rich flavor often marinated in olive oil with herbs and hot pepper flakes.

Salted Almonds

MAKES 2 CUPS
(500 ML)

Crisp freshly roasted nuts are a delicious accompaniment to a cheese platter and a glass of wine.

Variation

Spiced Nuts: Other seasonings may be added to the nuts, including chipotle chile powder, garam masala and ground ginger.

● **Preheat oven to 300°F (150°C)**

2 cups	blanched almonds	500 mL
1 tsp	olive oil	5 mL
1 tsp	kosher or sea salt	5 mL

1. In a large bowl, toss almonds with oil to coat. Spread nuts in a single layer on a baking sheet. Roast in preheated oven, stirring occasionally, until light golden, 20 to 25 minutes. Sprinkle with salt and toss nuts to season evenly. Serve cool or warmed.

Sesame Ginger Cashews

MAKES 2 CUPS
(500 ML)

A hint of sesame adds a whole new dimension to these rich spicy nuts.

● **Preheat oven to 375°F (190°C)**

1 tbsp	sesame oil	15 mL
1½ tsp	ground ginger	7 mL
½ tsp	kosher or sea salt	2 mL
2 cups	raw cashew nuts	500 mL

1. In a large bowl, combine oil, ginger and salt and mix to a paste. Add cashews and toss to coat nuts in spicy paste. Spread nuts in a single layer on a baking sheet. Roast in preheated oven, stirring occasionally, until light golden and aromatic, 10 to 12 minutes.
2. Transfer toasted nuts to a bowl and toss gently while still warm to redistribute the flavors and oils.

Mushroom Pinwheels

MAKES 1 CUP (250 ML) FOR ABOUT 36 PINWHEELS

Use this versatile mushroom mixture to create many hot party snacks. Here we encase the mushrooms in puff pastry, but you can also use as a filling for small phyllo pastry cups, mini vol-au-vent pastry shells, short-crust pastry shells, wonton wrappers, salad roll wrappers or gougères.

Variations

Mushroom-Stuffed Wontons: Place about 2 tsp (10 mL) mushroom mixture in center of each square wonton wrapper. Moisten edges of square and fold to make a triangle. Wrap outer corners into each other and pinch to seal. Deep-fry wontons in oil, in batches, until golden, 1 to 2 minutes. Transfer to a tray lined with paper towel. Serve warm with Asian Dressing and Dip (page 60). Best enjoyed right away. However, if it is more convenient to cook them ahead, let them cool then cover and refrigerate for up to 1 day. Place on a parchment-lined baking sheet and reheat in a 350°F (180°C) oven, 5 to 6 minutes.

Mushroom Gruyère Crostini: Arrange crostini on a baking sheet. Spread with mushroom mixture and top with shaved Gruyère cheese. Bake in 350°F (180°C) oven until cheese is melted, about 5 minutes.

- **Preheat oven to 400°F (200°C)**
- **Food processor**
- **2 baking sheets, lined with parchment paper**

2	packages (each ½ oz/14 g) dried porcini mushrooms	2
¼ cup	hot water	50 mL
8 oz	cremini mushrooms, quartered	250 g
1	shallot, roughly chopped	1
2	cloves garlic, roughly chopped	2
2 tbsp	olive oil	25 mL
1 tsp	finely chopped thyme	5 mL
½ tsp	finely chopped rosemary	2 mL
	Salt and freshly ground black pepper	
1 tbsp	sherry or Madeira	15 mL
1 lb	puff pastry	500 g
1	egg, beaten	1

1. In a bowl, cover porcini mushrooms with hot water. Set aside to soak for 10 minutes. Remove mushrooms, squeeze out water and chop roughly. Strain soaking liquid to remove any grit and reserve ¼ cup (50 mL). Set aside.

2. In a food processor, pulse porcini mushrooms, cremini mushrooms, shallot and garlic until finely chopped.

3. In a large skillet, heat oil over medium-high heat. Add mushroom mixture, thyme and rosemary and season lightly with salt and pepper. Sauté for 3 to 4 minutes. Deglaze pan with sherry, scraping up browned bits on bottom, and add porcini soaking liquid. Stir and cook until liquid is reduced and mushrooms are lightly browned, 2 to 3 minutes. Let cool.

4. On a lightly floured surface, roll puff pastry to make a rectangle 18 by 9 inches (45 by 23 cm) and spread with a thin layer of mushroom mixture. Roll up pastry, jelly-roll style, to make a compact cylinder. Cut roll into ½-inch (1 cm) slices. Arrange mushroom pinwheels on prepared baking sheet, about 2 inches (5 cm) apart. Pinwheels may be prepared ahead to this point. Cover and refrigerate for up to 4 hours.

5. Brush tops lightly with egg and bake in preheated oven until pastry is golden, 15 to 20 minutes. Serve warm.

Crab Cakes

*Tender cakes of
well-seasoned crabmeat
with a crisp golden crust
are delicious served as
an appetizer, or lunch
with baby greens tossed
in a light white wine
vinaigrette. Form the crab
mixture into bite-size
cakes as a popular
cocktail and party snack
with tarragon-scented
aïoli, herbed crème
fraîche, or Fresh Herb
Dressing and Dip
(page 75).*

Tip

Crab cakes are best enjoyed
right away. However, if it is
more convenient to cook
them ahead of time, let
them cool, then cover and
refrigerate for up to 1 day.
Place on a parchment-lined
baking sheet and reheat in a
preheated 350°F (180°C) oven
for 5 to 6 minutes.

Variation

Cocktail-Size Crab Cakes: To
form cocktail-size crab cakes,
use a tablespoon (15 mL)
measure or scoop and shape
into small patties, a scant
½ inch (1 cm) thick. Cook crab
cakes for 2 to 3 minutes per
side. Do not crowd pan. Place
on prepared baking sheet
while cooking remaining
cakes. Add more oil as
necessary between batches.
Serve hot.

- Baking sheet, lined with paper towel

1	can (1 lb/500 g) crab claw meat, drained	1
1 tbsp	finely grated fresh horseradish or prepared horseradish, drained	15 mL
¼ cup	finely diced daikon radish	50 mL
2 tbsp	thinly sliced chives	25 mL
1 tbsp	coarsely chopped tarragon	15 mL
1½ tsp	minced garlic	7 mL
1 tsp	kosher or sea salt	5 mL
½ tsp	cayenne pepper	2 mL
½ tsp	dry mustard powder	2 mL
¼ tsp	freshly ground black pepper	1 mL
2 tsp	hot pepper sauce	10 mL
1 tsp	Worcestershire sauce	5 mL
¼ cup	mayonnaise (approx.)	50 mL
3	egg whites, lightly beaten	3
2½ cups	panko or fresh bread crumbs, divided	625 mL
½ cup	vegetable oil, divided	125 mL

1. Pick through crabmeat and remove any stray bits of shell.

2. In a bowl, combine crabmeat, horseradish, radish, chives, tarragon, garlic, salt, cayenne, dry mustard, pepper, hot pepper sauce, Worcestershire sauce, ¼ cup (50 mL) mayonnaise, egg whites and ½ cup (125 mL) of the bread crumbs. Mix together lightly. Cover and refrigerate for 1 hour. Form a small amount of mixture into a ball shape to test whether mixture holds together. If it falls apart, add another tablespoon (15 mL) mayonnaise.

3. Pour the remaining bread crumbs into a medium bowl. To form crab cake, fill a ¼ cup (50 mL) measure, or scoop, with crab mixture. Form mixture into a ball and then flatten top and bottom to form a straight-sided disk, about ½ inch (1 cm) thick.

4. Place crab cakes, one at a time, in bowl of bread crumbs and press to coat on all sides with crumbs. Set aside on a rack. Discard any excess crumbs. You can make the cakes ahead to this point, place the rack on a baking sheet, cover and refrigerate for up to 4 hours.

5. In a large skillet, heat $\frac{1}{4}$ cup (50 mL) of the oil over medium-low heat just until oil begins to ripple. Add crab cakes, in batches, and cook, turning once, until cakes are nicely browned, 3 to 5 minutes per side. Do not crowd pan. Place on prepared baking sheet while cooking remaining cakes. Add more oil as necessary between batches. Serve hot.

Curried Scallop Cakes

Serve these delicate scallop cakes as an appetizer, or lunch with baby greens tossed in a light white wine vinaigrette, or shape the scallop mixture into bite-size cakes as a cocktail or party snack. Serve with Roasted Red Pepper Mayonnaise.

Tip

Scallop cakes are best enjoyed right away. However, if it is more convenient to cook them ahead of time, let them cool then cover and refrigerate for up to 1 day. Place on a parchment-lined baking sheet and reheat in a preheated 350°F (180°C) oven for 5 to 6 minutes.

- Food processor
- Baking sheet, lined with paper towel

1 lb	sea scallops, divided	500 g
2 tsp	butter	10 mL
½ cup	finely chopped onion	125 mL
2	green onions, finely chopped	2
2 tsp	curry powder	10 mL
Pinch	cayenne pepper	Pinch
	Salt and freshly ground black pepper	
1¼ cups	fresh bread crumbs	300 mL
3 tbsp	mayonnaise (approx.)	45 mL
1 tbsp	finely chopped cilantro	15 mL
1 tsp	dry mustard	5 mL
2	egg yolks, beaten	2
½ cup	all-purpose flour	125 mL
1	egg, beaten	1
2 cups	panko bread crumbs	500 mL
¼ cup	vegetable oil	50 mL
	Roasted Red Pepper Mayonnaise (page 241)	

1. In a food processor, pulse half the scallops to a soft paste. Finely chop remaining scallops by hand. In a large bowl, combine puréed and finely chopped scallops. Set aside.

2. In a small skillet, melt butter over medium heat. Add onion and green onions and sauté, until softened but not browned, 4 to 5 minutes. Stir in curry powder and cayenne and season lightly with salt and pepper. Let cool.

3. Add seasoned onions, fresh bread crumbs, 3 tbsp (45 mL) mayonnaise, cilantro, dry mustard and egg yolks to scallops. Mix together lightly. Cover and refrigerate for 1 hour. Form a small amount of mixture into a ball shape to test whether mixture holds together. If it falls apart, add another tablespoon (15 mL) mayonnaise.

4. Place flour, beaten egg and panko bread crumbs in separate bowls. To form an appetizer-size scallop cake, fill a $\frac{1}{4}$ cup (50 mL) measure, or scoop, with scallop mixture. Form mixture into a ball and then flatten top and bottom to form a straight-sided disk, about $\frac{1}{2}$ inch (1 cm) thick. To form cocktail-size scallop cakes, use a tablespoon measure (15 mL) or scoop and shape into small patties, a scant $\frac{1}{2}$ inch (1 cm) thick. Dip each cake first in flour, then in egg and lastly coat in bread crumbs. Set aside on a rack. Discard any excess flour, egg and bread crumbs. You can make the cakes ahead to this point, place the rack on a baking sheet, cover and refrigerate for up to 4 hours.

5. In a large skillet, heat oil over medium-low heat just until oil begins to ripple. Add scallop cakes, in batches, and cook until cakes are nicely browned, turning once, 3 to 5 minutes per side for appetizer-size cakes, or 2 to 3 minutes per side for cocktail-size ones. Set aside on prepared baking sheet. Serve hot with Roasted Red Pepper Mayonnaise.

Pissaladière

This onion-and-anchovy tart originated in Nice. It is traditionally formed in a rectangle and served in slices or squares. You can use short-crust pastry, pizza dough or puff pastry to make the crisp base. The herb-flavored caramelized onions are delicious as a filling for small tarts and a topping for crostini, garnished with shavings of Asiago or Parmesan cheese.

Tip

There is controversy among chefs as to the best method for caramelizing onions. Some insist on long, gentle cooking for about an hour to result in soft, uniformly golden, sweet onions. Others start onions off at high heat, stirring to start the browning and then reduce the heat to low for the softening period. I suspect the latter method is to save time in a busy kitchen, which is the way we do it in ours.

Variation

Caramelized Onions and Gruyère Crostini: Arrange crostini on a baking sheet. Spread with caramelized onions and top with shaved Gruyère cheese. Bake in preheated 350°F (180°C) oven until cheese is melted, about 5 minutes.

● **Preheat oven to 400°F (200°C)**

1	partially baked 9-inch (23 cm) flat pastry disk, or 9- by 5-inch (23 by 12.5 cm) partially baked pizza crust	1
	Caramelized Onions (see below)	
8	anchovy fillets, rinsed and dried	8
16	dry-cured Niçoise olives, halved and pitted	16
1 tbsp	extra virgin olive oil	15 mL

1. Spread the prepared pastry crust with an even layer of Caramelized Onions. Garnish top with anchovy fillets and olives. Drizzle with olive oil.

2. Bake in preheated oven until the bottom of the pastry is crisp and lightly browned, 10 to 15 minutes. Serve warm or at room temperature.

Caramelized Onions

Makes 2 cups (500 mL)

● **Butcher's string**

5 tbsp	olive oil, divided	75 mL
2 lbs	onions, chopped	1 kg
2	sprigs thyme	2
2	sprigs flat-leaf parsley	2
1	bay leaf	1
1	clove garlic, chopped	1
½ tsp	kosher or sea salt	2 mL
Pinch	freshly ground black pepper	Pinch
1 tbsp	balsamic vinegar, optional	15 mL

1. In a large skillet, heat 4 tbsp (60 mL) of the olive oil over medium-high heat. Add onions and stir until evenly colored, 8 to 10 minutes. Tie thyme, parsley and bay leaf together with butcher's string and add to onions with garlic, salt and pepper. Reduce heat to low and continue to cook, stirring occasionally, until onions are soft and a rich caramel color, 8 to 10 minutes. Discard herb bundle. Taste and adjust seasoning. Add a splash of balsamic vinegar, if desired.

Teriyaki Shrimp Skewers

Without doubt, shrimp and smoked salmon are always the first dishes to vanish at a party! Shrimp served hot from the grill with a tasty sauce are a special treat. The number of shrimp on the skewer will depend on the size of the shrimp you are using: two large shrimp per skewer is usually appropriate.

The Teriyaki Grilling Sauce is a classic and a standard in our kitchen. It's used to season many varieties of fish and seafood as well as pork tenderloin, spare ribs, flank steak and chicken wings.

- **Preheat indoor grill or barbecue grill to medium-high**
- **Twelve 8-inch (20 cm) bamboo skewers soaked in water for 30 minutes**

24	snow peas, trimmed	24
24	large shrimp, peeled and deveined	24
½ cup	Teriyaki Grilling Sauce, divided (see below)	125 mL
	Kosher or sea salt	

1. In a saucepan of boiling, lightly salted water, blanch snow peas for 30 seconds. Remove and plunge in ice water. Drain and set aside.
2. Wrap a snow pea around a shrimp and thread on a skewer. Wrap another snow pea around a shrimp and thread on the same skewer. Repeat threading the rest of the skewers with shrimp and snow peas.
3. Baste shrimp with ¼ cup (50 mL) Teriyaki Grilling Sauce and grill, turning once, until shrimp is resilient to the touch, 2 to 3 minutes per side. Serve hot, basted with remaining teriyaki sauce and sprinkled with salt.

Teriyaki Grilling Sauce

Makes 1 cup (250 mL)

½ cup	soy sauce	125 mL
¼ cup	mirin	50 mL
¼ cup	vegetable oil	50 mL
¼ cup	packed brown sugar	50 mL
2	cloves garlic, sliced	2
2	green onions, roughly chopped	2
1 tsp	minced gingerroot	5 mL

1. In a small saucepan, combine soy sauce, mirin, oil, brown sugar, garlic, green onions and ginger. Bring to a simmer over medium heat, stirring to dissolve sugar. Reduce heat and simmer, about 5 minutes. Strain and discard seasonings. Let cool.

Sweet Potato Samosas

Here we cheat a little and use handy wonton wrappers as the casing for a curried sweet potato filling. When time allows consider making authentic samosa dough (page 347). This dough is adapted from The Art of Indian Vegetarian Cooking *by Yamuna Devi.*

Tip

Other curried vegetable mixtures may be used as fillings for samosas, such as Gobi Masala (page 283). You will need about 1½ cups (375 mL) to stuff 24 samosas.

Variation

When time allows consider making authentic samosa dough (page 347) and hone your samosa-forming skills.

- **Deep-fryer or heavy-bottomed saucepan with basket**

1 tbsp	butter	15 mL
1	onion, chopped	1
1	clove garlic, chopped	1
1 tsp	curry powder	5 mL
½ tsp	ground cumin	2 mL
½ tsp	ground cinnamon	2 mL
¼ tsp	hot pepper flakes	1 mL
¼ tsp	fennel seeds	1 mL
2	sweet potatoes, peeled and diced	2
1 tbsp	freshly squeezed lemon juice	15 mL
	Salt and freshly ground black pepper	
2 tbsp	mango chutney	25 mL
1 tbsp	chopped cilantro	15 mL
24	wonton wrappers	24
	Vegetable oil for deep-frying	
	Tamarind Dipping Sauce (page 355) or Spinach Raita (page 356)	

1. In a large skillet, melt butter over medium heat. Add onion and sauté until softened and lightly browned, 6 to 8 minutes. Add garlic, curry powder, cumin, cinnamon, hot pepper flakes and fennel seeds and sauté for 1 to 2 minutes.

2. Add sweet potatoes and stir to coat in spicy onions. Add lemon juice and season lightly with salt and pepper. Reduce heat to low. Cover and cook, stirring occasionally, until sweet potatoes are soft, about 25 minutes. Remove from heat and stir in chutney and cilantro. Taste and adjust seasoning. Let cool.

3. Place about 2 tsp (10 mL) of the sweet potato mixture in center of each wonton square. Moisten edges of square and fold to make a triangle. Wrap outer corners into each other and pinch to seal.

4. Meanwhile, in deep-fryer, preheat oil to 350°F (180°C).

5. Deep-fry stuffed wontons in hot oil, in batches, until golden, 1 to 2 minutes. Transfer to paper towels. Serve hot with Tamarind Dipping Sauce or Spinach Raita.

Samosa Dough

Makes 24

● **Food processor**

2 cups	all-purpose flour	500 mL
½ tsp	sea salt	2 mL
⅓ cup	plain yogurt	75 mL
¼ cup	melted butter	50 mL
½ tsp	vegetable oil	2 mL

1. In a food processor, combine flour and salt. Add yogurt and melted butter and pulse a few times to make a crumbly mixture.
2. Turn mixture out onto a board and form into a ball. Knead dough until smooth, about 10 minutes. Place dough in a bowl. Coat lightly with oil and cover and set aside for 1 hour.
3. When ready to make samosas, on a lightly floured surface, roll dough ⅛ inch (3 mm) thick. Stamp out circles about 6 inches (15 cm) in diameter.
4. Cut each circle of dough in half. Dip your finger in water and moisten half of the straight edge of a semicircle of dough. Pick up the dough and bring the half with the dry edge over the half with the moistened edge overlapping by about ¼ inch (0.5 cm) to form a cone. Pinch to seal the seam (see Techniques, page 24).
5. Fill the cone with 1 tbsp (15 mL) of stuffing. Moisten the inside edges of the opening and pinch closed to make a secure seam. Place samosa, seam side down, on a baking tray in a cool spot while you complete assembling the rest. Deep-fry as described on page 346.

Tip

It takes practice to create a perfect samosa! Seal the edges of the pastry cone securely so that the stuffing stays inside and the samosa remains intact during deep-frying.

Sweet Potato Latkes with Caramelized Onions and Stilton

Bite-size latkes make irresistible party bites. We change the toppings and the garnishes with the season.

Tips

If preparing ahead, let cool, cover and refrigerate for up to 4 hours. Reheat latkes on a baking sheet in a preheated 350°F (180°C) oven for 3 to 4 minutes. Remove, add garnishes and return to the oven for 2 to 3 minutes.

Familiar onions with papery brown skin (known in the trade as "storage" onions) are strong and acidic. With slow cooking over medium-low heat the yellowish flesh becomes soft and transparent and the flavor becomes mellow and sweet. Sweet onions soften during cooking but do not caramelize in the same way as "storage" onions.

Variation

Sweet Potato Latkes with Caramelized Onions and Duck Confit: Replace Stilton cheese with a garnish of finely shredded Duck Confit (page 128).

- Baking sheet, lined with paper towel
- Preheat oven to 300°F (150°C)

1	sweet potato, peeled and grated (about 1 cup/250 mL)	1
½ cup	grated onion	125 mL
1	egg, beaten	1
3 tbsp	all-purpose flour	45 mL
1½ tsp	kosher or sea salt	7 mL
¼ tsp	freshly ground black pepper	1 mL
2 to 3 tbsp	vegetable oil or clarified butter	25 to 45 mL
1 cup	Caramelized Onions (page 344)	250 mL
1 cup	crumbled Stilton cheese	250 mL
2	sprigs thyme	2

1. Place grated sweet potato and onion in a large sieve. Drain off excess moisture and squeeze dry.

2. In a large bowl, combine sweet potatoes and onion with egg, flour, salt and pepper.

3. In a large skillet, heat 2 tbsp (25 mL) of the oil over medium heat. Working in batches, scoop 1½ tsp (7 mL) vegetable mixture into your hand and form into a small patty. Slip patty into hot oil and brown one side, 2 to 3 minutes. Turn and cook the other side until golden, about 2 minutes more. Repeat with remaining vegetable mixture, adding more oil to pan as needed. Place latkes on prepared baking sheet loosely covered with foil and keep warm in preheated oven. Before serving, top latkes with a small spoonful of Caramelized Onions and top with cheese. A tiny piece of a sprig of thyme is the finishing touch.

Pakoras

MAKES ABOUT 24 SNACKS

Crispy fritters of vegetables cooked in a spicy chickpea batter are a favorite snack. Serve with cooling Spinach Raita (page 356) or a Tamarind Dipping Sauce (page 355). Choose from a variety of vegetables, such as cauliflower florets, matchsticks of sweet potato, slivered bell peppers and spinach leaves.

Tip

Red onions are milder in flavor than familiar brown-skinned "storage" onions (see Tips, page 348). The bright color makes them attractive to use in salads and salsas and to cook on the grill. Some sweet onions, such as Vidalia, Walla Walla and Maui (named after the areas in which they are grown), are mild in flavor and have a balance of sweetness and sharpness that adds interesting flavor to salsas, salads and some cooked dishes.

- **Deep-fryer or heavy-bottomed saucepan with wire basket (see Tips, page 350)**
- **Preheat oven to 300°F (150°C)**

1½ cups	chickpea flour	375 mL
2 tsp	ground coriander	10 mL
2 tsp	garam masala, divided	10 mL
1 tsp	fine sea salt	5 mL
½ tsp	ground turmeric	2 mL
¼ tsp	cayenne pepper	1 mL
1 tbsp	vegetable oil or ghee	15 mL
1 tbsp	freshly squeezed lemon juice	15 mL
⅔ cup	cold water	175 mL
1	red onion, thinly sliced lengthwise (see Tip, left)	1
1	sweet potato, peeled and sliced into matchsticks	1
¼	cauliflower, broken into small florets	¼
	Vegetable oil for deep-frying	

1. In a large bowl, sift together chickpea flour, coriander, 1 tsp (5 mL) of the garam masala, salt, turmeric and cayenne. Make a well in the center. Add oil, lemon juice and ⅓ cup (75 mL) cold water and beat or whisk to make a smooth batter. Whisk in more water by the tablespoonful (15 mL), beating until batter has consistency of thick cream and coats the back of a spoon. Cover and set aside for 10 minutes.

2. Meanwhile, in deep-fryer, preheat oil to 350°F (180°C).

3. Beat batter again for 2 to 3 minutes. Pat vegetables dry with paper towel. Add red onion, sweet potato and cauliflower and stir well to coat. Working in batches, using a small ¼ cup (50 mL) measure, slip a portion of vegetable mixture into hot oil. Turn after 2 minutes to brown evenly. When nicely browned, 2 to 5 minutes, remove with a slotted spoon and place on a rack set on a baking sheet in preheated oven. Fry in small batches. Do not crowd the pan. Sprinkle pakoras with remaining garam masala before serving.

Spicy Coconut Shrimp with Mango Salsa

MAKES 24

Shrimp coated in a crisp golden batter and deep-fried are perennial favorites. Here they provide a taste of the tropics when we roll them in coconut and serve with a fresh Mango Salsa.

Tips

For successful deep-frying be sure that cooking oil is at the correct temperature. An electric deep-fryer has built-in temperature controls. If using a saucepan with wire basket, it's wise to invest in a deep-fry thermometer that can be attached to the side of the saucepan without touching the bottom. You may need to let oil reheat or cool down between batches.

The bread cube test: Lower a cube of fresh bread into hot oil. If it browns in 40 seconds the temperature is about 375°F (190°C), which is the desired temperature for frying most seafood and vegetables.

Preferred oils for deep-frying have a smoking point much higher than the temperature required to cook the food. Most popular are peanut, corn, safflower and soybean oil, since they are bland and have high smoking points.

- **Deep-fryer or large heavy saucepan with wire basket (see Tips, left)**
- **Preheat oven to 300°F (150°C)**
- **Wire rack on a baking sheet, lined with paper towel**

1½ cups	all-purpose flour, divided	375 mL
1 tsp	grated lime zest	5 mL
1 tsp	kosher or sea salt	5 mL
½ tsp	freshly ground black pepper	2 mL
½ tsp	cayenne pepper	2 mL
2	eggs yolks, beaten	2
1 tbsp	freshly squeezed lime juice	15 mL
1 cup	ice water	250 mL
2½ cups	unsweetened long shredded coconut	625 mL
24	large shrimp, peeled, deveined, tail on	24
	Vegetable oil for deep-frying (see Tips, left)	
	Mango Salsa (page 351)	

1. In a large bowl, combine 1 cup (250 mL) of the flour, lime zest, salt, pepper and cayenne. Make a well in the center and add beaten egg yolks, lime juice and ¾ cup (175 mL) ice water. Combine to form a batter. Add 2 to 3 tbsp (25 to 45 mL) extra water as needed to form a light batter. Do not overmix.

2. Place remaining flour and coconut in separate bowls. Pat shrimp dry. Dip each shrimp in flour, coat in batter and roll in coconut. Place on a rack. Discard any excess flour, batter and coconut.

3. Meanwhile, in deep-fryer, preheat oil to 375°F (190°C). Deep-fry shrimp, in batches, until nicely browned, 1 to 2 minutes, depending on size. Do not crowd pan. Transfer to prepared baking sheet. Set aside, loosely covered with foil in preheated oven until all shrimp are cooked. Serve hot with Mango Salsa on the side.

Mango Salsa

Makes 1½ cups (375 mL)

1	ripe mango, diced	1
¼ cup	finely diced red onion	50 mL
¼ cup	finely diced red bell pepper	50 mL
1	jalapeño pepper, seeded and finely diced	1
1 tbsp	freshly squeezed orange juice	15 mL
1 tbsp	red wine vinegar	15 mL
1 tbsp	chopped cilantro	15 mL
	Kosher or sea salt	

1. In a bowl, combine mango, red onion, bell pepper, jalapeño, orange juice, vinegar and cilantro. Season with salt to taste. Set aside for 1 hour for flavors to blend or for up to 4 hours. If keeping for more than 1 hour, add cilantro just prior to serving.

Cheese

The glory that is cheese has nothing to do with the ubiquitous orange slices wrapped in plastic. The glory is the "real" cheese — "milk's leap into immortality" as the U.S. writer Clifton Fadiman called it some 40 years ago. This is the cheese that has been made in farmsteads and dairies since first recorded by the Sumerians about 5,500 BC. This is a simple food packed with valuable nutrients of the milk from which it is made, a source of protein for the working man for centuries, as in the wedge of Cheddar and chunk of crusty bread of the legendary Ploughman's Lunch.

Following a period in the 1900s when industrialization of cheese production reached a peak, there is now a growing urge to return to cheeses of individual character and taste. Today's global distribution networks enable us to experience the great classic cheeses far from their home of origin at peak of flavor. We can feast on a splendid cave-aged Gruyère from the Swiss Alps, a creamy Roquefort Carles from the Rouergue region in France, or a fabulous Manchego made from milk of sheep that graze on La Mancha in Spain. Their unique flavor comes from high-quality milk provided by cows, sheep or goats that graze in regional pastures. They are produced and aged following centuries-old traditional cheese-making methods and the best are handled with infinite care throughout the stressful period of transportation to our markets.

Today, there is a burgeoning group of passionate artisan cheese-makers around the world who are developing new cheeses. A genuine artisan cheese is made by hand on the farm, or in small production at a local independent dairy, from milk (usually unpasteurized) from a single regional source using traditional cheese-making methods. The best artisan cheeses offer uniqueness of flavor and texture that relate to their "terroir." Clifton Fadiman would be very happy.

In the Kitchen
Buying and Storing Cheese

For more than 20 years at All The Best we have pursued a passionate quest to seek out the finest cheeses. It requires working closely with cheese importers and local artisan cheese-makers to find out what wonderful cheeses are at the perfect stage of ripeness. We encourage our customers to taste and discover their favorites, as we do. First you must *smell* to capture and assess the aroma, *look* to judge the appearance and texture, and, most importantly, *take time* to appreciate the first bite and then wait to enjoy the lingering finish.

Every fine cheese has a window of time when the flavor and texture have developed to the point of maximum enjoyment. For some the window is small. When you find a Normandy **Camembert** that has a distinct yet subtle aroma of mushrooms and a tinge of light reddish flecks on the bloomy rind take it home and enjoy on the same day. Firm cheeses, like aged **Cheddar** or firm **Comté**, are more robust, but even then it is best to use within a few days.

Buy cheese freshly cut from the wheel. Wrap the wedge in parchment or waxed paper, place it loosely in a heavy duty plastic bag and keep in the refrigerator, preferably in the vegetable drawer. A fine cheese suffers when tightly wrapped in plastic and stored at a temperature too cold and with little humidity.

Serving Cheese

For a cheese course to serve before dessert at a dinner party consider three to five cheeses that offer interesting variety of appearance, age, texture (soft to firm) and taste (mild to strong). The selection may feature cheeses made from different milks (cow, sheep or goat), cheeses from a particular country, classics from around the world, or, for the adventurous, offer a tasting of new or unfamiliar cheeses. Our best advice is to visit a reliable cheese merchant and make your choices based on which cheeses are at peak of condition that day. Allow about 1 oz (30 g) of each cheese for each person. If the cheese course is to be a main feature of a lunch or party allow about ½ oz (15 g) more per person. Serve cheese at room temperature. Remove from the refrigerator, still wrapped, 30 to 60 minutes before serving. Prepare only the amount you are serving at that time. Cheese dries out if left standing exposed to air for long periods and does not fare well when subjected to changing temperatures. Present cheeses on simple wooden boards or slate or marble slabs and provide a separate sharp knife for each cheese.

Fresh bread is the best accompaniment to cheese — baguette, rustic white or whole wheat breads. Rye is perfect with some firm cheeses, and raisin or walnut breads are wonderful with some **blues** and aged Cheddars. Plain crackers or crisp breads work well but avoid ones that are highly flavored that overwhelm the cheese.

Keep other accompaniments simple. Select fruit and condiments according to the cheese selection and the season: sweet pears, figs, melon and grapes, toasted almonds and walnuts complement salty cheeses; ripe strawberries are delicious with a **triple crème**; quince paste with **Manchego** or a drizzle of honey with **Parmigiano-Reggiano**. And, of course, take your cheese list to the wine store to find the wines to match.

Cooking with Cheese

Cook cheese over gentle heat. When exposed to high heat over a long period of time cheese becomes stringy and the fat tends to separate out. Slice, cube or grate cheese when adding to a dish so that it melts quickly and add toward the end of cooking. Add a cheese topping to a gratinéed dish at the end of cooking and set under a broiler for a few minutes to melt and brown,

watching carefully. Use semisoft cheeses, such as **Mozzarella**, **Fontina d'Aosta** or **Havarti**, sliced or coarsely grated. Finely grate firm and hard cheeses, such as **Parmesan** or **Asiago**.

Soft, fresh cheeses, such as **ricotta** are delicious in fillings for pastries and cannelloni, in lasagna and cheesecakes. Deli-style cream cheese, soft **chèvre** and tangy **feta** are quickly turned into savory dips and spreads. The great melting cheeses **Gruyère**, **Emmental** and **Appenzeller** are the foundation of a fondue, add richness and flavor to creamy sauces and make wonderful grilled sandwiches. Such regal hard cheeses as Parmigiano-Reggiano, **Sbrinz** and **Grana Padano** add ultimate flavor grated into risottos or pasta dishes. Creamy blues, like **Stilton**, **Roquefort** and **Ermite** are crumbled into soups or over salads, made into a spread or added to a filling. And if you have any pieces leftover, throw them in the food processor with a clove of garlic and a dash of white wine and whirl them all together to make a typically thrifty and tasty French spread called "le fromage fort."

Handy measurements
- 1 oz (30 g) cheese = 4 tbsp (60 mL) grated
- 2 oz (60 g) = ½ cup (125 mL) grated
- 8 oz (250 g) = 2 cups (500 mL) grated
- 8 oz (250 g) ricotta = 1 cup (250 mL)

Classic French Cheese Board
Arrange cheese on a wooden board or marble or slate slab. Provide a knife for each variety and a basket of breads or crackers. Allow about 1½ ounces (45 g) cheese per person (i.e. about 2 lbs/1 kg for a party of 20 guests when other food is being served). For a small group, reduce the selection to three cheeses to make a pleasing presentation.

- Saint-Maure (creamy goat's milk)
- Brie de Meaux (soft cow's milk)
- Beaufort (firm cow's milk)
- Roquefort (creamy sheep's milk blue)

Chèvre Tartlets

MAKES 24 TARTLETS

These little tarts are exceptionally tasty and are perfect for a luncheon or tea party as well as the cocktail hour. To offer a selection of small tarts, see the many suggested quiche fillings (Variations, page 249).

- **Preheat oven to 400°F (200°C)**
- **24 mini tartlet pan**
- **Food processor**

	Flaky Pie Pastry (page 409)	
8 oz	chèvre (soft goat's cheese)	250 g
½ cup	whipping (35%) cream	125 mL
¼ cup	butter, softened	50 mL
2	eggs, beaten	2
1 tsp	finely chopped thyme	5 mL
	Salt and freshly ground black pepper	
½ cup	Caramelized Onions (page 344)	125 mL

1. On a lightly floured surface, roll out pastry ⅛ inch (3 mm) thick and cut into 24 circles, each about 3 inches (7.5 cm) in diameter. Line mini tartlet pan with pastry.

2. In a food processor, combine chèvre, cream, butter, eggs, thyme, and salt and pepper to taste. Process until smooth.

3. Place 1 tsp (5 mL) of the Caramelized Onions in the bottom of each tart shell and fill with goat's cheese mixture.

4. Bake in preheated oven until pastry is cooked and filling is puffed, set and lightly browned, 15 to 20 minutes. Serve warm. Tartlets can be made up to 1 day ahead. Keep covered in the refrigerator and place on a baking sheet in a preheated 300°F (150°C) oven for about 10 minutes to warm before serving.

Yogurt Honey Dip

**MAKES 1 CUP
(250 ML)**

This sweet, lightly spiced dip is great to serve with snacks such as Pakoras (page 349).

1 cup	plain yogurt	250 mL
2 tsp	liquid honey	10 mL
¼ tsp	green cardamom seeds, toasted and ground	1 mL

1. In a small bowl, combine yogurt, honey and cardamom. Dip may be made ahead. Keep in a covered container in the refrigerator for up to 1 day.

Tamarind Dipping Sauce

**MAKES 1¼ CUPS
(300 ML)**

This is an excellent sauce to serve with Indian-inspired snacks. You will find that the tart-sweet flavors are also delicious as a dipping sauce for grilled chicken satays.

Food processor or blender

¼ cup	tamarind pulp (see Tips, page 290)	50 mL
1¼ cups	boiling water	300 mL
⅔ cup	raisins	150 mL
2 tsp	packed brown sugar or palm sugar	10 mL
¼ tsp	garam masala	1 mL

1. In a nonreactive bowl, combine tamarind and boiling water. Set aside for 30 minutes. With a fork, break up the softened pulp. Place a sieve over a bowl, pour in the tamarind mixture and force the pulp through the sieve, leaving skin and seeds behind. Discard skin and seeds.
2. In a food processor, combine tamarind liquid, raisins, brown sugar and garam masala and process until smooth. Transfer to a container, cover and refrigerate up to 4 days.

Spinach Raita

**MAKES ABOUT
2 CUPS (500 ML)**

*Here's a refreshing dish to
serve as a condiment with
curries or as a dip with
snacks such as Pakoras
(page 349).*

1 tbsp	vegetable oil	15 mL
1 lb	fresh spinach, trimmed	500 mL
	Salt and freshly ground black pepper	
1½ cups	plain yogurt	375 mL
1 tsp	grated lemon zest	5 mL
1 tbsp	freshly squeezed lemon juice	15 mL
2 tbsp	finely chopped cilantro	25 mL

1. In a large skillet, heat oil over medium heat. Add
   spinach, cover pan and cook, 3 to 4 minutes. Remove
   lid and continue to cook, stirring, until spinach is
   wilted and moisture is evaporated, 2 to 3 minutes more.
   Sprinkle with ¼ tsp (1 mL) salt and a pinch of pepper.
   Transfer to a bowl and let cool. Cover and refrigerate
   until needed, for up to 1 day.
2. About 1 hour before serving, chop spinach and squeeze
   out any remaining moisture. In a bowl, combine spinach
   with yogurt and lemon zest and juice. Stir in cilantro
   and salt and pepper to taste.

Cookies, Quick Breads and Yeast Breads

Rocky Road Cookies

**MAKES ABOUT
5 DOZEN COOKIES**

The best part of a Rocky Road Cookie is when you have chewy, toffee-like melted marshmallow, chocolate, nuts and buttery cookie all in one bite — and if it's just out of the oven it is even better!

Variations

Replace chocolate chunks with chocolate chips or chopped chocolate and pecans with walnuts, if you wish.

- **Preheat oven to 375°F (190°C)**
- **Baking sheets, lined with parchment paper**

2¼ cups	all-purpose flour	550 mL
1 tsp	baking soda	5 mL
½ tsp	salt	2 mL
1 cup	butter, softened	250 mL
¾ cup	granulated sugar	175 mL
¾ cup	packed brown sugar	175 mL
2	eggs	2
1 tsp	vanilla extract	5 mL
1¼ cups	semisweet chocolate chunks	300 mL
1 cup	mini marshmallows	250 mL
1 cup	coarsely chopped pecans	250 mL
¾ cup	butterscotch chips	175 mL

1. In a bowl, combine flour, baking soda and salt. Set aside.

2. In a large bowl, using an electric mixer on medium speed or a wooden spoon, beat butter and granulated and brown sugars until blended. Add eggs, one at a time, beating well after each. Beat in vanilla. With a wooden spoon, gradually add flour mixture, stirring until blended. Stir in chocolate, marshmallows, pecans and butterscotch chips. Mix well.

3. Drop dough by tablespoonfuls (15 mL), about 2 inches (5 cm) apart, onto prepared baking sheets. Bake in preheated oven until golden around edges, 7 to 11 minutes. Let cool for 5 minutes on sheets, then transfer to wire racks and let cool completely.

Cookie Tips

In our kitchen you will see the bakers creaming pounds of butter and sugar in a giant floor mixer and cracking dozens of eggs into a bowl to be added to cookie batters. At home, cookie making is made effortless with the use of a standing or hand-held electric mixer, but all you really need is a bowl, a wooden spoon and some good muscles. Place your bowl on a damp tea towel. This keeps the bowl steady and prevents it from "walking" across the counter as you beat and mix.

If you use a standing mixer you will find it handy to combine dry ingredients on a square of wax paper instead of a bowl. The paper can be formed into a cone shape, which makes it easy to add flour gradually into a mixing batter. You save some of the washing up, too.

Cookies quickly become overbaked and too crisp. Remove them from the oven when the edges are beginning to brown. Remember they continue to cook a little when they come out of the oven. If you like chewy cookies, underbake them by 1 to 2 minutes.

Parchment paper is invaluable in the kitchen. It even prevents melted marshmallows from sticking. If you are a passionate baker you might like to invest in a few Silpat baking pan liners. These silicone-covered glass mesh sheets come in various sizes, and are nonstick and reuseable. They replace greasing or lining pans.

Take note of how the heat circulates in your oven. Every oven has its idiosyncrasies and hot spots. In order to bake cookies and cakes evenly do not crowd the oven. Bake one sheet at a time or arrange sheets in top and bottom third of the oven. Rotate the sheets during baking.

Storage Tips

Enjoy freshly baked cookies with a minimum of fuss. Our cookie recipes include a good proportion of butter so the raw cookie dough freezes well. Pack cookie dough firmly into a freezer container. Place plastic wrap over the surface and seal with a tight-fitting lid. Label and date. For even greater convenience, scoop prepared cookie dough into desired portions and place on baking sheets. Place in the freezer until solidly frozen, about 1 hour. Transfer frozen cookie dough scoops into freezer bags. Press out as much air as possible and seal securely. Freeze for up to 6 months. Don't forget to date and label. When ready to bake, let dough come to room temperature. Form and bake cookies as directed.

Buttery shortbreads freeze well. Freeze when completely cool as soon after baking as possible. Arrange cookies in layers between sheets of parchment paper in a freezer container with a tight-fitting lid. Label and date. Freeze for up to 4 months. Remove from freezer and let stand at room temperature in packaging for several hours before serving. For best quality, only remove from the freezer the amount of shortbreads that will be enjoyed on the same day.

Cherries 'n' Chunks Cookies

MAKES ABOUT
5 DOZEN COOKIES

This has to be one of our all-time favorite cookies. Sometimes we bake mini Cherries 'n' Chunks and drizzle them with melted white chocolate for a tea party. Dried cherries are a bit of a luxury, but worth it with every bite.

- Preheat oven to 375°F (190°C)
- Baking sheets, lined with parchment paper

2¼ cups	all-purpose flour	550 mL
1 tsp	baking powder	5 mL
½ tsp	baking soda	2 mL
½ tsp	salt	2 mL
1 cup	butter, softened	250 mL
¾ cup	granulated sugar	175 mL
¾ cup	packed brown sugar	175 mL
2	eggs	2
1 tsp	almond extract	5 mL
1½ cups	chopped white chocolate	375 mL
1½ cups	dried cherries	375 mL
1½ cups	slivered almonds	375 mL

1. In a bowl, combine flour, baking powder, baking soda and salt. Set aside.

2. In a large bowl, using an electric mixer on medium speed or a wooden spoon, beat butter and granulated and brown sugars until blended. Add eggs, one at a time, beating well after each. Beat in almond extract. With a wooden spoon, gradually add flour mixture, mixing until blended. Stir in chocolate, dried cherries and almonds with a wooden spoon. Mix well.

3. Drop dough by tablespoonfuls (15 mL), about 2 inches (5 cm) apart, on prepared baking sheets. Bake in preheated oven until golden around edges, 9 to 12 minutes. Let cool for 5 minutes on sheets, then transfer to wire racks and let cool completely.

Nuts in the Bakery

We use many varieties of nuts in our bakery and each variety adds distinct flavor to baked cookies, cakes, loaves, breads and desserts. Almonds, walnuts, pecans, hazelnuts, macadamia nuts and pine nuts are staples. Always make sure that the nuts you purchase are fresh. They tend to go rancid quickly, especially in warm cupboards. For short storage time toast nuts and store in a covered container in the refrigerator; for longer periods, store in the freezer and toast just before using.

Orange Cranberry Oat Cookies

**MAKES ABOUT
3 DOZEN COOKIES**

This is a great cookie for the lunch box. They keep well until the cookie jar is discovered!

Tips

Old-fashioned or large-flake rolled oats are larger with thicker flakes so they give cookies a more "oaty" taste and rustic appearance.

Corn syrup in the batter contributes to a cookie with chewy texture. If you like crisp cookies, bake them a little longer.

Variations

Oat and Seed Cookies:
Consider substituting a mix of nutritious nuts and seeds for a portion of the oatmeal. Include sweetened flaked coconut, sesame seeds, flax seeds, sunflower seeds, green pumpkin seeds or chopped pecans in your favorite combination.

Replace cranberries with chocolate or butterscotch chips for a more decadent treat.

Add 1/2 cup (125 mL) sweetened flaked coconut to the dough.

- Preheat oven to 350°F (180°C)
- Baking sheets, lined with parchment paper

1¼ cups	all-purpose flour	300 mL
1 tsp	baking soda	5 mL
¾ tsp	salt	3 mL
1 cup	butter, softened	250 mL
1½ cups	packed brown sugar	375 mL
1	egg	1
1 tbsp	corn syrup (see Tips, left)	15 mL
1 tbsp	grated orange zest	15 mL
3½ cups	old-fashioned rolled oats (see Tips, left)	875 mL
1½ cups	dried cranberries	375 mL

1. In a bowl, combine flour, baking soda and salt. Set aside.
2. In a large bowl, using an electric mixer on medium speed or a wooden spoon, beat butter and brown sugar until blended. Add egg and beat well. Beat in corn syrup and orange zest. With a wooden spoon, gradually add flour mixture, mixing until blended. With a wooden spoon, stir in oats and cranberries. Mix well.
3. Drop dough by tablespoonfuls (15 mL), about 2 inches (5 cm) apart, on prepared baking sheets. Press flat with a floured fork or palm of your hand. Bake in preheated oven until golden and slightly firm to the touch, 13 to 17 minutes. Let cool for 5 minutes on sheets, then transfer to wire racks and let cool completely.

Decadent Chocolate Cookies

**MAKES ABOUT
4 DOZEN COOKIES**

*Is it a brownie, or is it
a cookie? This fudgy
cookie is for serious
chocolate-lovers. Loaded
with chocolate, they are
completely irresistible
warm from the oven,
perhaps paired with a
bowl of super deluxe
vanilla ice cream and
sliced strawberries.*

Tips

Remove cookies from the
oven when the center is still
soft. They'll firm up on cooling.

Vanilla is native to the tropical
rain forests of Mexico and
Central America. The dark
brown pods are "sweated" in
the sun and then cured for 6
to 9 months, a process that
develops vanillin, which gives
the pods their unique flavor
and aroma. We recommend
that you use only pure vanilla
extract in all your baking.

Variations

Replace chocolate chunks with
chocolate chips, if you wish.

For a black and white version,
replace semisweet chocolate
chunks with white chocolate.

- **Preheat oven to 375°F (190°C)**
- **Baking sheets, lined with parchment paper**

⅔ cup	all-purpose flour	150 mL
½ tsp	baking powder	2 mL
¼ tsp	salt	1 mL
8 oz	semisweet chocolate, chopped	250 g
3 oz	unsweetened chocolate, chopped	90 g
½ cup	butter	125 mL
3	eggs	3
1¼ cups	granulated sugar	300 mL
1 tsp	vanilla extract (see Tips, left)	5 mL
2 cups	semisweet chocolate chunks	500 mL
1 cup	coarsely chopped pecans	250 mL

1. In a bowl, combine flour, baking powder and salt. Set aside.

2. In a saucepan over low heat, melt chopped semisweet and unsweetened chocolate and butter, stirring until smooth. Let cool.

3. In a large bowl, using an electric mixer on high speed, beat eggs and sugar until pale and thick, about 5 minutes. With a wooden spoon, stir in melted chocolate mixture and vanilla. Stir in flour mixture, mixing until smooth. Stir in chocolate chunks and pecans. Mix well.

4. Drop dough by tablespoonfuls (15 mL), about 2 inches (5 cm) apart, on prepared baking sheets. Bake in preheated oven just until tops start to crack and insides are still moist, 8 to 12 minutes. Let cool for 10 minutes on sheets or until firm enough to move, then transfer to wire racks and let cool completely.

Norwegian Lace Cookies

MAKES ABOUT
4 DOZEN COOKIES

Light and crisp, these cookies are a delicious accompaniment to a bowl of ice cream, gelato or fresh fruit.

Tip
Use quick-cooking oats in this recipe. Old-fashioned or instant oats will not result in cookies of crisp, fine texture.

Variations
Add a little spice, such as ½ tsp (2 mL) ground cinnamon or ginger, to the dry ingredients, or the grated zest of an orange or lemon to the batter, for a change in flavor.

Preheat oven to 350°F (180°C)

Baking sheets, lined with parchment paper

1 cup	quick-cooking rolled oats (see Tip, left)	250 mL
1 cup	finely chopped walnuts	250 mL
3 tbsp	all-purpose flour	45 mL
1 tsp	baking powder	5 mL
½ tsp	salt	2 mL
½ cup	butter, softened	125 mL
1 cup	packed brown sugar	250 mL
1	egg	1
1 tsp	vanilla extract	5 mL

1. In a bowl, combine oats, walnuts, flour, baking powder and salt. Set aside.

2. In a large bowl, using an electric mixer on medium speed or a wooden spoon, beat butter and brown sugar until blended. Add egg and vanilla, beating until smooth. With a wooden spoon, stir in nut mixture. Mix well.

3. Drop by rounded teaspoonfuls (5 mL), about 2 inches (5 cm) apart, on prepared baking sheets. Bake in preheated oven until golden, 5 to 9 minutes. Let cool for 5 minutes on sheets, then transfer to wire racks and let cool completely.

Lemon Sugar Cookies

**MAKES ABOUT
3½ DOZEN COOKIES**

*Lemon zest adds
wonderful fresh flavor
to a tender crisp sugar
wafer. This is a very
versatile cookie that
can be modified to suit
many occasions.*

Tip

Chill dough for about
30 minutes for easy rolling. Use
your favorite cookie cutters.
Larger cookies will require a
longer baking time. If you wish
to decorate the cookies after
they are cool, omit the sugar
sprinkle before baking.

Variations

Holiday Cookies: Replace lemon
zest and juice with 1 tsp (5 mL)
vanilla. Use your favorite cookie
cutters for the season, such as
trees and Santas at Christmas;
bunnies and eggs at Easter;
or pumpkins at Halloween.
Sprinkle with colored sugar or
decorate with icing.

Jammies: Cut cookie rounds,
each 1½ inches (4 cm). Stamp
out a small shape (a heart,
star or circle) in half of cookie
rounds. These will form top
of a sandwich cookie. Bake
cookies as directed but
reduce baking time to 12 to
16 minutes. When cool, place
cookies without the cut out,
good side down, and spread
with raspberry or apricot jam.
Dust good side of cookies with
the cut out with confectioner's
sugar and place on top of jam.
Press cookies together gently
to form a cookie sandwich.

- Preheat oven to 325°F (160°C)
- 2-inch (5 cm) round cookie cutter
- Baking sheets, lined with parchment paper

2 cups	all-purpose flour	500 mL
½ tsp	baking powder	2 mL
¼ tsp	salt	1 mL
½ cup	butter, softened	125 mL
1 cup	granulated sugar	250 mL
1	egg	1
1 tbsp	grated lemon zest	15 mL
1 tbsp	lemon juice	15 mL
	Coarse or granulated sugar	

1. In a bowl, combine flour, baking powder and salt. Set aside.

2. In a large bowl, using an electric mixer on medium speed or a wooden spoon, beat butter and sugar until blended. Add egg and lemon zest and juice, beating until smooth. With a wooden spoon, gradually add flour mixture, mixing until blended.

3. On a lightly floured surface, roll out dough to ¼-inch (0.5 cm) thickness. Cut into 2-inch (5 cm) rounds with a floured cookie cutter, rerolling scraps. Place on prepared baking sheets, about 1 inch (2.5 cm) apart. Sprinkle with coarse sugar. Bake in preheated oven until golden around edges, 15 to 20 minutes. Let cool for 10 minutes on sheets, then transfer to wire racks and let cool completely.

Eggs

There is something about the egg that has captivated humankind since the plasma cooled and whatever marine life they were before developed, a few billion years later, into chickens. Ancient Egyptians knew that the great god Ptah created the egg, bypassing the first chicken entirely, from the sun and the moon; North American Indians, on the other hand, held that the world was created by the Great Spirit bursting forth from a giant golden egg. No word here, either, on where that egg came from. Maybe after all a hen is merely the egg's way of making another egg.

Today, given to more localized pleasures, we have our own certainty: Cent per gram, the egg should be valued as the greatest food value available to us — "as close to perfection," in the words of one American cooking maven, "as this world affords." Low in calories, high in protein, all the essential vitamins but one, impressive amounts of iron and phosphorus — add a glass of fresh O.J. to make up for the missing C, and perfection is at hand. Inexpensive, too: selective breeding has produced hens that lay more eggs than they can hatch, so egg production per hen today is well over 300 — four times more than what it was a century ago.

There was a time, in the '70s, when fear of excess dietary cholesterol gave eggs a hard time. Taste great, but bad for the heart. With time came wisdom: a study of 27,000 subjects by the American College of Nutrition has shown that the risk of cardiovascular disease in men and women did not increase with increased egg consumption. To top it off, thanks to less fat and more nutrients in their diet, hens now produce eggs with 25 percent less cholesterol than they did in the '70s.

So no guilt any more with an egg a day, for most of us. There are still some people with habitually high blood cholesterol levels, and for these we suggest egg whites alone. Gently fried, they work well as a go-with in sandwiches, and in recipes calling for one egg yolk, two whites can often be used instead. Whites also contain the egg's full supply of potassium, which fights heart disease and rheumatoid arthritis, and are an excellent source of protein.

In the Kitchen

Eggs are graded as to the quality of their shell, the size of air cell and yolk and the firmness of the white. Grades AA, A and B make it to the supermarkets in the U.S. In Canada only Grade A eggs are sold in grocery stores. Sizes range from **Pee Wee** to **Jumbo**. The most commonly used sizes are **Medium** (U.S. 21 ounces per dozen; Canada 40 to 55 grams each), **Large** (U.S. 24 ounces per dozen; Canada 56 to 62 grams each) and **Extra-large** (U.S. 27 ounces per dozen; Canada 63 to 69 grams each). One large whole egg yields 3 tbsp (45 mL). One large egg yolk yields 1 tbsp (15 mL) and one large egg white yields 2 tbsp (25 mL). When substituting one size for another, take note of the weight and volume.

Brown or white, organic eggs, omega-3 eggs and free-range eggs all have some benefits over the stock supermarket supply. Pastured eggs, that is, eggs from true free-range hens raised on grass, are best of all — with less cholesterol, twice as much omega-3, three times more vitamin E, and four to six times more vitamin D than any of them. But first find the farm that produces them, and expect to pay for all those benefits when you do. The taste will be a revelation.

The Best Gingerbread

There is some controversy about whether a gingerbread cookie should be slightly chewy or crisp! This buttery gingerbread is crisp and spiced just right. Our pastry chefs create and decorate whimsical gingerbread cookies to suit every season and occasion, and particularly at holiday time the activity reaches fever pitch.

- Cookie cutters (gingerbread boys and girls), about 2½ inches (6 cm)
- Baking sheets

6½ cups	all-purpose flour	1.625 L
4 tsp	ground cinnamon	20 mL
4 tsp	ground ginger	20 mL
1 tsp	ground cloves	5 mL
1 tsp	baking soda	5 mL
¼ tsp	salt	1 mL
2 cups	butter, softened	500 mL
2 cups	packed dark brown sugar	500 mL
1 cup	light (fancy) molasses	250 mL
	Decorative (Royal) Icing (page 367)	

1. In a bowl, combine flour, cinnamon, ginger, cloves, baking soda and salt. Set aside.

2. In a large bowl, using an electric mixer on medium speed or a wooden spoon, cream butter and brown sugar until blended. Add molasses and beat until smooth. On low speed or with a wooden spoon, gradually add flour mixture, mixing until blended. Divide gingerbread dough into 2 disks. Wrap securely in parchment or plastic wrap and refrigerate for 30 minutes or for up to 8 hours.

3. On a lightly floured surface, roll dough out to ⅛- to ¼-inch (3 mm to 0.5 cm) thickness. Stamp out shapes with floured cookie cutters as desired. Place on baking sheets, about 1 inch (2.5 cm) apart. Bake in preheated oven until firm and lightly browned, 10 to 15 minutes, depending on size of cutouts. Be vigilant, as cookies brown quickly in the last few minutes. Let cool for 10 minutes on baking sheets, then transfer to racks to cool completely. Gingerbread becomes crisp when cool. Decorate with icing when completely cooled.

Decorative (Royal) Icing

Makes 3 cups (750 mL)

3	egg whites (see Tips, right)	3
½ tsp	cream of tartar	2 mL
3 to 4 cups	sifted confectioner's (icing) sugar	750 mL to 1 L
1 tsp	vanilla extract, optional	5 mL
	Gel paste colors (see Tips, right)	

1. In a large bowl, using an electric mixer on medium-high speed or with a large whisk, beat egg whites with cream of tartar until frothy. Add icing sugar, ½ cup (125 mL) at a time, and beat until mixture is smooth and shiny. Add extra icing sugar by the spoonful until the icing holds soft peaks. Add vanilla, if using. Divide icing into small bowls and add gel paste colors as needed.

Tips

This recipe contains raw egg whites. If you are concerned about the safety of using raw egg whites, use 6 tbsp (90 mL) pasteurized liquid egg whites and/or meringue powder instead. Meringue powder is readily available at the supermarket and each brand provides good instructions for use.

In our kitchen, the pastry chefs use gel paste colors to color icing. Divide white icing into bowls and add color as needed, a tiny bit at a time; we dip the paste from the pot with a wooden toothpick. The basic colors (red, yellow, blue and black) are all you need. To get intense red or black you will need to add a larger amount of color paste.

Gingersnaps

**MAKES ABOUT
4 DOZEN COOKIES**

We love the warm, spicy flavor of ginger and use it in the bakery in many forms — ground ginger, crystallized ginger, freshly grated gingerroot, preserved ginger in syrup and even pickled ginger. These spicy cookies are a perennial favorite and are delicious with a bowl of lemon or mango sorbet.

Tip

For crisp cookies, press the balls flat with the bottom of a glass dipped in sugar. If you like chewy cookies, do not flatten before baking.

Variations

For an extra hit of ginger, add 2 tbsp (25 mL) minced gingerroot to the dough with the egg, or add 2 to 3 tbsp (25 to 45 mL) chopped crystallized ginger.

- Preheat oven to 350°F (180°C)
- Baking sheets, lined with parchment paper

2 cups	all-purpose flour	500 mL
2 tsp	baking soda	10 mL
1 tsp	ground cinnamon	5 mL
1 tsp	ground ginger	5 mL
½ tsp	ground cloves	2 mL
¼ tsp	ground allspice	1 mL
¼ tsp	salt	1 mL
¼ tsp	ground black pepper	1 mL
¾ cup	butter, softened	175 mL
1 cup	granulated sugar	250 mL
1	egg	1
¼ cup	fancy (light) molasses	50 mL
	Granulated sugar for coating	

1. In a bowl, combine flour, baking soda, cinnamon, ginger, cloves, allspice, salt and pepper. Set aside.

2. In a large bowl, using an electric mixer on medium speed or a wooden spoon, beat butter and sugar until blended. Add egg and molasses, beating until smooth. With a wooden spoon, gradually add flour mixture, mixing until blended.

3. Shape dough into 1-inch (2.5 cm) balls. Roll in sugar and place on prepared baking sheets, about 2 inches (5 cm) apart. Bake in preheated oven until edges are starting to brown, 10 to 12 minutes. Let cool for 10 minutes on sheets, then transfer to wire racks and let cool completely.

Nut Biscotti

*Biscotti originated in the
Veneto region in Italy.
The dough is usually
not overly sweet and is
twice baked to produce
hard, crisp cookies perfect
for dipping into vino
santo, or to accompany
an espresso. This "nutty"
version is packed with
chunky almonds.*

Tip

Knead the almonds into the
dough with your hands, if it
is easier.

Variations

Replace half of the almonds
with ¾ cup (175 mL) dried
cranberries and include
orange zest instead of lemon.

Dip one end of the cooled
biscotti in melted semisweet
chocolate, if you wish.

- Preheat oven to 350°F (180°C)
- Baking sheet, lined with parchment paper

2 cups	all-purpose flour	500 mL
⅓ cup	ground hazelnuts	75 mL
1¼ tsp	baking powder	6 mL
¼ tsp	salt	1 mL
2	eggs	2
¾ cup	granulated sugar	175 mL
½ cup	sunflower oil	125 mL
1 tbsp	grated lemon zest	15 mL
1 cup	whole unblanched almonds	250 mL

1. In a bowl, combine flour, ground hazelnuts, baking powder and salt. Set aside.

2. In a large bowl, whisk together eggs, sugar, oil and lemon zest until smooth. Add flour mixture, stirring with a wooden spoon until dough comes together. Stir in almonds.

3. Divide dough in half. Shape each half into a log about 8 inches (20 cm) long. Place logs, about 4 inches (10 cm) apart, on prepared baking sheet. Flatten to about 3 inches (7.5 cm) wide. Bake in preheated oven until light golden, for 35 minutes.

4. Leave oven on and remove logs from baking sheet. Let cool on a rack for 15 minutes. Transfer to a cutting board. Cut on a slight diagonal into ½-inch (1 cm) thick slices. Arrange cut side up on baking sheet and return to the oven to bake for 10 minutes. Turn slices over and bake until crisp and golden, 5 to 10 minutes more. Transfer to wire racks and let cool completely.

Butter

Butter is something unique in the world of animal fats. No animals are killed to make it. Butter can transform anything it touches, starting with melting on the tongue. It heightens the flavors of everything we eat and adds a sense of luxury, close to sin, while doing so. No imitation, no matter how trans-fat free, comes close. Life can never be so troubled, its prospects never so dire, that butter, judiciously applied, would not provide surcease and sudden pleasure — if only until you apply it again.

For centuries butter was considered a peasant food, even in the north, and the great and the good ignored it except, when pushed, as a substitute for oil in their lamps. But with the Renaissance came the people in between, the middle class, who liked it a lot — and who were further encouraged by the Reformation in the 16th century, when butter was no longer banned during fasting periods or Lent.

Gradually butter's status grew, and as it grew it became expensive and a prerogative of the rich, who had previously favored lard for cooking. And then in the latter part of the 20th century its status dropped, amid absurdly exaggerated claims that it was a death trap for all of us. In a century North American consumption dropped some 75 percent. It is far too good a staff of life to stay that way. We must come to our senses and realize that butter is good for us.

Our butter is 80 percent fat, 50 percent of that saturated, but it may boost our immune system and help lower bad LDL cholesterol levels. Also in there: Vitamins A, D, E and K, zinc, iodine, lecithin and copper.

In the Kitchen

Mass-produced and highly regulated (including no more than 16 percent moisture, 1.5 percent milk solids and 2.5 percent salt), butter can be stored for long periods in the refrigerator — indeed may be frozen for months before it reaches the market shelves. The result is fluctuating quality and a certain uniformity of flavor. Where possible, seek out small private butter producers making butter from grass-fed cows with fat content in the high 80s and consequently lower moisture levels. The product will be a revelation.

Sweet cream butters, made from pasteurized fresh cream, predominate in North America and the United Kingdom.

Cultured butter, from pasteurized fermented cream, is the favorite in continental Europe. Both can be salted to add taste — notably when used on bread with jams. In our kitchen we use only freshly churned unsalted (sweet) butter. Our chefs prefer to control and add salt, as needed.

European-style butter, a little more expensive with a higher butterfat content than regular butter, is good for sauces to create a true "butter" taste and mouth feel; available in specialty food stores.

Whipped butter is aerated with nitrogen gas and designed to be spreadable. It is not recommended for cooking.

Ghee and clarified butter are often used interchangeably. Both are melted butter — but they are not the same thing. Ghee is cooked after the butter is melted, which gives it a higher smoke point than butter. Thus it can be heated to higher temperatures than clarified butter. It also has more flavor and will keep longer, sometimes for more than a century.

Maple Shortbread

Over the years this maple-flavored shortbread has become one of our signature cookies. We cut them out in a maple leaf shape and sprinkle them with real maple sugar to make them very special. They've even been sent to Ottawa, our federal capital, to be presented at a state occasion!

Tip

Maple sugar is made from the crystals left when maple sap is boiled past the syrup stage until almost dry. It has a wonderful sweet, true maple taste. About 85 percent of maple syrup produced in the world is made in Canada, New England and New York State. If you can't find maple sugar, simply sprinkle cookies with coarse granulated sugar.

- **Preheat oven to 325°F (160°C)**
- **3-inch (7.5 cm) maple leaf cookie cutter**
- **Baking sheets**

2 cups	all-purpose flour	500 mL
2 tbsp	cornstarch	25 mL
1/4 tsp	salt	1 mL
1 cup	butter, softened	250 mL
1/2 cup	packed dark brown sugar	125 mL
1 tbsp	maple extract	15 mL
3/4 cup	granulated maple sugar (see Tip, left)	175 mL

1. In a bowl, combine flour, cornstarch and salt. Set aside.

2. In a large bowl, using an electric mixer on medium speed or a wooden spoon, cream butter, brown sugar and maple extract until blended. On low speed or with a wooden spoon, gradually add flour mixture, mixing until blended. Knead by hand to form a smooth dough.

3. On a lightly floured surface, roll out dough to 1/4-inch (0.5 cm) thickness. Cut into maple leaves using a floured cookie cutter. Place on baking sheets, about 1 inch (2.5 cm) apart. Sprinkle generously with maple sugar. Bake in preheated oven until starting to brown around edges, 15 to 20 minutes. Let cool for 10 minutes on sheets, then transfer to wire racks and let cool completely.

Ginger Lime Shortbread

The buttery cookies known as shortbreads originated in Scotland way back in the 15th century and are usually associated with the holiday season — a tin of shortbreads makes a great gift. Originally, shortbreads included finely ground oats but today, starting from the basic mix of butter, sugar and flour, our shortbreads appear flavored in dozens of ways and in many different shapes and sizes.

Tips

Shortbreads keep well. Store in a well-sealed container in a cool spot for up to 1 month. Keep very aromatic shortbreads in separate containers. The lime and ginger flavors in this shortbread will permeate other cookies in the container. They can be frozen, but the texture will be altered slightly.

A sliver of crystallized ginger placed on top before baking looks great.

- **Preheat oven to 325°F (160°C)**
- **2-inch (5 cm) round cookie cutter**
- **Baking sheets**

1¾ cups	all-purpose flour	425 mL
½ cup	cornstarch	125 mL
1 tsp	ground ginger	5 mL
¼ tsp	salt	1 mL
1 cup	butter, softened	250 mL
½ cup	packed brown sugar	125 mL
2 tsp	grated lime zest	10 mL
½ cup	finely chopped crystallized ginger	125 mL

1. In a bowl, combine flour, cornstarch, ground ginger and salt. Set aside.

2. In a large bowl, using an electric mixer on medium speed or a wooden spoon, cream butter, brown sugar and lime zest until blended. With a wooden spoon, gradually add flour mixture, mixing until blended. Knead by hand to form a smooth dough. Knead in crystallized ginger.

3. On a lightly floured surface, roll out dough to ¼-inch (0.5 cm) thickness. Cut into rounds with floured cookie cutter. Place on baking sheets, about 1 inch (2.5 cm) apart. Bake in preheated oven until starting to brown around edges, 15 to 25 minutes. Let cool for 10 minutes on sheets, then transfer to wire racks and let cool completely.

Brown Sugar Chocolate Shortbread

MAKES ABOUT 3½ DOZEN COOKIES

This melt-in-the-mouth shortbread with the caramel taste of brown sugar and shavings of rich chocolate is one of my personal favorites. A bowl of fresh raspberries and one of these shortbreads is my idea of the perfect dessert.

Tip

Chop chocolate with a sharp chef's knife to get a mixture of shavings and pieces, which give the shortbread an attractive appearance and delicious crunch.

Variations

Replace chopped chocolate with chips or chunks.

Replace semisweet chocolate with bittersweet chocolate.

Add ½ cup (125 mL) chopped pecans or hazelnuts, chopped crystallized ginger or chopped tart dried cherries to the dough along with the chocolate.

- **Preheat oven to 325°F (160°C)**
- **Baking sheets**

2 cups	all-purpose flour	500 mL
2 tbsp	cornstarch	25 mL
¼ tsp	salt	1 mL
1 cup	butter, softened	250 mL
½ cup	packed dark brown sugar	125 mL
1 tsp	vanilla extract	5 mL
¾ cup	chopped semisweet chocolate (see Tip, left)	175 mL

1. In a bowl, combine flour, cornstarch and salt. Set aside.

2. In a large bowl, using an electric mixer on medium speed or a wooden spoon, cream butter, brown sugar and vanilla until blended. With a wooden spoon, gradually add flour mixture, mixing until blended. Knead by hand to form a smooth dough. Work in chocolate until evenly distributed.

3. On a lightly floured surface, roll dough out to ¼-inch (0.5 cm) thickness. Cut into 2-inch (5 cm) squares with a knife. Place on baking sheets, about 1 inch (2.5 cm) apart. Bake in preheated oven until golden around edges, 15 to 25 minutes. Let cool for 10 minutes on sheets, then transfer to wire racks and let cool completely.

Apple Cinnamon Streusel Loaf

This moist and delicious loaf is the perfect lunchbox treat. Change the flavor by using different varieties of firm apple. Granny Smith and Golden Delicious keep their shape well during baking and each provides a distinctive taste.

Variations

Replace apple with pear.

Replace cinnamon with ginger.

- Preheat oven to 350°F (180°C)
- 9- by 5-inch (23 by 12.5 cm) loaf pan, greased and lined with parchment paper

2 cups	all-purpose flour	500 mL
1 tsp	baking powder	5 mL
1 tsp	ground cinnamon	5 mL
½ tsp	baking soda	2 mL
¼ tsp	salt	1 mL
½ cup	butter, softened	125 mL
¾ cup	packed brown sugar	175 mL
2	eggs	2
½ cup	sour cream	125 mL
½ cup	unsweetened apple juice	125 mL
1 tsp	vanilla extract	5 mL
1½ cups	peeled diced apples (2 small apples)	375 mL
	Streusel (see below)	

1. In a bowl, combine flour, baking powder, cinnamon, baking soda and salt. Set aside.

2. In a large bowl, using an electric mixer on medium speed or a wooden spoon, beat butter and brown sugar until blended. Add eggs, one at a time, beating until smooth. Add sour cream, apple juice and vanilla. Mix well.

3. On low speed or with a wooden spoon, add flour mixture, mixing until blended. Stir in apple. Spread batter into prepared pan. Sprinkle streusel over top. Bake in preheated oven until a tester inserted in center comes out clean, 65 to 75 minutes. Let cool for 15 minutes in pan on a wire rack, then remove from pan and let cool completely on rack.

Streusel

Makes about ⅔ cup (150 mL)

⅓ cup	all-purpose flour	75 mL
⅓ cup	packed brown sugar	75 mL
3 tbsp	butter, cold	45 mL
1 tsp	ground cinnamon	5 mL
¼ tsp	ground ginger	1 mL

1. In a bowl, combine flour, brown sugar, butter, cinnamon and ginger, mixing with a pastry blender or your fingertips until mixture resembles coarse crumbs. Refrigerate streusel for 15 minutes before sprinkling on cake.

Give It a Rise

Most of our baking recipes include chemical leavening agents in addition to the natural method of incorporating airiness by careful mixing and/or beaten egg whites. The most familiar is double-acting baking powder. Different brands on the market contain various blends of ingredients but in most cases the action is caused by two acid salts — monocalcium phosphate and sodium aluminum sulphate. One reacts when in contact with a liquid and the other responds to heat to create air bubbles, which cause a batter to rise. The combination is convenient since it allows for a more continuous rising action over a longer period of time. It has a shelf life of up to 1 year and, once the package is opened, effectiveness diminishes over time. Our pastry chefs recommend a non-aluminum baking powder to produce a more tender, better tasting pastry (sometimes you may be aware of a metallic taste to many commercial baked products).

To substitute 1 tsp (5 mL) double-action baking powder, combine ¼ tsp (1 mL) baking soda, ½ tsp (2 mL) cream of tartar and ½ tsp (2 mL) cornstarch.

Cream of tartar is made from tartaric acid, a sediment left in wine bottles after fermentation that is purified and ground to a fine powder. When beating egg whites, a pinch of cream of tartar is sometimes added to make the beaten whites more stable.

Baking soda (bicarbonate of soda or sodium bicarbonate) is familiar in the home. It is an effective neutralizer of acids, and a useful cleaner and deodorizer in the refrigerator. In baking it is activated when in contact with an acidic ingredient to produce carbon dioxide that causes a batter to rise. Such acidic ingredients include buttermilk, molasses, non-alkalized cocoa powder, dark brown sugar and citrus juices. Always mix baking soda with dry ingredients first and if blending with wet ingredients, add it at end of blending. Bake as soon as possible.

Big Batch Bran Muffins

*This was where it all
began! These muffins,
made with natural bran
and buttermilk, were the
first products we made
in our small countertop
mixer when All The
Best opened its doors
25 years ago. The batter
is prepared ahead and is
ready to be scooped and
baked as needed.*

Tips

Measure oil first then honey
and molasses. The sticky
stuff will slip easily out of the
measuring cup.

In all cake and muffin baking
have your ingredients at room
temperature before starting
to mix for easy blending.

Wheat bran is the outer layer
of the wheat kernel that is high
in carbohydrates, calcium and
fiber. Wheat germ is the highly
nutritious core of the wheat
kernel. We add bran and
wheat germ to some of our
breads, muffins, cookies and
loaves for hearty nutty flavor
and added health benefit.

Variations

Add raisins, chopped dates or
apricots to the mixture either
when mixing or when ready
to bake.

Replace whole wheat flour
with all-purpose for a less
"bran" taste.

● **Muffin pan, greased or lined with paper muffin cups**

6½ cups	natural bran (see Tips, left)	1.625 L
4 cups	whole wheat flour	1 L
7 tsp	baking soda	35 mL
1½ tsp	salt	7 mL
8	eggs	8
⅔ cup	packed brown sugar	150 mL
3 cups	buttermilk	750 mL
1⅓ cups	sunflower oil	325 mL
1½ cups	liquid honey	375 mL
1½ cups	light (fancy) molasses	375 mL

1. In a bowl, combine bran, flour, baking soda and salt. Set aside.

2. In a large bowl, whisk together eggs, brown sugar, buttermilk, sunflower oil, honey and molasses until smoothly blended. Add flour mixture. Mix well. Cover and refrigerate overnight or for up to 6 weeks.

3. Preheat oven to 400°F (200°C).

4. Spoon batter into prepared muffin cups, filling almost full.

5. Bake in preheated oven until top springs back when lightly touched, 20 to 25 minutes. Let cool for 10 minutes in pan on a wire rack, then remove from pan and let cool.

Cranberry Orange Loaf

MAKES 1 LOAF

Keep a supply of cranberries in your freezer to enjoy this loaf year round.

Tips

Chopping the cranberries distributes the fruit more evenly through the batter.

Add a sprinkling of sugar over the batter before baking for a nice glistening finish.

Variations

Replace cranberries with blueberries or chocolate chips.

Mixed Berry Loaf: Replace orange zest with lemon zest and replace cranberries with a mixture of fresh berries such as blueberries, raspberries, blackberries or strawberries.

- Preheat oven to 350°F (180°C)
- 9- by 5-inch (23 by 12.5 cm) loaf pan, greased and lined with parchment paper

1½ cups	all-purpose flour	375 mL
½ cup	granulated sugar	125 mL
2 tsp	baking powder	10 mL
½ tsp	baking soda	2 mL
¼ tsp	salt	1 mL
1	egg	1
1¼ cups	sour cream	300 mL
⅓ cup	butter, melted	75 mL
1 tbsp	grated orange zest	15 mL
1 cup	cranberries, thawed if frozen, chopped	250 mL

1. In a bowl, combine flour, sugar, baking powder, baking soda and salt. Set aside.

2. In a large bowl, whisk together egg, sour cream, melted butter and orange zest until smooth.

3. Add flour mixture in 3 additions, gently stirring after each addition until smooth. Fold in cranberries. Spread batter evenly in prepared pan. Bake in preheated oven until tester inserted in center comes out clean, 50 to 55 minutes. Let cool for 15 minutes in pan on a wire rack, then remove from pan and let cool completely on rack.

Raisin Scones

An old-fashioned favorite that has stood the test of time. They're at their best warm from the oven.

Tip

If you don't have buttermilk, put 2 tbsp (25 mL) lemon juice in a measuring cup and fill to 1¼ cups (300 mL) with milk. Let stand for 5 minutes, then stir.

Variations

Replace raisins with dried cranberries and lemon zest with orange zest.

For special occasions and afternoon teas, turn out the dough onto a floured board and pat into a rectangle about ¾ inches (2 cm) thick. Stamp out small scones with a floured 1½-inch (4 cm) round cutter. Brush tops with cream and dust with sugar. Serve with Devonshire cream or whipped cream and strawberry jam.

- **Preheat oven to 425°F (220°C)**
- **Baking sheet, lined with parchment paper**

2⅓ cups	cake flour	575 mL
¼ cup	granulated sugar	50 mL
2½ tsp	baking powder	12 mL
½ tsp	baking soda	2 mL
½ tsp	salt	2 mL
½ cup	cold butter, cut into cubes	125 mL
½ cup	raisins	125 mL
1 tbsp	grated lemon zest	15 mL
1¼ cups	buttermilk	300 mL
1 tbsp	buttermilk, milk or cream	15 mL
	Coarse sugar for finishing	

1. In a large bowl, combine flour, sugar, baking powder, baking soda and salt, mixing to blend. Using a pastry blender or 2 knives, cut in butter until mixture resembles coarse crumbs. Stir in raisins and zest.

2. Add buttermilk all at once, stirring lightly with a fork until a soft dough forms. Using ¼ cup (50 mL) measure, drop dough onto baking sheet, at least 2 inches (5 cm) apart. Let stand for 10 minutes. Brush tops with buttermilk and sprinkle with coarse sugar. Bake in preheated oven until golden, 12 to 15 minutes. Serve warm.

Cheddar 'n' Chive Scones

*Add to the bread basket
and serve with soup, beef
stew, roast ham, chili or
with a salad for lunch.*

Tip

It is important to use very
cold butter when making
scones so that it is easier
to distribute the fat evenly
throughout the mixture.

Variations

Replace Cheddar with Swiss
cheese.

Add ⅓ cup (75 mL) diced
cooked bacon along with the
cheese.

Add 1 to 2 tbsp (15 to 25 mL)
grated Parmigiano-Reggiano
cheese to spice up the mix.

- **Preheat oven to 400°F (200°C)**
- **Baking sheet, lined with parchment paper**

2 cups	all-purpose flour	500 mL
1 tbsp	baking powder	15 mL
¾ tsp	salt	3 mL
⅓ cup	cold butter, cut into cubes (see Tip, left)	75 mL
1½ cups	shredded sharp (old) Cheddar cheese	375 mL
2 tbsp	chopped fresh chives or green onions	25 mL
1¼ cups	milk	300 mL

1. In a large bowl, combine flour, baking powder and salt. With a pastry blender or 2 knives, cut in butter until mixture resembles coarse crumbs. Stir in cheese and chives.

2. Add milk all at once, stirring lightly with a fork until a soft dough forms. Using ⅓ cup (75 mL) measure, drop dough onto baking sheet. Bake in preheated oven until golden, 18 to 22 minutes. Serve warm.

Glazed Lemon Pound Cake

A wonderful treat to enjoy in many ways. Serve with a bowl of fresh strawberries, use as a base for strawberry shortcake and trifle or dunk in melted chocolate in fondue. Grill until lightly charred and serve with a mix of peaches and blueberries. Or just enjoy with a cup of tea.

Tip

Citrus fruit release more juice at room temperature than when used straight from the refrigerator. Grate citrus before juicing; it's hard to zest a squished lemon half!

Variations

Replace lemon zest, juice and glaze with a mixture of lemon and lime, or orange.

Early in the year, use zest and juice of a blood orange and coat the warm loaf with a rosy pink glaze.

- Preheat oven to 350°F (180°C)
- 9- by 5-inch (23 by 12.5 cm) loaf pan, greased and lined with parchment paper

1½ cups	all-purpose flour	375 mL
½ tsp	salt	2 mL
¼ tsp	baking powder	1 mL
¼ tsp	baking soda	1 mL
½ cup	butter, softened	125 mL
1 cup	granulated sugar	250 mL
2	eggs	2
1 tbsp	grated lemon zest	15 mL
⅓ cup	sour cream	75 mL
3 tbsp	freshly squeezed lemon juice	45 mL

Lemon Glaze

½ cup	sifted confectioner's (icing) sugar	125 mL
1 tbsp	freshly squeezed lemon juice	15 mL

1. In a bowl, combine flour, salt, baking powder and baking soda. Set aside.

2. In a large bowl, using an electric mixer on medium speed or a wooden spoon, beat butter and sugar until blended. Add eggs, one at a time, beating lightly after each addition until smooth. Then beat vigorously until thick and creamy. Add lemon zest.

3. On low speed or with wooden spoon, add flour mixture in 3 additions, alternately with sour cream and lemon juice and mixing until blended. Spread evenly in prepared pan. Bake in preheated oven until tester inserted in center comes out clean, 55 to 60 minutes. Let cool for 15 minutes in pan on a wire rack.

4. *Lemon Glaze:* In a bowl, combine confectioner's sugar and lemon juice until smooth. Remove loaf from pan and place on a wire rack. Spoon Lemon Glaze over top while warm. Let cool completely.

Banana Bread

MAKES 1 LOAF

Our customers expect to find freshly baked banana bread on our shelves every day. It's a favorite for school lunch boxes. Lots of ripe bananas make this version very moist and flavorful.

Tip

To achieve a rich banana flavor use very ripe bananas. If you are working with a wooden spoon, mash the bananas with a fork before beating with the sugar.

Variations

Divide batter into 3 (5¾ by 3¼ by 2 inch/15 by 8 by 5 cm) small foil loaf pans to make mini banana breads; reduce baking time to 35 to 45 minutes. Or scoop into paper-lined muffin cups to make banana cupcakes; reduce baking time to about 20 minutes.

Add ½ cup (125 mL) chopped pecans or walnuts, coconut or chocolate chips to the batter.

● **Preheat oven to 350°F (180°C)**
● **9- by 5-inch (23 by 12.5 cm) loaf pan, greased and lined with parchment paper**

2 cups	all-purpose flour	500 mL
1 tsp	baking soda	5 mL
½ tsp	salt	2 mL
½ tsp	ground cinnamon	2 mL
¼ tsp	ground allspice	1 mL
3	large ripe bananas, cut into chunks	3
1 cup	granulated sugar	250 mL
2	eggs	2
⅓ cup	sunflower oil	75 mL

1. In a bowl, combine flour, baking soda, salt, cinnamon and allspice. Set aside.

2. In a large bowl, using an electric mixer on medium speed or a wooden spoon, beat bananas and sugar until almost smooth, about 3 minutes. Add eggs, one at a time, beating lightly after each addition. Beat in oil. On low speed or with a wooden spoon, add flour mixture, beating just until blended. Spread evenly in prepared pan.

3. Bake in preheated oven until tester inserted in center comes out clean, 55 to 60 minutes. Let cool for 15 minutes in pan on a wire rack, then remove from pan and let cool completely on rack.

Pumpkin Loaf

This spicy moist loaf is a personal favorite and part of our fall and Thanksgiving tradition. A sprinkling of toasted pumpkin seeds on top adds a pleasing crunch.

Tip

Be sure to buy pumpkin purée not pumpkin pie filling. The pie filling has sugar and spices added to it.

• **Preheat oven to 350°F (180°C)**
• **9- by 5-inch (23 by 12.5 cm) loaf pan, greased and lined with parchment paper**

1½ cups	all-purpose flour	375 mL
⅔ cup	granulated sugar	150 mL
1 tsp	baking powder	5 mL
1 tsp	baking soda	5 mL
1 tsp	ground cinnamon	5 mL
½ tsp	ground nutmeg	2 mL
½ tsp	ground cloves	2 mL
¼ tsp	salt	1 mL
2	eggs	2
1 cup	canned pumpkin purée (not pie filling) (see Tip, left)	250 mL
⅓ cup	sunflower oil	75 mL
½ cup	raisins	125 mL
2 tbsp	green pumpkin seeds	25 mL

1. In a bowl, combine flour, sugar, baking powder, baking soda, cinnamon, nutmeg, cloves and salt. Set aside.

2. In a large bowl, with a wooden spoon, beat together eggs, pumpkin and oil until smooth. Gradually add flour mixture, beating until blended. Stir in raisins. Spread batter evenly in prepared pan. Sprinkle pumpkin seeds over top.

3. Bake in preheated oven until tester inserted in center comes out clean, 55 to 60 minutes. Let cool for 15 minutes in pan on a wire rack, then remove from pan and let cool completely on rack.

Cornbread

MAKES 1 LOAF

Customers come from across the city to pick up this rich buttery cornbread at our store. It's an All The Best classic. Serve warm with soups, chili or grilled fish. Grill the cornbread until lightly charred to serve with your breakfast eggs.

Variation

Cheese and Pepper Cornbread: Stir ⅔ cup (150 mL) shredded sharp (old) Cheddar cheese, ¼ cup (50 mL) diced roasted red peppers, 1 finely chopped green onion and 1 to 2 tbsp (15 to 25 mL) finely chopped jalapeño pepper into the batter after the dry ingredients.

- **Preheat oven to 400°F (200°C)**
- **9-inch (23 cm) square baking pan, greased and lined with parchment paper**

1½ cups	yellow cornmeal	375 mL
1 cup	all-purpose flour	250 mL
⅓ cup	granulated sugar	75 mL
1 tbsp	baking powder	15 mL
1 tsp	salt	5 mL
2	eggs	2
1½ cups	buttermilk	375 mL
¾ cup	butter, melted and cooled	175 mL

1. In a bowl, combine cornmeal, flour, sugar, baking powder and salt. Set aside.

2. In a large bowl, whisk together eggs, buttermilk and melted butter. Add flour mixture, stirring with a wooden spoon just until blended. Do not overmix. Spread batter in prepared pan. Bake in preheated oven until tester inserted in center comes out clean, 25 to 30 minutes. Serve warm.

Fruit and Nut Bread

Tips

If you are making the bread by hand (without the aid of a stand mixer with dough hook) in Step 3, combine sponge, flour, salt and water in a bowl and mix to form a dough. Turn out on a lightly floured surface and knead until smooth and elastic, about 10 minutes. Knead in citrus peel, cherries and raisins, then add pecans. Set aside and continue with recipe.

To add interesting flavor and texture, our baker likes to include a mix of ¼ cup (50 mL) dark Thompson raisins and ½ cup (125 mL) golden Sultana raisins.

- Stand mixer with paddle attachment (see Tips, left)
- Baking sheet, lined with parchment paper

Sponge

1½ tsp	active dry yeast	7 mL
6 tbsp	lukewarm water	90 mL
⅔ cup	bread flour	150 mL

Bread Dough

2 cups	bread flour	500 mL
2 tbsp	granulated sugar	25 mL
1½ tsp	kosher or sea salt	7 mL
¾ cup	raisins (see Tips, left)	175 mL
½ cup	currants	125 mL
¼ cup	mixed candied citrus peel	50 mL
¼ cup	dried cherries	50 mL
1¼ cups	roughly chopped toasted pecans	300 mL

1. *Sponge:* In a mixer bowl, stir yeast into warm water and let stand until mixture begins to froth, about 5 minutes. With a wooden spoon, stir flour into yeast mixture, mixing thoroughly. Cover and set aside in a warm, draft-free place until doubled in bulk, 1 to 1½ hours.

2. *Bread Dough:* In a stand mixer fitted with dough hook, combine sponge mixture, flour, sugar, salt and ½ cup plus 1 tsp (130 mL) water. Mix at medium speed for 3 minutes. Add raisins, currants, citrus peel and cherries and mix for 2 minutes. Add pecans and mix at low speed for 1 minute. Do not overmix. Cover bowl and set aside in a warm, draft-free place until doubled in bulk, about 2 hours.

3. Divide dough into 2 equal portions. On a lightly floured surface, pat each portion of dough into a rectangle about 8 by 5 inches (20 by 12.5 cm). Roll each rectangle of dough, jelly-roll style, into an 8-inch (20 cm) log and pinch seams closed. Place loaves, seam side down, on a prepared baking sheet, at least 6 inches (15 cm) apart. Set aside, loosely covered, until doubled in bulk, 1 to 2 hours.

4. Meanwhile, preheat oven to 400°F (200°C).

5. With a sharp knife, make 3 diagonal slashes in the top of each loaf. Bake in preheated oven until loaves sound hollow when tapped on the bottom, about 30 minutes.

Focaccia

Every day we bake a batch of these savory breads. We change the toppings with the seasons or to accompany a special soup or salad on the weekly menu.

Tips

Suggested focaccia toppings:

Tapenade (page 324 or store-bought), baby arugula and grated Grana Padano cheese.

Quartered fresh figs, prosciutto, shredded mozzarella, grated Grana Padano cheese and chopped tarragon.

Sliced roasted butternut squash, sliced red onion, grated Asiago cheese and grated Grana Padano cheese.

Slices of fresh mozzarella and cherry tomatoes and basil leaves.

Cherry tomatoes, pitted ripe olives and chopped oregano.

Variation

Focaccia slab for sandwiches: Make a double batch of focaccia dough. Line 15- by 10-inch (38 by 25 cm) rimmed baking sheet with parchment and dust with durum semolina or cornmeal. After the first rise, spread batter on sheet and set aside, loosely covered in a warm, draft-free place to proof until doubled in bulk, 1 to 1½ hours. Dimple the top of the dough with your fingertips, drizzle with oil and sprinkle with dried rosemary and sea salt. Bake as in Step 5.

Baking sheet, lined with parchment, dusted with durum semolina or fine cornmeal

1 tsp	active dry yeast	5 mL
1¼ cups	lukewarm water	300 mL
3 tbsp	extra virgin olive oil	45 mL
1½ tsp	kosher or sea salt	7 mL
1⅔ cups	bread flour	400 mL
	Coarse salt	

1. In mixer bowl, stir yeast into warm water and let stand for 5 to 10 minutes until mixture begins to froth and double in volume.

2. In a stand mixer fitted with dough hook, combine yeast mixture, oil, salt and flour. Mix at medium speed until dough resembles a very thick pancake batter, about 8 minutes. Stop occasionally to scrape down the sides of the bowl until everything is well mixed. Cover bowl and set aside in a warm, draft-free place until doubled in bulk, 1 to 1½ hours.

3. Moisten your hands with olive oil. Scoop up dough and divide into 2 portions. Loosely form each portion into a ball. Place balls on prepared baking sheet, at least 6 inches (15 cm) apart and gently pat down to form 2 flat-topped disks, about 8 inches (20 cm) in diameter. Set aside, loosely covered to proof for 1 hour.

4. Meanwhile, preheat oven to 400°F (200°C).

5. Add toppings of your choice (see Tips, left) and a sprinkling of coarse salt. Bake in preheated oven until loaves sound hollow when tapped on the bottom, 18 to 20 minutes.

Cinnamon Buns

MAKES 10 BUNS

On one visit to New York, I saw a very long line up of people waiting in the basement of a department store early in the morning. Being curious, I followed my nose to front of the line and discovered that the attraction was cinnamon buns, fresh from the oven! These, too, are worth waiting for.

Tip

Cut one of the corners off the bottom of a small freezer bag to make a handy disposable piping bag for the icing.

- Stand mixer with dough hook attachment
- Baking sheet, lined with parchment paper

2 tsp	active dry yeast	10 mL
½ cup	lukewarm water	125 mL
3½ cups	all-purpose flour	875 mL
⅔ cup	granulated sugar	150 mL
1 tsp	kosher or sea salt	5 mL
1 cup	lukewarm milk	250 mL
3	eggs	3
1¼ cups	butter, softened, divided	300 mL
1 cup	packed brown sugar	250 mL
1 tbsp	ground cinnamon	15 mL
1¼ cups	sifted confectioner's (icing) sugar	300 mL
3 tbsp	milk	45 mL
⅛ tsp	vanilla extract	0.5 mL

1. In a mixer bowl, stir yeast into warm water and let stand for 5 to 10 minutes until mixture begins to froth and double in volume.

2. In a stand mixer fitted with dough hook, combine flour, sugar and salt. Form a well in the center of the bowl. Combine milk, 2 eggs and yeast mixture and pour into the well. Add ¾ cup (175 mL) of the soft butter. Mix at low speed until dry ingredients are incorporated with liquid. Raise speed to medium and mix until a smooth, soft ball of dough forms around the dough hook, about 5 minutes.

3. Cover bowl and set aside to proof until doubled in bulk, about 1½ hours. Punch dough down and let it rest for 20 minutes.

4. Turn out dough onto a lightly floured surface and gently roll into a rectangle about 15- by 7-inches (37.5 by 18 cm). Roll so that the longest side of the rectangle is closest to you. Lightly spread the remaining butter over the surface of the dough, leaving a 1-inch (2.5 cm) border unbuttered at the top.

5. In a bowl, combine brown sugar and cinnamon. Sprinkle mixture evenly over buttered dough. Beat remaining egg and brush along the top bare strip of dough. Starting from the bottom of the rectangle, gently roll the dough, jelly-roll style, into a log about 3 inches (7.5 cm) thick. Cut the log into slices about $1\frac{1}{2}$ inches (4 cm) wide.

6. Arrange slices, flat side down, on prepared baking sheet, about 2 inches (5 cm) apart. Set aside, loosely covered, to proof until doubled in bulk, about $1\frac{1}{2}$ hours.

7. Meanwhile, preheat oven to 350°F (180°C).

8. Bake in preheated oven until golden, 8 to 10 minutes. Transfer buns from baking sheet to a wire rack and let cool.

9. In a bowl, mix confectioner's sugar, milk and vanilla until smooth. Drizzle or spread icing over top of buns.

Chelsea Buns

MAKES 7 BUNS

This sweet treat made from an egg-enriched bread dough coiled around a sweet filling of currants, sugar, cinnamon and lemon zest originated in The Bun House of Chelsea in London in the 18th century. Our version is made more decadent by a caramel topping that includes pecans and cherries.

- **7-inch (18 cm) round cake pan, lightly greased**
- **Candy thermometer**
- **Stand mixer with paddle attachment (see Tips, page 384)**

Caramel Topping

10	pecan halves	10
10	dried cherries	10
½ cup	packed brown sugar	125 mL
3 tbsp	butter	45 mL
3 tbsp	corn syrup	45 mL

Chelsea Sponge

1 tsp	active dry yeast	5 mL
6 tbsp	lukewarm milk	90 mL
⅓ cup	bread flour	75 mL

Chelsea Dough

3 tbsp	butter, softened, divided	45 mL
2 tbsp	granulated sugar	25 mL
½ tsp	kosher or sea salt	2 mL
1	egg	1
¾ cup + 2 tbsp	all-purpose flour	200 mL
¼ cup	packed brown sugar	50 mL
2 tbsp	sultana raisins	25 mL
2 tbsp	currants	25 mL
2 tbsp	chopped walnuts	25 mL
½ tsp	ground cinnamon	2 mL
Pinch	grated nutmeg	Pinch
	Grated zest of 1 lemon	

1. *Caramel Topping:* Sprinkle pecans and cherries evenly in bottom of prepared cake pan.
2. In a saucepan over medium heat, combine brown sugar, butter and corn syrup. Heat, stirring, until mixture reaches 270°F (138°C) on a candy thermometer. Immediately remove from heat and carefully pour hot syrup into cake pan. Set aside.
3. *Chelsea Sponge:* In a bowl, stir yeast into warm milk and let stand for 5 to 10 minutes until mixture begins to froth and double in volume.

4. With a wooden spoon, beat flour into yeast mixture, mixing thoroughly. Cover bowl and set aside in a warm, draft-free place until doubled in bulk, about 1 hour.

5. *Chelsea Dough:* In a stand mixer fitted with paddle attachment, beat 2 tbsp (25 mL) of the butter with granulated sugar and salt until creamy. Add sponge mixture, egg and flour and mix at low speed for 8 minutes. Cover bowl and set aside to proof until doubled in bulk, $1\frac{1}{2}$ to 2 hours.

6. In a bowl, combine brown sugar, raisins, currants, walnuts, cinnamon, nutmeg and lemon zest.

7. Turn out dough onto a lightly floured surface and gently roll into a square about 7 by 7 inches (18 by 18 cm). Lightly spread remaining butter over surface of dough edge to edge. Sprinkle with an even layer of brown sugar mixture, leaving about $\frac{1}{2}$-inch (1 cm) border. Gently roll dough jelly-roll style into a log. Place seam side down on work surface and cut log into slices about 1 inch (2.5 cm) wide.

8. Arrange one slice, flat side down, in middle of caramel-lined cake pan and place the other rolls around the edge of the pan with the seam side facing inward, resting against the center roll. Set aside, loosely covered to proof until doubled in bulk, about $1\frac{1}{2}$ hours.

9. Meanwhile, preheat oven to 350°F (180°C).

10. Place pan on a baking sheet and bake in preheated oven until golden brown and sounds hollow when tapped on top, about 25 minutes. Let stand for a few minutes. Carefully turn out onto a rack set over a plate. Use a heat-resistant spatula to scrape the cake pan of any delicious caramel-coated pecans and cherries that may be left behind. Serve warm.

Orange Raisin Crown

A special occasion bread that is rich, buttery and slightly sweet. Twist dough into a crown or braid or bake in a loaf pan. This bread makes unbelievably good French toast.

- **Stand mixer with paddle attachment (see Tips, page 384)**
- **Baking sheet, lined with parchment paper**

Sponge

2 tsp	active dry yeast	10 mL
7 tbsp	lukewarm milk	105 mL
⅔ cup	bread flour	150 mL

Bread Dough

3½ tbsp	butter, softened	52 mL
3 tbsp	granulated sugar	45 mL
1 tsp	kosher or sea salt	5 mL
2	eggs	2
1¼ cups	all-purpose flour	300 mL
	Grated zest of 1 orange	
⅔ cup	raisins	150 mL
2 tbsp	coarse sugar	25 mL

1. *Sponge:* In a bowl, stir yeast into warm milk and let stand for 5 to 10 minutes until mixture begins to froth.

2. With a wooden spoon, stir flour into yeast mixture, mixing thoroughly. Cover bowl and set aside in a warm, draft-free place until doubled in bulk, about 1 hour.

3. *Bread Dough:* In a stand mixer fitted with paddle attachment, beat butter with sugar and salt until creamy. Add sponge mixture, one egg and flour and mix at low speed for 6 minutes. Add orange zest and raisins and mix for 2 minutes. Cover bowl and set aside in a warm, draft-free place to proof until doubled in bulk, about 2 hours.

4. On a lightly floured surface, turn out dough and gently roll into a rope about 18 inches (45 cm) long. Slightly flatten rope and coil up into a large circle, starting from the center. Flatten the outside end of the dough rope and tuck it underneath.

5. Place loaf, flat side down, on prepared baking sheet and set aside, loosely covered to proof until doubled in bulk, about 2 hours.

6. Beat remaining egg and brush over loaf and sprinkle with sugar. Bake in preheated 350°F (180°C) oven until loaf sounds hollow when tapped, 20 to 24 minutes.

Desserts

Old-Fashioned Shortcakes

MAKES ABOUT 12 SHORTCAKES

A rich, slightly sweet biscuit is the foundation of a fabulous summer dessert when served warm with fresh berries and mounds of lightly sweetened whipped cream.

Tip

Use a food processor to combine the dry ingredients. Add chunks of cold butter and pulse to form coarse crumbs. Turn into a large bowl.

Variations

Strawberry Shortcakes: Bake shortcakes as indicated in recipe. Rinse and hull 4 cups (1 L) strawberries, slice into quarters and sprinkle with 3 to 4 tbsp (45 to 60 mL) granulated sugar, depending on sweetness of fruit. Set aside for 30 minutes to let juices run. Split warm shortcakes in half. Spoon strawberries and juice on the bottom half and add a generous mound of whipped cream. Place the other half of the shortcake on top. Savor every bite!

Peach Blueberry Shortcakes: Follow recipe but replace strawberries with 6 ripe sliced peaches and 1 cup (250 mL) blueberries. Toss with 3 tbsp (45 mL) granulated sugar and 1 tbsp (15 mL) rum. Set aside for 30 minutes to let juices run. Proceed with recipe.

- **Preheat oven to 425°F (220°C)**
- **Baking sheet, lined with parchment paper**
- **1½-inch (4 cm) round biscuit or cookie cutter**

3 cups	cake flour, sifted	750 mL
¼ cup	granulated sugar	50 mL
1 tbsp	baking powder	15 mL
½ tsp	salt	2 mL
¼ tsp	baking soda	1 mL
	Grated zest of 1 lemon	
½ cup	cold butter, cut into cubes	125 mL
1	egg, lightly beaten	1
½ to ⅔ cup	half-and-half (10%) cream, divided	125 to 150 mL
	Extra cream or egg wash	
	Coarse sugar	
	Crème Chantilly, optional	

1. In a large bowl, combine flour, granulated sugar, baking powder, salt, baking soda and lemon zest, mixing to blend. Using a pastry blender or 2 knives, cut in butter until mixture resembles coarse crumbs.

2. Make a well in center of flour mixture. In a measuring cup, combine egg and ½ cup (125 mL) of the cream. Add all at once to dry ingredients and toss lightly with a fork or spatula until no dry flour remains. Sprinkle with a little more cream if needed to form a soft dough.

3. Turn out dough onto a floured board and pat into a rectangle about 1½ inches (4 cm) thick. Stamp out shortcakes with a floured cutter. Place shortcakes on prepared baking sheet, about 2 inches (5 cm) apart. Or drop dough by the scant ¼ cup (50 mL) measure onto prepared baking sheets, about 2 inches (5 cm) apart. Brush tops with cream or egg wash and sprinkle with coarse sugar. Bake in preheated oven until tops are golden and crisp, 12 to 15 minutes. Serve warm with Crème Chantilly, if desired.

Crème Chantilly

Makes 2 cups (500 mL)

1 cup	whipping (35%) cream, chilled (see Tip, right)	250 mL
1 tbsp	granulated sugar	15 mL
½ tsp	vanilla extract	2 mL

1. In a large bowl, using an electric mixer or a large whisk, beat cream with sugar until soft peaks form. Add vanilla and beat until cream forms soft, fluffy mounds. Do not overbeat or you'll end up with grainy cream and eventually butter. Refrigerate until serving for up to 1 hour.

Tip

For best results, chill cream, bowl and whisk before whipping. Whipped cream may be prepared up to 1 hour ahead. Refrigerate and beat again lightly before serving.

Fall Fruit Compôte

A selection of seasonal fruits simmered in flavored syrup is a staple in the fall and winter sweet kitchen. Enjoy spooned over strained yogurt or ice cream, in a trifle, as the fruit in a winter fruit shortcake or simply with a topping of whipped cream or crème fraîche with a Norwegian Lace cookie (page 363) on the side.

Variation

Add a splash of cognac or aged rum to ward off winter chills.

½ cup	granulated sugar	125 mL
2	pears, sliced	2
2	firm apples, sliced	2
4	Italian prune plums, sliced	4
½ cup	raisins	125 mL
1	strip lemon zest or 1 slice (¼ inch/0.5 cm) gingerroot	1

1. In a saucepan over medium heat, combine ½ cup (125 mL) water and sugar, stirring until sugar dissolves.
2. Add pears, apples, plums, raisins and lemon zest. Bring to a boil. Reduce heat to low and simmer until fruit is tender, 10 to 15 minutes. Remove from heat, discard lemon zest and let cool. Serve warm or chilled.

Panna Cotta

Literally translated from the Italian, panna cotta means "cooked cream." It is a deliciously delicate dessert of softly jelled cream, traditionally flavored with citrus and served with caramel, chocolate or fruit coulis.

Tip

Serve chilled with lightly sugared berries or fruit compote, or drizzle with Chocolate Ganache (page 416) or caramel.

Variation

Add other flavorings to scald with the cream, such as 1 tbsp (15 mL) instant coffee granules, a strip of lemon or orange zest, a slice of crystallized ginger, 1 tbsp (15 mL) Earl Grey tea or ½ tsp (2 mL) culinary lavender. Reduce vanilla to 1 tsp (5 mL). Strain and discard flavorings.

Six 6-oz (175 mL) ramekins

3¼ cups	whipping (35%) cream	800 mL
⅓ cup	granulated sugar	75 mL
1 tbsp	vanilla extract	15 mL
1 tbsp	unflavored gelatin powder	15 mL
⅓ cup	cold water	75 mL

1. In a saucepan over medium heat, combine cream, sugar and vanilla. Bring cream to a simmer, stirring until sugar dissolves. Do not boil. Remove from heat.

2. Dissolve gelatin in water. Let stand for 5 minutes to soften and stir into scalded cream.

3. Strain cream into ramekins and refrigerate overnight to set.

Raspberry Coulis

Wonderful fresh fruit sauces can be made from many different fruits. Raspberries, blueberries, blackberries and strawberries, alone or in combination, and the puréed fruit of mango, papaya or peach are all delicious to serve as the finishing touch to many desserts, with ice creams and sorbets or to create a truly decadent fruit sundae.

● **Food processor or blender**

½ cup	granulated sugar	125 mL
2 cups	raspberries, fresh or frozen, thawed	500 mL
½ tsp	grated orange zest	2 mL
1 tbsp	orange-flavored liqueur, optional	15 mL

1. *To make sugar syrup:* In a small saucepan over medium heat, combine sugar and ½ cup (125 mL) water, stirring until sugar dissolves and mixture just reaches a boil. Remove from heat and let cool.

2. In a food processor or blender, purée raspberries. Press raspberry purée through a sieve to remove seeds.

3. In a bowl, combine sieved raspberry purée, orange zest, orange-flavored liqueur, if using, and sweeten to taste with sugar syrup. (You may not need to add all the syrup.) Refrigerate in a covered container until ready to use or for up to 1 week.

Lemon Curd

This luxurious cream made with eggs, sugar and butter and flavored with citrus makes a delicious filling for tarts and layer cakes and is used as a flavoring for mousses, creams and frostings.

Tips

Lemon curd is best enjoyed when freshly made but may be refrigerated for up to 2 weeks. It may also be frozen but the flavor and texture will change slightly.

Scrub the skins of regular citrus fruits well before using or seek out organic citrus fruit. The flavor of the grated zest is then uncompromised by sprays and preserving chemicals.

Zest lemons directly into the mixing bowl. The lemon oil that sprays from the fruit skin as you grate adds valuable concentrated flavor and aroma. This, however, does not work when making lemon meringues since the lemon oil will interfere with the successful beating of egg whites.

Variation

Make the curd with the juice and zest of other citrus fruits, such as limes, oranges, blood oranges or pink grapefruit. Taste the freshly squeezed juices; they may need to have lemon juice added for extra zip.

7	egg yolks	7
3/4 cup	granulated sugar	175 mL
1 1/2 tsp	grated lemon zest	7 mL
1/2 cup	freshly squeezed lemon juice	125 mL
1/2 cup	butter, softened	125 mL

1. In a large, heatproof glass or nonreactive bowl, whisk egg yolks, sugar and lemon juice to blend. Place bowl over a saucepan of barely simmering water over medium heat. (Make sure the bowl does not touch the water.) Cook, stirring constantly with a wooden spoon or heat-resistant spatula, until mixture is smooth and thickened and coats the back of the spoon, 10 to 15 minutes (see Tip, page 174). When you run your finger down the back of the spoon the curd or custard should hold its shape. Be careful not to overcook. The eggs continue to thicken the curd a little as it cools. Adjust the heat so that the mixture does not get too hot or you will scramble the eggs.

2. Remove bowl from heat and strain mixture into a clean bowl. Whisk in butter, 2 to 3 tbsp (25 to 45 mL) at a time, and zest until smooth and butter is completely incorporated. For smoother, richer consistency use an immersion blender. Place plastic wrap directly on the surface of the curd to prevent a skin from forming. Let cool completely. Refrigerate until needed (see Tips, left).

Lemon Mousse

MAKES 8 CUPS (2 L)

A light and luscious dessert that is particularly popular in summer when fresh berries are at their sweetest to serve alongside.

Tip

If the mousse has to stand at room temperature for a short while before being served, you may stabilize it by adding gelatin. Dissolve 2 tsp (10 mL) unflavored gelatin powder in 2 tbsp (25 mL) cold water. Let stand for 5 minutes to soften. Melt gelatin completely by heating in the microwave at Medium (50%) power, or by setting in a saucepan over low heat for 1 minute. Fold gelatin thoroughly into room temperature lemon curd before folding into whipped cream.

3 cups	whipping (35%) cream, chilled	750 mL
2 cups	Lemon Curd (page 397), at room temperature	500 mL

1. In a large bowl, whip cream until it forms medium soft fluffy mounds — just beyond the soft peak stage. Set aside.

2. Gently fold Lemon Curd into cream until completely incorporated. Transfer to a serving bowl or individual dessert glasses and refrigerate until serving for up to 1 hour.

Pastry Cream

**MAKES 2 CUPS
(500 ML)**

This rich pastry cream is the foundation for many desserts. Use as a creamy base in a fruit tart, layer with cake and fruit in a trifle, or simply lighten with whipped cream and serve with fruit.

⅔ cup	whipping (35%) cream	150 mL
⅔ cup	whole (3.25%) milk, divided	150 mL
1	egg yolk	1
1	egg	1
⅓ cup	granulated sugar	75 mL
Pinch	salt	Pinch
2 tbsp + 1 tsp	cornstarch	30 mL
1½ tsp	vanilla extract	7 mL

Tip

Sometimes recipes include instruction to beat eggs yolks and sugar "until they form a ribbon." This technique prepares the egg yolks so that they can be heated without becoming grainy. It also incorporates air to lighten the finished custard. As you gradually beat sugar into egg yolks the mixtures thickens to the point when you can lift the whisk, or beater, out of the bowl and the egg mixture falls back into the bowl forming a soft ribbon that melts slowly into the surface of the mixture.

Variations

Flavor cream by adding grated citrus zest, grated chocolate, coffee or orange-flavored liqueur, rum or cognac.

Place cream in the refrigerator for 30 minutes until just chilled but still creamy. Fold in 1 cup (250 mL) whipped cream. Spoon into parfait glasses and garnish with fresh berries. Let chill until serving, 4 to 6 hours.

1. In a saucepan over medium heat, bring cream and ⅓ cup (75 mL) of the milk to a boil. Immediately remove from heat.

2. In a large, heatproof bowl, whisk together egg yolk, egg, sugar and salt until thick and pale, the "ribbon stage" (see Tip, left). Mix together remaining milk with cornstarch and blend into egg mixture. Gradually pour hot cream into egg mixture and whisk until smooth.

3. Place bowl on top of a saucepan of barely simmering water over medium heat. (Make sure the bowl does not touch the water.) Cook, stirring constantly with a wooden spoon or heat-resistant spatula, until mixture is smooth and thickened and coats the back of the spoon, 10 to 15 minutes (see Tip, page 174). When you run your finger down the back of the spoon the curd or custard should hold its shape. Be careful not to overcook. The eggs continue to thicken the cream a little as it cools. Remove from heat and stir in vanilla.

4. Pour pastry cream into a bowl and let cool. Place plastic wrap directly on the surface of the cream to prevent a skin from forming. Spread the cream into a fully baked tart shell or incorporate into other desserts while still lukewarm.

Meringues

MAKES ABOUT
2 DOZEN 3-INCH
(7.5 CM) MERINGUES

Perfect homemade meringues are light, crumble sweetly and melt in the mouth. Form and bake meringues in various sizes and shapes. Fill meringue nests with ice cream or sorbet and drizzle with fruit coulis or chocolate sauce or add a scoop of lemon mousse and top with fresh berries for an instant irresistible dessert.

Variations

Meringue Layers: Create sensational desserts with meringue disks, layers of whipped cream and fresh berries. Draw the outline of three 8-inch (20 cm) circles on parchment-lined baking sheets. Using a spatula, or a piping bag and ½-inch (1 cm) tip, make an even layer of meringue inside the circles about ½ inch (1 cm) high. Follow Step 3.

Lemon Meringues: Add 1 tsp (5 mL) very finely grated lemon zest with cornstarch and confectioner's sugar.

Chocolate Meringues: Add 1 tbsp (15 mL) unsweetened cocoa powder with cornstarch and confectioner's sugar.

Hazelnut Meringues: Fold ¼ cup (50 mL) toasted and finely ground hazelnuts into meringue mixture.

- **Preheat oven to 200°F (100°C)**
- **Baking sheets, lined with parchment**

5	egg whites	5
½ cup	granulated sugar	125 mL
1 tbsp	cornstarch	15 mL
1 cup	sifted confectioner's (icing) sugar	250 mL

1. In a large bowl, using an electric mixer, whip egg whites to combine. On high speed, gradually add sugar, beating to stiff peak stage. Fold in cornstarch and confectioner's sugar.

2. Drop by tablespoons (15 mL) onto prepared baking sheets, about 2 inches (5 cm) apart.

3. Bake in preheated oven for 20 minutes. Turn heat off and leave meringues in oven until meringues are dried out, 3 to 4 hours. Lift a meringue off the baking sheet to test; the bottom should be completely baked and dry. Transfer to wire racks and let cool completely.

What is This About "Peaks"?

Egg whites whisk more successfully when at room temperature and a few days old. Save egg whites from making curds and custards to use later. They will keep for up to 2 days in a covered container in the refrigerator or frozen for up to 4 months. Thaw in the refrigerator and use as fresh.

Use a clean, grease-free, large, glass, copper or stainless-steel bowl; avoid aluminum. Using an electric mixer or a large whisk, beat the egg whites rapidly at high speed to keep them smooth and prevent moisture from separating out. Test how stiffly the egg whites are beaten by gently pulling the beater or whisk out of the bowl. At the soft peak stage, the beaten egg whites form voluminous soft mounds, and when you lift the beaters the peaks fall quite quickly back into the bowl. At medium peak stage the peaks hold longer and begin to fall over at the tips. At stiff peak stage the tips of the peaks of egg white keep their points.

The same "peak" terms are often applied to whipped (35%) cream. The cream, bowl and whisk should be chilled. For accompanying fruits and desserts, soft billowy cream is best. For folding into mousses you need to beat a bit longer closer to medium peak stage. If you continue to beat cream past stiff peaks it'll eventually end up as butter!

Rice Pudding

This is a comforting dessert that is popular throughout the year and at all times of day. Our rice pudding is extra rich and creamy, but it is almost as comforting when made with just whole milk.

2½ cups	whipping (35%) cream	625 mL
2 cups	whole (3.25%) milk	500 mL
¾ cup	granulated sugar	175 mL
⅔ cup	Arborio rice	150 mL
1½ tsp	vanilla extract	7 mL
½ tsp	ground cinnamon	2 mL

1. In a large saucepan, combine cream, milk, sugar, rice and vanilla. Place over medium heat, stirring until mixture gently comes to a boil. Reduce heat to low and simmer, stirring occasionally, until rice is cooked and pudding is rich and creamy, 25 to 30 minutes. Serve warm or chilled sprinkled with cinnamon.

Raisin Pecan Bread Pudding

An old-fashioned dessert with lasting appeal that reaches new heights when served with a warm pouring custard, such as Bourbon Custard (page 403).

Variation

Use cubes of egg bread or panettone to make an extra-delicious bread pudding.

● **Preheat oven to 400°F (200°C)**
● **9- by 5-inch (23 by 12.5 cm) shallow baking dish, buttered**

3½ cups	bread cubes, 1 inch (2.5 cm) square	875 mL
3	eggs	3
¾ cup	granulated sugar	175 mL
1 tsp	vanilla extract	5 mL
1 tsp	ground cinnamon	5 mL
¼ tsp	freshly grated nutmeg	1 mL
2 tbsp	melted butter, cooled	25 mL
1 cup	whole (3.25%) milk	250 mL
⅓ cup	raisins	75 mL
¼ cup	roughly chopped toasted pecans	50 mL

1. Place cubed bread in prepared baking dish. Set aside.
2. In a large bowl, using an electric mixer on high, beat eggs until light and fluffy. Add sugar, vanilla, cinnamon, nutmeg and melted butter and beat until well blended. Beat in milk. Stir in raisins and pecans. Pour egg mixture over bread and let stand for 30 minutes.
3. Place in preheated oven. Reduce heat to 350°F (180°C) and bake until topping is golden brown and the custard just springs back when gently tapped, 25 to 35 minutes. Serve warm.

Bourbon Custard

MAKES 2 CUPS (500 ML)

There's a quip about food in England that says… "if you can't put mustard on it, put custard on it"! Making custard to accompany whatever was served for dessert at Sunday lunch was probably my first culinary experience. I have to admit that the main ingredient was a scoop of ubiquitous Bird's custard powder! It was later that I discovered the delight of smooth, rich, creamy custard made with fresh egg yolks, sugar and milk.

Tip
Beat 1 tsp (5 mL) cornstarch into the egg yolk mixture. This helps to reduce the risk of scrambling the eggs since the mixture can withstand a few degrees more heat.

Variation
Replace Bourbon and vanilla with other flavors to complement your fruit or dessert. Try grated citrus zest, rum, cognac, orange-flavored liqueur, single malt whiskey, Calvados, Poire William or Kirsch.

⅔ cup	whipping (35%) cream	150 mL
⅔ cup	whole (3.25%) milk	150 mL
3	egg yolks	3
¼ cup	granulated sugar	50 mL
1 tbsp	melted butter, cooled	15 mL
1 tsp	vanilla extract	5 mL
1 tbsp	Bourbon	15 mL

1. In a saucepan over medium-low heat, combine cream and milk. Bring just to a boil.

2. In a bowl, whisk egg yolks. Gradually whisk in sugar, butter and vanilla. Beat until mixture is pale yellow and forms a ribbon (see Tip, page 399). Slowly pour hot creamy milk over yolk mixture, whisking to combine.

3. Place bowl on top of a saucepan of barely simmering water over medium heat. (Make sure the bowl does not touch the water.) Cook mixture, stirring constantly with a wooden spoon or heat-resistant spatula, until smooth and thickened and coats the back of the spoon, 10 to 15 minutes (see Tip, page 174). Do not bring mixture close to simmering point or eggs will scramble.

4. Remove from heat. Strain through a fine sieve into a clean bowl and stir in Bourbon. Serve warm. If made ahead, place plastic wrap directly on the surface of the custard to prevent a skin from forming. Let cool completely. Refrigerate until needed for up to 2 days. Warm over low heat, stirring constantly.

Tiramisù

The recipe for this decadent dessert was brought to our kitchen by Mario Totaro, our pastry chef, who comes from Agnone, in southern Italy. Agnone is a city famous for making bells that ring in Catholic churches around the world. The translation for tiramisù is "pick-me-up." Legend has it that the dessert originated in a restaurant near Venice. Courtesans who worked above the restaurant needed a sweet Marsala or brandy-doused restorative after rigorous amorous adventures. In our version the "pick-me-up" is espresso and Tia Maria, which is deliciously effective!

Tip

This recipe contains raw eggs. If you are concerned about the safety of using raw eggs, use pasteurized egg whites and pasteurized whole eggs instead.

13- by 9-inch (33 by 23 cm) shallow serving dish

3¼ cups	brewed espresso, divided	800 mL
1¼ cups	coffee-flavored liqueur, divided	300 mL
2⅓ cups	whipping (35%) cream, chilled	575 mL
4	eggs, separated (see Tip, left)	4
½ cup	granulated sugar	125 mL
3 cups	mascarpone cheese, softened (see Tip, right)	750 mL
48	ladyfingers	48
2 tbsp	unsweetened Dutch-process cocoa powder	25 mL

1. In a bowl, combine 3 cups (750 mL) of the brewed espresso and 1 cup (250 mL) of the coffee-flavored liqueur. Set aside.

2. In a bowl, using an electric mixer, whip cream until soft peaks form. Set aside. In another bowl with clean beaters, beat egg whites to soft peak stage. Set aside.

3. In a large bowl, combine egg yolks, sugar and remaining ¼ cup (50 mL) of espresso. Whisk until thick and creamy.

4. Using an electric mixer at low speed, add mascarpone to egg yolk mixture, ½ cup (125 mL) at a time. Blend until completely smooth after each addition. Slowly add remaining ¼ cup (50 mL) coffee-flavored liqueur. Using a large spatula, gently fold in beaten egg whites and then fold in whipped cream. Set aside.

5. *To assemble the Tiramisù:* Dip ladyfingers in espresso and coffee liqueur mixture and arrange an even layer on the bottom of serving dish. Spread half of the mascarpone-cream mixture on top of the ladyfingers. Arrange another layer of soaked ladyfingers on top of the mascarpone and fill the dish with the rest of the mascarpone cream. Dust the surface lightly with cocoa powder. Refrigerate overnight or at least 24 hours before serving.

How to Fold in Egg Whites

Folding beaten egg whites and whipped cream into a mixture is usually the last stage of mixing and contributes to the lightness of the cake or pastry. Use a clean, wide-bladed spatula, or an equally clean hand. Don't be intimidated by egg whites! It's best to make few decisive folds than lots of hesitant ones. Fold into mixture in 3 stages.

1. Scoop one-third of the beaten egg whites onto batter and, with a few decisive strokes, blend them in. This lightens the batter and makes the "folding" part easier.
2. Scoop half of the remaining egg whites onto batter and make a cutting action through the middle of the mixture right down to the bottom of the bowl. Flip the mixture back over itself. Turn the bowl a quarter turn (90°) and repeat the cutting motion. Continue until only a few light streaks of egg white remain.
3. Scoop remaining egg white onto the mixture and continue cutting, flipping and turning the bowl until no streaks of egg white remain.

Tip

Mascarpone is a decadent, delicately flavored triple-crème cheese originating in Lombardy. It is a treat for special occasions since the butterfat content is 90%! Mascarpone is most frequently used in desserts or to accompany sweet fruits. Torta is a luscious combination of layers of mascarpone and creamy Gorgonzola cheese that is fabulous after dinner with sliced pears, figs, dates and toasted walnuts.

Variation

Assemble Tiramisù in individual dessert ramekins or martini glasses.

Chocolate

All round, it must be the single most-welcome taste in the world, giving an extra fillip to joy and a calming balm to woe. The word comes from the Mexican Aztecs (*xocolatl*), who associated it with the goddess of fertility and reserved its consumption for warriors, priests and the nobility. Beans of the cacao, chocolate's parent, were used for taxation; 100 beans could buy a slave, 12 a courtesan.

As a drink it was a particular favorite at the court of the Aztec emperor Montezuma II: he is said to have drunk 50 gold goblets of chocolate a day (proclaiming it, among other things, an aphrodisiac), and in the early 16th century introduced the drink to his nemesis, the Spanish conquistador Hernán Cortés, whom he had warmly welcomed. Without much in the way of thanks (he was after the gold), Cortés then put Montezuma's people to the sword by the thousands, and took the elixir back to Spain. It became a court favorite there, too, and the rest is 500 years of western history. Montezuma, of course, had his revenge, and it continues among visitors to this day.

Some two-thirds of the world's cacao is now grown in western Africa, and chocolate is generally defined as any product made primarily from cocoa solids (from the cacao bean) and cocoa butter (a vegetable fat from the bean, which was introduced by the Swiss chocolatier Rodolphe Lindt in 1879 and gives the chocolate bar the essential meltability we know and love today). Today artisan chocolatiers have taken chocolate up another notch. We are learning to differentiate varieties of cocoa beans as to their place of origin, like organic Sambirano from Madagascar or Forasteros from Ghana, and to recognize the impact on flavor of variety and growing conditions. "Organic" or "fair trade" labels are important factors.

In the Kitchen

Baking chocolate (aka **bitter, unsweetened**) contains a high percentage (50 percent and up) of chocolate liquor (cocoa solids and cocoa butter) and no sugar. The chocolate flavor is deeper, making it the preferred choice of bakers and premium chocolate makers.

Dark chocolate has vanilla and sugar added to chocolate liquor to produce chocolate of varying sweetness, from bittersweet to semisweet to sweet. This is a wide umbrella, covering at least 35 percent chocolate liquor for bittersweet to 15 percent for sweet. Bittersweet usually contains less sugar than semisweet.

Milk chocolate (a minimum 10 percent chocolate liquor) is a sweet chocolate that contains added milk powder or condensed milk. Despite the growing popularity of darker varieties, milk still rules the roost, accounting for 80 percent of total chocolate sales.

White chocolate is hardly chocolate at all, since it contains no cocoa solids, only butter, milk solids, and sugar and vanilla.

Cocoa powder is the ground, pressed substance left over after cocoa butter has been extracted from the chocolate liquor. It is available as American "natural" cocoa powder and European "Dutch-process." It's not recommended to substitute one for the other in recipes. Regular cocoa powder is more acidic and is paired with an alkaline ingredient like baking soda to create carbon dioxide bubbles that cause cakes to rise. In **Dutch-process cocoa** the beans are treated with an alkaline solution that removes some of the acidity, resulting in a more mellow flavor: it is paired with an acid ingredient like baking powder in baking.

Peach and Pink Plum Crisp

Seasonal fruit topped with a golden streusel topping is one our most popular family desserts. We wait impatiently for the harvest of wonderful fruits grown on the Niagara Peninsula, just a short distance to the south of our kitchen. When peach season arrives the bakery sometimes combines juicy freestone peaches with luscious pink plums to make a splendid crisp. Serve warm with your favorite ice cream, crème fraîche or yogurt.

Tip
Using a food processor, blend flour, sugar and spices. Add chilled butter, cut in chunks. Pulse until mixture forms pea-size crumble pieces.

Variations
Use other fruits alone or in combination, according to the season. Favorites include apples, strawberries and rhubarb, a mix of fresh berries, blackberries and apples. Vary the flavoring to suit.

In the streusel topping, replace half of the flour with quick-cooking rolled oats or granola. Add slivered almonds, pecans, shredded coconut or hazelnuts, too, if you wish.

- Preheat oven to 350°F (180°C)
- 8-cup (2 L) shallow baking dish, lightly buttered

6 to 8	peaches, peeled, sliced	6 to 8
6 to 8	red plums, quartered	6 to 8
¼ cup	all-purpose flour	50 mL
¼ cup	packed brown sugar, or to taste	50 mL
¼ cup	granulated sugar, or to taste	50 mL
1 tsp	grated lemon zest	5 mL
½ tsp	ground cinnamon	2 mL
	Streusel (see below)	

1. In a large bowl, combine peaches and plums with flour, brown and granulated sugars, lemon zest and cinnamon.
2. Spread fruit evenly in prepared dish and cover with a layer of streusel. Place dish on a baking sheet. Bake in preheated oven until top is golden and fruit is bubbling up around the topping, 45 to 50 minutes. Let stand for 10 to 15 minutes before serving.

Streusel

- Makes 2 cups (500 mL)

1 cup	all-purpose flour	250 mL
½ cup	packed brown sugar	125 mL
1 tsp	ground cinnamon	5 mL
¼ tsp	ground ginger	1 mL
½ cup	butter, cut into pieces	125 mL

1. In a large bowl, combine flour, brown sugar, cinnamon, ginger and butter, mixing with a fork until blended. Use your fingertips to complete forming a crumbly mixture.

Sweet Short-Crust Pastry

Tips

For a blind-baked pastry shell for pies, squares and tarts: Prepare a partially baked shell for pies, squares and tarts that are to be filled and then baked. Prepare a fully baked shell for pies, squares and tarts that are filled with a completely cooked filling, such as a mousse, a curd or custard topped with fresh fruit.

You may find the following method helps you to handle pastry. Cut a template of parchment slightly larger than the baking pan and dust with flour. Roll out the pastry on the parchment. For a rectangular baking sheet, lift the parchment and slide it into the pan with an overlap on all sides. Trim the pastry even with the edge of the pan. To line a pie plate, cut a circle template of parchment and roll pastry on parchment. Trim to fit. Slide parchment circle onto a cutting board and place a pie plate upside down on pastry circle. Flip cutting board and pie plate over. Remove board and parchment. Trim edges even with the edge of the pie plate. Refrigerate as directed.

● 15- by 10-inch (38 by 25 cm) rimmed baking sheet, lined with parchment, or two 9-inch (23 cm) tart pans or pie plates

1 cup	butter, softened	250 mL
⅔ cup	granulated sugar	150 mL
2	eggs	2
4 cups	cake flour	1 L

1. In a large bowl, using an electric mixer on medium-low speed or with a wooden spoon, cream butter and sugar until blended. Add eggs, one at a time, until incorporated. Blend in flour until just combined. Do not overmix.

2. Form dough into 1 or 2 balls and flatten into a disk. Wrap in plastic wrap and refrigerate for 2 hours. Remove from refrigerator 30 minutes before using. If pastry is too cold or too warm, it is difficult to handle.

3. On a lightly floured surface, roll out pastry ¼ inch (0.5 cm) thick and about 2 inches (5 cm) larger than your baking sheet or tart pan on all sides. Roll the pastry around the rolling pin. Position the rolling pin at the edge of a parchment-lined baking sheet or over the tart pan, and gently unroll to cover the sheet or pan. Gently press pastry into the baking sheet or tart pan. Trim edges even with the sides of the sheet or pan. Cover with plastic wrap and chill for 1 hour.

4. Meanwhile, preheat oven to 375°F (190°C).

5. When ready to bake, prick the bottom of the pastry shell with a fork. Place a sheet of parchment or foil on top of the pastry and fill with pastry weights or dried beans. Bake in preheated oven until edges are light golden and the pastry on the bottom looks dry, 15 to 20 minutes.

6. Remove liner and beans and return the pastry shell to the oven for about 5 minutes more for a partially baked shell, and 10 to 12 minutes more for a fully baked shell (see Tips, left). Let cool completely before filling unless otherwise directed in the recipe.

Flaky Pie Pastry

MAKES ENOUGH PASTRY FOR ONE 9-INCH (23 CM) TWO-CRUST PIE, 2 QUICHE SHELLS OR TWELVE 3-INCH (7.5 CM) TARTS

Even though we now make dozens of pies, tarts and quiches every day, we still make pastry by hand as we did when we first opened the store 25 years ago. There is no other way to have a pie with real homemade texture and taste. In this pastry we add shortening to contribute to a flaky texture and butter for flavor and richness.

Tips

To assemble a two-crust pie: See Techniques, Perfecting Pastry, page 21.

A fully baked and cooled pie shell can be set aside, loosely wrapped, in a cool spot for several hours or overnight before filling.

For convenience, line pie plates with pastry and store in the freezer, well wrapped for up to 1 month. Do not thaw before baking.

- Food processor
- 9-inch (23 cm) tart pan or pie plate

2 cups	all-purpose flour	500 mL
1/2 tsp	salt	2 mL
2/3 cup	shortening, chilled, cut into pieces	150 mL
1/4 cup	butter, chilled, cut into pieces	50 mL
1/3 cup	ice cold water	75 mL

1. In food processor, combine flour and salt. Add shortening and butter and pulse until large crumbs form. Drizzle with water and pulse 2 to 3 times until crumbs are uniformly coated with moisture and clumps are beginning to form.

2. Transfer mixture to a large bowl. Form crumbly mixture into a ball and flatten into a disk. If using pastry to make a two-crust pie, divide the pastry ball into 2 disks, one slightly larger than the other. Wrap in plastic wrap and refrigerate for 2 hours. If pastry is too cold or too warm, it is difficult to handle. After pastry has rested, remove from refrigerator 30 minutes before you are ready to roll.

3. *For a single-crust pie:* On a lightly floured surface, roll out pastry 1/8 inch (3 mm) thick and about 1 inch (2.5 cm) larger than the pie plate. Roll pastry around the rolling pin. Position the rolling pin over the pie plate, and slowly unroll to cover the pan. Gently press pastry into pie plate. Trim edge to 1/2 inch (1 cm) and tuck underneath around the edge of the pie plate. Crimp to form an attractive edging. Cover with plastic wrap and chill for 1 hour.

4. Meanwhile, preheat oven to 350°F (180°C).

5. When ready to bake, prick the bottom of the pastry shell with a fork. Place a sheet of parchment or foil on top of the pastry and fill with pastry weights or dried beans. Bake in preheated oven until edges are light golden and the pastry on the bottom looks dry, 12 to 15 minutes.

6. Remove liner and beans and return the pastry shell to the oven for about 5 minutes more for a partially baked shell and 7 to 10 minutes more for a fully baked shell (see Tips, left). Let cool completely before filling.

Lemon Coconut Squares

A buttery, crisp crust with tart, creamy lemon topping and a layer of sweet coconut that rises to the top. It's a treat for after lunch, to accompany afternoon tea or to serve in small bites at a party.

Variation

Lemon Tart: Prepare a partially baked Sweet Short-Crust Pastry shell in a 9-inch (23 cm) fluted tart pan with removable base, or a 9-inch (23 cm) pie plate. Prepare lemon filling using ¾ cup (175 mL) granulated sugar, ¼ cup (50 mL) all-purpose flour, 4 eggs and 6 tbsp (90 mL) lemon juice. Omit coconut. Bake for 25 to 30 minutes.

● **Preheat oven to 350°F (180°C)**

1½ cups	granulated sugar	375 mL
7 tbsp	all-purpose flour	105 mL
7	eggs	7
¾ cup	freshly squeezed lemon juice	175 mL
3 cups	unsweetened long shredded coconut	750 mL
	Sweet Short-Crust Pastry shell for squares, partially baked (page 408)	

1. In a large bowl, combine sugar and flour.
2. In a bowl, whisk eggs until light. Slowly add beaten eggs to flour-sugar mixture and combine using an electric mixer on medium speed or with a wooden spoon. Add lemon juice and mix until blended. Do not overmix.
3. Spread coconut in an even layer over bottom of partially baked pastry shell. Pour lemon mixture over coconut. Bake in preheated oven until edge of crust and coconut topping is just beginning to brown and lemon filling is set, 30 to 35 minutes. Let cool completely on baking sheet on a wire rack. Cut into squares.

Pecan Squares

The delicious pecan filling may be baked into a pan of squares, a splendid tart for dessert, or mini tarts for a party. Be sure the pecans are fresh.

Tip

We often prepare trays of bite-size sweets for parties. On those occasions we put slabs of squares in the freezer for 1 hour. It is then easier to cut the slabs into small, neat shapes.

Variation

Pecan Tart: Prepare a partially baked Sweet Short-Crust Pastry shell in a 9-inch (23 cm) fluted tart pan with removable base, or a 9-inch (23 cm) pie plate. Prepare half amount of pecan filling. Bake for 30 to 35 minutes.

Preheat oven to 350°F (180°C)

½ cup	butter, softened	125 mL
1½ cups	packed brown sugar	375 mL
1 cup	corn syrup	250 mL
6	eggs	6
1 tbsp	vanilla extract	15 mL
1 tbsp	dark rum	15 mL
1 tsp	salt	5 mL
4 cups	toasted pecan halves	1 L
	Sweet Short-Crust Pastry shell for squares, partially baked (page 408)	

1. In a large bowl, using an electric mixer on medium speed or with a wooden spoon, cream butter, brown sugar and corn syrup until blended.

2. In another bowl, whisk together eggs, vanilla, rum and salt. Add to butter mixture and whisk until well blended.

3. Spread pecans in an even layer over the bottom of partially baked pastry shell. Pour butter mixture over pecans. Bake in preheated oven until edge of crust and pecan filling is just set and browning nicely, 35 to 40 minutes. Let cool completely on baking sheet on a wire rack. Cut into squares.

Date Squares

This classic square has a perfect balance of sweet, salt, fruit and crumble. The flavor is enhanced by a made-from-scratch date filling and a buttery crumble crust.

15- by 10-inch (38 by 25 cm) rimmed baking sheet, lined with parchment paper

Date Filling

7 cups	chopped dried dates	1.75 L
1½ cups	granulated sugar	375 mL
¼ cup	freshly squeezed lemon juice	50 mL

Oat Streusel

4¼ cups	quick-cooking oats	1.05 L
4 cups	all-purpose flour	1 L
1¾ cups	packed brown sugar	425 mL
1 tbsp	baking soda	15 mL
2 tsp	salt	10 mL
2½ cups	butter	625 mL

1. *Date Filling:* In a large saucepan, combine dates 3½ cups (825 mL) water, sugar and lemon juice. Bring to a boil over medium heat, stirring occasionally. Reduce heat to low and simmer, stirring often, until dates are tender and liquid is absorbed, about 20 minutes. Remove from heat and let cool.

2. *Oat Streusel:* In a large bowl, using an electric mixer fitted with paddle attachment or with a wooden spoon, combine oats, flour, sugar, baking soda and salt. Add butter and mix on medium speed until blended and mixture is crumbly.

3. Spread half of the streusel in the bottom of prepared baking sheet and press to make an even packed layer. Place in refrigerator for 2 hours or in the freezer for 30 minutes.

4. Meanwhile, preheat oven to 350°F (180°C).

5. Spread date filling evenly in the pan and top with an even layer of the remaining streusel. Bake in preheated oven until streusel topping is lightly browned, 35 to 40 minutes. Let cool completely on baking sheet on a wire rack. Cut into squares.

Fudge Brownies

Everyone has their own idea of the perfect brownie and this one is a winner. It is fudgy and dense with rich chocolate flavor. You could add a chocolate frosting but it is not needed; just drizzle with dark chocolate or dust with confectioner's sugar.

Tip

Melt chocolate in the microwave in a glass bowl at Medium (50%) power for 1 minute. Stir and return to oven for 30 to 60 seconds more.

Variation

Spoon batter into lightly greased mini muffin tins to make popular two-bite brownies and bake until a tester inserted in the center comes out with some crumbs attached, 20 to 25 minutes — a great lunchbox treat.

- **Preheat oven to 350°F (180°C)**
- **8-inch (20 cm) square baking pan, lightly greased**

1 cup	all-purpose flour	250 mL
Pinch	salt	Pinch
²⁄₃ cup	butter	150 mL
½ cup	unsweetened chocolate, coarsely chopped	125 mL
¼ cup	chopped semisweet chocolate	50 mL
1 cup	granulated sugar	250 mL
3	eggs	3
1 tsp	vanilla extract	5 mL

1. In a bowl, combine flour and salt. Set aside.
2. Place butter, unsweetened and semisweet chocolate in a stainless-steel or glass bowl on top of a saucepan of barely simmering water over medium heat. (Make sure the bowl does not touch the water.) Stir frequently as butter and chocolate melts and remove bowl from heat when chocolate is about three-quarters melted. Let cool.
3. In a large bowl, using an electric mixer on medium speed, beat sugar, eggs and vanilla until mixture is light and pale colored. On low speed, slowly add chocolate, mixing until combined. Add flour and stir with a wooden spoon just to combine. Don't overmix.
4. Spread evenly in prepared pan. Bake in preheated oven until top is shiny and a tester inserted in center comes out with some crumbs adhering, 35 to 40 minutes. Let cool in pan. Cut into squares.

Fresh Raspberry Tart

Fresh Raspberry Tart

MAKES ONE 9-INCH (23 CM) TART

Crisp buttery pastry, tangy light lemon cream and sweet berries — a summer dessert that is pure delight!

Variations

Fresh Raspberry Tartlets: Stamp out Sweet Short-Crust Pastry into 3-inch (7.5 cm) rounds and press into small tart tins. Line each tart shell with a square of foil and pastry weights or beans and fully bake. Let cool. Fill each tart with about 1 tbsp (15 mL) Lemon Mousse and top with fresh raspberries. Sprinkle lightly with sugar or confectioner's sugar just before serving.

Substitute other fruits for the raspberries, such as a mix of blackberries and raspberries, wild blueberries or small ripe strawberries. Just be sure the fruit is ripe, perfect, a similar size and gorgeous.

Substitute a filling of Pastry Cream (page 399) for Lemon Mousse and top with fruit.

	Lemon Mousse (page 398)	
1	fully baked Sweet Short-Crust Pastry Shell (page 408)	1
1½ cups	raspberries	375 mL
1 tbsp	fine granulated sugar or confectioner's (icing) sugar	15 mL

1. Spoon freshly made Lemon Mousse in an even layer in prepared tart shell. Arrange raspberries, stem end down, in closely packed circles on top of the mousse. Refrigerate until serving. This tart is best enjoyed the same day it is made.

2. At serving time, sift a light sprinkling of sugar over raspberries.

Raisin Pecan Butter Tarts

This pastry with gooey brown sugar filling is a Canadian original. Ex-patriot Canadians have been known to suffer severe butter tart withdrawal symptoms, and battles wage on what is judged to be the best of butter tarts. Essentially, the pastry must be rich and flaky and the filling should almost, but not quite, be ready to drip at the first bite. Mini butter tarts are the hit of every party.

Tip

Sometimes the buttery filling rises up and over the edge of the pastry making a caramel edge to the tarts. It tastes scrumptious but makes it difficult to remove the tarts from the pan. It's best to run the tip of a sharp paring knife around the edge of each tart while the filling is still hot (be careful the filling can burn!). Remove the tarts from the pan to a rack as soon as they are cool enough to handle.

Variations

Maple Pecan Tarts: Replace corn syrup with pure maple syrup.

Mini Butter Tarts: Stamp out pastry in 3-inch (7.5 cm) rounds and press into lightly buttered mini muffin or tart tins. Reduce baking time to 20 to 25 minutes.

- **Preheat oven to 300°F (150°C)**
- **4-inch (10 cm) round cookie cutter**
- **Muffin tin, lightly greased**

	Flaky Pie Pastry (page 409)	
1¼ cups	packed brown sugar	300 mL
1 cup	corn syrup	250 mL
¼ cup	butter, melted	50 mL
2	eggs	2
2 tsp	vanilla extract	10 mL
½ cup	raisins, optional	125 mL
½ cup	toasted pecan pieces, optional	125 mL

1. Remove prepared pastry from refrigerator and let rest at room temperature for 30 minutes. On a lightly floured surface, roll dough ¼ inch (0.5 cm) thick. Stamp out rounds with floured 4-inch (10 cm) round cookie cutter. Press pastry circles gently into prepared muffin tin. Chill for 30 minutes.

2. In a large bowl, using an electric mixer on medium speed or with a whisk, combine brown sugar and corn syrup until blended. Add melted butter. In a measuring cup, whisk together eggs and vanilla. Slowly add to mixture, mixing until well combined.

3. Sprinkle raisins and pecan pieces evenly in the bottom of each tart shell, if using, and fill three-quarters full with brown sugar mixture. Bake in preheated oven until pastry is golden and filling is bubbling, 35 to 45 minutes. Let tarts stand in tins for 10 minutes. Transfer to a wire rack and let cool completely.

Silky Chocolate Tart

8 oz	semisweet chocolate, finely chopped	250 g
1½ cups	whipping (35%) cream	375 mL
1 tbsp	liquid honey	15 mL
	Hazelnut Crust, baked and chilled (page 417)	
1 tbsp	unsweetened Dutch-process cocoa powder	15 mL
12	toasted whole hazelnuts or ¼ cup (50 mL) coarsely chopped toasted hazelnuts (see Tips, page 417)	12

1. Place chocolate in a large heatproof bowl.
2. In a small heavy-bottomed saucepan over medium heat, bring cream to a boil. Immediately remove from heat and pour over chocolate. Let stand for 1 minute, while chocolate softens. Add honey and stir until smooth. Let cool.
3. Pour chocolate filling into hazelnut crust. Refrigerate until set, about 3 hours.
4. Place cocoa powder in a small fine sieve and lightly dust surface of tart. Decorate tart with whole hazelnuts, grouped in threes, or with a pattern of coarsely chopped hazelnuts. Let chill until serving, for at least 2 hours. This tart is best enjoyed the same day it is made.

Tip

A light dusting of cocoa powder or confectioner's (icing) sugar, or a combination of the two, is often used as a simple elegant finish to tarts and cakes. Cut out a cardboard template the size of the tart or cake and create a pattern, or simply cut a curving shape, or a checkerboard that covers part of the surface. Place the template on the surface or slightly above it and dust cocoa or confectioner's (icing) sugar over the exposed part. Carefully lift off the template.

Variation

Silky Chocolate Mini Tarts: Line about twenty-four 3-inch (7.5 cm) tart shells with Hazelnut Crust (page 417) and bake. Fill each tart shell with about 1 tbsp (15 mL) chocolate filling. Decorate with whole hazelnuts or chopped hazelnuts or top with a raspberry to make delicious individual desserts.

Chocolate Ganache

The chocolate filling of Silky Chocolate Tart is a variation of chocolate ganache, a dense, delectable chocolate cream that is used when warmed as a rich sauce to drizzle over ice cream or sundaes and as a glaze for cakes and, when chilled, forms the center for chocolate truffles.

In a saucepan over medium-low heat, bring 1 cup (250 mL) whipping (35%) cream to a boil. Immediately pour over 8 oz (250 g) semisweet chocolate in a heatproof bowl, let stand for 1 minute and stir until smooth. Flavor ganache with 2 tbsp (25 mL) liqueur, if you wish. Hazelnut liqueur, Kahlúa, Cointreau, Framboise, Cognac or Armagnac are all delicious additions. Transfer ganache from bowl to a clean container. Cover and refrigerate until needed. Place cold ganache in a bowl set over a saucepan of barely simmering water to soften when needed.

Hazelnut Crust

A sweet crust of ground hazelnuts and butter is delicious paired with chocolate. It is also the basis of the classic German Linzertorte with a filling of raspberry preserves.

Tip

Hazelnuts are toasted and skins removed before using. Preheat oven to 350°F (180°C). Spread nuts in a single layer on a rimmed baking sheet. Bake until hot to the touch and fragrant, shaking the tray occasionally so nuts toast evenly, 7 to 10 minutes. Spread a clean tea towel on a work surface and scoop the nuts into the middle. Grab sides of the towel to make a bundle and roll nuts around. The toasted brown skins will flake off. When nuts are cool enough to handle, rub off any loose remaining skin with your fingers. Don't be concerned if all the skin does not come off, some flecks of brown add to the appearance and most of the bitterness has been toasted away.

Variation

Linzer Thumbprint Cookies: Scoop Hazelnut Crust dough into 1 tbsp (15 mL) portions and arrange on a parchment-line baking sheet, 3 inches (7.5 cm) apart. Make an indent in top of each cookie and fill with ½ tsp (2 mL) raspberry preserves. Bake in a 375°F (190°C) oven until lightly browned, about 20 minutes.

- Preheat oven to 350°F (180°C)
- 9-inch (23 cm) fluted tart tin with removable base

⅓ cup	butter, softened	75 mL
3 tbsp	granulated sugar	45 mL
¾ cup	ground toasted hazelnuts	175 mL
½ cup	all-purpose flour	125 mL

1. In a large bowl, using an electric mixer on medium speed or with a wooden spoon, cream together butter and sugar. Add hazelnuts and flour and combine on low speed or with a wooden spoon to form a soft dough. Do not overmix. Form into a ball and pat into a disk. If dough is too soft to handle, wrap and refrigerate.

2. Working with small pieces of the dough, press evenly into tart tin. Trim edges even with the sides of the tin. Cover with plastic wrap and refrigerate for 1 hour.

3. When ready to bake, place a sheet of parchment or foil on top of the hazelnut shell and fill with pastry weights or dried beans. Bake in preheated oven until shell is lightly browned, about 15 minutes. Remove liner and beans and return the pastry shell to the oven for 5 to 10 minutes, or until golden and firm. Let cool completely.

It's the Berries Pie

SERVES 6

There are few things as good as a freshly baked homemade fresh fruit pie. Serve with ice cream, honeyed crème fraîche or lightly sweetened vanilla-scented whipped cream.

Tips

Lay a piece of foil loosely on top of the pie if pastry is browning too quickly and the fruit is not yet bubbling.

Bumbleberry bushes do not exist! When a pie is labeled "bumbleberry" at the market it is made with a combination of berries and fruits, usually a mix of blackberries, blueberries, raspberries and/or cranberries combined with apples and rhubarb.

● **Preheat oven to 400°F (200°C)**
● **9-inch (23 cm) pie plate**

	Flaky Pie Pastry (page 409)	
1½ cups	raspberries	375 mL
1½ cups	strawberries, sliced	375 mL
1 cup	wild blueberries	250 mL
1 tbsp	freshly squeezed lemon juice	15 mL
¼ cup	all-purpose flour	50 mL
¼ cup	granulated sugar	50 mL
1	egg, lightly beaten with 1 tbsp (15 mL) water	1
1 tbsp	coarse sugar	15 mL

1. Remove prepared pastry from refrigerator and let rest at room temperature for 30 minutes.

2. Meanwhile, in a large bowl, combine raspberries, strawberries, blueberries and lemon juice. Add flour and sugar and toss gently. Set aside.

3. On a lightly floured surface, roll the larger pastry disk into a circle ¼ inch (0.5 cm) thick. Line pie plate with pastry and fill with prepared fruit, mounding slightly in the center. Brush edge of pastry with egg wash.

4. On a lightly floured surface, roll other disk of pastry into a circle ¼ inch (0.5 cm) thick. Gently place over fruit. Press edges of pastry together and trim with a small sharp knife. Crimp to form a decorative edge. Brush top of pie with egg wash and cut 2 or 3 long slits in the top to allow steam to escape. Sprinkle with coarse sugar.

5. Place pie on a baking sheet and bake in lower half of preheated oven for 20 minutes. Reduce heat to 350°F (180°C) and continue to bake until pastry is golden and fruit is bubbling, 35 to 45 minutes. Let stand for 10 minutes before serving.

Peach Sour Cream Pie

Juicy ripe peaches, sour cream, brown sugar and a dash of rum combine in a heavenly pie.

Variation

Apple Sour Cream Pie: Replace peaches with about 6 thinly sliced Northern Spy, Mutsu or Jonagold apples. Sprinkle the top with cinnamon and sugar.

- **Preheat oven to 400°F (200°C)**
- **9-inch (23 cm) pie plate**

	Flaky Pie Pastry (page 409)	
¾ cup	sour cream	175 mL
¼ cup	all-purpose flour	50 mL
¼ cup	granulated sugar	50 mL
¼ cup	packed brown sugar	50 mL
1 tsp	ground cinnamon	5 mL
1 tbsp	rum	15 mL
6 to 8	ripe peaches, peeled and sliced	6 to 8
1	egg, lightly beaten with 1 tbsp (15 mL) water	1
1 tbsp	coarse sugar	15 mL

1. Remove prepared pastry from refrigerator and let rest at room temperature for 30 minutes.

2. Meanwhile, in a large bowl, combine sour cream, flour, granulated and brown sugars, cinnamon and rum. Add peaches and toss gently. Set aside.

3. On a lightly floured surface, roll the larger pastry disk into a circle ¼ inch (0.5 cm) thick. Line pie plate with pastry and fill with prepared fruit, mounding slightly in the center. Brush edge of pastry with egg wash.

4. On a lightly floured surface, roll other disk of pastry into a circle ¼ inch (0.5 cm) thick. Gently place over fruit. Press edges of pastry together and trim with a small sharp knife. Crimp to form a decorative edge. Brush top of pie with egg wash and cut 2 or 3 long slits in the top to allow steam to escape. Sprinkle with coarse sugar.

5. Place pie on a baking sheet in lower half of preheated oven and bake for 20 minutes. Reduce heat to 350°F (180°C) and continue to bake until pastry is golden and fruit is bubbling, 35 to 45 minutes. Let stand for 10 minutes before serving.

Apple Cinnamon Crumble Pie

No matter how many different fancy fruit pies we bake, apple is still the runaway favorite. Served with a scoop of good vanilla ice cream it's hard to beat! Northern Spy apples would be our first choice for a great apple pie, but use your favorite apple that holds its shape during cooking, has a firm texture and a good tangy flavor such as Rome Beauties, Gravenstein or Jonagold. If apples are a sweeter variety, cut back on sugar a little and add a dash of lemon juice. This is a single-crust pie with a crumble topping.

Variation

Strawberry Rhubarb Streusel Pie: In a large bowl, combine 2 cups (500 mL) strawberries, halved or quartered, depending on size, and 2 cups (500 mL) rhubarb, sliced into 1-inch (2.5 cm) pieces. Replace brown sugar in fruit filling with granulated sugar and increase flour to ⅓ cup (75 mL). Reduce cinnamon to ½ tsp (2 mL) and add ½ tsp (2 mL) ground ginger and 1 tsp (5 mL) grated lime zest.

- **Preheat oven to 400°F (200°C)**
- **9-inch (23 cm) pie plate**

	Flaky Pie Pastry (page 409)	
¼ cup	all-purpose flour	50 mL
¼ cup	packed brown sugar	50 mL
1 tsp	ground cinnamon	5 mL
3	large apples, peeled and thinly sliced	3
	Streusel (page 407)	
1	egg, lightly beaten with 1 tbsp (15 mL) water	1

1. Remove a disk of prepared pastry from refrigerator and let rest at room temperature for 30 minutes.

2. Meanwhile, in a large bowl, combine flour, brown sugar and cinnamon. Add apples and toss gently.

3. On a lightly floured surface, roll pastry into a circle ¼ inch (0.5 cm) thick and about 11 inches (27.5 cm) in diameter. Line pie plate with pastry. Fold about ½ inch (1 cm) pastry underneath around the edge. Crimp to form a neat high border. Fill with prepared fruit, mounding slightly in the center. Cover with a layer of streusel. Brush edge of pastry with egg wash.

4. Place pie on a baking sheet and bake in lower half of preheated oven for 20 minutes. Reduce heat to 350°F (180°C) and continue to bake until streusel is golden and fruit is bubbling, 35 to 40 minutes. Let stand for 10 minutes before serving.

Apples

At first bite, it's strange that the apple should ever have been connected with sin. How could anything so juicy, so fundamentally good for us, be fruit's Delilah? The short answer is Eve, who tempted Adam with it. But did she? The Bible says nothing of the kind: Genesis mentions only that God forbade the eating of the fruit of the tree of the knowledge of good and evil. Early rabbis, apple-shunners to a man, suggested the fruit was, among others, the fig, carob pods and grapes. Modern Biblical researchers favor the pomegranate (which may be even better for us than the apple). It was left to the Christians, particularly artists in France and Germany from about the 12th century, to pin the sin on the apple — perhaps because their Latin scholars couldn't resist a pun: *Malus*, apple; *malum*, evil. Thus *Malus domestica* = forbidden fruit.

The forbidden part was a joke long before then. The apple has been cultivated for more than 3,000 years, and now there are some 10,000 different varieties grown around the world, more than 2,500 of them cultivated in the U.S.

Old standards and newly developed varieties abound. The available choice is largely dependent on the climate of your region; many apple varieties just do not thrive in temperatures that go below minus 30°F (minus 34°C).

As for the apple a day keeping the doctor away: Many serious studies have extolled the apple's virtue, never its sin. They assert that it lowers bad cholesterol, blood pressure and risk of stroke, fights heart disease, prostate and colon cancers, type 2 diabetes, asthma, and the neurodegenerative diseases Parkinson's and Alzheimer's. But whatever you do to the apple, do NOT peel it. Therein lies the bulk of the quercetin, the powerful antioxidant that is the apple's prime health source.

In the Kitchen

For pies and general baking, the **Rome Beauty**, originating in Ohio in the early 1800s, is a cook's prime choice. Splendidly round and deeply red, it holds its shape and cooks better than it tastes in the hand. Among other good bakers: **Northern Spy** (a favorite in our northern kitchen), **Golden Delicious**, **Fuji** and **Ida-Red**.

For pie baking, select varieties that hold their shape and have distinct flavor. Try making a blend of tart, tangy **Granny Smith**, **Gravenstein** or **Northern Spy** with sweeter **Fuji**, **Jonagold** or **Mutsu**. Five of the best multipurpose apples are the Golden Delicious, Granny Smith, **McIntosh**, the still-rare **Mutsu**, and the **Newton-Pippin**.

Golden Delicious is large, yellow and very sweet; bruises easily.

Granny Smith is light green, crisp, juicy and less sweet than the Delicious. It originated in Australia in the 1860s and didn't arrive in North America till 1972. It's the symbol of the Beatles' Apple Records.

Mutsu (aka **Crispin**) is a Golden Delicious cross rapidly growing in popularity; spicy, sweet, slight anise flavor. Great for applesauce and for slicing in salads; it browns slowly.

McIntosh was developed in Ontario, Canada in 1796. It's great for snacking, salads and applesauce; less great for baking.

Newton-Pippin is yellowy green. It's the most famous colonial American apple; fine for eating and for cider making. "They have no apples here," wrote Thomas Jefferson from Paris in the 1780s, "to compare with our Newton-Pippin."

Pumpkin Pie

As soon as orange pumpkins ripen in the fields at the end of summer, customers come looking for our pumpkin pies. It might have something to do with the fact that the perfectly spiced filling is rich with cream and a hint of brandy! Pumpkin Pie is the essential ending to a Thanksgiving feast. Serve chilled, perhaps with a spoonful of lightly sweetened vanilla- or brandy-flavored whipped cream on the side (see Crème Chantilly, page 393).

Tip

Do not overcook pumpkin pie or the filling will dry out and crack. It is better to remove pie from the oven when the filling is puffed around the edges and just beginning to be firm in the center. Residual heat will continue to cook the eggs further as it rests.

● **Preheat oven to 350°F (180°C)**
● **9-inch (23 cm) pie plate**

2	eggs	2
¼ cup	granulated sugar	50 mL
3 tbsp	packed brown sugar	45 mL
1½ cups	canned pumpkin purée (not pie filling) (see Tip, page 382)	375 mL
1½ tsp	ground cinnamon	7 mL
1 tsp	ground ginger	5 mL
¼ tsp	freshly grated nutmeg	1 mL
¼ tsp	salt	1 mL
⅔ cup	whipping (35%) cream	150 mL
1½ tbsp	brandy	22 mL
	9-inch (23 cm) Sweet Short-Crust Pastry shell in 9-inch (23 cm) pie plate, partially baked (page 408)	

1. In a large bowl, using an electric mixer on medium speed or with a whisk, beat eggs and granulated and brown sugars together until combined and smooth and pale in color. Add pumpkin, cinnamon, ginger, nutmeg and salt. In electric mixer or using a wooden spoon, stir to combine. Fold in cream and brandy.

2. Place partially baked pastry shell on a baking sheet. Fill with pumpkin mixture. Bake in preheated oven until pastry is golden and filling is set, 40 to 45 minutes. Let stand for 10 minutes before serving.

Vanilla Cheesecake

This is a classic New York–style cheesecake. Serve chilled with sliced strawberries.

Tips

A low oven temperature and a pan of water in the oven provides a moist atmosphere to help prevent cheesecake from cracking.

Cool cake slowly to help prevent cracking. If time permits, turn off heat after 45 minutes and allow cheesecake to cool in the oven.

- **Preheat oven to 325°F (160°C)**
- **8-inch (20 cm) springform pan, lined with parchment**

	Graham Cracker Crust (see below)	
¾ cup	butter, softened	175 mL
1¾ lbs	cream cheese, softened	875 g
1 cup	granulated sugar	250 mL
4	eggs	4
1½ tsp	vanilla extract	7 mL
3 tbsp	all-purpose flour	45 mL

1. Press crust into prepared pan and refrigerate.
2. In a large bowl, using an electric mixer on medium-low speed or with a wooden spoon, cream butter until light and smooth. Add cream cheese, 4 oz (125 g) at a time, and blend until smooth. Gradually add sugar and continue to blend until smooth. Beat in eggs, one at a time. Add vanilla. Sprinkle flour over mixture and mix well to combine. Do not overmix or the cheesecake will be spongy instead of creamy, as desired.
3. Place a shallow pan half-filled with boiling water on the lower rack in the oven to add moisture. Place crust-lined pan on a baking sheet and pour in cream cheese mixture. Bake in preheated oven for 20 minutes. Reduce heat to 300°F (150°C) and continue baking until top of cheesecake no longer looks wet and cake is beginning to pull away from the sides of the pan, 60 to 70 minutes more. Let cool in pan on a wire rack. Remove from pan, peel away parchment and refrigerate for at least 8 hours. Best enjoyed within 2 days of making.

Graham Cracker Crust

Makes one 8-inch (20 cm) crust

1 cup	graham cracker crumbs	250 mL
⅓ cup	melted butter	75 mL
2 tbsp	granulated sugar	25 mL

1. In a bowl, combine graham cracker crumbs, melted butter and sugar. Mix well. Press into pan or pie plate according to recipe directions. Refrigerate until needed.

Lime Mousse Cheesecake

Here's a light, refreshing summer dessert to serve with wild blueberries.

● **8-inch (20 cm) springform pan, lined with parchment on the bottom, sides greased**

	Graham Cracker Crust (page 423)	
1 cup	whipping (35%) cream, chilled	250 mL
14 oz	cream cheese, softened	425 g
	Grated zest and juice of 3 limes	
1 cup	granulated sugar	250 mL
2 tsp	unflavored gelatin powder	10 mL

1. Press Graham Cracker Crust into prepared springform pan and refrigerate.
2. In a bowl, whip cream until stiff peaks form. Set aside.
3. In a large bowl, using an electric mixer on medium-low speed or with a wooden spoon, blend cream cheese and lime zest until smooth. Gradually add sugar and continue to blend until smooth. Add lime juice.
4. In a glass measuring cup or bowl, soften gelatin in ¼ cup (50 mL) water. Let stand for 5 minutes to soften. Melt gelatin completely by heating in the microwave at Medium (50%) power, or by setting in a saucepan over low heat, for 1 minute. Fold gelatin thoroughly but gently into cheese mixture. Do not overmix. Using a large spatula, fold one-third whipped cream into batter until incorporated. Gently fold in the rest of the whipped cream.
5. Spoon batter over crust, smoothing top. Cover and place in refrigerator to set overnight. Release from springform pan and transfer to a platter at serving time. This cheesecake is best enjoyed within 2 days of making.

Rhubarb Upside-Down Cake

This simple cake is made special with a caramel fruit topping. Serve as a treat with tea or at brunch or for a family dessert with crème fraîche or whipped cream flavored with grated orange zest.

Tip

Rhubarb's sweet-tart flavor and rosy red color is eagerly awaited after a gray winter. Choose wild field rhubarb over hothouse rhubarb for its bright flavor. Select firm, medium-size stalks with a good amount of rosy red color. Chop the rhubarb into 1-inch (2.5 mL) pieces.

Variation

Line the pan with different fruit of the season and flavor the batter accordingly. Pitted cherries with a hint of almond extract in the batter, halved apricots, peaches or plums with cinnamon, sliced pears or pineapple with ginger.

- Preheat oven to 350°F (180°C)
- 8-inch (20 cm) round cake pan, lightly greased

Glaze

⅓ cup	butter	75 mL
½ cup	packed brown sugar	125 mL
1 cup	chopped rhubarb (see Tip, left)	250 mL

Cake

1¼ cups	all-purpose flour	300 mL
½ tsp	baking powder	2 mL
¼ tsp	baking soda	1 mL
¼ tsp	salt	1 mL
⅓ cup	butter, softened	75 mL
½ cup	granulated sugar	125 mL
2	eggs	2
1 tsp	vanilla extract	5 mL
¾ cup	sour cream	175 mL

1. *Glaze:* In a small saucepan over medium heat, combine butter and brown sugar. Cook, stirring constantly, until sugar dissolves and mixture is bubbling, about 5 minutes. Pour into prepared pan and arrange an even layer of rhubarb over top.

2. *Cake:* In a bowl, combine flour, baking powder, baking soda and salt. Set aside.

3. In a large bowl, using an electric mixer on medium speed or with a wooden spoon, beat butter and sugar until batter is pale-colored, light and fluffy. Add eggs, one at a time, beating lightly after each addition until smooth. Add vanilla and beat on high speed until thick.

4. On low speed or with a wooden spoon, add flour mixture, alternately with sour cream until blended, making 3 additions of flour and 2 of sour cream. Spread batter over rhubarb, making the sides a little higher than the center. Bake in preheated oven until cake is beginning to pull away from the sides of the pan and a tester comes out clean, 40 to 45 minutes.

5. Let cake stand in pan for 2 to 3 minutes. Invert a cake platter over pan and carefully invert cake onto platter then remove pan. Be careful not to burn yourself with hot glaze. Serve warm or at room temperature.

Fresh Ginger Cake

SERVES 6 TO 8

My first encounter with an out-of-this-world moist, spicy ginger cake was in Alice Waters' restaurant Chez Panisse in Berkeley, California. After one bite I decided it was a cake that our customers would love. Our chefs went to work and this cake has indeed become a favorite. We finish the cake with a dusting of confectioner's sugar or a drizzle of white or dark chocolate. It is delicious unadorned as a snack with tea, or for dessert serve with Sauternes-poached pears, candied apple slices, lemon or rum-flavored custard or orange-scented whipped cream.

Tips

Grate fresh gingerroot until very fine to avoid any stringy fibrous bits in the cake.

Add 1 tbsp (15 mL) finely chopped crystallized ginger to the batter for those who love ginger.

- **Preheat oven to 350°F (180°C)**
- **8-inch (20 cm) round cake pan, lightly greased and lined with parchment paper**

1 cup	all-purpose flour	250 mL
½ tsp	baking soda	2 mL
½ tsp	ground cinnamon	2 mL
¼ tsp	ground cloves	1 mL
¼ tsp	freshly ground black pepper	1 mL
Pinch	salt	Pinch
⅔ cup	sunflower oil	150 mL
⅔ cup	light (fancy) molasses	150 mL
½ cup	granulated sugar	125 mL
2	eggs	2
¼ cup	freshly grated gingerroot	50 mL
1 tbsp	confectioner's (icing) sugar	15 mL

1. In a bowl, sift together flour, baking soda, cinnamon, cloves, pepper and salt. Set aside.

2. In a large bowl, using an electric mixer on medium speed or with a whisk, beat oil, molasses and sugar until smooth. Lightly beat in eggs and ginger. On low speed or with a wooden spoon, add dry ingredients alternately with ¼ cup (50 mL) water, making 3 additions of flour mixture and 2 of water, beating until just blended. Pour batter into prepared pan, smoothing top. Bake in preheated oven until top springs back and a tester inserted in the center comes out clean, 50 to 60 minutes.

3. Let cake stand in pan for 10 minutes. Run a knife around the inside of pan to release the cake and turn out onto a cake board or plate. Remove parchment. Invert onto a wire rack and let cool. Lightly dust top with confectioner's sugar before serving.

Chocolate Almond Cake

This dense flourless chocolate cake makes a delicious dessert. Serve with whipped cream and fruit.

- Preheat oven to 300°F (150°C)
- 8-inch (20 cm) round cake pan, lightly greased and lined with parchment paper

¾ cup	butter, softened	175 mL
1½ cups	semisweet chocolate, finely chopped	375 mL
1¼ cups	granulated sugar	300 mL
1 cup	ground almonds	250 mL
¾ cup	unsweetened Dutch-process cocoa powder	175 mL
¼ tsp	salt	1 mL
7	eggs, beaten	7
1 tsp	vanilla extract	5 mL
	Chocolate Ganache (page 416) or confectioner's (icing) sugar	

1. In a bowl placed over a saucepan containing 1 inch (2.5 cm) barely simmering water, combine butter, chocolate and sugar. (Make sure the bowl does not touch the water). Stir over low heat until chocolate is almost melted. Remove from heat and stir until smooth. Let cool.

2. In a large bowl, combine almonds, cocoa and salt. Pour chocolate mixture over almonds and using an electric mixer on low speed or with a wooden spoon, mix well. Add eggs in 3 additions and vanilla, beating well after each addition. Spread batter into prepared cake pan, smoothing top. Bake in preheated oven until cake begins to pull away from the sides of the pan and a tester inserted in the center comes out with a few moist crumbs attached, 1¼ to 1½ hours.

3. Let cake stand in pan for 10 minutes. Run a knife around the inside of pan to release the cake and turn out onto a cake board or plate. Remove parchment. Invert cake onto a wire rack. Let cool. Drizzle top with Chocolate Ganache, or dust top with confectioner's sugar.

Vanilla Chiffon Cake

SERVES 8 TO 10

This light-textured cake is a favorite for birthdays and special occasions.

Tip

Make a small vertical notch in one side of the cake. Slice into 3 equal horizontal layers with a long sharp, serrated knife. When you reassemble the cake, line up the notches. A chilled, or frozen cake is easier to cut.

Variations

Lemon Chiffon Cake: Replace water in cake batter with ¼ cup (50 mL) freshly squeezed lemon juice. Add grated zest of a lemon with the sugar in Step 2. Spread Lemon Curd (page 397) or Lemon Mousse (page 398), between the layers instead of the Vanilla Frosting.

Vanilla Chiffon Cupcakes: Spoon batter into 18 cups of muffin tins, lightly greased and lined with parchment or paper liners. Reduce baking time to 20 minutes. Top with Vanilla Frosting when cool.

Use Fudge Frosting (page 431) between layers and on top.

- Preheat oven to 350°F (180°C)
- 8-inch (20 cm) round cake or springform pan, with 3-inch (7.5 cm) sides, lightly greased and lined with parchment on the bottom

1 cup	cake flour, sifted	250 mL
¾ cup	all-purpose flour	175 mL
1 cup	granulated sugar, divided	250 mL
1½ tsp	baking powder	7 mL
½ tsp	salt	2 mL
4	eggs, separated	4
½ cup	lukewarm water	125 mL
⅓ cup	sunflower oil	75 mL
1½ tsp	vanilla extract	7 mL
	Vanilla Frosting (page 429)	

1. In a bowl, sift together cake and all-purpose flours, ⅓ cup (75 mL) of the sugar, baking powder and salt. Set aside.

2. In a large bowl, using an electric mixer on medium speed or with a whisk, beat ⅓ cup (75 mL) of sugar with egg yolks, water, oil and vanilla until well combined. Add flour mixture, one-third at a time, and blend on low speed until smooth.

3. In a bowl, using a whisk or with clean beaters of an electric mixer, beat egg whites. Gradually add remaining sugar until stiff peaks form. Using a large spatula, fold one-third of egg whites into batter until incorporated. Gently fold in the remaining egg whites. Spoon batter into prepared cake pan, smoothing top (for cupcakes, see Variations, left). Bake in preheated oven until top of the cake is golden and springs back when lightly touched and a tester inserted in the center comes out clean, about 50 minutes.

4. Let cake stand in the pan for 10 minutes. Run a knife around the inside of pan to release the cake and turn out onto a cake board or plate. Remove parchment. Invert onto a wire rack and let cool completely.

5. Cut cake horizontally into 3 equal layers (see page 431). Spread frosting. Reassemble cake and frost the top and sides. Set aside in a cool spot. This cake is best enjoyed the same day it is made.

Vanilla Frosting

Makes 4 cups (1 L), enough for one 3-layer cake

½ cup	whole (3.25%) milk	125 mL
12 oz	butter, softened	375 g
4½ cups	sifted confectioner's (icing) sugar, divided	1.125 L
1 tbsp	vanilla extract	15 mL
Pinch	salt	Pinch

1. In a small saucepan, bring milk almost to a boil over medium heat. Immediately remove from heat.

2. In a large bowl, using an electric mixer on medium speed or with a wooden spoon, cream butter until smooth. Add half of the confectioner's sugar, vanilla, salt and milk and blend until smooth. Add remaining sugar and mix until thick and light.

Frosting a Cake

Scoop a portion of frosting into a small bowl. This is your working bowl as you make the initial "crumb" layer and prevents the rest of the frosting from getting spoiled with crumbs. Trim cake layers of any crusty bits and brush surface clean with a pastry brush. Put a dab of frosting on the cake board, or decorating turntable, and put bottom cake layer in place. Spread with a thin layer of filling. Repeat with the other two layers, lining up the notches (see Tip, page 428). With an offset spatula (palette knife), spread a thin layer of frosting on the top and sides of the cake. Place in the refrigerator to chill for 30 minutes. Spread top and sides of cake with finishing layer of frosting. Use more frosting than you think you need. It creates a smoother finish and it's easier to remove excess frosting than to have to add more. Make decorative swirls. If you want a smooth finish, dip spatula in hot water and make smooth sweeping strokes across top and around sides. Sprinkle with coarse sugar to add a crisp shine or dust with cocoa powder. Create a decorative motif by drizzling with sieved raspberry jam. Finish with pieces of fresh fruit or berries, and for the kids a generous topping of Smarties or crushed chocolate bar is always a hit.

Tip

If frosting is too soft, place in the refrigerator to firm up. Frosting may be kept in refrigerator in a covered container for up to 7 days or freeze for up to 3 months. Thaw in the refrigerator. Bring to room temperature and rewhip before using.

Chocolate Buttermilk Cake

This favorite birthday cake has a rich chocolate flavor and the essential fudgy buttercream frosting.

Tips

Replace brewed coffee with 1 tsp (5 mL) instant coffee granules dissolved in 3 tbsp (45 mL) water.

Dutch-process cocoa powder has been treated to reduce the acidity that is found in natural cocoa powder. The process darkens the color and provides a rich mellow chocolate flavor particularly suited for delicate cakes, pastries, creams and icings. It contains no sugar. If using natural cocoa powder in recipes that include a large amount of Dutch-process it is necessary to add baking soda, or increase the specified amount of baking soda, to compensate for the increased acidity.

Variation

Chocolate Buttermilk Cupcakes: Spoon batter into 18 cups of muffin tins, lightly greased or lined with parchment or paper liners. Reduce baking time to about 20 minutes. Top with Fudge Frosting when cool.

- **Preheat oven to 350°F (180°C)**
- **8-inch (20 cm) round cake or springform pan, with 3-inch (7.5 cm) sides, lightly greased and lined with parchment paper on the bottom**

1¼ cups	all-purpose flour	300 mL
1 cup	unsweetened Dutch-process cocoa powder (see Tips, left)	250 mL
½ tsp	each baking soda and baking powder	2 mL
Pinch	salt	Pinch
½ cup	butter, softened	125 mL
⅓ cup	sunflower oil	75 mL
¾ cup	granulated sugar	175 mL
¾ cup	packed brown sugar	175 mL
3	eggs	3
1¼ cups	buttermilk	300 mL
3 tbsp	brewed coffee (see Tips, left)	45 mL
	Fudge Frosting (page 431)	

1. In a bowl, sift together flour, cocoa powder, baking soda, baking powder and salt. Set aside.

2. In a large bowl, using an electric mixer on medium speed or with a wooden spoon, beat butter, oil and granulated and brown sugars until well combined and pale in color. Add eggs, one at a time, beating until smooth after each addition.

3. In a measuring cup or bowl, combine buttermilk and coffee. With a wooden spoon, stir flour mixture into butter mixture, alternately with buttermilk, making 3 additions of flour and 2 of buttermilk, and blend until smooth. Spread batter into prepared cake pan, smoothing top. Bake in preheated oven until top of cake springs back when lightly touched and a tester inserted in the center comes out clean, about 1 hour.

4. Let cake stand in pan for 10 minutes. Run a knife around the inside of pan to release the cake and turn out onto a cake board or plate. Remove parchment. Invert onto a wire rack and let cool completely.

5. Cut cake horizontally into 3 equal layers (see page 431). Spread about ¾ cup (175 mL) Fudge Frosting between each layer. Reassemble cake and frost the top and sides. Refrigerate until serving.

Fudge Frosting

Makes 4 cups (1 L), enough frosting for one 3-layer cake

7 oz	semisweet chocolate, cut into small chunks	210 g
½ cup	butter, softened	125 mL
4½ cups	sifted confectioner's (icing) sugar	1.125 L
Pinch	salt	Pinch
⅔ cup	half-and-half (10%) cream	150 mL
1 tbsp	vanilla extract	15 mL

1. In a saucepan over low heat, combine chocolate and butter, stirring, until chocolate is almost melted. Remove from heat and stir until smooth. Let cool to lukewarm.

2. In a large bowl, using an electric mixer on low speed or with a wooden spoon, mix together confectioner's sugar and salt. Slowly add cream and vanilla. Add lukewarm chocolate mixture and beat until smooth and thick.

Slicing a Cake before Frosting

Use a sharp, long knife with serrated edge and make smooth sawing motions to slice the cake into layers.

1. Trim cake of any crusty edges and remove all crumbs from your work surface.
2. Make one small vertical cut down the side of the cake. This will be a helpful guide when you line up the layers to reassemble the cake.
3. Hold the cake firmly on top with the flat of your hand to guide the knife while you cut in even horizontal layers.

Tip

If frosting is too soft, place in the refrigerator to firm up. Frosting may be kept in the refrigerator in a covered container for up to 7 days or freeze for up to 3 months. Thaw in the refrigerator. Bring to room temperature and rewhip before using.

Carrot Cake

SERVES 8 TO 10

An all-time favorite cake: light, moist and packed with good things. Here we bake a layer cake for special occasions, but for everyday snacking, bake batter in a square baking pan to make a single layer cake — and don't forget the icing.

Variation

Carrot Cupcakes: Spoon batter into 18 cups of muffin tins, lightly greased or lined with parchment or paper liners. Reduce baking time to about 20 minutes. Spread tops with Cream Cheese Frosting when cool and decorate with chopped walnuts.

- Preheat oven to 350°F (180°C)
- 8-inch (20 cm) round cake or springform pan, with 3-inch (7.5 cm) sides, lightly greased and lined with parchment paper on the bottom

1⅓ cups	all-purpose flour	325 mL
2 tsp	baking soda	10 mL
1¼ tsp	ground cinnamon	6 mL
½ tsp	ground allspice	2 mL
½ tsp	freshly grated nutmeg	2 mL
½ tsp	salt	2 mL
1 cup	granulated sugar	250 mL
¾ cup	sunflower oil	175 mL
2	eggs	2
1½ tsp	vanilla extract	7 mL
1 cup	grated carrots	250 mL
⅓ cup	drained, crushed pineapple	75 mL
½ cup	unsweetened shredded coconut	125 mL
¾ cup	chopped walnuts, divided	175 mL
	Cream Cheese Frosting (page 433)	

1. In a bowl, sift together flour, baking soda, cinnamon, allspice, nutmeg and salt. Set aside.

2. In a large bowl, using an electric mixer on medium speed or with a whisk, beat sugar and oil until smooth. Lightly beat in eggs and vanilla. On low speed or with a wooden spoon, add flour mixture, beating until just blended. Stir in carrots, pineapple, coconut and ½ cup (125 mL) of the walnuts. Pour batter into prepared pan, smoothing top. Bake in preheated oven until a tester inserted in the center comes out clean, 60 to 70 minutes.

3. Let cake stand in pan for 10 minutes. Run a knife around the inside of pan to release the cake and turn out onto a cake board or plate. Remove parchment. Invert onto a wire rack and let cool completely.

4. Cut cake horizontally into 3 equal layers (see page 431). Spread Cream Cheese Frosting between layers. Reassemble cake and spread a smooth frosting layer on top and sides. Decorate top with remaining chopped walnuts.

Cream Cheese Frosting

Makes about 4 cups (1 L)

½ cup	butter, softened	125 mL
12 oz	cream cheese, softened	375 g
1 tsp	vanilla extract	5 mL
6 cups	sifted confectioner's (icing) sugar	1.5 L

1. In a large bowl, using an electric mixer on medium speed or with a wooden spoon, cream butter until smooth. Add cream cheese, 4 oz (125 g) at a time, and blend until smooth. Add vanilla. Gradually add confectioner's sugar and blend on low speed until smooth. Use immediately or refrigerate until needed. Bring to room temperature before using and mix with a few strokes of a rubber spatula to ensure a smooth consistency.

Variation

Spiced Cream Cheese Frosting: Follow recipe left and add ½ tsp (2 mL) ground ginger, ½ tsp (2 mL) ground cloves, ½ tsp (2 mL) ground allspice and 2 tbsp (25 mL) dark rum. Mix to combine well.

Spiced Apple Cake

Warmly spiced with cardamom and cinnamon, this cake is a popular fall dessert.

- Preheat oven to 350°F (180°C)
- 8-inch (20 cm) round cake or springform pan, with 3-inch (7.5 cm) sides, lightly greased and lined with parchment paper on the bottom

2 cups	all-purpose flour	500 mL
1 tsp	baking powder	5 mL
1 tbsp	ground cardamom	15 mL
1 tsp	ground cinnamon	5 mL
½ tsp	baking soda	2 mL
½ tsp	salt	2 mL
1 cup	butter, softened	250 mL
1 cup	packed brown sugar	250 mL
3	eggs	3
1 tsp	vanilla extract	5 mL
1 cup	sour cream	250 mL
¾ cup	finely chopped apple	175 mL
	Spiced Cream Cheese Frosting (Variation, page 433)	
	Fall Fruit Compôte, optional (page 394)	
	Glazed Apple Slices (page 435) or chopped walnuts for decoration	

1. In a large bowl, sift together flour, baking powder, cardamom, cinnamon, baking soda and salt. Set aside.

2. In a large bowl, using an electric mixer on medium speed or with a wooden spoon, beat butter and brown sugar until batter is pale colored and light and fluffy (see Tip, page 174). Add eggs, one at a time, beating until smooth after each addition. Add vanilla.

3. Add flour mixture alternately with sour cream, making 3 additions of flour and 2 of sour cream, and blend until smooth. Stir in apple. Spread batter into prepared cake pan, smoothing top. Bake in preheated oven until top of the cake springs back when lightly touched and a tester inserted in the center comes out clean, 50 to 60 minutes.

4. Let cake stand in pan for 10 minutes. Run a knife around the inside of pan to release the cake and turn out onto a cake board or plate. Remove parchment. Invert onto a wire rack and let cool completely.

5. Cut cake horizontally into 3 equal layers. Spread Spiced Cream Cheese Frosting on bottom layer. Add second cake layer and spread with frosting. Add top cake layer and spread a smooth frosting layer on top. Decorate top with Glazed Apple Slices or chopped walnuts.

Glazed Apple Slices
Peel, core and slice 1 apple. In a small skillet over medium-high heat, melt 1 tbsp (15 mL) butter. Add apple slices and 1 tbsp (15 mL) brown sugar. Cook, stirring occasionally, until sugar is melted and apples are soft and golden, about 5 minutes. Let cool.

Index

Library and Archives Canada Cataloguing in Publication

Rodmell, Jane, 1938–
  All the best recipes : 300 delicious and extraordinary recipes / Jane Rodmell.

Includes index.
ISBN 978-0-7788-0223-5

1. Cookery. I. Title.

TX714.R63 2009   641.5   C2009-902212-5